FOURTH EDITION

Case Approach to
Counseling and Psychotherapy

About the Author

Gerald Corey is a professor in both the Human Services Department and the Counseling Department at California State University at Fullerton, where for ten years he was the coordinator of the Human Services Department. He received his doctorate in counseling from the University of Southern California. A Diplomate in Counseling Psychology, American Board of Professional Psychology, he is a National Certified Counselor and a California licensed psychologist. He is a Fellow of the American Psychological Association (Counseling Psychology) and a Fellow of the Association for Specialists in Group Work. Jerry teaches both undergraduate and graduate courses in group counseling, professional ethics, and theories and techniques of counseling, and he conducts experiential groups and training and supervision workshops. He also presents workshops for professional organizations and at various universities. Along with his wife, Marianne Schneider Corey, and other colleagues, he offers weeklong residential personal-growth groups and residential training and supervision workshops each summer. Recently Jerry made a two-part videotape, *The Art of Integrative Counseling and Psychotherapy* (available from Brooks/Cole), demonstrating his integrated approach to counseling as applied to Ruth, the central case in this text.

Other recent books that Jerry has authored or co-authored (all published by the Brooks/Cole Publishing Company) are:

- *Theory and Practice of Counseling and Psychotherapy*, Fifth Edition (and *Manual*) (1996)
- *Theory and Practice of Group Counseling*, Fourth Edition (and *Manual*) (1995)
- *Becoming a Helper*, Second Edition (1993)
- *I Never Knew I Had a Choice*, Fifth Edition (1993)
- *Issues and Ethics in the Helping Professions*, Fourth Edition (1993)
- *Groups: Process and Practice*, Fourth Edition (1992)
- *Group Techniques*, Second Edition (1992)

FOURTH EDITION

Case Approach to Counseling and Psychotherapy

Gerald Corey
California State University, Fullerton
Diplomate in Counseling Psychology,
American Board of Professional Psychology

Brooks/Cole Publishing Company
I(T)P™ An International Thomson Publishing Company

Pacific Grove • Albany • Bonn • Boston • Cincinnati • Detroit • London • Madrid • Melbourne
Mexico City • New York • Paris • San Francisco • Singapore • Tokyo • Toronto • Washington

A CLAIREMONT BOOK

Sponsoring Editor: *Claire Verduin*
Marketing Team: *Margaret Parks and Nancy Kernal*
Editorial Associate: *Patsy Vienneau*
Production Coordinator: *Fiorella Ljunggren*
Production: *Cecile Joyner, The Cooper Company*
Manuscript Editor: *William Waller*

Permissions Editor: *May Clark*
Interior Design: *Vernon T. Boes*
Interior Illustration: *John and Judy Waller*
Cover Design: *Sharon Kinghan*
Typesetting: *Kachina Typesetting*
Cover Printing: *Phoenix Color Corporation*
Printing and Binding: *Quebecor/Fairfield*

For more information, contact:

BROOKS/COLE PUBLISHING COMPANY
511 Forest Lodge Road
Pacific Grove, CA 93950
USA

International Thomson Editores
Campos Eliseos 385, Piso 7
Col. Polanco
11560 México D. F. México

International Thomson Publishing Europe
Berkshire House 168-173
High Holborn
London WC1V 7AA
England

International Thomson Publishing GmbH
Königswinterer Strasse 418
53227 Bonn
Germany

Thomas Nelson Australia
102 Dodds Street
South Melbourne, 3205
Victoria, Australia

International Thomson Publishing Asia
221 Henderson Road
#05-10 Henderson Building
Singapore 0315

Nelson Canada
1120 Birchmount Road
Scarborough, Ontario
Canada M1K 5G4

International Thomson Publishing Japan
Hirakawacho Kyowa Building, 3F
2-2-1 Hirakawacho
Chiyoda-ku, Tokyo 102
Japan

Printed in the United States of America

10 9 8 7 6 5 4

Library of Congress Cataloging-in-Publication Data

Corey, Gerald.
    Case approach to counseling and psychotherapy / Gerald Corey. —
4th ed.
        p. cm.
    Includes bibliographical references.
    ISBN 0-534-26580-4
    1. Psychotherapy—Case studies.   2. Counseling—Case studies.
3. Case method. I. Title.
RC465. C67   1996   95-15146
616.89' 14—dc20   CIP

THIS BOOK IS PRINTED ON ACID-FREE RECYCLED PAPER

In memory of Bill Waller,
our manuscript editor,
whose spirit lives in the pages of this book

About the Contributors

James Robert Bitter, Ed.D., is a professor, as well as the chairperson, of human development and learning at East Tennessee State University. He has a range of experience in applying Adlerian principles to the counseling of children and families. His scholarly activities include publications in the areas of family mapping and family constellation, created memories and early recollections, and family reconstruction. He has been associated with Virginia Satir's Avanta Network of trainers.

William Blau, Ph.D., has a private practice and teaches as an adjunct associate professor at the California School of Professional Psychology, in Los Angeles. Although his theoretical orientation is psychoanalytic, he often uses techniques from other approaches. His specialty areas include clinical biofeedback and the psychotherapy of psychotic people. Blau and his wife, Cathey Graham Blau, LCSW, work together in teaching stress management and providing couples therapy.

David J. Cain, Ph.D., A.B.P.P., was the founder and editor of the *Person-Centered Review* and founder of the Association for the Development of the Person-Centered Approach. For more than 20 years he has been a client-centered therapist, teacher, supervisor, and consultant. He is a Diplomate in Clinical Psychology of the American Board of Professional Psychology and a member of the Center for Studies of the Person. He teaches at Chapman University and has a private practice in Carlsbad, California.

Susan C. Carlin-Finch, M.A., M.M.F.T., is a Ph.D. candidate at the University of Southern California and is employed as a mediator/family counselor by the Los Angeles Superior Court's Mediation and Conciliation Service. Current research interests include fertility management as a normal couple process and evaluation of court-based parent education programs.

Barbara Brownell D'Angelo, Ph.D., a California-licensed psychologist with a behavioral orientation, taught in the Human Services Program at California State University at Fullerton and was a counselor in the Counseling Center there. She later had a private practice in psychotherapy in Santa Ana, California. She is currently completing her first novel and is vice president of Real Time Instruments in Lake Forest, California.

Frank M. Dattilio, Ph.D., A.B.P.P., is on the faculty of psychiatry at the University of Pennsylvania School of Medicine and Hospital and is a clinical psychologist in private practice. He was one of the first to apply cognitive therapy to couples and families. He has authored or co-authored several books and more than 70 professional publications worldwide. Dattilio is also a clinical member and approved supervisor of the American Association for Marriage and Family Therapy and has been a visiting lecturer at many universities internationally.

John M. Dusay, M.D., is a psychiatrist in private practice in San Francisco and an associate clinical professor at the University of California at San Francisco. He was a protégé of Eric Berne and is a founding member and past president of the International Transactional Analysis Association. He has written and lectured extensively on transactional analysis.

Albert Ellis, Ph.D., is the founder and director of the Institute for Rational-Emotive Therapy in New York. He is considered the grandfather of the cognitive-behavioral approaches, and he continues to work hard at developing REBT. Ellis has written about 700 journal articles and authored or co-authored over 50 books. He sees as many as 80 clients a week and gives about 200 talks and workshops to professionals each year.

Rainette Eden Fantz, Ph.D., was one of the founders of the Gestalt Institute of Cleveland. She was the chairwoman of the Institute's Intensive Post Graduate Training Program, she worked with groups, and she conducted special-interest workshops. Fantz drew from her extensive background as an artist, musician, and actress to enrich her therapy. She died in 1994.

Linda Gilbert, Ph.D., is the executive director of the Southern California Institute for Rational-Emotive Therapy. She is director of Psychological Services and Stress Management at Loma Linda University's Center for Health Promotion and is an associate professor in the Schools of Medicine and Public Health at the university.

William Glasser, M.D., is the founder and president of The Institute for Control Theory, Reality Therapy and Quality Management in Canoga Park, California. He presents many workshops each year, both in this country and abroad. His practical approach continues to be popular among a variety of practitioners and teachers. He has written a number of books on reality therapy and control theory.

Arnold A. Lazarus, Ph.D., A.B.P.P., is distinguished professor in the Graduate School of Applied and Professional Psychology at Rutgers University. He is a Diplomate in Clinical Psychology of the American Board of Professional Psychology. His writings include numerous books and professional papers. He developed the multimodal approach, a broad-based, systematic, and comprehensive approach to behavior therapy.

Mary E. Moline, Ph.D., is a professor in the Department of Family Psychology at Seattle Pacific University and is a licensed marriage, family, and child counselor. For 15 years she has taught courses that emphasize training in marriage and family therapy at the graduate level. She has co-authored two books and is a clinical member and an approved supervisor of the American Association for Marriage and Family Therapy.

Donald Polkinghorne, Ph.D., is a professor of counseling psychology at the University of Southern California and a licensed psychologist. He served as president of the Division of Theoretical and Philosophical Psychology of the American Psychological Association, as a consulting editor of the *Journal of Phenomenological Psychology,* and as a member of the editorial boards of the *Journal of Counseling Psychology* and the *Journal of Humanistic Psychology.* Among his many publications are works on phenomenological research methods and existential psychotherapy and on social values.

Jon L. Winek, Ph.D., received his graduate training at the University of Southern California, where he received master degrees in both sociology and marital and family therapy, as well as a doctorate in sociology. He is a faculty member in the Department of Human Development and Psychological Counseling at Appalachian State University and in private practice in Boone, North Carolina. One of his interests is how wider social issues such as race, culture, gender, and class affect individuals and their families.

Robert E. Wubbolding, Ed.D., is professor of counseling at Xavier University in Cincinnati and the director of the Center for Reality Therapy in Cincinnati. He is also the director of training for the Institute for Reality Therapy in Los Angeles. He has taught reality therapy cross-culturally throughout Asia and Europe and has written seven books on reality therapy.

Contents

Preface

Case Approach to Counseling and Psychotherapy reflects my increasing emphasis on the use of demonstrations and the case-approach method to bridge the gap between the theory and practice of counseling. Students in the courses I teach have found that a demonstration in class often clears up their misconceptions about how a therapy actually works. This book is an attempt to stimulate some of the unique learning that can occur through seeing a therapeutic approach in action. It also gives students a chance to work with cases from the vantage point of nine counseling approaches: psychoanalytic, Adlerian, existential, person-centered, Gestalt, reality, behavior, cognitive-behavior, and family systems.

The format of this book provides an opportunity to see how each of the various therapeutic approaches is applied to a single client, Ruth Walton, who is followed throughout the book. A feature of the text is an assessment of Ruth's case by one or more consultants in each of the nine theoretical perspectives. Highly competent practitioners assess and treat Ruth from their particular theoretical orientation; most of them have provided sample dialogues to illustrate their style of working with Ruth. In certain cases I was able to enlist the founder of a theory to describe what his approach to working with Ruth would be. For example, William Glasser offers an assessment of her in the context of control theory and illustrates his interventions using reality therapy. Arnold Lazarus, the founder of multimodal therapy, provides an overview of how he would assess Ruth's functioning with his BASIC I.D. framework. And Albert Ellis describes his analysis of Ruth and demonstrates his style in providing rational emotive behavior therapy (REBT).

New to this fourth edition is the inclusion of family systems therapy, in which Frank Dattilio demonstrates a cognitive-behavioral approach to family therapy with Ruth. Also in this chapter, Mary Moline demonstrates the importance of working with Ruth from a systemic perspective. I work with Moline when she brings the entire Walton family together for a family therapy session. Finally, Jon Winek and Susan Carlin-Finch present their work as co-therapists with another family.

The nine theory chapters use a common format, allowing for comparisons among approaches. This format includes the guest commentary or commentaries, followed by my way of working with Ruth from that particular perspective. I discuss the theory's basic assumptions, an initial assessment of Ruth, the goals of therapy, and the therapeutic procedures to be used. The therapeutic process is concretely illustrated by client/ therapist dialogues, which are augmented by process commentaries explaining the rationale for my interventions. Questions for Reflection help readers apply the material to their personal lives and offer guidelines for continuing to work with Ruth within each of the theoretical orientations. A second case is then presented as a further illustration of how the concepts and techniques of each approach can be applied, and students are again asked to deal with the case within a specific theoretical framework.

After the theory chapters, Chapter 11 brings the approaches together and helps students develop their own therapeutic styles. I demonstrate how I would counsel Ruth in an integrated fashion by drawing on most of the therapeutic approaches. Guidelines are also provided for working with Ruth as a member of various cultural groups.

Ideally, *Case Approach to Counseling and Psychotherapy* will be used as part of an integrated learning series that I have written for courses in counseling theory and practice. This book can supplement the core textbook to enhance students' learning of theory by letting them see counseling in action. In the textbook, *Theory and Practice of Counseling and Psychotherapy*, Fifth Edition (Brooks/Cole, 1996), students are given an overview of the key concepts and techniques of the nine models of contemporary therapy. The accompanying *Student Manual* contains many experiential activities and exercises designed to help students apply the theories to themselves and connect theory with practice. Unless readers have had a course in counseling theory or have at least read a textbook covering the range of standard approaches, they may have trouble working with the cases in this book, for it is not designed as a substitute for a text surveying the counseling theories.

A videotape set, *The Art of Integrative Counseling and Psychotherapy*, illustrates my own integrative perspective in working with Ruth. In Part 1 ("Techniques in Action") there are short clips of Ruth's therapy sessions from the initial phase to termination. In Part 2 ("Challenges for the Counselor") the focus is on issues such as resistance, transference, and countertransference as they apply to working with Ruth. This video brings together several of the therapies that are discussed in this book. Information can be obtained from the Brooks/Cole Publishing Company, Pacific Grove, CA 93950.

Acknowledgments

A number of professors have reviewed this book, and I have used their responses in refining the present material. I am most appreciative of the diversity of reviewer reactions, which helped bring more reality and clarity to the cases.

I also appreciate both the support and the challenge given by those teachers of counseling courses and clinicians who read the revised manuscript and provided specific and helpful comments for improving the effectiveness of the case presentations. These people are Madeline Alford and William Cottrell, Jr., both of Lamar University in Port Arthur, Texas; Robert Haynes, psychology internship director at the Atascadero State Hospital in California; Barbara Herlihy of the Loyola University at New Orleans; Thomas Hodgson, of Empire State College of SUNY in New York; Michael Nystul, of New Mexico State University; Beverly Palmer, of California State University at Dominguez Hills; and Jorja Manos Prover. Emmy van Deurzen-Smith reviewed the chapter on existential therapy; Joseph Zinker reviewed the chapter on Gestalt therapy; and the chapter on family systems therapy was reviewed by Patrick Callanan, Marianne Schneider Corey, Irene Goldenberg, Arthur Horne, and Patrick McGrath. Two of my undergraduate students, Pamela Cuervo and Christiana Woodward, reviewed the entire manuscript and provided insightful and useful suggestions. Indeed, my students were my most demanding critics!

I am particularly indebted to those individuals who reviewed a chapter in their area of expertise and who also contributed by writing about their way of working with Ruth from their particular therapeutic perspective. Most of the original contributors updated and expanded their selections in this edition, and there are several new ones. A complete list of the contributors appears on pp. vi–x.

Recognition goes to members of the staff of the Brooks/Cole Publishing Company who have given extra time and attention to this revised edition, particularly Claire Verduin and Fiorella Ljunggren. I want to acknowledge my special appreciation to Cecile Joyner, who guided the production of the book, and to Bill Waller, the manuscript editor, whose sensitivity and editorial skills contributed in important ways to the readability and interest of this text.

Special thanks are extended to Marianne Schneider Corey, my wife and colleague, for her support and her contributions to this revision. Based on her clinical experiences as a marriage and family therapist, she went over each case, challenging me to pay attention to subtle yet important nuances.

Finally, I want to acknowledge the people with whom I have worked in groups and workshops and the students in my human services and counseling courses at California State University at Fullerton. For over 23 years at this university, I have learned more from these people than I ever learned taking courses and reading textbooks. Indeed, through these encounters I have developed many of the themes that appear in this book. The struggles and life themes of these people appear in disguised form in the cases presented in this book.

Gerald Corey

CHAPTER ONE

Introduction and Overview

STRUCTURE OF THE BOOK

Even after reading about a theory of therapy and discussing it in class, students sometimes still have unclear notions about how to apply it. I began experimenting with asking my students to volunteer for a class demonstration in which they served as "clients." Seeing concepts in action gave them a clearer picture of how therapists from various approaches work. This book illustrates nine therapies in action and gives you experience in working with different cases. It also shows you how to selectively borrow concepts and techniques from all of the major therapeutic approaches. Additionally, it encourages you to integrate techniques that are appropriate to your client population into a style that is an expression of who you are as a person. From my perspective, effective counseling involves the personality of the therapist even more than the technical skills that he or she employs. In order to apply techniques appropriately, it is essential to consider your personal style and theoretical orientation in relation to each client's unique life situation.

Before this large task of developing a personalized approach can be accomplished, however, it is necessary to know the basics of each of the theories and to have some experience with these therapies. This book aims to provide a balance between describing the way therapists with a given orientation might proceed with a client and challenging you to try your hand at showing how you would proceed with the same client.

This initial chapter deals with methods of conceptualizing a case, as well as providing background material on the central figure in this book, Ruth Walton. Her intake form and autobiography can be referred to frequently as you work with her in the nine theory chapters. Ruth is not an actual client. I have created her by combining many of the common themes that I observe in my work with clients. Thus, in her case and in all of the other cases in this book, the clients have a basis in fact, but details have given them a new identity. In this way, I believe, the clients represent some of those you may meet.

Ruth appears in each of the chapters on individual theories (Chapters

2–10). These chapters begin with commentaries by one or more "outside consultants" on her case. Each consultant was given Ruth's background information and also read my perspective on her for the theory under discussion. Then, this representative wrote a section describing the following:

- the core concepts and goals of his or her therapeutic approach
- the themes in Ruth's life that might serve as a focus for therapy
- an assessment of her dynamics, with emphasis on her current life situation
- the techniques and procedures that would probably be used in counseling her
- illustrations of the therapy in action through dialogue between Ruth and the therapist

You will notice that the consultants' sections in the first three chapters, dealing with the psychoanalytic, Adlerian, and existential approaches, are more detailed than those in subsequent chapters in order to provide you with richer background information on Ruth. Having seen these three perspectives, each dealing with the same data on the same case, you will have a good framework for working with Ruth from the other theoretical orientations. You will also notice that there are two invited consultants for Chapter 7 (on reality therapy), Chapter 8 (on behavior therapy), and Chapter 10 (on family systems therapy). Due to the diversity of the approach, there are three invited consultants for Chapter 9 (on cognitive-behavior therapy). There were several reasons for asking an additional therapist to contribute a commentary for these chapters. The first presentation in these chapters is usually made by a key figure in the approach: William Glasser (the founder of reality therapy), Arnold Lazarus (a pioneer in clinical behavior therapy), and Albert Ellis (the founder of rational emotive behavior therapy and grandfather of cognitive-behavior therapy). The second (or third) presentation in these chapters features another expert in reality therapy, behavior therapy, cognitive-behavior therapy, transactional analysis, or family systems therapy. These sections demonstrate that practitioners in the same theoretical orientation, though subscribing to some basic concepts, have a diversity of styles and apply these concepts in practice in unique ways.

After this opening section or sections, I look at the approach's basic assumptions, make an initial assessment of Ruth, and examine the theory's therapeutic goals and procedures. The therapeutic process is made concrete with samples of dialogues between Ruth and me, along with process commentaries to provide an explanation of the direction that therapy is taking.

You are encouraged to become an active learner by evaluating the manner in which the consultants and I work with Ruth from each of the nine theoretical perspectives. You are asked to show how you would work with her as your client, using the particular approach being considered in the chapter. To guide you in thinking of ways to work with her, I provide questions. I also suggest that besides reflecting on these questions by yourself, you arrange to work with fellow students in small discussion groups and explore various approaches.

Following Ruth's case in Chapters 2–10 there is a case for additional practice. This supplementary case shows you how the same therapy approach can be applied to a client with different life themes and issues. It also allows me to describe techniques different from those employed with Ruth. As with the case of Ruth, you are invited to become an active participant and show how you would continue working with each of these cases if the client were referred to you. You will learn the nine therapy systems best if you think and work within the general framework of each theory. You will also be able to determine from what aspects of that approach you would most like to draw as you begin putting together your own synthesis, your personal counseling style.

You can further enhance your learning by participating in a variety of role-playing exercises in which you "become" the client under discussion and also by participating in group discussions based on the cases. Rather than merely reading about these cases, you can use them to stimulate reflection on ways in which you have felt like the given client. Thus, as you read about Ruth, Moe, Marion, the Field family, and others, it will help if you think about the degree to which you see yourself in these people. In experiential practice sessions you can also draw on your own concerns in becoming the counselor. Think of as many ways as possible to use these cases as a method of stimulating introspection and providing lively class discussion.

In Chapter 11 you are encouraged to consider the advantages of eventually developing your own counseling theory and style. Such an integrative, or *eclectic, perspective* of counseling entails selecting concepts and methods from various sources and theories. It does not necessarily refer to developing a new theory; rather, it emphasizes a systematic integration of underlying principles and techniques of the various therapy systems. Those who call themselves eclectic range from practitioners who haphazardly pick and choose to those who seriously look for ways to validate their own personal perspective. I am not endorsing a sloppy eclecticism of grabbing at any technique that appears to work. Instead, I encourage you to strive to build a unified system that fits you and is appropriate for the particular setting in which you practice. It is also essential that you be willing to challenge your basic assumptions, test your hypotheses as you practice, and revise your theory as you confirm or disconfirm your clinical hunches.

Although it may be unrealistic to expect you to complete the formulation of your personal perspective while reading this book, my hope is that you will begin this process. Toward this end I suggest that you develop your own reading program, emphasizing those theories that you find the most valuable in understanding and working with a diverse range of clients. At the end of each of the theory chapters you will find reading suggestions. The "Recommended Supplementary Readings" are a few selected works that you may find useful if you want to learn more about each theory.

OVERVIEW OF THE THERAPEUTIC PERSPECTIVES

In the chapters to follow, as mentioned, the case of Ruth will be analyzed and discussed from various therapeutic perspectives. For each of these perspectives we will consider its basic assumptions, its view of how to assess clients, its goals for therapy, and its therapeutic procedures. This section presents the essence of the various approaches. As a way of laying the foundation for developing an eclectic, integrative approach, we will look for common denominators among the nine perspectives and also differences among them.

Basic Assumptions

When therapists make initial contact with a client, their theoretical perspective determines what they look for and what they see. It largely determines the focus and course of therapy, and it influences their choice of therapeutic strategies and procedures. As you develop your counseling stance, pay attention to your own basic assumptions. Developing a counseling perspective is more involved than merely accepting the tenets of a particular theory or combination of theories. Your theoretical approach is an expression of your unique life experiences.

How do theoretical assumptions influence practice? Your view about the assessment of clients, the goals that you think are important in therapy, the strategies and techniques that you employ to reach these goals, the way in which you divide responsibility in the client/therapist relationship, and your view of your role and functions as a counselor are largely determined by your theoretical orientation.

Attempting to practice counseling without at least a general theoretical perspective is somewhat like flying a plane without a map and without instruments. But a counseling theory is not a rigid structure that prescribes the specific steps of what to do in therapeutic work. Instead, a theoretical orientation is a set of general guidelines that you can use to make sense of what you are doing.

One way to approach the basic assumptions underlying the major theoretical orientations is to consider four categories under which most of the contemporary systems fall. These are (1) the *psychodynamic approaches*, which stress insight in therapy (psychoanalytic and Adlerian therapy); (2) the *experiential and relationship-oriented approaches,* which tend to stress feelings and subjective experiencing (existential, person-centered, and Gestalt therapy); (3) the *cognitive and behavioral approaches,* which stress the role of thinking and doing and tend to be action oriented (behavior therapy, rational emotive behavior therapy, other cognitive-behavioral approaches, and reality therapy), and (4) *family systems theory,* an orientation stressing that the individual can be understood only in light of understanding the entire system of which he or she is a part. (Actually, Adlerian therapy, which I classify as a psychodynamic approach, could be placed in the cognitive-behavioral camp as well, for in some respects it foreshadowed the current interest in the cognitive therapies.) Although I have separated the theories into four general camps, in reality many common denominators will become evident as you study the theories, so this categorization is somewhat arbitrary. Overlapping concepts and themes make it difficult to neatly compartmentalize these theoretical orientations. What follows is a thumbnail sketch of the basic assumptions underlying each of these nine therapeutic systems.

Psychoanalytic therapy.   The psychoanalytic approach views people as being significantly influenced by unconscious motivation, conflicts between impulses and prohibitions, defense mechanisms, and early childhood experiences. Because the dynamics of behavior are buried in the unconscious, treatment consists of a lengthy process of analyzing inner conflicts that are rooted in the past. Therapy is largely a process of restructuring the personality; therefore, clients must be willing to commit themselves to an intensive, long-term process.

Adlerian therapy.   According to the Adlerian approach, people are primarily social beings, influenced and motivated by societal forces. Human nature is viewed as creative, active, and decisional. The approach focuses on the unity of the person and on understanding the individual's subjective perspective. Adler holds that inherent feelings of inferiority immediately initiate a striving for superiority. He asserts that we acquire inferiority feelings, which stem from childhood, and that we then develop a style of life aimed at compensating for such feelings and becoming the master of our fate. The style of life consists of our views about ourselves and the world and of distinctive behaviors that we adopt in the pursuit of our life goals. We can shape our own future by actively and courageously taking risks and making decisions in the face of unknown consequences. Clients are not viewed as being "sick" and needing to be "cured"; rather, they are seen as discouraged and needing encouragement to correct mistaken self-perceptions. Counseling is not simply a matter of an expert therapist making prescriptions for change. It is a collaborative effort, with the client and the therapist actively working on mutually accepted goals.

Existential therapy.   The existential perspective holds that we define ourselves by our choices. Although outside factors restrict the range of our choices, we are ultimately the authors of our lives. We are thrust into a meaningless world, yet we are challenged to accept our aloneness and create a meaningful existence. Because we have the capacity for awareness, we are basically free. Along with our freedom, however, comes responsibility for the choices we make. Existential practitioners contend that clients often lead a "restricted existence," seeing few if any alternatives to limited ways of dealing with life situations and tending to feel trapped or helpless. The therapist's job is to confront these clients with their restricted life and to help them become aware of their own part in creating this condition. As an outgrowth of the therapeutic venture, clients are able to recognize outmoded patterns of living, and they begin to accept responsibility for changing their future.

Person-centered therapy. The person-centered approach rests on the assumption that we have the capacity to understand our problems and that we have the resources within us to resolve them. Seeing people in this light means that therapists focus on the constructive side of human nature and on what is *right* with people. This approach places emphasis on feelings about the self. Clients can move forward toward growth and wholeness by looking within rather than focusing on outside influences. They are able to change without a high degree of structure and direction from the therapist. What they need from the therapist is understanding, genuineness, support, acceptance, caring, and positive regard.

Gestalt therapy. The Gestalt approach is based on the assumption that people must find their own way in life and accept personal responsibility if they hope to achieve maturity. The therapist's task is to provide a climate in which clients can fully experience their here-and-now awareness and can recognize how they are preventing themselves from living in the present. Clients carry on their own therapy as much as possible by doing experiments aimed at change and finding their own meanings. They are encouraged to experience their conflicts directly instead of merely talking about them. In this way they gradually expand their own level of awareness and integrate the fragmented and unknown aspects of themselves.

Reality therapy. From the perspective of reality therapy, counselors have the task of challenging clients to look at their current behavior to help them assess how much what they are doing is getting them what they want. A basic assumption is that if clients examine their wants and needs, they will be in a better position to determine if what they are doing is working effectively for them. The approach also aims at getting clients to explore their perceptions, share their wants, and make a commitment to counseling. Clients then explore the direction in which their behavior is taking them, and they make an evaluation of what they are doing. They create a plan of action to make the changes they want. Because clients can directly control what they are doing and thinking more than they can control what they are feeling, behavior becomes the focus of therapy. Clients can gain effective control of their lives if they are willing to accept responsibility for their actions.

Behavior therapy.   Although behavior therapy assumes that people are basically shaped by learning and sociocultural conditioning, this approach focuses on the client's ability to eliminate maladaptive behavior and acquire constructive behavior. Behavior therapy is a systematic approach that begins with a comprehensive assessment of the individual to determine the present level of functioning as a prelude to setting therapeutic goals. After the client establishes clear and specific behavioral goals, the therapist typically suggests strategies that are most appropriate for meeting these stated goals. It is assumed that clients will make progress to the extent that they are willing to practice new behaviors in real-life situations. Continual evaluation is a way to determine how well the procedures and techniques are working.

Cognitive-behavioral approaches.   From the perspective of rational emotive behavior therapy (REBT), our problems are caused by our perceptions of life situations and our thoughts, not by the situations themselves, not by others, and not by past events. Thus, it is our responsibility to recognize and change self-defeating thinking that leads to emotional and behavior disorders. REBT also holds that people tend to incorporate these dysfunctional beliefs from external sources and then continue to indoctrinate themselves with this faulty thinking. To overcome irrational thinking, therapists use active and directive therapy procedures, including teaching, suggestion, and giving homework. REBT emphasizes education, which means that the therapist functions as a teacher, and the client as a learner. Although REBT is didactic and directive, it mainly tries to get people to think, feel, and act for themselves, in their own right. It reeducates clients to do their own thinking. Therapists have the job of consistently encouraging and challenging clients to do what is necessary to make long-lasting and substantive change.

Other cognitive-behavioral therapies share some of the assumptions of REBT. Many of these approaches assume that people are prone to learning erroneous, self-defeating thoughts but that they are capable of unlearning them. People perpetuate their difficulties through their self-talk. But by pinpointing their cognitive errors and by correcting them, they can create a more self-fulfilling life for themselves. Cognitive restructuring plays a central role in these therapies. People are assumed to be able to make changes by listening to their self-talk, by learning a new internal dialogue, and by learning coping skills needed for behavioral changes.

Family systems therapy.   The final approach is grounded on the assumption that the individual cannot be fully understood apart from the family system. A basic principle is that a change in one part of the system will result in a change in other parts of the system. If the family unit changes in significant ways, these changes have an impact on the individual. Like-wise, if the individual in a system (family) makes changes, the entire unit will be affected. Thus, therapy involves assessing and treating an in-dividual's concerns within the context of the interaction among family members.

The transactions that occur between the individual and other family members influence the individual's concept of self, relationship with oth-ers, and world views. From a systemic perspective, being a healthy person involves both a sense of belonging to the family system and also having a sense of separateness and individuality. The client's problem is generally viewed as being a symptom of how the system is functioning. The assump-tions of the family systems model are in contrast to those of the intrapsy-chic theories, which conceptualize an individual's problems as the result of internal conflicts. Some of the assumptions of family therapy include the notion that a client's behavior may (1) serve a function or a purpose for the family, (2) be the result of the system's inability to function effectively, and (3) result from dysfunctional patterns that are passed on from generation to generation. Conceptually, the therapist intervenes with individual clients in ways that will enable them to deal more effectively with significant people in their lives, whether or not these other people are physically present in the therapy session.

Cultural and individual differences emerging from basic assumptions

The contemporary theories of therapeutic practice are grounded on assumptions that are part of Western culture. Many of these assumptions are not appropriate when they are applied to non-Western cultures. The basic assumptions of the nine orientations described above emphasize values such as choice, the uniqueness of the individual, self-assertion, and the strengthening of the ego. Therapeutic outcomes that these systems stress include improving assertive coping skills (by changing the environ-ment, changing one's coping behavior, and learning to manage stress). By contrast, non-Western orientations focus on interdependence, play down individuality, and emphasize the losing of oneself in the totality of the cosmos. Counseling from an Asian perspective, for example, reflects the life values associated with a focus on inner experience and acceptance of one's environment.

Whereas the Western therapeutic approaches are oriented toward change, non-Western approaches focus more on the social framework than on the development of the individual. Applying the Western world's model of therapy to the Chinese culture does have certain limitations. Likewise, this model has its limitations when it is applied to many ethnic and cultural groups such as Asian Americans, Latinos, Native Americans, and African Americans. Seeking professional help is not customary for many client populations, and they will typically turn first to informal systems (family, friends, community).

The point is that counselors need to be aware of the basic assumptions underlying their theoretical orientations. In an increasingly pluralistic society, there is an ethical imperative to avoid forcing all clients to fit into a mold that is not appropriate for their cultural background. Therefore, we need to learn how our assumptions influence practice.

Perspectives on Assessment

Some approaches stress the importance of conducting a comprehensive assessment of the client as the initial step in the therapeutic process. The rationale is that specific counseling goals cannot be formulated and appropriate strategies cannot be designed until a thorough picture of the client's past and present functioning is formed. In this section I describe various views of the role of assessment in therapy. I also present some ways of conceptualizing an individual case, emphasizing what information to gather during the initial stages of therapy.

Psychoanalytic therapy.   Psychoanalysts assume that normal personality development is based on dealing effectively with successive psychosexual and psychosocial stages of development. Faulty personality development is the result of inadequately resolving a specific developmental conflict. Therapists are interested in the client's early history as a way of understanding how past situations have contributed to a dysfunction. Projective personality testing—techniques such as the Rorschach test or the Thematic Apperception Test, which are designed to tap a client's unconscious processes—may be used to identify themes running through the client's life. This approach emphasizes the importance of comprehensive assessment techniques as a basis for understanding personality dynamics and the origin of emotional disorders. However, some analysts shy away from gathering information, preferring to let it unfold during the process of analytic therapy.

Adlerian therapy.   Assessment is a basic part of Adlerian therapy. The initial session focuses on creating a relationship based on trust and cooperation. Soon after this cooperative relationship is established, the therapist conducts a comprehensive interview to gather specific information, including an assessment of the client's family constellation, birth order, parental relationship and family values, and early recollections. Clients are often asked to complete a detailed lifestyle questionnaire. (You will see an example of a lifestyle questionnaire in Chapter 3.)

Therapists devote attention to how the family structure has influenced the client's development. Childhood experiences are connected to the shaping of one's unique style of life, which includes one's views of self, others, and the world. Therapists identify major patterns that appear in the questionnaire and thus get a picture of the client's basic personality. This process helps clarify "basic mistakes" (faulty perceptions and assumptions about life) and assets (strengths and resources) that the client has developed and has carried through into present functioning. This assessment provides a direction for the course of therapy.

Existential therapy.   Existentially oriented counselors maintain that the way to understand the client is by grasping the essence of the person's subjective world. The primary purpose of existential clinical assessment is to understand the assumptions that clients use in structuring their existence. This approach is different from the traditional diagnostic framework, for it focuses not on understanding the individual from an external perspective but, instead, on grasping the essence of the client's inner world.

Person-centered therapy.   In much the same spirit as existential counselors, person-centered therapists maintain that assessment and diagnosis are detrimental, because they are external ways of understanding the client. They believe that (1) the best vantage point for understanding another person is through his or her subjective world; (2) the practitioner can become preoccupied with the client's history and thus neglect present attitudes and behavior; and (3) therapists can develop a judgmental attitude, shifting too much in the direction of telling clients what they ought to do. Focusing on gathering information about a client can lead to an intellectualized conception about the person. The client is assumed to be the one who knows the dynamics of his or her behavior, and for change to occur, the person must experience a perceptual change, not simply receive data. Thus, therapists listen actively, attempt to be present, and allow clients to identify the themes that they choose to explore.

Gestalt therapy.   Like the two previous approaches, Gestalt therapy does not gather information about clients as a prerequisite to counseling. It does not use diagnostic labels, because it sees them as an escape from full participation in the client/therapist relationship. Assessment and diagnostic procedures can foster talking about a client's life, whereas the focus of Gestalt therapy is gaining awareness by direct experiencing. The premise is that the salient points in a person's developmental history will surface as the client pays attention to where he or she is stuck in the present. Themes that run through a person's life will become evident during the therapeutic process itself.

Reality therapy.   Assessment of clients is typically not a formal process; psychological testing and diagnosis are not generally a part of this approach. Through the use of skillful questioning, however, reality therapists help clients make an assessment of their present behavior. They have little interest in learning the causes of an individual's current problems or in gathering information about the client's past experiences. Instead, the focus is on getting clients to take a critical look at what they are doing now and then to determine the degree to which their present behavior is effective. This informal assessment directs clients to pay attention to their pattern of wants, needs, perceptions, successes, and personal assets to evaluate whether their lives are moving in the direction they want.

Behavior therapy.   The behavioral approach begins with a comprehensive assessment of the client's present functioning, with questions directed to past learning that is related to current behavior patterns. It includes an objective appraisal of specific behaviors and the stimuli that are maintaining them. Some of the reasons for conducting a thorough assessment at the outset of therapy are that (1) it identifies behavioral deficiencies as well as assets, (2) it provides an objective means of appraising both a client's specific symptoms and the factors that have led up to the client's malfunctioning, (3) it facilitates the selection of the most suitable therapeutic techniques, (4) it specifies a new learning and shaping schedule, (5) it is useful in predicting the course and the outcome of a particular clinical disorder, and (6) it provides a framework for research into the effectiveness of the procedures employed.

Multimodal therapy, developed by Lazarus, is an example of a broad-based, systematic, and comprehensive approach to behavior therapy. It calls for technical eclecticism, but it remains firmly grounded on social-learning theory. In the multimodal orientation a comprehensive assessment process attends to each area of a client's BASIC I.D. (behavior, affect, sensation, imagery, cognition, interpersonal relationships, and drugs and biological factors). Interactive problems throughout each of these seven areas are identified, and appropriate techniques are selected to deal with each difficulty.

Cognitive-behavioral approaches.   The assessment used in cognitive-behavioral therapy is based on getting a sense of the client's patterns of thinking. Attention is paid to various beliefs that the client has developed in relation to certain events. Therapists are not merely concerned with gathering data about past events but are also alert to evidence of faulty thinking and cognitive distortions that the client has incorporated. Once rigid, unrealistic, absolutist ideas have been identified, the therapeutic process consists of actively undermining self-defeating beliefs and substituting constructive ones.

Family systems therapy.   In most systemic approaches, both the therapist and the client are involved in the assessment process. Some systemic practitioners will assist clients in tracing the highlights of their family history and in identifying issues in their family of origin. The premise underlying the significance of understanding and assessing one's family of origin is that the patterns of interpersonal behavior learned there will be repeated in other interactions outside the family. Individuals may be asked to identify what they learned from interacting with their parents, from observing their parents' interactions with each other, and from observing how each parent interacted with each sibling. Clients may also identify the rules governing interactions in their family. These family precepts include unspoken rules, messages given by parents to children, myths, and secrets. Family rules may be functional or dysfunctional. Part of the assessment process will probably deal with family goals, structure (functional versus dysfunctional), decision-making processes, power structure, communication styles, history and life cycle, and multigenerational patterns that reveal a unified picture of the family's dynamics.

The place of assessment and diagnosis in counseling and case management

Assessment consists of evaluating the relevant factors in a client's life to identify themes for further exploration in therapy. Diagnosis, which is sometimes part of the assessment process, consists of identifying a specific category of psychological problem based on a pattern of symptoms. There are several types of diagnosis. *Medical diagnosis* is the process of examining physical symptoms, inferring causes of physical disorders or diseases, providing a category that fits the pattern of a disease, and prescribing an appropriate treatment. *Psychological diagnosis* entails identifying an emotional or behavioral problem and making a statement about the current status of a client. It includes stipulating the possible causes of the individual's emotional, psychological, and behavioral difficulties. It also entails suggesting the appropriate therapeutic techniques to deal with the identified problem and estimating the chances for a successful resolution. *Differential diagnosis* consists of distinguishing one form of psychiatric disorder from another by determining which of two (or more) diseases or disorders with similar symptoms the person is suffering from. The 1994 edition of the American Psychiatric Association's *Diagnostic and Statistical Manual of Mental Disorders* (DSM-IV) is the standard reference for the nomenclature of psychopathology.

A practioner's view of diagnosis will depend on his or her theoretical orientation, as we have seen. For instance, psychoanalytically oriented therapists tend to favor diagnosis as one way of understanding how past situations have contributed to an individual's dysfunction. Practitioners with a behavioral orientation also favor diagnosis, for they emphasize observation and other objective means of appraising both a client's specific symptoms and the factors that have led up to the person's malfunctioning. Such an assessment process allows them to employ techniques that are appropriate for a particular disorder and to evaluate the effectiveness of a treatment program. On the other side of the issue are person-centered practitioners, who maintain that diagnosis is not essential for counseling because it tends to pull therapists away from a subjective way of understanding their clients and fosters an external conception about them.

Regardless of your theoretical orientation, it is likely that you will be expected to work within the framework of the DSM-IV if you are counseling in a community agency. Even if you are in private practice, you will have to provide a diagnosis on the client's claim form if you accept insurance for mental-health services. Because you will need to think within the framework of assessing and diagnosing clients, it is essential that you become familiar with the diagnostic categories and the structure of the DSM-IV.

My own perspective on assessment

I see assessment, broadly construed, as a legitimate part of therapy. The assessment process does not necessarily have to be completed during the intake interview, nor does it have to be a fixed judgment that the therapist makes about the client. It is a continuing process that focuses on understanding the person. Ideally, assessment is a collaborative effort that is part of the interaction between the client and the therapist. Both should be involved in discovering the nature of the client's presenting problem, a process that begins with the initial sessions and continues until therapy ends. The questions that are helpful for a therapist to consider during this early assessment phase are:

- What are my immediate and overall reactions to the client?
- What is going on in this person's life at this time?
- What are the client's main assets and liabilities?
- What are his or her resources for change?
- Is this a crisis situation, or is it a long-standing problem?
- What does the client primarily want from therapy, and how can it best be achieved?
- What should be the focus of the sessions?
- What major factors are contributing to the client's current problems, and what can be done to alleviate them?
- In what ways can an understanding of the person's cultural background shed light on developing a plan to deal with the person's problems?
- What significant past events appear to be related to the client's present level of functioning?
- What specific family dynamics might be relevant to the person's present struggles and interpersonal relationships?
- On what support systems can the client rely in making changes? Who are the significant people in the client's life?
- What are the prospects for meaningful change, and how will we know when that change has occurred?

As a result of questions such as these, therapists will develop tentative hypotheses, and they can share them with their clients as therapy proceeds. This process of assessment does not have to result in classifying the client under some clinical category. Instead, counselors can describe behavior as they observe it and encourage clients to think about its meaning.

In this way assessment becomes a process of thinking about issues *with* the client, rather than a mechanical procedure conducted by an expert therapist. From this perspective, assessment and diagnostic thinking are vital to the therapeutic procedures that are selected, and they help practitioners conceptualize a case.

Even if counselors are required to diagnose someone for administrative or insurance reasons, they are not bound rigidly to that view of their client. The diagnostic category is merely a framework for viewing and understanding a pattern of symptoms and for making treatment plans. It is not necessary to restrict clients to a label or to treat them in stereotypical ways. It is essential that practitioners be aware of the dangers of labeling and adopt a tentative stance toward diagnosis. As therapy progresses, additional data are bound to emerge, which may call for a modification of an original diagnosis.

General guidelines for assessment

The intake interview typically centers on making the assessment described earlier and prescribing an appropriate course of treatment. As we have seen, depending on the practitioner's orientation, this assessment may take various forms. For example, Adlerians look for ways in which the family structure has affected the client's development, whereas a psychoanalytic practitioner is interested in intrapsychic conflicts. This section will present a fairly comprehensive scheme for conceptualizing an individual case. After looking at several intake forms and case summary forms, I have pulled together some guidelines that might be helpful in thinking about how to get significant information and where to proceed with a client after making an initial assessment. Below are ten areas that are a basic part of conceptualizing an individual case:

1. *Identifying data.* Get details such as name, age, sex, appearance, ethnic background, socioeconomic status, marital status, religious identification, and referral source (who referred the client, and for what purpose?).

2. *Presenting problem(s).* What is the chief complaint? This area includes a brief description, in the client's own words, of the immediate problems for which he or she is seeking therapy. The presenting situation includes a description of the problems, how long they have existed, and what has been done to cope with them.

3. *Current living circumstances.* Information to collect here includes marital status and history, family data, recent moves, financial status, legal problems, basic lifestyle conflicts, support systems, and problems in personal relationships.

4. *Psychological analysis and assessment.* What is the client's general psychological state? For example, how does the person view his or her situation, needs, and problems? What is the client's level of maturity? Is

there evidence of detrimental influences in the client's life? What are the person's dominant emotions? Is the client excited, anxious, ashamed, or angry? This phase of assessment entails describing the client's ego functioning, including self-concept, self-esteem, memory, orientation, fantasies, ability to tolerate frustration, insight, and motivation to change. The focus is on the client's view of self, including perceived strengths and weaknesses, the person's ideal self, and how the client believes that others view him or her. What is the client's level of security? What ability does the person have to see and cope with reality, make decisions, assert self-control and self-direction, and deal with life changes and transitions? Standardized psychological tests of intelligence, personality, aptitudes, and interests may be used. Another assessment procedure is the *mental-status examination*, which is a structured interview leading to information about the client's psychological level of functioning. This examination focuses on areas such as appearance, behavior, feeling, perception, and thinking. Under the behavior category, for example, the counselor making the assessment will note specific dimensions of behavior, including posture, facial expressions, general body movements, quality of speech, and behavior in the interview situation. Under the thinking category it is important to assess factors such as the client's intellectual functioning, orientation, insight, judgment, memory, thought processes, and any disturbances in thinking. The mental-status examination is also used to screen for psychosis.

5. *Psychosocial developmental history.* The focus here is on the developmental and etiological factors relating to the client's present difficulties. Five types can be considered: (1) precipitating factors—for example, maturational or situational stress, school entry, divorce, or death of a parent; (2) predisposing factors—for example, parent/child relationships and other family patterns, personality structure, and hereditary or constitutional factors; (3) contributory factors—for example, a current or past illness or the problems of family members; (4) perpetuating factors—for example, secondary gains such as the sympathy that a sufferer from migraine headaches elicits; and (5) sociocultural factors—that is, customs, traditions, family patterns, and cultural values.

From a developmental perspective the following questions could be asked: How well has the client mastered earlier developmental tasks? What are some evidences of conflicts and problems originating in childhood? What were some critical turning points in the individual's life? What were some major crises, and how were they handled? What key choices did the client make, and how are these past decisions related to present functioning? How did the client's relationships within the family influence development? What was it like for the client to be in the family? What are family relationships like now? How are the client's cultural experiences related to his or her personality? This section might conclude with a summary of developmental history, which could include birth and early development, toilet training, patterns of discipline, developmental delays, educational experiences, sexual development, social development, and the influence of religious, cultural, and ethical orientations.

6. *Health and medical history.* What is the client's medical history? What was the date of the client's last consultation with a physician, and what were the results? Is there any noticeable evidence of recent physical trauma or neglect (for example, battering, welt marks, bruises, needle marks, sloppy clothing, sallow complexion)? What is the client's overall state of health? This section should include an assessment of the client's mental health. Has the client been in previous treatment for the present problem? Has there been a prior hospitalization? Has the client been taking medications? What were the outcomes of previous treatments? Is there any history of emotional illness in the family? It is important to be alert to signs that may indicate an organic basis for a client's problem (such as headaches, sudden changes in personal habits or in personality, and other physical symptoms). Regardless of the therapist's orientation, it is essential to rule out organic causes of physical symptoms before proceeding with psychotherapy.

7. *Adjustment to work.* What work does the client do or expect to do? How satisfied is the client with work? What is the meaning of employment to the person? Does he or she have future plans? What are the benefits and drawbacks of work? What is the client's work history? Has the person had long-term employment or a history of work problems? What is the balance between work and leisure? What is the quality of the client's leisure time? "Work" is used in the broad sense, whether or not the person receives pay for it. For instance, it would be important to inquire about a woman's satisfaction with her work as a housewife and mother, even if she is not formally employed.

8. *Lethality.* Is the client a danger to self or others? Is he or she thinking about suicide or about hurting someone or something? Does the client have a specific plan either for committing suicide or for harming another person? Does the client have the means available to kill himself or herself? Have there been prior attempts at self-destruction or violent behavior toward others? Is the client willing to make a no-suicide contract as a condition of beginning therapy?

9. *Present human relationships.* This area includes a survey of information pertaining to spouse, siblings, parents, children, friends, colleagues, and other social ties. Included are the person's level of sexual functioning, family beliefs and values, and satisfaction derived from relationships. What are the client's main problems and conflicts with others? How does he or she deal with conflict? What support does the client get from others?

10. *Summary and case formulation.* Provide a summary of the client's major defenses, core beliefs, and self-definition of current problems, strengths, and liabilities, and make an assessment. What are the major recommendations? What is the suggested focus for therapeutic intervention? This formulation might specify the frequency and duration of treatment, the preferred therapeutic orientation, and the mode of treatment.

The client might be included in the assessment process as a collaborator, which tends to set the stage for a shared therapeutic venture.

After the initial assessment of the client is completed, a decision is made whether to refer the person for alternative or additional treatment. Again, it is important to include the client in this decision-making process. If the client is accepted by the therapist, the two can discuss the assessment results. This information can be used in exploring the client's difficulties in thinking, feeling, and behaving and in setting treatment goals. Assessment can be linked directly to the therapeutic process, forming a basis for developing methods of evaluating how well the counselor's procedures are working to achieve the client's goals. Because most work settings require an intake interview, familiarity with these assessment procedures is essential.

Therapeutic Goals and Procedures

After the initial comprehensive assessment of a client, *therapeutic goals* need to be established. These goals will vary, depending in part on the practitioner's theoretical orientation. For example, psychoanalytic therapy is primarily an insight approach that aims at regressing clients to very early levels of psychological development so that they can acquire the self-understanding necessary for major character restructuring. It deals extensively with the past, with unconscious dynamics, with transference, and with techniques aimed at changing attitudes and feelings. At the other extreme is reality therapy, which focuses on evaluating current behavior so that the client can develop a realistic plan leading to more effective ways of behaving. Reality therapy is not concerned with exploring the past, with unconscious motivation, with the transference that clients might develop, or with attitudes and feelings. It asks the key question "What is the client doing now, and what does the client want to be doing differently?" It assumes that the best way to change is by focusing on what one is doing and thinking. If these dimensions change, it is likely that the client's feelings and physiological reactions will also change.

Therapeutic goals are diverse and include restructuring personality, finding meaning in life, creating an I/thou relationship between the client and the counselor, eliminating dysfunctional beliefs, helping clients look within themselves to find answers, substituting effective behaviors for maladaptive ones, facilitating individual differentiation from the family system, and correcting mistaken beliefs and assumptions. Given this wide range, it is obvious that the perspectives of the client and the therapist on goals will surely have an impact on the course of therapy and on the therapeutic interventions chosen.

Despite this diversity of goals, all therapies share some common denominators. They aim at optimizing the individual's autonomy—that is, at intervening to encourage the client to make changes that will lead to self-reliance. To some degree they also have the goal of identifying what the client wants and then modifying the person's thoughts, feelings, and behaviors.

Each theoretical orientation focuses on a particular dimension of human experience as a route to changing other facets of personality. For example, both Adlerian and cognitive-behavior therapists emphasize the client's cognitions under the assumption that if they are successful in modifying beliefs and thought processes, behavioral changes will follow, and feelings will eventually be modified.

Selecting *therapeutic techniques*, then, depends on whether a counselor's goals are oriented toward changing thoughts, feelings, or behaviors. Psychoanalytic therapists, for example, are primarily concerned that their clients acquire *insights* into the nature and causes of their personality problems. They employ techniques such as free association, analysis of dreams, interpretation of resistance, and analysis of transference as tools to uncover the unconscious and lead to the desired insight. Gestalt therapists are interested in helping clients fully experience what they are *feeling* moment to moment; they use a wide range of exercises and experiments designed to intensify this experiencing of emotions. Rational emotive behavior therapists are mainly concerned that clients identify and uproot dysfunctional *thinking*, and they use a variety of cognitive (as well as behavioral and emotive) techniques. Behavior therapists are interested in helping clients decrease or eliminate unwanted *behaviors* and increase adaptive ones. Thus, they employ many procedures aimed at teaching clients new behaviors. Whatever techniques you employ, it is essential to keep the needs of your client in mind. Some clients relate best to cognitive techniques, others to techniques designed to change behavior, and others to techniques aimed at eliciting emotional material. The same client, depending on the stage of his or her therapy, can profit from participating in all of these different techniques.

As a therapist you would do well to think of ways to take techniques from all of the approaches so that you are able to work with a client on *all levels* of development. Take the case of Ruth, with whom you will become very familiar in this book. At the outset your interventions may be directed toward getting her to identify and express feelings that she has kept bottled up for much of her life. If you listen to her and provide a place where she can experience what she is *feeling*, she is likely to be able to give more expression to emotions that she has distorted and denied.

As her therapy progresses, you may well direct interventions toward getting her to think about critical choices she made that still have an influence in her life. At this time in her therapy you are likely to shift the focus from exploration of feelings to exploration of her attitudes, her *thinking processes*, her values and her basic beliefs. Still later your focus may be more on helping her develop *action programs* in which she can experiment with new ways of *behaving*, both during the sessions and outside of them.

In addition to working with Ruth as an individual, there may be significant therapeutic value in bringing in members of her family of origin, her current family, and significant others. Seeing Ruth as a part of a system will provide another dimension that can deepen therapy. It is not a matter of working with one aspect of Ruth's experiencing while forgetting about the other facets of her being; rather, it is a case of selecting a focus for a particular phase of her therapy. The challenge that you will face as you encounter Ruth (and the other "clients" in this book) is how to utilize an *integrative approach* as you draw on a variety of techniques to help clients work through their struggles.

In working within a multicultural framework, it is especially important for counselors to use techniques flexibly. Clients should not be forced into a strict mold. Rather, techniques are most effective when they are tailored to what the individual client needs, which means that therapists will have to modify their strategies. Some clients will resist getting involved in techniques that are aimed at bringing up and expressing intense emotions. Highly confrontive techniques may close down some clients. In such cases it may be best to focus more on cognitive or behavioral techniques or to modify emotive techniques that are appropriate for the client. On the other hand, some clients need to be confronted if they are to move. Confrontation at its best is an act of caring. It is designed to challenge clients to examine what they are thinking, feeling, and doing. Relying strictly on supportive techniques with certain clients will not provide the impetus they need to take the steps necessary to change. Techniques work best when they are designed to help clients explore thoughts, feelings, and actions that are within their cultural environment. Again, the value of bringing the client into the counseling process as an informed partner and a collaborator with the therapist cannot be overemphasized.

The rest of this section summarizes the goals of therapy from the various theoretical perspectives and some of the techniques commonly used by each of the nine therapeutic approaches. Also addressed are these questions: When are clients ready to terminate therapy? How are the outcomes of therapy evaluated?

Psychoanalytic therapy. The main goal is to resolve intrapsychic conflicts, toward the end of reconstructing one's basic personality. Analytic therapy is not limited to problem solving and learning new behaviors; there is a deeper probing into the past in order to develop one's level of self-understanding.

From the psychoanalytic perspective all techniques are designed to help the client gain insight and bring repressed material to the surface so that it can be dealt with consciously. Major techniques include gathering of life-history data, dream analysis, free association, and interpretation and analysis of resistance and transference. Such procedures are aimed at increasing awareness, gaining intellectual and emotional insight, and beginning a working-through process that will lead to the reorganization of personality.

When are clients ready to leave therapy? How are the outcomes of therapy evaluated? Psychoanalytic clients are ready to terminate their sessions when they and the therapist agree that they have clarified and accepted their emotional problems, have understood the historical roots of their difficulties, and can integrate their awareness of past problems with present relationships.

Adlerian therapy.   Therapists help clients develop social interest, provide encouragement to discouraged individuals, and facilitate insight into clients' mistaken ideas (notions) and their personal assets. Adlerian practitioners are not bound by any set of prescribed techniques. They may use a variety of methods that are suited to the unique needs of their clients. A few of these therapeutic procedures are attending, encouragement, confrontation, paradoxical intention, interpretation of the family constellation and early recollections, suggestions, homework assignments, and summarizing.

Because Adlerians stress a democratic approach, the client and therapist typically discuss and decide on termination. The stress on goal alignment gives both of them a frame of reference to assess the outcomes of therapy.

Existential therapy.   The principal goal is to challenge clients to recognize and accept the freedom they have to become the author of their life. Therapists confront them on ways in which they are avoiding their freedom and the responsibility that accompanies it.

The existential approach places primary emphasis on understanding the client's current experience, *not* on using therapeutic techniques. Thus, counselors are not bound by any prescribed techniques, so they can borrow tactics from other schools of therapy. Interventions are used in broadening the ways in which clients live in their world.

The issues of termination and evaluation are typically resolved through an open exchange between the client and therapist. Since the client generally makes the choice to enter therapy, it seems fitting that it be his or her choice and responsibility to decide when to leave therapy. If clients continue to rely on the therapist for this answer, they are not yet ready to terminate. However, therapists are given the latitude to express their reactions and views about the person's readiness for termination. The choices that clients are making and the changes in their perceptions of themselves in their world are the basis for an evaluation of therapeutic outcomes.

Person-centered therapy.   The person-centered approach seeks to provide a climate of understanding and acceptance through the client/therapist relationship that will enable clients to come to terms with aspects of themselves that they have denied or disowned. Other goals are enabling clients to move toward greater openness, trust in themselves, willingness to be a process rather than a finished product, and spontaneity.

Because this approach places primary emphasis on the client/therapist relationship, it specifies few techniques. It minimizes directive intervention, interpretation, questioning, probing for information, giving advice, collecting history, and diagnosis. Person-centered therapists maximize active listening, reflection, and clarification. Current formulations of the theory stress the full and active participation of the therapist as a person in the therapeutic relationship.

In keeping with the spirit of person-centered therapy, it is the client who largely determines when to stop coming for therapy. Likewise, the therapist assumes that clients can be trusted to determine the degree to which therapy has been successful for them. As clients increasingly assume an inner locus of control, they are in the best position to assess the personal meaning of their therapeutic venture.

Gestalt therapy.   The goal of the Gestalt approach is to challenge clients to move from environmental support to self-support and to assist them in gaining awareness of moment-to-moment experiencing. Clients are encouraged to experience directly, in the present, their struggles with "unfinished business" from their past. This process allows them to integrate fragmented parts of their personality.

A wide range of techniques is designed to intensify experiencing and to resolve emotional conflicts. Gestalt therapy stresses confrontation of discrepancies and of ways in which clients are avoiding responsibility for their feelings. The client engages in role playing by performing all of the various parts and polarities, thus gaining greater awareness of inner conflicts. Techniques commonly used are dialogue with conflicting parts of oneself, exaggeration, focusing on body messages, staying with particular feelings, reexperiencing past unfinished situations in the here and now, and working with dreams. Clients interpret their own dreams.

Clients are ready to terminate therapy when they become increasingly aware of what they are thinking, feeling, and doing in the present moment. When they have recognized and worked through their unfinished business, they are ready to continue therapy on their own. As with the other experiential therapies (existential and person-centered) the evaluation of therapeutic outcomes is rooted in the client's subjective experience and perceptions about the changes that have occurred.

Reality therapy.   The overall goal of reality therapy is to help individuals find more effective ways of meeting their needs for belonging, power, freedom, and fun. The approach challenges clients to make an assessment of their current behavior to determine if what they are doing and thinking is getting them what they want from life. As clients become aware of the ineffective behaviors they are using to control the world, they are then more open to learning alternative ways of behaving.

Reality therapy is active, directive, and didactic. The therapist assists clients in making plans to change specific behaviors that they determine are not working for them. Skillful questioning and a variety of behavioral methods are often used to encourage clients to evaluate what they are doing. If they decide that their present behavior is not effective, they develop a specific plan for change and make a commitment to follow through.

When clients are more effectively fulfilling their wants and needs and when they have gained (or regained) control of their world, they are ready to leave counseling. This approach has the advantage of being anchored in a specific plan for change. This plan is not nebulous, but specific, which allows objective evaluation of outcomes.

Behavior therapy.   The main goal is to eliminate clients' maladaptive behavior patterns and replace them with more constructive ones. Therapists identify thought patterns that lead to behavioral problems and then teach new ways of thinking that are designed to change the clients' ways of acting.

The main behavioral techniques are systematic desensitization, relaxation methods, reinforcement, modeling, assertion training, self-management programs, behavioral rehearsal, coaching, and other multi-modal techniques. Assessment and diagnosis are done at the outset to determine a treatment plan. "What," "how," and "when" questions are used (but not "why" questions).

This approach has the advantage of specifying clear and concrete behavioral goals that can be monitored and measured. Because therapy begins with an assessment of baseline data, the degree of progress can be evaluated by comparing the client's behavior on a given dimension at any point in the therapy with the baseline data. Moreover, assessment and treatment occur simultaneously. The client is frequently challenged to answer the question "Is what we are doing in here helping you make the changes you desire?" With this information, clients are in the best position to determine when they are ready to terminate.

Cognitive-behavioral approaches.   The goal is to eliminate clients' self-defeating outlooks on life and assist them in acquiring more tolerant and rational views of life. Clients are taught how they incorporated self-defeating beliefs, how they are maintaining this faulty thinking, what they can do to undermine such thinking, and how they can teach themselves new ways of thinking that will lead to changes in their ways of behaving and feeling.

Typically, REBT practitioners use a variety of cognitive, affective, and behavioral techniques. Procedures are designed to get the client to critically examine present beliefs and behavior. *Cognitive* methods include disputing irrational beliefs, carrying out cognitive homework, and changing one's language and thinking patterns. *Emotive* techniques include role playing, REBT imagery, and shame-attacking exercises. A wide range of active and practical *behavioral* procedures is used to get clients to be specific and committed to doing the hard work required by therapy. Cognitive-

behavioral approaches insist on client participation in homework assignments both during and outside of the therapeutic sessions. Individuals will
rarely change a self-defeating belief unless they are willing to act consistently against it. Clients are ready to terminate when they give up their
*must*urbatory thinking. When they no longer badger themselves with
"shoulds," "oughts," and "musts" and when they replace their irrational
and self-destructive beliefs with rational and constructive ones, they do not
need formal therapy. Therapeutic outcomes can be evaluated by looking at
the specific cognitive, affective, and behavioral changes demonstrated by
the client.

Family systems therapy.   Depending on the specific orientation of a family systems practitioner, this approach has a variety of goals, some of which
are resolving the presenting problems of the client and the family; resolving a family crisis as quickly and efficiently as possible; creating an environment where new information can be infused into a system, allowing the
family to evolve on its own; restructuring a system so that autonomy by all
family members is encouraged; changing the rules and patterns of interaction among family members; teaching communication skills; and teaching
problem-solving skills.

Change occurs by working with both the family system and the individual. The family therapy process may involve helping each member to
individuate as well as to become a productive member of the family. The
focus is on changing dysfunctional family structures and patterns. Change
occurs both in the family sessions and through directives aimed at practicing skills outside of therapy. Through identifying coalitions and alliances
within the family, the therapist also facilitates change.

My perspective on the integration of goals and techniques

I attempt to integrate goals from most of the major theories by paying
attention to changes that clients want to make in how they typically think,
feel, and behave. My early interventions are aimed at helping clients
identify specific ways in which they want to be different. Once they have
formulated concrete goals, it is then possible to utilize a variety of techniques that foster modification of thinking processes, feelings, and ways of
behaving.

In counseling culturally diverse client populations, it is important to
consider the degree to which the general goals and methods employed are
congruent with the cultural background and values of clients. It is essential
that both the therapist and the client recognize their differences in goal
orientation. For example, it can be a therapeutic mistake to encourage
some clients to learn to be assertive with their parents and tell them exactly
what they are thinking and feeling. An Asian-American client might hold
to the value that it is rude to confront one's parents and that it is inappropriate to bring out conflicts. The therapist who would push such a

client to be independent and to deal with conflicts within the family would probably alienate this person. Interdependence, thinking about what is best for the social group, and striving for harmony may be the dominant values operating in this culture. It becomes critical that therapists listen to their clients and enter their perceptual world. The process of therapy is best guided by the particular goals and values of each client, not by what the therapist thinks is best. Questions that therapists can frequently ask of their clients are "Why are you seeking counseling from me?" "What is it that you would like to explore?" and "What is it about yourself or your life situation that you would most want to change?" By staying focused on what their clients want, therapists can greatly reduce the dangers of imposing their goals.

Having considered a survey of nine therapy perspectives from the vantage point of their basic assumptions, views of assessment, goals of therapy, and therapeutic procedures, we are now ready to consider a specific case. As you study Ruth's case, look for ways in which you can apply what you have just read in gaining a fuller understanding of her.

THE CASE OF RUTH

The themes in Ruth's life are characteristic of those of many clients I have worked with individually and, especially, in groups. As mentioned earlier, I took typical struggles from a number of clients and based a clinical picture on them. Pulled together, these common themes form Ruth. Her intake form, reproduced here, and autobiography will provide you with much of the information you need to understand and work with her. Each of the theory chapters will provide you with extra information. As you read the next nine chapters, I suggest that you refer back to this information about Ruth to refresh you on some of the details and themes in her life.

Ruth's Autobiography

As a part of the intake process the counselor asked Ruth to bring the autobiography that she had written for her counseling class. Although most therapists do not make it a practice to ask their clients to write an autobiography, I think that doing so can be a beneficial experience for the client, as a way of reviewing significant life experiences, as well as a useful tool to give the therapist insight into the client's self-perception. Ruth wrote:

Something I've become aware of recently is that I've pretty much lived for others so far. I've been the superwoman who gives and gives until there is little left to give. I give to my husband, John. I've been the "good wife" and the "good mother" that he expects me to be. I do realize that I need John, and I'm afraid he might leave me if I change too much. I've given my all to seeing that my kids grow up decently, but even though I'm trying my best, I often worry that I haven't done enough.

When I look at my life now, I must admit that I don't like what I see. I don't like who I am, and I certainly don't feel very proud of my body. I'm very overweight, and despite my good intentions to lose weight I just can't seem to get rid of the pounds. I've always enjoyed eating and often eat too much. My family nagged me as a child, but the more they wanted me to stop, the more I seemed to eat, sometimes to the point of making myself sick. I make resolutions to start an exercise program and stick to a diet, but I've yet to find a way to follow through with my plans.

One of the things I do look forward to is becoming a teacher in an elementary school. I really think this would make my life more meaningful. Right now I worry a lot about what will become of me when my kids leave and there is just John and myself in that house. I know I should at least get out there and get that job as a substitute teacher in a private school that I've wanted (and have an offer for), yet I drag my feet on that one, too.

One big thing that troubles me a lot is the feeling of panic I get more and more of the time. I don't remember ever feeling that bad. Often during the day, when I'm trying to do well at school, I feel dizzy, almost like fainting, and have a hard time breathing. Sometimes I'll be sitting in class and get hot flashes, and then I sweat profusely, which is really embarrassing to me. At times my hands start to tremble, and I'm afraid that others will notice this and think I'm weird. And sometimes when I'm sitting in class or even doing shopping, my heart is racing so fast that I worry I'll die of a heart attack. Then there are times when I wake up at night with my heart beating very fast, in a cold sweat, and sometimes shaking. I feel a terrible sense of doom, but I don't know what over. I get so scared over these feelings, which just seem to creep up on me at the times I least expect them. It makes me think that maybe if I don't get better control of myself, I might go crazy. I know that I worry about death—about my dying—a lot. Maybe I still fear going to hell. As a kid I was motivated by fear of fire and brimstone. Nine years ago I finally broke away from my strong fundamentalist church, because I could see that it was not me. Somehow, taking that philosophy class in the community college years ago got me to thinking about the values I was taught. It was the gospel, and who was I to question? So, when I was 30, I made the break from the fundamentalist religion that I had so closely lived by. I'm now attending a less dogmatic church, yet I still feel pangs of guilt that I am not living by the religion my parents brought me up with. They haven't formally disowned me, but in many ways I think they have. I know I'll never win their approval as long as I stay away from the religion that's so dear to them. But I find it more and more difficult to live by something I don't believe in. The big problem for me is that I so often feel lost and confused, wanting some kind of anchor in my life. I know what I don't believe, but I still have little to replace those values that I once lived by. I sometimes wonder if I really discarded those values, because I so often hear the voices of my parents inside my head!

As a part of my college program I took a course that was an introduction to counseling, and that opened my eyes to a lot of things. One of our guest speakers was a licensed clinical psychologist, who talked about the value of counseling for people even though they are not seriously disturbed. I began to consider that maybe I could benefit from getting some counseling. Up until that time I had always thought you had to be a psycho before going to a psychotherapist. I see that I could work on a lot of things that I've neatly tucked away in my life. Yet even though I think I've almost made the decision to seek therapy, there is still this nagging fear within me, and I keep asking myself questions. What if I find out things about me that I don't like? What will I do if I discover there's nothing inside of me? What if I lose John while I'm getting myself together? I so much want those magical answers. All my life I've had clear answers to every question. Then nine years ago, when I became a questioner to some extent, I lost those neat answers. What if I open Pandora's box and too much comes out and I get even more overwhelmed than I already am?

What I most want from therapy is that the therapist will tell me what I have to do and push me to do it, so that I can begin to live before it's too late. The trouble is that I think I could settle for my nice and comfortable life that I have now, even though a great part of it is driving me nuts. Sure, it's boring and stale, but I don't have to make any decisions either. Then again it's uncomfortable to be where I am. But new decisions are so scary for me to make. I'm scared I'll make the wrong decisions and that in doing so I'll ruin not only my life but John's life and the future of my kids. I feel I owe it to them to stay in this marriage. I guess I'm trapped and don't see a way out. And that would be the last straw if my father ever found out that I was seeing a counselor! He'd tell me I was foolish—that all the answers to life are found in the Bible. Sometimes I wonder if I should turn my life over to God and let Him take over. I so much wish He would take over! I don't know what lies ahead. I'm afraid and excited at the same time.

Diagnostic Impressions of Ruth

While I was making an earlier revision of this book, I had a telephone call from Michael Nystul, a professor of counseling at New Mexico State University, who told me that he was using *Case Approach to Counseling and Psychotherapy* for one of his summer classes. "Dr. Corey," he asked, "what diagnosis would you give Ruth? My students are discussing her case, and they were interested in getting your opinion about her diagnostic category."

"Well," I replied, "I generally don't think in diagnostic terms, so I would be hard pressed to give Ruth a diagnosis."

"But if you *had* to give her a diagnosis," he insisted, "what would it be?"

CLIENT'S INTAKE FORM

AGE	SEX	RACE	MARITAL STATUS
			Married
39	Female	Caucasian	**SOCIOECONOMIC STATUS** Middle class

APPEARANCE

Dresses meticulously, is overweight, fidgets constantly with her clothes, avoids eye contact, speaks rapidly.

LIVING SITUATION

Recently graduated from college as an elementary-education major, lives with husband (John, 45) and her children (Rob, 19, Jennifer, 18, Susan, 17, and Adam, 16).

PRESENTING PROBLEM

Client reports general dissatisfaction. She says her life is rather uneventful and predictable, and she feels some panic over reaching the age of 39, wondering where the years have gone. For two years she has been troubled with a range of psychosomatic complaints, including sleep disturbances, anxiety, dizziness, heart palpitations, and headaches. At times she has to push herself to leave the house. Client complains that she cries easily over trivial matters, often feels depressed, and has a weight problem.

HISTORY OF PRESENTING PROBLEM

Client made her major career as a housewife and mother until her children became adolescents. She then entered college part time and obtained a bachelor's degree. She has recently begun work toward a credential in elementary education. Through her contacts with others at the university she became aware of how she has limited herself, how she has fostered her family's dependence on her, and how frightened she is of branching out from her roles as mother and wife.

Ruth completed a course in introduction to counseling that encouraged her to look at the direction of her own life. As a part of the course she participated in self-awareness groups, had a few individual counseling sessions, and wrote several papers dealing with the turning points in her own life. One of the requirements was to write an extensive autobiography that was based on an application of the principles of the counseling course to her own personal development. This course and her experiences with fellow students in it acted as a catalyst in getting her to take an honest look at her life. Ruth is not clear at this point who she is, apart from being a mother, wife, and student. She realizes that she does not have a good sense of what she wants for herself and that she typically lived up to what others in her life wanted for her. She has decided to seek individual therapy for the following reasons:

HISTORY OF PRESENTING PROBLEM (CONT'D)

• A physician whom she consulted could find no organic or medical basis for her physical symptoms and recommended personal therapy. In her words, her major symptoms are these: "I sometimes feel very panicky, especially at night when I'm trying to sleep. Sometimes I'll wake up and find it difficult to breathe, my heart will be pounding, and I'll break out in a cold sweat. I toss and turn trying to relax, and instead I feel tense and worry a lot about many little things. It's hard for me to turn off these thoughts. Then during the day I'm so tired I can hardly function, and I find that lately I cry very easily if even minor things go wrong."

• She is aware that she has lived a very structured and disciplined life, that she has functioned largely by taking care of the home and the needs of her four children and her husband, and that to some degree she is no longer content with this. Yet she reports that she doesn't know what "more than this" is. Although she would like to get more involved professionally, the thought of doing it does frighten her. She worries about her right to think and act selfishly, she fears not succeeding in the professional world, and she most of all worries about how becoming more professionally involved might threaten her family.

• Her children range in age from 16 to 19, and all of them are now finding more of their satisfactions outside of the family and the home and are spending increasing time with their friends. Ruth sees these changes and is concerned about "losing" them. She is having particular problems with her daughter Jennifer, and she is at a loss how to deal with Jennifer's rebellion. In general, Ruth feels very much unappreciated by her children.

• In thinking about her future, she is not really sure who or what she wants to become. She would like to develop a sense of herself apart from the expectations of others. She finds herself wondering what she "should" want and what she "should" be doing. Ruth does not find her relationship with her husband, John, at all satisfactory. He appears to be resisting her attempts to make changes and prefers that she remain as she was. But she is anxious over the prospects of challenging this relationship, fearing that if she does, she might end up alone.

• Lately, Ruth is experiencing more concern over aging and losing her "looks." All of these factors combined have provided the motivation for her to take the necessary steps to initiate individual therapy. Perhaps the greatest catalyst that triggered her to come for therapy is the increase of her physical symptoms and her anxiety.

PSYCHOSOCIAL HISTORY

Client was the oldest of four children. Her father is a fundamentalist minister, and her mother, a housewife. She describes her father as distant, authoritarian, and rigid; her relationship with him was one of unquestioning, fearful adherence to his rules and standards. She remembers her mother as being critical, and she thought that she could never do enough to please her. At other times her mother was supportive. The family demonstrated little affection. In many ways Ruth took on the role of caring for her younger brother and sisters, largely in the hope of winning the approval of the parents. When she attempted to have any kind of fun, she encountered her father's disapproval and outright scorn. To a large extent this pattern of taking care of others has extended throughout her life.

One critical incident took place when Ruth was 6 years old. She reported: "My father caught me 'playing doctor' with an 8-year-old boy. He lectured me and refused to speak to me for weeks. I felt extremely guilty and ashamed." It appears that Ruth carried feelings of guilt into her adolescence and that she repressed her own emerging sexuality.

In her social relationships Ruth had difficulty in making and keeping friends. She felt socially isolated from her peers because they viewed her as "weird." Although she wanted the approval of others, she was not willing to compromise her morals for fear of consequences.

She was not allowed to date until she completed high school; at the age of 19 she married the first person she had dated. She used her mother as a role model by becoming a homemaker.

We exchanged our views on a possible diagnosis for Ruth. Since several possible diagnoses seemed to fit in her case, I began thinking about the process a practitioner goes through in attempting to identify the most appropriate diagnostic category for a client. I then asked several of my colleagues at the university who were familiar with Ruth's case to suggest a diagnosis. Interestingly, I got a variety of interpretations, each with a good supporting rationale. I also asked some of those who were reviewing this manuscript to give me their impressions of the most appropriate diagnostic category for Ruth. As you might suspect, there was a variety of diagnostic impressions.

At this point you are just beginning to familiarize yourself with Ruth. I suggest that you consider what your provisional diagnosis would be for her, knowing what you do at this time. Examine some of the various diagnostic classifications in the DSM-IV and some of the provisional diagnoses given below. Justify the diagnosis you select on the basis of the information presented above. Keep in mind this matter of formulating a tentative diagnosis as you read through the following nine chapters. In learning about the various approaches to counseling Ruth, you may find new evidence or emerging patterns of behavior that warrant modifying your original diagnosis.

Rather than identifying one specific major disorder, I will describe a number of possible provisional diagnoses that *may* be appropriate for Ruth's case. As you review the nine different theories, consider the following diagnostic classifications to see which category you think best fits the case of Ruth.

Adjustment disorder.   The key feature of adjustment disorders is the development of clinically significant emotional or behavioral symptoms in response to psychosocial stressors. Some stressors may accompany specific developmental events, such as beginning school, becoming a parent, having children leave home, and failing to attain educational or career goals. There is some basis for giving Ruth a diagnosis of adjustment disorder, possibly with anxiety. She is experiencing some key developmental crises. A number of stressors are resulting in symptoms such as nervousness, worry, and fear of separation from major figures in her life. She could also be classified as adjustment disorder, unspecified, which reflects symptoms such as physical complaints, social withdrawal, or work or academic inhibition.

Panic disorder.   Individuals who have unexpected panic attacks typically describe their fear as intense and report that they feel as if they are going to die, lose control, or have a heart attack. In general, Ruth presents evidence of an anxiety disorder; specifically, her pattern of symptoms meets the diagnostic criteria for panic attack: palpitations of the heart, sweating, shortness of breath, dizziness, trembling, hot flashes and cold sweats, fear of dying, and fear of losing control or going crazy.

Dysthymic disorder. The essential feature of a dysthymic disorder is chronic depression, which occurs for most of the day on more days than not for at least two years. Individuals with such a disorder often describe their condition as feeling "down in the dumps." When people experience a depressed mood, they often manifest some of the following symptoms: overeating, insomnia, low energy or fatigue, low self-esteem, difficulty in making decisions, and feelings of hopelessness. At times, individuals are self-critical and view themselves as uninteresting or incapable. Ruth appears to fit this picture. She exhibits a long-term depressed mood that is part of her character but not severe enough to be considered major depression. She also manifests dependent personality traits in that she consistently puts the needs of others ahead of herself and has low self-esteem. She exhibits a number of physical complaints but does not indicate any serious physical disease necessitating surgery or other severe medical intervention.

Identity problem. Ruth's patterns fit the syndrome of identity problem. The main features of this classification include uncertainty about long-term goals, career choice, friendship patterns, sexual orientation and behavior, moral and religious values, and group loyalties. Affected clients respond to their uncertainty with anxiety and depression and are preoccupied about their lack of a sense of self. These people doubt themselves in everyday situations. One of the most common questions asked by the person with an identity disorder is "Who am I?"

I asked two of the reviewers of this edition of *Case Approach to Counseling and Psychotherapy* to provide their diagnostic perspectives on Ruth's case. They are Michael Nystul, who was introduced earlier, and Beverly Palmer, professor of psychology at California State University at Dominguez Hills.

Nystul's DSM-IV diagnosis

The three key factors I use to facilitate the process of a differential diagnosis are onset, severity, and duration. Normally, I would explore these three issues within the context of a clinical interview, which would include a mental-status exam. In this instance, I must base my diagnostic impressions on Ruth's autobiography.

The DSM-IV provides guidelines for a comprehensive assessment leading to a diagnosis. There are five categories, called axes, in the DSM-IV that can be used by clinicians in formulating a treatment plan:

Axis I. Clinical disorders; other conditions that may be a focus of clinical attention
Axis II. Personality disorders; mental retardation
Axis III. General medical conditions
Axis IV. Psychosocial and environmental problems
Axis V. Global assessment of functioning

As I read Ruth's autobiography, the major symptoms that stood out for me were anxiety and depression (Axis I disorders). The primary considerations for a differential diagnosis in this case appear to be an adjustment disorder with mixed anxiety and depressed mood, a panic disorder without agoraphobia, or a dysthymic disorder. Ruth's diagnosis could be an adjustment disorder if her anxiety and depression occurred within three months of a stressor and persisted for over six months and her symptoms did not fulfill the criterion of an Axis I disorder such as a panic disorder or dysthemic disorder.

In terms of Axis II, I would want to rule out a dependent personality disorder. The history suggests that "she has fostered her family's dependence on her" and has "pretty much lived for others." If she did not meet the full criterion for a dependent personality disorder, I would record "dependent personality features" on Axis II, if I believed Ruth had prominent maladaptive personality features relating to dependency.

I would record "none" on Axis III (general medical conditions), because the history notes that a physician did not find anything medically wrong with Ruth.

Axis IV requires a listing of the psychosocial and environmental problems that Ruth has experienced within the last year (or longer if she had experienced a posttraumatic stress disorder). A stressor that would be included for Ruth is discord with child. (The history suggested Ruth was having significant problems with Jennifer.) If my clinical interview suggested marital discord, that would also be included on Axis IV.

Axis V allows for the determination of Ruth's Global Assessment of Functioning (GAF). Based on the DSM's guidelines, I would estimate her current GAF to be 60, which would indicate that she has moderate symptoms or moderate difficulty in social/occupational or school functions.

Palmer's DSM-IV diagnosis

Ruth's case is difficult to diagnose because she is a compilation of a number of clients. Yet the DSM-IV category of panic disorder without agoraphobia (300.01) is the one most supported by the evidence presented throughout the book. She experiences unexpected panic attacks and is worried about having additional attacks. The symptoms of a panic attack she experiences are dizziness, heart palpitations, difficulty breathing, sweating, and a fear of dying. All of these symptoms occur within a ten-minute period and usually occur during the evening when she is trying to sleep. Presently, there is no evidence that she has agoraphobia (anxiety about being in a place from which escape might be difficult, which often causes the person to not want to leave her house). However, her therapist would want to monitor her for agoraphobia, since recurrent panic attacks can develop into panic disorder with agoraphobia. Ruth shows signs of yet another DSM-IV disorder: eating disorder not otherwise specified (307.50)—specifically, binge eating disorder. She reports eating more than she should when she is depressed and being very overweight. She also ate to the point of making herself sick when she was a child, and she has tried exercise and dieting but is unable to stick to either. Thus, it appears that she eats, in a discrete period of time, an amount of food that is larger than most people would eat and that she experiences a lack of control over eating during these episodes.

Ruth has two other DSM-IV conditions: a phase of life problem (V62.89) and an identity problem (313.82). She is concerned about what her life will be like after her children leave home or if she begins a professional job, and these concerns are characterized by the existential therapist as components of a midlife crisis. She is struggling with the identity issues of finding the values she does believe in and who she is apart from the expectations of others. Ruth is also having conflicts with her teenage daughter and with her husband, but it is difficult to determine whether these relational problems are causing clinically significant symptoms or significant impairment in family functioning. Thus, two other DSM-IV conditions, a partner relational problem (V61.12), and a parent–child relational problem (V61.20), are probably not warranted from the evidence given.

As important as ruling in a particular diagnosis is ruling out other possible diagnoses. Ruth mentions several times that she feels "depressed" and that she eats more when she is depressed. Yet, there are not enough symptoms of depression to diagnose a mood disorder such as dysthymic disorder. Her tiredness during the day is due to the panic attacks that cause her insomnia. If she had "depression," she would feel tired even though she had had a good night's sleep, and her insomnia (typically early-morning awakening) would not be due to worrying or panic attacks. She does have low self-confidence and some guilty feelings, but she needs at least three of the symptoms listed for dysthymia for at least two years for this diagnosis to be made. So, although "depression" is a catch-all term that many patients use to explain their present condition, it is not an accurate term to be applied in this case. The difference between self-diagnosis and a therapist's diagnosis is often in the degree of understanding of the psychological, social, and biological theories that are the foundation of the DSM-IV categories. Of course, sometimes beneath the panic attacks and anxiety is a depression that can pop up once the panic attacks are alleviated. Another factor that must be eliminated when making the diagnosis of panic attacks is that there is no substance use or general medical condition (such as hyperthyroidism) that might cause the symptoms Ruth reports. She did have a recent checkup by a physician, which is always a wise recommendation for every therapist to make during the initial assessment.

The DSM-IV is a multiaxial system of diagnosis, and so far I have given only Axis I diagnoses. Axis II is used to diagnose personality disorders or personality features that might also be the focus of treatment. Sometimes a person can have only an Axis I or only an Axis II diagnosis, but usually a person has diagnoses on both axes, and the two axes influence each other in treatment. In the case of Ruth there is no Axis II diagnosis (V71.09), although she does show a few dependent personality features. As the behavior therapist says, Ruth has trouble stating her viewpoints clearly, and she often accepts projects in which she does not want to get involved. She admits dragging her feet in getting the substitute schoolteacher job she wants, which may be an indication of the dependent personality trait of having difficulty initiating projects or doing things on her own. Since Ruth shows only three dependent personality traits, she does not have the full-blown picture of dependent personality disorder. The therapist also has to be careful that those traits typical of the socialization of a woman Ruth's age are not pathologized into dependent personality disorder.

Axis III is the place to indicate the results of her recent medical consultation and her problem with being overweight. Her physical condition and physical problems interact with her psychological problems reported on Axes I and II, so it is important to record them in this multiaxial system of diagnosis. For example, her being overweight affects her self-esteem, and her self-esteem affects her weight. Also, her panic attacks might be treated by medication as well as by psychological means, so health professionals from all fields need to communicate with one another. This multiaxial system is an ideal way to start this communication.

Axis IV is the place to record any social or environmental factors in Ruth's life. She reports relational problems with her daughter and with her husband, so it is on this axis that these social issues are recorded as problems with her primary support group.

The final axis, Axis V, is used to report Ruth's overall level of functioning. The usual way of recording this is by using the GAF scale. Ruth has some moderate symptoms, such as occasional panic attacks, which cause her to have some difficulty in her functioning at home, so she receives a GAF score of between 51 and 60.

One important axis is missing from the DSM-IV, and that is one that records Ruth's strengths. She has many strengths; she has recently pursued higher education successfully, and she has good insight into her present condition as well as a thirst for exploring her future directions. Her strengths will be used in treatment just as much as will her difficulties, so it would be important to have a record of them with the DSM-IV system of diagnosis.

In looking over the provisional diagnoses described above, what patterns do you see in these assessments taken as a group? Which ones do you tend to agree with the most, and why? If you do not agree with a particular diagnostic formulation, give your reasons. What are your legal and ethical responsibilities when diagnosing Ruth? Under what circumstances, if any, would you be likely to share your diagnostic impressions with her?

This section on diagnostic procedures with Ruth is necessarily brief in keeping with the purposes of this book. I encourage you to consult the

DSM-IV as a reference tool. My intention in introducing this handbook as a resource is to introduce you to the categories and labeling system that are part of the assessment and diagnostic process. If you are interested in ordering a copy of the DSM-IV, see further information given in the "Recommended Supplementary Readings."

RECOMMENDED SUPPLEMENTARY READINGS

The following books can be used in conjunction with this casebook. For the theory chapters that deal with the case of Ruth, the listed books can provide a theoretical background that will enable you to better grasp the basic dynamics of the case. If you have not had a course in counseling theories, it will be especially important to do some supplementary reading on the foundations of the various approaches.

American Psychiatric Association. (1994). *Diagnostic and statistical manual of mental disorders* (4th ed.). Washington, DC: Author.

This is the official guide to a system of classifying psychological disorders. It is a resource to consult to identify patterns of emotional and behavioral disturbances. It gives specific criteria for the classifications and shows the differences among the various disorders. In addition to describing neurotic, psychotic, and personality disorders, this revised edition also deals with a variety of other disorders pertaining to developmental stages, substance abuse, moods, sexual and gender identity, eating, sleep, impulse control, and adjustment.

If you are interested in obtaining a copy of the DSM-IV, contact:

American Psychiatric Press, Inc.
1400 K Street, N.W., Suite 1101
Washington, DC 20005
Telephone: (800) 368-5777

Corey, G. (1996). *Theory and practice of counseling and psychotherapy* (5th ed.). Pacific Grove, CA: Brooks/Cole. This text deals with all of the theories covered in this casebook by examining themes such as key concepts, the therapeutic process, therapeutic techniques, and evaluation.

Corsini, R., & Wedding, D. (Eds.). (1995). *Current psychotherapies* (5th ed.). Itasca, IL: F. E. Peacock. This book contains an in-depth discussion of all of the theories covered in this casebook. The authors of the chapters on various theories are considered experts in their field.

Cottone, R. R. (1992). *Theories and paradigms of counseling and psychotherapy*. Needham Heights, MA: Allyn & Bacon. The author has chapters on psychoanalytic therapy, rational emotive behavior therapy, person-centered therapy, Gestalt therapy, and behavior therapy, and he has five chapters dealing with systemic and relational paradigms.

Gilliland, B., James, R. K., & Bowman, J. T. (1994). *Theories and strategies in counseling and psychotherapy* (3rd ed.). Needham Heights, MA: Allyn & Bacon. This text has separate theory chapters dealing with the following orientations: psychoanalytic, Adlerian, Jungian, person-centered, Gestalt, transactional analysis, behavioral, reality, cognitive, trait-factor, and eclectic.

Hansen, J. C., Rossberg, R. H., & Cramer, S. H. (1994). *Counseling: Theory and process* (5th ed.). Needham Heights, MA: Allyn & Bacon. This book deals with most of the theories covered in this casebook, and it also discusses the counseling process.

Ivey, A. E., Ivey, M. B., & Simek-Morgan, L. (1993). *Counseling and psychotherapy: A multicultural perspective* (3rd ed.). Needham Heights, MA: Allyn & Bacon. This text provides a good foundation for the traditional theories of counseling and therapy, and it includes an emphasis on the multicultural dimensions of theory and practice.

Orcutt, F. L., & Prell, J. R. (1994). *Integrative paradigms of psychotherapy.* Needham Heights, MA: Allyn & Bacon. As the name implies, this book deals more with an integrative perspective than it does with separate theories.

Prochaska, J. O., & Norcross, J. C. (1994). *Systems of psychotherapy: A transtheoretical analysis.* (3rd ed.). Pacific Grove, CA: Brooks/Cole. The authors have separate theory chapters on all the approaches covered in this casebook, and they also have useful chapters on gender- and culture-sensitive therapies and on integrative therapies.

Schultz, D., & Schultz, S. E. (1995). *Theories of personality* (5th ed.). Pacific Grove, CA: Brooks/Cole. This is an excellent survey text that provides a good foundation for understanding the counseling theories presented in this casebook.

Sptizer, R. L., Gibbon, M., Skodol, A. E., Williams, J. B. W., & First, M. B. (1994). *DSM-IV casebook.* Washington, DC: American Psychiatric Association. This book is a collection of case vignettes that grew out of the authors' experiences. Updated to include information from the DSM-IV, this book helps both students and clinicians visualize disorders through the use of clinical vignettes. If you are interested in obtaining a copy of the DSM-IV Casebook, you can contact:

American Psychiatric Press, Inc.
1400 K Street, N.W., Suite 1101
Washington, DC 20005
TELEPHONE: (800) 368-5777

Wedding, D., & Corsini, R. J. (Eds.). (1995). *Case studies in psychotherapy.* Itasca, IL: F. E. Peacock. This book consists of brief verbatim accounts of a variety of theoretical approaches to case histories. It stresses application of techniques advocated by different schools of therapy.

CHAPTER TWO

Case Approach to Psychoanalytic Therapy

INTRODUCTION

In this chapter and the eight to follow I assume the identity of a therapist from the particular orientation being considered. As much as possible I attempt to stay within the spirit of each specific approach, but I again want to emphasize that you will be seeing my interpretation and my own style. There are many differences in therapeutic style among practitioners who share the same theoretical orientation. Thus, there is no "one right way" of practicing psychoanalytic therapy or any of the other systems. I encourage you to do your best in assuming each of the separate theoretical perspectives as you follow the case of Ruth and take up the other case example in each chapter. Doing this will help you decide which concepts and techniques you want to incorporate into your own therapeutic style.

In each of these nine chapters I am Ruth's therapist. I have read her intake form and her autobiography before meeting her for the first time. In these chapters I give an overview of the particular theory by describing the following: the basic assumptions underlying practice, my initial assessment of Ruth, the goals that will guide our work, and the therapeutic procedures and techniques that are likely to be employed in attaining our goals. A section on the therapeutic process shows samples of our work together. It is illustrated with dialogues between Ruth and me, along with an ongoing process commentary that explains my rationale for the interventions that I make and the general direction of her therapy.

Before I demonstrate my way of working with Ruth from each of the perspectives, there is at least one section written by an expert in each of the theoretical orientations. It is a good practice for counselors to consult with other practitioners at times, for doing so provides them with ideas of other ways to proceed with a client. In working with Ruth, I am using this model of consultation. Background data on Ruth's case were sent to a well-known representative of each approach, who was asked: "How would you assess Ruth's case? What themes would you probably focus on? What procedures would you be likely to use? How would you expect the therapeutic process to unfold? The contributions of these consultants are used to introduce each therapeutic approach.

A PSYCHOANALYTIC THERAPIST'S PERSPECTIVE ON RUTH, by William Blau, Ph.D.

Assessment of Ruth

Psychoanalytic perspective and overview of case material.   As a psychoanalytically oriented therapist I suspect that Ruth's background descriptions of her parents, her siblings, and herself are less than objective. Moreover, I predict that the areas of inaccuracy will turn out to be clues to the core of her personality problems. I anticipate finding that her symptoms (anxiety attacks, overeating, fear of accomplishment, panic over being 39, fear of abandonment, and so forth) can be interpreted as outward manifestations of unconscious conflicts that have their origins in childhood experiences and defensive reactions to these experiences that were necessary to her as a child. I suspect, given her intelligence and motivation, that her current exacerbation of symptoms is related to her recognition of discrepancies between what makes sense to her logically and what seems to drive her emotions and behavior. I hypothesize that Ruth is experiencing a split (a struggle between opposing dimensions of herself). This conflict is between the part of her that wants to change and the other part of her that clings to old patterns that were once necessary and have helped her maintain mental stability all her life. Although some of her defenses seem maladaptive from my perspective, I believe I cannot give her the most effective help unless I can fully understand *why* her patterns of defense seem necessary to her *now* and why, once, they were necessary to her psychological survival.

In contrast to some therapeutic practitioners, I am very interested in why Ruth thinks, feels, and behaves as she does. I have no interest in excusing her behavior or condemning others, but I believe that her problems can be most fully helped by answering the "why" as well as the "what" questions regarding her life. I believe that this fundamental interest in the "whys" of an individual client's experience and behavior is a critical distinction between analytic therapy and other approaches.

Unraveling the dynamics of her history and filling in the story of her life with newly emerging memories will be an ongoing part of Ruth's treatment; hence, this aspect of assessment is never complete, although it becomes less important in the final phases of treatment.

Assessing Ruth's suitability for analytic therapy.   Before establishing a contract to do analytic therapy with Ruth, I would need to ascertain if she was a good candidate for the treatment and if she had the perseverance and resources to make this approach the treatment of choice. Assessment of her need for analytic therapy would include determining whether she wants and needs to understand the unconscious roots of her neurosis. If simply teaching her about the pathological nature of some of her behavior would lead to significant change, she would probably not need analytic therapy. Didactic approaches would suffice. I suspect, however, that Ruth does not consciously know why she reacts in symptomatic ways, and I suspect that she is repeatedly frustrated when she has been given good advice by others (or by herself) but still finds the old patterns persisting.

As a psychoanalytic therapist I believe that the economics of treatment, both in terms of financial arrangements and also in the investment of time and energy in therapy, cannot be separated from the process of therapy or expectations for a successful outcome. I would assess the degree of commitment Ruth brings to the initial sessions and would establish not only her ability to pay for a lengthy course of treatment but also the relationship of her method of payment to the dynamics of treatment. Her case history indicates that she works as a housewife and student and fears abandonment. Would the therapy be financed by her husband, either directly or through insurance? Would her university be providing the treatment as a health benefit, and, if so, would her eligibility end once she obtained her teaching credential? These issues are important not only to ensure continuation of treatment but also to understand the role of the fee in the dynamics of the therapy. If, for example, Ruth's husband is financing the therapy, how will that affect her struggles for independence?

Ruth's case history does include a number of factors suggesting that she could be a good candidate for analytic treatment. Her autobiography shows her to be a woman for whom understanding the meaning of her life is important and for whom achieving individuation is a meaningful goal. Her autobiography also shows that she has the ability to look at herself from a somewhat objective perspective. Her need for symptom alleviation is sufficient to provide strong motivation for change, yet her symptoms are not currently incapacitating.

Ruth fantasizes that the therapist will tell her what to do with her life and take the place of her father and the God of her childhood religion. In contracting with her for treatment, I would let her know that fulfillment of this fantasy is not provided by analytic psychotherapy; however, this would by no means end the issue. Despite the formal contract I anticipate that she will continue to demand that the therapist take charge of her life. This aspect of transference will be of ongoing significance in treatment. On the whole, Ruth is the sort of client for whom analytically oriented psychotherapy might be indicated.

Diagnosis.   DSM-IV diagnosis of Ruth is of limited value. It is necessary in that physical causes for Ruth's symptoms must be ruled out. Analytic therapy is more clearly indicated for some disorders than for others, and some disorders require extensive modification of technique. But traditional diagnosis is limited in that the individual's ability to form a therapeutic alliance, which is the key issue in assessment for analytic treatment, is largely independent of diagnosis.

From a diagnostic standpoint (once it has been demonstrated that Ruth is not suicidal or homicidal) the most important issues would be to determine the role of organic factors in her symptomatology and to determine if she should be referred for medication.

Ruth's reported unhappiness with her life could be her way of expressing symptoms of depression that might be helped by medication in addition to psychotherapy. If she is depressed "for most of the day, for more days than not," a DSM-IV diagnosis of dysthymic disorder should be considered. Her panic attacks could be related to a cardiac condition, and her "hot flashes" and other psychophysiological symptoms could have organic as well as psychodynamic origins.

In DSM-IV terms, Ruth meets the following diagnostic criteria:

- 301.01: panic disorder without agoraphobia
- 313.82: identity problem

Neither of these diagnostic categories, in my opinion, conveys a feeling for Ruth as she is described in her autobiography and intake form. DSM-IV diagnoses tend to reify symptom clusters rather than promoting understanding of the client as a person.

Panic attacks are the essential elements of the panic disorder diagnosis, and I would strongly consider treating these attacks initially with the cost-effective techniques of psychophysiological counseling and biofeedback rather than psychoanalytic psychotherapy. DSM-IV diagnoses of panic disorder are coded as either with or without agoraphobia. I specified "without agoraphobia" because Ruth doesn't describe herself as being unduly afraid to travel or to be in crowds or similar social or confining situations. Nevertheless, at times she "has to push herself to leave the house," according to her intake form. This statement suggests that agoraphobia is a potential symptom. If agoraphobic symptoms develop or if further case-history information indicates that DSM-IV criteria for agoraphobia are presently met, the diagnosis should be changed to 300.21, panic disorder with agoraphobia.

The DSM-IV category of identity problem is descriptive of the contents of Ruth's concerns. However, it is not a "clinical disorder" in DSM-IV terms, and it minimizes the intensity of her very real suffering.

The real, human Ruth presents a blending of neurotic symptoms and existential concerns. Her symptoms seem to be at a critical stage and could flower into an eating disorder, a counterphobic impulsive behavior, a generalized anxiety disorder, or a psychosomatic conversion disorder, as well as agoraphobia or a dysthymic disorder as discussed above. Her difficulties in establishing a sense of self suggest that her individuation is an important goal of treatment. I do not anticipate overtly psychotic symptoms, and her basic reality testing appears sufficiently stable that she can be expected to undergo some degree of regression in the course of treatment without danger of precipitating a psychotic break.

Key Issues and Themes in Working with Ruth

Intrapsychic conflicts and repression of childhood experiences.   As a psychoanalytically oriented psychotherapist I accept the role of detective in ferreting out the secrets of the past that are locked away in Ruth's unconscious. Although I am guided by theory to suspicious content areas, her psyche and the secrets therein are uniquely hers, and it is ultimately she who will know the truth of her life through her own courage and perceptions.

I suspect that the psychosexual aspects of Ruth's relationships with her parents (and possibly her siblings) remain key conflict areas for her, even now. In the classical Freudian model of healthy development, she would have experienced early libidinal attraction to her father, which she would eventually have replaced with normal heterosexual interests in male peers; likewise, her feelings of rivalry with her mother for her father's affection would have been replaced with identification with her mother. In the ideal model, moreover, she would have experienced rebellion against parental constraints, particularly during the developmental period associated with toilet training and also in adolescence.

In reality Ruth appears to have superficially avoided normal rebellion and to have repressed her sexuality except for adopting a wifely role with the first man she dated. Although she followed the format of using her mother as role model and having children by an acceptable husband, she apparently abdicated in the struggles of sexuality, rebellion, and identification, leaving these conflicts unresolved. Her conscious recollections of her parents are of a rigid, fundamentalist father and a "critical" mother. I would be interested in knowing what these parents were really like, as perceived by Ruth in childhood. How did her father handle his feelings for his children? Did his aloofness mask strongly suppressed incestuous feelings that she intuitively sensed? Were these ever acted out?

A Freudian view of her father's harsh reactions to Ruth's "playing doctor" would emphasize the Oedipus/Electra aspects of this father/daughter encounter. Her father's refusal to speak to her for weeks after this incident suggests jealousy rather than simply moral rejection of childhood sexual activity. This suspicion is supported by the parentally imposed isolation of the children that delayed dating until after high school. Ruth's attempts to win her father's approval by supplanting the role of mother (by caring for her younger siblings) is also consistent with these Oedipus/Electra dynamics. Ruth internalized her father's overtly negative attitude to sexuality.

If these hypotheses are correct, a theme in therapy will be Ruth's reexperiencing of the sensual aspects of her attachment to her father and his response to her. As she is able to first "own" these feelings and memories and then to relinquish the fantasy of fulfillment with her father, she can become open to an adult relationship in which her sexuality is appreciated rather than scorned or distorted.

Although there is no direct evidence of sexual abuse in the case material, the family dynamics are such that there is the possibility of actual incestual acts by the father, the memories of which have been repressed by Ruth. Even more likely is the pattern wherein the father's incestuous feelings were not overtly acted out but were so intense that he developed defenses of reaction formation and projection, labeling her sexuality (rather than his) as reprehensible. The jealous response of Ruth's mother is consistent with either of the above patterns of paternal behavior, but the mother's response is more pathological (and more pathogenic) if actual abuse occurred.

Oedipus/Electra feelings by both parent and child are considered part of normal development. However, intense conflicts and guilt regarding these feelings or experiences are very common in clients seeking counseling or psychotherapy, and all too often, actual molestation is eventually determined to have occurred.

Regardless of the details of the actual memories and buried feelings unearthed in the therapy, the analytic therapist is alert for indications of psychological traumas in the client's early life, psychic wounds that may be associated with a family *secret* that the client has needed to protect from exposure through suppression, denial, and repression. The probability of a secret being at the heart of Ruth's neurosis is increased by the indication in the case material that she was socially isolated and that her lack of relationships outside the family was enforced by the parents, at least in terms of dating. The entire family may have lived with their unspoken secrets in relative isolation. Although incestuous themes in one form or another are the most common secrets unearthed, other "unthinkable" secrets may be at the center of the repression—namely, the hidden mental illness, homosexuality, or alcoholism of a family member.

To what extent is Ruth bringing themes from her family of origin to her present family? She defines her husband only by what he is not (her father) and by his potential to reject her (as her father had rejected her). Does she know the man she married at all, or is he merely a stand-in for the real man in her life? Is her husband's apparent rejection of her attempts at personal growth a facet of his personality, or is he being set up? Her reaction to her daughter Jennifer may very likely be related to her own failure to rebel. Acceptance and nurturance by Ruth of the suppressed child-rebel aspect of herself may well improve her relationship with her daughter.

Symptoms and Psychodynamics

A psychoanalytic approach views psychological symptoms as active processes that give clues to the client's underlying psychodynamics. Some acute symptoms are valuable in that they alert the client that something is wrong. Other symptoms, particularly when chronic, may be extremely resistant to intervention and may severely impair or even threaten the life of the client.

Ruth's symptoms (assuming that organic factors are absent or minimal) suggest compatibility with psychoanalytically oriented therapy. I would use analytic theory to help understand the role of anxiety in her life and the methods she uses to control her anxiety.

I view Ruth's current existential anxiety as related to these issues: Her early training by her parents clearly made individuation (in the object-relations sense) a very scary proposition for her; hence, any attempt toward individuation is anxiety-provoking. She is, therefore, terrified not only of acting impulsively but also of acting independently. She hopes to make her own choices in life but also hopes that her therapist will make her decisions for her.

Ruth's symptom of overeating probably gratifies her need for affection, but a psychoanalytic approach to this symptom would also explore its developmental origin. Oral gratification is the primary focus of libidinal energy in the earliest stage of development. Symptoms associated with this stage can appear if the client suffered deprivation during this period *or* if the period was relatively gratifying. If the symptom relates to early deprivation, the adult is fixated on getting the satisfaction never adequately obtained during the childhood stage. I am inclined to suspect that Ruth's overeating is regressive, and that she experienced her most satisfactory developmental stage in infancy when she may have been accepted by her mother and when her libidinal needs could be satisfied at her mother's breast without being labeled "sexual" by her father. This hypothesis is supported by her having a relatively intact adult personality and a reasonable amount of ego strength. She is able to seek therapy for her needs to individuate without having had to exhibit the extreme problems in social living (suicide attempts, inability to maintain any relationship, and failure to tolerate the stresses of mothering) that are diagnostic of the borderline syndrome. Significant deprivation during the "pre-oedipal" stages of early childhood, particularly the oral stage, is associated, in analytic thinking, with psychosis, sociopathic character formation, and borderline/narcissistic personality disorders. Ruth's current mental status suggests problems at the later stages of development in which Oedipus/Electra dynamics are prominent. This distinction is relevant to her treatment in that the treatment of pre-oedipal conditions requires more deviation from traditional technique than does the treatment of neurotic states, which have their origins primarily in the later developmental stages.

Ruth's weight problem also has psychodynamic meaning. Being overweight may lead to her feeling sexually unattractive and, therefore, less likely to be faced with sexual arousal. To the degree that her morality is based on compliance with authority rather than on personal choice, she would be tempted by anyone demanding sex from an authoritative position. Moreover, her overweight may be directly related to Oedipus/Electra themes. She may be in some sense saving her sexuality for her father or for a fantasy hero who will break the spell cast by her father. If her overweight has been more severe since she began experiencing the "empty-nest" syndrome, her obesity may represent a symbolic pregnancy.

Ruth's increasing difficulty in leaving home suggests a fear of meeting others who might threaten the stability of her marriage. This symptom is consistent with the dynamics of her overweight.

The exacerbation of physical symptoms and anxiety is cited in the background information as being the catalyst for Ruth's seeking therapy at this time. A psychoanalytic approach to these symptoms would explore the "secondary gain" associated with each symptom. A symptom is expected to include elements of both sides of an intrapsychic conflict. For instance, a headache might serve to keep her sexually distant from her husband while also providing a pretext for avoiding social contacts that might threaten the marriage.

Analytic therapy provides a means for treating Ruth's symptoms, but only in the context of broader treatment of her psychological problems. Some psychosomatic, phobic, and eating disorders can be treated directly, and at lesser expense, by nonanalytic therapies. When the client wants understanding as well as symptom relief or when the "secondary gain" of the symptom leads to either failure of the direct approach or to the substitution of a new symptom for the old one, analytic therapy is indicated. Ruth gives evidence of multiple symptoms and of a desire to examine her life. Hence, consideration of analytic therapy rather than a symptom-focused behavioral approach is reasonable.

Treatment Techniques

Psychoanalytically oriented psychotherapy versus psychoanalysis. The treatment approach I propose for Ruth is psychoanalytically oriented psychotherapy rather than psychoanalysis. This choice does not indicate a theoretical disagreement with the methods of classic analysis; psychoanalytic psychotherapy is a form of analytic treatment that has advantages and disadvantages compared with classical psychoanalysis. In classical analysis the analyst adopts a "blank-screen" approach in which expressions of the real analyst/client relationship are minimized in order to promote development of the client's transference relationship with the analyst. Transference leads the client to react to the analyst as if he or she were a significant person from the client's past life.

Psychoanalytic therapy does not require the blank-screen approach, is less frustrating to the patient, allows the therapist more flexibility in technique, is less costly, may be shorter in duration, and provides "support" for the patient's least maladaptive defenses. Hence, it is often the treatment of choice. The drawbacks of analytic psychotherapy as compared with psychoanalysis are directly related to the advantages. The variations in technique lead to a lowering of expectations, as many aspects of the client's personality will remain unanalyzed due to elimination of the blank screen and the consequent intrusion of aspects of the "real" relationship between therapist and client into the analysis of their "as-if" transference relationship. If, for example, Ruth is in analysis with me, free-associating from the couch, and she states her belief that I disapprove of some feeling or behavior of hers, I can be reasonably sure that she is reacting to me as if I were some other figure in her life. In contrast, if she makes the same assertion in face-to-face psychotherapy, my actual nonverbal behavior (or prior self-disclosure of any sort) may have given her valid clues to my actual (conscious or unconscious) disapproval of her feelings or behavior. I can never know the exact degree to which her response is a transference response as opposed to a response to my "real" behavior in our "real" relationship. In psychoanalytically oriented psychotherapy with Ruth I must keep in mind that every aspect of our interaction will have a mix of "real" and "as-if" components. To the degree that I participate in the "real" relationship by providing support, by giving advice, or by sharing an opinion or personal experience, I am limiting my ability to maintain an analytic stance to the material she presents.

Although significant therapeutic work is possible using this model, I must be very sensitive to the meanings that Ruth will attribute to my "real" interactions with her. If I disapprove of a particular act or intention of hers, for example, I can reasonably expect her to assume that I approve of all her reported acts or intentions to which I have *not* expressed disapproval. Thus, although I am free to use the "real" as well as the "as-if" relationship in making therapeutic interventions, I am not free to vacillate in my therapeutic stance without risk of doing harm.

The therapeutic contract.   I form as clear a therapeutic contract as possible with Ruth, explaining the goals, costs, and risks of the treatment as well as briefly describing the methods and theory of psychotherapy. I make my expectations regarding payment explicit, including the analytic rule that fees are charged for canceled sessions. This contractual clarity regarding fees has therapeutic implications in that Ruth's obligation to me for my services is specified at the outset of treatment. Thereafter, she can feel free of any additional requirement to meet my needs, and I can interpret any concerns that she does express about my needs in terms of the "as-if" relationship. As indicated in the assessment section above, the method by which she pays for the sessions is significant. Ideally, she should pay enough to be motivated to make good use of each hour, but she should not be placed under a financial strain that will create a hardship or precipitate a premature termination of treatment.

A treatment schedule of two or three sessions per week, each session lasting 50 minutes, is typical for psychoanalytically oriented therapy. Any planned vacations in the next six months or so, by either Ruth or me, should be noted, and therapy should not commence shortly before a vacation.

Other aspects of the contract include confidentiality (and its limitations), the degree to which I am available for emergencies or other between-session contacts, and an admonition to generally avoid making major life decisions during the course of treatment. The latter "rule" for clients in analysis is relevant to Ruth. She indicates that she wants a therapist to make decisions for her, and I have some concern about the possibility of her leaping to decisions while experiencing regression in the course of treatment.

Free association.   Free association is a primary technique in psychoanalysis and is the "basic rule" given to clients. In my therapy with Ruth I emphasize the technique of free association at certain times, such as when she comments that she doesn't know what to talk about. However, we have verbal interaction in addition to her free associations, even in the early phases of therapy. I often instruct her to express her associations to her dreams, to elements of her current life, and to memories of her past life, particularly new memories of childhood events that emerge in the course of treatment.

Dreams, symptoms, jokes, and slips.   Dreams are considered the "royal road" to the unconscious, and I encourage Ruth to report her dreams and to associate to them. As an analytically oriented therapist I conceptualize each of her dreams as having two levels of meaning, the manifest content and the latent meaning. Analytic theory postulates that each dream is a coded message from her unconscious, a message that can be interpreted so as to understand the unconscious wish that initiated the dream and the nature of the repression that forced the wish to be experienced only in disguised form. Hypotheses about the latent meaning of dream symbols can be derived from theory, but the actual interpretation of her dream elements is based on her own unique associations to her dream symbols.

In addition to dreams, the hidden meanings inherent in Ruth's symptoms are subject to analysis. Her presenting symptoms, manifestations of resistance, memories, and spontaneous errors (slips of the tongue) are clues to her underlying dynamics. The wordplay involved in slips of the tongue is meaningful, as may be any intentional joke or pun made or recalled by her in a session.

Interpretations of resistance and content.   My initial interpretations are of resistance, and I follow the rule of interpreting the resistance that Ruth presents relative to a content area before actually interpreting the content. I recognize that every accurate interpretation is an assault on her defenses, and I know that she will react to the interpretation as a threat to her present adjustment. Hence, in choosing the timing of a particular interpretation, I am guided by her readiness to accept it as well as by my sense of its accuracy. I also follow the general rule that more inferential interpretations should be made in the later stages of therapy after a therapeutic alliance and trust have been established. Early interpretations should be minimally inferential, often only noting a correspondence. For example, commenting to Ruth that she wrote less in her autobiography about her mother than she did about her father is much less inferential than interpreting her overeating as a defense against sexuality.

Many interpretations, particularly in the later stages of therapy, relate to her transference reactions and are geared to helping her work through childhood-based conflicts in the context of her therapeutic relationship with me.

The following brief dialogue begins with the here and now and ends with an insight about the past:

RUTH: I worry I'm just hiding in my therapy. It's an indulgence; I should be using your time to fix my problems, not just to talk about anything I like.

THERAPIST: What's being hidden here?

RUTH: That I'm not really working. I tell myself I'm going to a doctor's appointment, but you just listen, and I just play around with my thoughts.

THERAPIST: Is it OK to play here, at your doctor's appointment?

RUTH: Of course not. This is work; we're not playing. You wouldn't see me if I were here to play, Dr. Blau.

THERAPIST: There was a time when your father didn't speak to you for weeks.

RUTH: That was about playing doctor too! Do I still think it's sinful to explore? My dad would be shocked at some of the thoughts I've explored here.

THERAPIST: How would he react?

RUTH: He'd be . . . Oh, I just remembered how he looked then. He got red in the face and stammered. His brow got sweaty. He punished me, for my sin.

THERAPIST: For whose sin?

RUTH: Maybe . . . for his own. I hardly knew anything about sex when he decided I was bad; maybe his thinking about me being sexual made *him* feel guilty or something.

THERAPIST: But you're the one who got punished.

RUTH: Yeah. I got punished for what *he* thought and felt, not for what I actually did.

In this example I follow a hunch that Ruth's concern about "playing" at her "doctor's" appointment might have associations to the childhood incident when she was punished for "playing doctor." Her acceptance of this association sets the stage for the final interpretive exchange and insight.

Even the best interpretations are only hypotheses that are presented to the client for consideration. Premature interpretations can be harmful, even if correct. As a therapist, I keep an open mind about the meaning of Ruth's thoughts, feelings, memories, dreams, and fantasies, and I rarely make interpretations about the actuality of past events, imagined or remembered. Although I use my hunches to promote the process of freeing repressed memories, I do not treat my hunches about the past as if they were facts to be imposed on the client's reality.

Transference and countertransference.   Ruth's experience in therapy is both gratifying and frustrating. It is gratifying in that we spend each hour focusing on her life. Her needs, hopes, disappointments, dreams, fantasies, and everything else of importance to her are accepted as meaningful, and she need not share center stage with anyone else. It is her hour, and I listen to everything without criticizing her or demanding that she see anything my way or do anything to please me. My sustained, active attention to and interest in her are different from any other interpersonal interaction. Other people in her life insist on wanting things from her, or they want to criticize her, or at the very least they expect her to be as interested in them as they are in her.

But the sessions are also frustrating. Ruth wants help, and all I seem to do is listen and occasionally ask a question or comment on what she has said. Do I like her? Or am I only pretending to be interested because that's what I am paid for? When, she wonders, will the therapy start helping? When will she find out how to resolve her issues about her marriage and her boring life?

Given this mixture of gratification and frustration, it is not surprising that Ruth begins to see *me* as a source of both of those emotions. Moreover, it is not surprising that she will "transfer" onto me attributes of others in her life who have been sources of gratification and frustration to her. Hence, she begins to react to me as if I were her father, mother, or other significant figure.

The permissiveness of the sessions also allows Ruth to regress—to feel dependent and childlike and to express her thoughts and feelings with little censorship. I take almost all the responsibility for maintaining limits; she need only talk. Her regression is fostered to the degree that I maintain the classic analytic stance, and it is ameliorated to the degree that I interact with her in terms of our "real" relationship—for example, by expressing empathy.

Ruth's past haunts her present life and interpersonal relationships, and to an even greater degree it haunts her relationship with me. But the distortions projected onto me exist in a controlled interpersonal setting and, therefore, are amenable to interpretation and resolution. The therapeutic session provides a structure in which the nature of her conflicts can be exposed and understood, not only in the sense of intellectual insight but also in the analysis of their actual impact on her perceptions and feelings about me and the therapeutic relationship.

The therapeutic relationship provides gratification and frustration for the therapist as well as for the client. My therapeutic task includes monitoring not only the content of the sessions but also my feelings that grow out of this relationship. There are aspects of Ruth that I like and others that I dislike. I find her dependency both appealing and irritating. I enjoy the positive attributes she projects onto me, and I experience some hurt when she projects negative attributes onto me. Nevertheless, I must minimize indulgence in these reactions and concentrate instead on ensuring that my participation consistently promotes her self-understanding and individuation. Although she is free to demand anything and everything from me, I must deny myself almost all the rewards of a "real" relationship with her.

Understanding the theory of therapeutic techniques helps me keep my perspective, as does recollection of my own therapy. The therapy I have received is useful to me in understanding the psychotherapeutic experience from the client's point of view, and it helps me understand some of my conflicts that could impair my effectiveness as a therapist. Nevertheless, my adherence to the ideal role is imperfect. To some extent I inadvertently let my feelings and conflicts distort my perceptions of Ruth. My distortions include my projecting onto her attributes of significant figures in my own life; I experience countertransference. Although I can minimize countertransference, it can never be eliminated. Therefore, to minimize the negative impact of my countertransference on Ruth's treatment, I monitor my feelings about her and my reactions toward her, and I periodically discuss my treatment of her, including these feelings, with a trusted colleague. Voluntary consultation about my feelings and interventions is, in my opinion, an effective method for assessing and minimizing deleterious effects of countertransference. If I find myself uncomfortable discussing a particular aspect of Ruth's treatment, I suspect that countertransference is at work. Consultations must be conducted so as to protect her confidentiality; this usually includes her releasing of the information and my altering information about her identity during the consultation.

My scrutiny of my countertransference reactions to Ruth may be of value in helping me understand her; often my unconscious reactions to a client give clues to that patient's dynamics and to the reactions that others have to the patient. Countertransference can be used in the service of the therapy if it can be understood and controlled. My monitoring of my countertransference feelings serves as a major source of clinical information about the client. If I were to find my countertransference to be having a significant negative effect on Ruth's treatment, I would, after consultation, enter therapy myself and either refer her to a colleague or continue to treat her under supervision.

Some aspects of countertransference may be partially inseparable from the conscious motivation of the therapist to engage in the arduous work of psychotherapy. As I work actively with Ruth to break the spell cast on her in her past, I apply my understanding of the nature of the spell and of the "magic" needed to break it. As I engage in this struggle, I run the countertransference risk of becoming invested in the hero role, thereby fostering her dependence and prolonging her regression. But to some extent I have opted for this role by choosing the profession of psychotherapist. Thus, by participating in Ruth's life as the hero she has dreamed of, I am fulfilling my own not-so-unconscious needs. But if I am to stay a hero in the sense of being a good therapist, I must renounce the role of hero to Ruth at precisely the moment in therapy in which I have released her from the past's constricting spell.

JERRY COREY'S WORK WITH RUTH FROM A PSYCHOANALYTIC PERSPECTIVE

Basic Assumptions

As I work with Ruth within a psychoanalytic framework, I am guided by both the psychosexual perspective of Sigmund Freud and the psychosocial perspective of Erik Erikson. My work with her is also influenced to some extent by contemporary psychoanalytic trends, which are often classified in terms of ego psychology and object-relations theory. I am moving beyond Freud to illustrate that contemporary psychoanalysis is an ever-evolving system rather than a closed and static model.

The *psychosexual theory*, as seen in traditional Freudian psychoanalysis, places emphasis on the internal conflicts of an individual during the first six years of life. This theory assumes that certain sexual and aggressive impulses are repressed during these formative years, because if they were to become conscious, they would produce extreme anxiety. Although these memories and experiences are buried in the unconscious, they exert a powerful influence on the individual's personality and behavior later in life.

The *psychosocial theory*, developed primarily by Erikson, emphasizes sociocultural influences on the development of personality. It assumes that there is a continuity in human development. At the various stages of life, we face the challenge of establishing an equilibrium between ourselves and our social world. At each crisis, or turning point, in the life cycle we can either successfully resolve our conflicts or fail to resolve them. Failure to resolve a conflict at a given stage results in fixation, or the experience of being stuck. It is difficult to master the psychosocial tasks of adulthood if we are psychologically stuck with unresolved conflicts from an earlier period of development. Although such a failure does not necessarily doom us to remain forever the victim of fixations, our lives are, to a large extent, the result of the choices we make at these stages.

The more recent work in the *psychoanalytic approach* is represented by the writings of Margaret Mahler, Heinz Kohut, and Otto Kernberg, among others. Contemporary psychoanalytic practice emphasizes the origins and transformations of the self, the differentiation between the self and others, the integration of the self with others, and the influence of critical factors in early development on later development. Predictable developmental sequences are noted in which the early experiences of the self shift in relation

to an expanding awareness of others. Once self/other patterns are established, they influence later interpersonal relationships. Human development can best be thought of as the evolution of the way in which
individuals differentiate self from others. One's current behavior in this
work is largely a repetition of the internal patterning during one of the
earlier stages of development.

In viewing Ruth's case, I make the assumption that her early development is of critical importance and that her current personality problems are
rooted in repressed childhood conflicts. Borrowing from Kohut's thinking,
I surmise that she was psychologically wounded during childhood and
that her defensive structure is an attempt to avoid being wounded again. I
expect to find an interweaving of old hurts with new wounds. Thus, I pay
attention to the consistency between her emotional wounding as a child
and those situations that result in pain for her today. Much of our
therapeutic work is aimed at repairing the original wounding.

The work of repairing early wounds takes time. Therefore, I expect to
see Ruth at least a couple of times a week for a minimum of three years.
Two of the reasons that therapy will take so long are that it entails a
reliving of early childhood memories and events and that the client must
do some basic reorientation. I am interested in a structural change in Ruth,
not in mere problem solving or in removal of symptoms. I see therapy as
an uncovering process that delves into repressed experiences. I assume
that for many years a person such as Ruth has been storing away conflicts,
intense feelings, and other impulses. Even though she may not be conscious of it, these repressed feelings influence her current behavior. It
would also be important to pay attention to the social and cultural factors
influencing her present struggles.

I make many of these assumptions before meeting a client. The psychoanalytic perspective on the developmental process provides me with a
conceptual framework that helps me make sense of an individual's current
functioning. Although I do not force my client into this theoretical mold, I
do make certain general assumptions about the normal sequence of human
development.

Assessment of Ruth

The following assessment is based on a few initial sessions with Ruth, her
intake form, and her autobiography. Her relationships with her parents are
critically important from a therapeutic standpoint. She describes her father
as "distant, authoritarian, and rigid." My hunch is that this view of her
father colors how she perceives all men today, that her fear of displeasing
her husband is connected to her fear of bringing her father displeasure,
and that what she is now striving to get from her husband is related to
what she wanted from her father. I expect that she will view me and react
to me in many of the same ways she responded to her father. Through this

transference relationship with me she will be able to recognize connecting patterns between her childhood behavior and her current struggles. For example, she is fearful of displeasing her husband, John, for fear he might leave. If he did, there would be a repetition of the pattern of her father's psychological abandonment of her after she had not lived up to his expectations. She does not stand up to John or ask for what she needs out of fear that he will become disgruntled and abandon her. She is defending herself against being wounded by him in some of the same ways that she was by her father.

From a psychosexual perspective I am interested in Ruth's early childhood experiences in which she developed her personal sexuality. Her father's response when he caught her in an act of sexual experimentation needs to be considered as we work with her present attitudes and feelings about sex. As a child and adolescent she felt guilty and ashamed over her sexual feelings. She internalized many of her father's strict views of sexuality. Because her father manifested a negative attitude toward her increased sexual awareness, she learned that her sexual feelings were evil, that her body and sexual pleasure were both "dirty," and that her curiosity about sexual matters was unacceptable. Her sexual feelings became anxiety provoking and were thus rigidly controlled. The denial of sexuality that was established at this age has been carried over into her adult life and gives rise to severe conflicts, guilt, remorse, and self-condemnation. Like Dr. Blau, I have a hunch that her weight problem is partially associated with her denial of sexuality. She does not allow herself to experience sexual attraction to men, nor does she allow herself to enjoy a sexual relationship with her husband. If she is not physically and sexually attractive either to herself or to others, she will not have to deal with anxiety.

Viewing Ruth from a psychosocial perspective will shed considerable light on the nature of her present psychological problems. As an infant she never really developed a basic trust in the world. She learned that she could not count on others to provide her with a sense of being wanted and loved. Throughout her early childhood she did not receive affection, a deprivation that now makes it difficult for her to feel that she is worthy of affection. The task of early childhood is developing *autonomy*, which is necessary if one is to gain a measure of self-control and any ability to cope with the world. In Ruth's case she grew up fast, was never allowed to be a child, and was expected to take care of her younger brothers and sisters. Although she seemed to be "mature" even as a child, in actuality she never became autonomous.

Ruth will not feel truly independent until she feels properly attached and dependent. This notion means that to be independent, one must be able to depend on others. Ruth, however, never felt a genuine sense of attachment to her father, whom she perceived as distant, or to her mother, whom she viewed as somewhat rejecting. For Ruth to have developed genuine independence, she would have needed others in her life whom she could count on for emotional support. But this support was absent from her background. During the school-age period she felt inferior in social relationships, was confused about her sex-role identity, and was unwilling to face new challenges. During adolescence she did not experience an identity crisis, because she did not ask basic questions of life. Rather than questioning the values that had been taught to her, she compliantly accepted them. In part, she has followed the design established by her parents when she was an adolescent. She was not challenged to make choices for herself or to struggle to find meaning in life. In her adulthood she managed to break away from her fundamentalist religion, yet she could not free herself of her guilt over this act. She is still striving for her father's approval, and she is still operating without a clearly defined set of values to replace the ones she discarded. A major theme of her life is her concern over how to fill the void that she fears will result when her children leave home.

Psychoanalytic theory provides a useful perspective for understanding the ways in which Ruth is trying to control the anxiety in her life. As one of her primary ego defenses she readily accepted her parents' rigid morality, because it served the function of controlling her impulses. Further, there is a fundamental split within her between the "good girl" and the "bad girl." Either she keeps in control of herself and others by doing things for them, or she gets out of control when she enjoys herself, as she did when she was "playing doctor." She feels in control when she takes care of her children, and she does not know what she will do once they leave home. Coupled with this empty-nest syndrome is her ambivalence about leaving the security of the home by choosing a career. This change brings about anxiety because she is struggling with her ability to direct her own life as opposed to defining herself strictly as a servant of others. This anxiety will be a focal point of therapy.

Goals of Therapy

The goal of our analytically oriented work will be to gradually uncover unconscious material. In this way Ruth will be able to use messages from the unconscious to direct her own life instead of being driven by her defensive controls. Therapy is aimed at the promotion of integration and ego development. The various parts of her self that she has denied will become more connected. The ideal type of identity is an autonomous self, which is characterized by self-esteem and self-confidence, capable of intimacy with others.

Therapeutic Procedures

I suspect that a major part of our work will entail dealing with resistance, at least at the start of therapy. In spite of the fact that Ruth has come to therapy voluntarily, any number of barriers will make her progress slow at times. She has learned to protect herself against anxiety by building up defenses over the years, and she will not quickly surrender them. As we have seen, some of her primary defenses are repression and denial. The chances are that she will have some ambivalence about becoming aware of her unconscious motivations and needs. Merely gaining insight into the nature of her unconscious conflicts does not mean that her therapy is over, for the difficult part will be the exploration and working through of these conflicts.

I mentioned earlier that therapy would be a long process. One of the reasons is that much of our time will be devoted to exploring Ruth's reactions to me. I expect that I will become a significant figure in her life, for I assume that she will develop strong feelings toward me, both positive and negative. She will probably relate to me in some of the same ways that she related to her father. Working therapeutically with this transference involves two steps. One is to foster this development of transference; the second consists of working through patterns that she established with significant others in her past as these feelings emerge toward me in the therapy relationship. This second step is the core of the therapy process. *Working through* refers to repeating interpretations of her behavior and overcoming her resistance, thus allowing her to resolve her neurotic patterns. Although I do not use a blank-screen model, keeping myself mysterious and hidden, in this type of intensive therapy the client is bound to expect me to fulfill some of her unmet needs. She will probably experience again some of the same feelings she had during her childhood. How she views me and reacts to me will constitute much of the therapeutic work, for this transference material is rich with meaning and can tell her much about herself.

In addition to working with Ruth's resistances and with any transference that develops in our relationship, I will probably use a variety of other techniques to get at her unconscious dynamics. Dream analysis is an important procedure for uncovering unconscious material and giving her insight into some areas of unresolved problems. I will ask her to recall her dreams, to report them in the sessions, and then to learn how to free-associate to key elements in them. Free association, a major procedure in our therapy, involves asking her to clear her mind of thoughts and preoccupations and to say whatever pops into her head without censoring, regardless of how silly or trivial it may be. This procedure typically leads to some recollection of past experiences and, at times, to a release of bottled-up feelings. Another major technique at my disposal is interpretation, or pointing out and explaining to Ruth the meanings of behavior manifested by her dreams, her free-association material, her resistances, and the nature of our relationship. Timed properly, these interpretations (or teachings) can help her assimilate new learning and uncover unconscious material more rapidly. This, in turn, will help her understand and deal with her life situation more effectively.

The Therapeutic Process

The crux of my therapeutic work with Ruth consists of bringing her past into the present, which is done mainly through exploring the transference relationship. My aim is to do more than merely facilitate recall of past events and insight on her part; instead, I hope that she will see patterns and a continuity in her life from her childhood to the present. When she realizes how her past is still operating, character change is possible, and new options open up for her.

Elements of the process

Exploring Ruth's transference.   After Ruth has been in therapy for some time, she grows more disenchanted with me because she does not see me as giving enough. For instance, she becomes irritated because I am not willing to share anything about my marriage or my relationships with my children. She says that I give her very analytical responses, when she is simply trying to get to know something about me personally. She complains that she is the one doing all the giving and that she is beginning to resent it. Here is a brief sample of a session in which we talk about these feelings:

RUTH: I want you to be more of a real person to me. It feels uncomfortable for you to know so much about me, when I know so little about you.
JERRY: Yes, it's certainly the case that I know a lot more about your life than you know about mine and that you're more vulnerable than I am.
RUTH: Well, you seem so removed and distant from me. You're hard to reach. This is not easy for me to say . . . uhm . . . I suppose I want to know what you really think of me. You don't tell me, and I'm often left wondering what you're feeling. I work hard at getting your approval, but I'm not sure I have it. I get the feeling that you think I'm bad.
JERRY: Has anyone else made you feel like this?
RUTH: Well, ah . . . you know that I always felt this way around my father. No matter what I did to get his approval, I was never really successful. And that's sometimes the way I feel toward you.

I am consciously not disclosing much about my reactions to Ruth at this point because she is finally bringing out feelings about me that she has avoided for so long. I encourage her to express more about the ways in which she sees me as ungiving and unreachable and as not being what she wants. It is through this process of exploring some of her persistent reactions to me, I hope, that she will see more of the connection between her unfulfilled needs from the past and how she is viewing me in this present relationship. At this stage in her therapy she is experiencing some very basic feelings of wanting to be special and wanting proof of it. By working over a long period with her transference reactions, she will eventually gain insight into how she has given her father all the power to affirm her as a person and how she has not learned to give herself the approval she so much wants from him. I am not willing to reassure her, because I want to foster the expression of transference.

Working with Ruth's internalized mother. At another period in Ruth's therapy we spend many sessions exploring her relationship to her mother. We focus on how she felt toward her mother as a child and how she feels toward her now. As a child Ruth attempted to become to her father what her mother was, but she never managed to replace her mother in her father's eyes. She tried by becoming "mother" to her younger brother and sisters and by working as hard as she could for recognition. But this was to no avail, for she did not get the recognition that she wanted from either her father or her mother. Much later in her sessions we explore the parallels between her giving to her brother and sisters and the way in which she has devoted much of her adult life to giving to her own children, only to feel a lack of appreciation and recognition for her efforts at being a good mother.

Process commentary

I am not working with Ruth from the perspective of classical psychoanalysis. Rather, I am drawing from psychosocial theory and from concepts in the newer psychoanalytic thinking, especially from Kohut's work. I direct much of our therapy to the exploration of Ruth's old issues, her early wounding, and her fears of new wounds. The bruises to her self that she experiences in the here and now trigger memories of her old hurts. Especially in her relationship with me, she is sensitive to rejection and any signs of my disapproval. Therefore, much of our therapeutic effort is aimed at dealing with the ways in which she is now striving for recognition as well as the ways in which she attempted to get recognition as a child. In short, she has a damaged self, and she is susceptible to and fearful of further bruising. We discuss her attachments, how she tried to win affection, and the many ways in which she is trying to protect herself from suffering further emotional wounds to a fragile ego.

As Ruth's therapy progresses, she is able to let more material rise to consciousness. We focus on the conflicts between her id (the impulsive and "spoiled-brat" side of her personality, which craves indulgence in physical gratification immediately), and her superego (her conscience and all the morals and standards that she has incorporated into her self-system). It is obvious that Ruth has an extremely strong superego, one that is based on some unrealistically high standards of perfection and that punishes with guilt. Through her therapy, I hope, she will learn to relax the boundaries of her superego so that she will not be controlled by its demands for perfection.

Much of Ruth's work involves going back to early events in her life—recalling them and the feelings associated with them—in the hope that she can be free from the restrictions of her past. She comes to realize that her past is an important part of her and that some old wounds will take a long time to heal.

One of the major ways in which Ruth gains insight into her patterns is by learning to understand her dreams. We regularly focus on their meanings, and she free-associates to some symbols. She has a very difficult time giving up control and simply allowing herself to say freely whatever comes to mind in these sessions. She worries about "saying the appropriate thing," and of course this is material we examine in the sessions. Dream work is one of the major tools to tap her unconscious processes.

Ruth also discovers from the way she responds to me some key connections between how she related to significant people in her life. She looks to me in some of the same ways that she looked to her father for approval and for love. I encourage her recollection of feelings associated with these past events, so that she can work through barriers that are preventing her from functioning as a mature adult.

Questions for Reflection

As you continue working with the nine therapeutic approaches described in this book, you will have many opportunities to apply the basic assumptions and key concepts of each theory to your own life. Some of the questions below will assist you in becoming more involved in a personal way. The rest of the questions are designed to give you some guidance in beginning to work with Ruth. They are intended to help you clarify your reactions to how the consultant and I worked with her from each of the therapeutic perspectives. Select the questions for reflection that most interest you:

1. Blau emphasizes the importance of understanding the "whys" of a client's experience and behavior. What advantages and disadvantages do you see in this focus?
2. Blau suggests that the psychosexual aspects of Ruth's relationships with her parents, and possibly her siblings, still represent key conflict areas in her present behavior. In what ways may her early experiences be having a significant impact on her life today? How might you explore these dynamics with her?
3. Do you share the emphasis of this approach on the importance of Ruth's father in her life? How might you go about exploring with her the ways in which conflicts with her father are related to some of her present conflicts?
4. Reflecting on your own childhood, what do you consider to be some significant events that still have an impact on your life today? (How did you get approval or disapproval? How much trust did you feel toward significant people in your life? What attitudes did you develop toward sex? How were your dependency needs met?)

5. Do you think that your relationships with your mother or father influence your life today, especially the ways in which you relate to significant women and men? What might you not have received from either parent that you are now seeking from other people?
6. What is one of the most significant themes (from the analytic perspective) that you would focus on in your sessions with Ruth?
7. How might you respond to Ruth if she challenged you over your aloofness and your unwillingness to give of yourself personally? Might you become defensive if she compared you to her father and accused you of being just like him? If you were more revealing, how do you expect that your therapy would be any different with her?
8. In what ways would you encourage Ruth to go back and relive her childhood? How important is delving into the client's early childhood in leading to personality change?
9. What defenses do you see in Ruth? How do you imagine you would work to lessen these defenses?
10. Blau discusses the importance of both the therapist's "real" relationship and the "as-if" relationship with Ruth. How might you differentiate between her transference reactions and her "real" reactions to you?

MOE: A RESISTIVE CLIENT
WHO ESCAPES WITH ALCOHOL

Moe has been in therapy with me for one year. Besides describing his character and what he is doing in therapy, I will give a running commentary explaining why I am proceeding as I am and clarifying what is occurring between us.

Some Background Data

Moe, who is 37 years old, originally became involved in analytically oriented therapy with me on the recommendation of his physician. It was clear to the doctor that he had a major drinking problem, which was a manifestation of more deeply rooted personality problems. Initially, he resisted seeing himself as a "problem drinker." Using the DSM-IV, I gave him a tentative general diagnosis of *substance abuse*. Moe exhibits the symptoms of *borderline personality disorder*. He shows impulsive binge behavior, engages in frantic efforts to avoid real or imagined abandonment, shows a pattern of unstable and intense interpersonal relationships, displays inappropriate and intense anger, manifests affective instability due to a marked reactivity of mood, and has a disturbed and unstable self-image. It appears that Moe has no significant medical problems or medical history. It also appears that he has problems with his primary support group (V61.9) and occupational problems (V62.2). Finally, his Global Assessment of Functioning (GAF) score is in the moderate range, probably around 51–55. As an adjunct to his individual therapy with me, he agreed to join Alcoholics Anonymous, which he now continues in by his choice.

So far in therapy we have done a lot of reviewing of Moe's early childhood years, which were rather traumatic. His mother died when he was 10, and his father sent him to a private boarding school in another state, feeling that he could not manage to bring up Moe by himself. Moe felt abandoned by both his parents: by his mother, who had died and left him, and by his father, just when he had most needed love, companionship, and support.

Moe has had three marriages, each of which ended when his wife left. Typically, each woman grew tired of his continual drinking binges and all that went with his alcoholism: getting fired from job after job, not being a father to his children, being abusive both verbally and physically to her, and being extremely dependent on her. Moe decided that he did not have what it took to keep a wife, and he grew increasingly bitter toward women. They *all* left him when he was most in need of them. Clearly, one of his conflicts is his dependency on women and his hostility toward them.

In his work life Moe feels a great deal of anger toward a former boss who fired him from his executive position in a business firm. He has complained that when "I was broke, financially and personally, my boss took my job away from me instead of giving me the support I needed." In Moe's eyes important men always let him down. His father sent him away, and his boss sent him away; what few male friends he did have broke contact with him, mainly because they felt put off by his drinking.

Moe has many ambivalent feelings toward me, which we have been working on in our sessions. He feels a liking and respect for me, and he says he needs me. He also feels hostility, fears letting himself "become dependent" on me, and in many ways is constantly defying me and testing me to see if I will be like other men in his life. We are now working on his *resistance* and his feelings toward me.

Highlights of Moe's Therapy

My goals in working with Moe.   Thinking within the analytic framework, I see psychotherapy as a process that should foster major character changes in Moe. This reconstruction will be accomplished by assisting him to become aware of his unconscious needs and motives. Examples of some of his unconscious dynamics are his dependency on strong women to take care of him and his conflicts with his bosses, whom he views as authority figures. My focus will be on using therapeutic methods designed to open the doors to his unconscious processes. I work on the assumption that it is necessary to recall and relive early childhood memories and experiences. These experiences will be reconstructed, discussed, interpreted, and analyzed with the aim of significantly changing his personality. Although I do not want to focus therapy entirely on his drinking, it will be imperative that we deal with his alcoholism. I will address the unconscious motivations and dynamics associated with his drinking as well as with some of his other passive/aggressive and highly dependent character traits. As Moe and I continue our sessions, I identify and diagnose him as a passive/aggressive client who is using alcohol as one of his major defenses and escape mechanisms.

To unlock Moe's unconscious, I focus on past experiences, such as the impact of his mother's death on him, his being sent away to a private boarding school, and other occasions when he felt a sense of abandonment and rejection. I pay special attention to linking these traumatic situations and feelings from the past with present situations. Working with some of his reactions toward me and his expectations of me, I help him gradually acquire self-understanding.

Moe begins to learn about his ego defenses.   Moe is gradually developing some insights into the typical defenses he uses to deal with anxiety. He is acquiring this understanding through talking about subjects that he typically avoids and through my interpretations. I am attempting to teach him the meaning of certain patterns of behavior by pointing out significant connections between dreams and his everyday behavior, by working with his resistances, and by exploring early events with him. For example, Moe will need to recognize that he typically numbs his feelings of sadness. By denial and avoidance he attempts to deaden himself to the hurt and abandonment he felt first as a child, when his mother died, and later as an adult, when his wives divorced him. He does this most strikingly by drinking. Moe is beginning to understand that *denial* is a way in which he has continued to deceive himself and thus ward off anxiety. In particular, his alcoholism is a fact that he has denied; he has kept himself from looking at his inability to handle alcohol by placing blame on others and looking to external events for his personal failures. If reality is too painful for him to accept, he typically ignores it.

Working with Moe's alcoholism.   Moe has a pattern of substance abuse. It would be a mistake to treat only his symptoms while ignoring the chemical dependency itself. Theoretically, I view the dynamics of his drinking problem as a fixation at an infantile level (oral stage). He is still unconsciously striving to be loved and taken care of in a way that is more appropriate to an infant. Part of my role will be to assist him in developing insight into the connection between many of his personality problems and his addiction to alcohol. As is true for most alcoholics, he feels socially isolated, unable to love others or receive love from them; he feels chronic guilt; he experiences depression and self-pity frequently; and he feels frightened in interpersonal relationships. Alcohol, a depressant drug, probably promotes or deepens the depression that he experiences. Sexual dysfunctions are common among alcoholics, as are broken marriages. Eventually, Moe will have to be confronted in a caring and concerned manner with his substance abuse. He is continuing his drinking even though he is in treatment. At this point he is using excuses, rationalization, denial, and minimizations. If I am well versed in the alcoholic's confused system of beliefs, all of these defenses can be effectively dealt with and eventually turned around and used as information leading to insight on his part. Yet timing is critical. At this point he is not likely to "hear" interpretations pertaining to his drinking problem, so we begin with the exploration of issues that are less threatening for him to consider. Eventually, however, his problem of chemical dependency will need to be thoroughly dealt with in therapy. It is a good sign that Moe has agreed to attend AA meetings. I think it would be a helpful adjunct to his therapy with me if he continued attending these meetings. There is no reason why we cannot work on the problem of his substance abuse and his underlying personality problems at the same time.

Procedures and Techniques Used with Moe

Keep in mind that the techniques I employ with Moe are part of the framework of psychoanalytically oriented therapy (rather than psychoanalysis). The techniques of free association, dream analysis, interpretation and analysis of resistance, and interpretation of the transference relationship are all routes to bringing out unconscious dynamics. The assumption is that the main way for Moe to change is to acquire insight and to work through places in his life where he got stuck. This is a relatively slow process that demands both patience and commitment.

Free association.   A basic tool for uncovering repressed material is free association, which consists of expressing whatever comes to mind, regardless of how painful, illogical, or irrelevant it may seem. At times I might begin a session with a free-association exercise that goes something as follows:

JERRY: Moe, I'd like you to close your eyes and try to clear your mind for a time. Let yourself say aloud whatever comes to your mind. Try not to make any sense out of what you're saying; just report any reactions, thoughts, and feelings you're experiencing. Simply flow with your words with as little censorship as possible.

The purpose of this exercise is to encourage Moe to become more spontaneous and to uncover unconscious processes. During this time I pay attention to patterns in his associations, especially noting areas where he tends to block or censor. In one session, for example, it is evident that he is censoring any information pertaining to the times he physically abused his wife in each of his marriages. This blocking is important to interpret and analyze. I am interested in identifying the patterns and themes that become apparent through his therapy sessions. I simply listen carefully to what he is saying, how he is saying it, and what he is not saying. I may use this free-association technique with a particular word, especially when he makes a significant "slip." For example, in one session Moe inadvertently refers to "Mother" when he is talking about one of his former wives. Using this as a clue, I ask him to free-associate to the word *mother*. His associations are "Never there . . . strong . . . doesn't care . . . all alone . . . [a long pause] lonely . . . dead and gone" [another pause, and he begins sobbing].

Following up on Moe's slip leads him to uncover some painful feelings toward his mother, which provide therapeutic material. This example shows that the free-association process may lead to a recall of past experiences that release intense feelings, which can then be explored in depth. In a later session we come back to explore the implications of Moe's slip in referring to his ex-wife as "Mother." This leads to a series of discussions of his dependency on and resentment of women.

Working with Moe's dreams.   I am extremely interested in Moe's dreams, for I see them as a rich avenue to tapping his unconscious wishes, fears, conflicts, needs, desires, and impulses. At times, he is reluctant to report his dreams, saying that he has "forgotten" them or that he has not been dreaming lately. Sometimes he does bring in a dream, and my task is to work with him to uncover its disguised meaning by studying the symbols involved. Again, when it is appropriate, I attempt to teach him about himself and his current conflicts through interpreting the meanings of his dreams. The following excerpts represent the manner in which we work.

Moe reports a dream in which several large women are chasing him with clubs. He is frightened that they will catch him and beat him to a pulp. They get closer to him, he trips . . . Then he wakes up in a panic.

I ask Moe to free-associate with every element in the dream, even though every aspect is not necessarily symbolic. His associations to this dream are as follows:

MOE: I'm afraid of those big clubs. They have thorns on them, and if I get hit, that could be it for me! Where can I run to and hide? I'm afraid I can't run fast enough, that I'll get caught and they'll hurt me. These women seem to hate me, and they want to do me in! I feel so helpless and scared. This is the way I felt so often when I was a child. I felt that I'd get hurt, and nobody would be around to protect me. I'm afraid I'll make a mistake, that I'll trip up, and that my mother will punish me by beating me. I tried to do my best, but I was always afraid I'd do the wrong thing and get hit. I remember wishing that my father would protect me, but he just looked the other way.

From these associations Moe begins to understand the meaning of his dream: "The women are my mother and other strong and oppressive women in my life who have the power and desire to hurt me. Nobody will protect me from the wrath of women!"

His dream contains interesting symbolism, which he avoids and which I choose not to interpret at this stage of his therapy. It seems to me that clear oedipal themes are being expressed unconsciously in his dream. Yet I need to be careful of introducing an interpretation or material that he does not seem ready to consider as being part of him. Even though I don't share with him my interpretation of the oedipal content of his dream, I do keep this in the background, and it provides me with more clues to some of his struggles. Moreover, it should be emphasized that I do not rely on one dream to uncover meaningful connections between his past and his present struggles. A dream is an additional resource for learning about his psychodynamics. Taken in conjunction with other material, it can provide clues to solving a puzzle.

I should add that dream analysis is not a simple matter, and the therapist needs to know a great deal about the client's life to accurately interpret a given dream. It takes years of clinical experience and study to explore dreams from a psychoanalytic perspective.

Working with Moe's resistance.   Resistance is Moe's way of avoiding opening the doors to unconscious material. Thus, a basic technique in analytic therapy is interpreting these avoidance patterns so that the client can begin to work through these barriers. Moe understands that his resistances are something to be understood and worked with in therapy, for they are ways of learning about some painful reality in his past.

Some manifestations of Moe's resistance that I have observed are:

- not remembering many of his dreams
- avoiding exploring sexual and aggressive themes in his dreams
- "forgetting" to show up for some appointments
- being late to some sessions
- talking about superficial topics
- his failure to pay some of his bills on time
- his insistence at times that I tell him what to talk about in the session
- his typical style of looking outside of himself for reasons to justify any failures on his part
- attending a session drunk

I see avoidance behavior, in whatever form it may take, as part of Moe's defenses against the anxiety that is aroused in him when he gets close to unconscious content. How do I deal with his resistances? First of all, they are not just something to be overcome. Both he and I need to recognize that his resistances are valuable indications of his defenses against anxiety, and they need to be understood and worked with. Generally, I call attention to the more readily observable resistances and work with these behaviors first. I take care not to criticize him, for that would be likely to increase his resistance. Also, I do not make dogmatic pronouncements, telling him what a certain pattern of behavior means; instead, I ask him to think for himself about some of these patterns and what they may indicate.

Working with our relationship.   As I mentioned earlier, Moe's reactions to me represent a rich resource for understanding conflicts that stem from relationships to significant people in his past. At times he treats me in many ways as a father figure—sometimes, the father he feels he had and at other times, the father he wishes he had had.

Moe goes through a period of several months expecting me to "kick him out" of therapy. He feels that because he has not been a cooperative and ideal patient, I will abandon him by refusing to see him in therapy any longer. Of course, there is a connection between what he experienced with his father and what he fears he will experience with me. We work in depth on these feelings that I will not be there when he needs me, sorting out what this means to him. We also explore some of his expectations and needs of me. In a very hostile way he continues asserting that I would not have the slightest interest in being with him if I were not being paid for the relationship. He feels resentment that he has to pay high fees to be listened to and cared about. We explore the reality of this situation as well as some of his own narcissism relating to his expectation that he be cared about unconditionally on his terms. He continues thinking that I am not providing enough direction and that merely letting him struggle will not get him anywhere. I agree that I provide little structure, telling him that this is part of my therapy approach. Instead, I deal with his reactions toward being in a situation in which I will not meet his demands and in which he has to decide what to bring up in his sessions.

We are devoting much of our time in current sessions to exploring Moe's dependency on me, which is primarily manifested by his wanting me to make important decisions for him. He looks to me for advice on how to proceed in life; when such advice is not forthcoming, he typically reacts with some hostile remark. He also has loving feelings for me, which are frightening to him. He is learning that he denies these positive feelings at times, so that he can remain angry.

Most of Moe's resistances that emerge from the sessions are an unconscious attempt to set me up to dislike him and ultimately to reject him. This follows the pattern of his significant relationships in the past. Related to his resistive behavior is the importance of maintaining my own objectivity. I must not get caught up in my own feelings and counterdefensive reactions toward him. If I get entangled in countertransference (my own defensive reactions that are a manifestation of my unconscious conflicts), I miss opportunities to help him work through places where he is now stuck. By remaining objective and by not overreacting personally to his behavior, I am able to foster his transference toward me so that we can analyze and interpret it. His reactions to me provide rich clues to the ways in which he was emotionally wounded as a child and to how much of his current behavior is unconsciously aimed at defending him against being wounded again.

Paradoxically, the very thing that Moe wants to avoid—being rejected and abandoned—he is unconsciously repeating. The difficult and time-consuming part of our therapy consists of his gradually becoming aware of ways in which he is replicating earlier interpersonal relationships. Once he gains insight into how he is bringing his past into present relationships in a self-defeating way, we will have to work through these barriers to his growth. In an early session, for example, he disclosed to me his appreciation for how much I had done for him and how much I meant to him. After expressing his affection and respect for me, he seemed very embarrassed and then made some indirect and sarcastic remarks. The next session he showed up 30 minutes late and drunk. The following week we dealt at length with his having appeared for his appointment drunk. He expressed his fear that I had judged him and had decided that he was a worthless person with no hope of getting better. Instead, I confronted him with what he had done and then explored with him the meaning of his behavior. I did not judge him as a worthless person, and I did not abandon him, even though on some levels he was setting me up to do so, as he had set up other significant people to criticize and eventually leave him.

By staying focused on the unconscious meanings of Moe's behavior and by not reacting to him in negative ways that he is used to from past experiences, I am teaching him that there can be a new ending to certain life dramas. Thus, in this transference situation we have the basis for him to learn new lessons about interpersonal relationships. Moe is acquiring the ability to perceive people differently than he perceived his parents.

I see Moe as a very dependent person, one who is looking for me to "feed" him. In his childhood he was deprived of the love and guidance he so much needed. Now in this relationship with me he is hoping that I will meet some of his infantile needs by protecting him, reassuring him, telling him that he is a special patient, approving of him, recognizing any progress he makes in therapy, and in many ways replacing the father that he never had. Rather than merely meeting his dependency needs, I am more interested in his coming to understand how he is repeating in his relationship with me some of his ineffective attempts to be recognized as a child. If I cater to his wants, I merely support his passivity and his helplessness.

The core of much of our work in therapy consists of Moe's becoming aware of those feelings that he had toward men such as his father and his boss that he is now projecting onto (or attributing to) me. Because these transference feelings are so essential for him to both understand and to *work through* in his relationship with me, I want to foster a climate in which they can be recognized, brought out into the open, discussed, and analyzed. The goal is that he will eventually no longer need to make men such as myself into father figures and thus keep himself as a "little boy." I hope that he can work through the transference relationship with me successfully, giving a *new ending* to our relationship and escaping the self-destructive ending he has had with other significant people in his life.

In order to create a therapeutic climate that will better enable Moe to both recognize the nature of his intense feelings toward me and work through (resolve) these feelings, I do not engage in much self-disclosure. By hiding many of my reactions from him, I keep myself an ambiguous figure. Because of this ambiguity his manner of perceiving and responding to me will be largely a matter of his projections, which we work with in therapy.

If I am to be therapeutic for Moe, I must be aware of any of my own unresolved conflicts that can easily surface in my relationship with him. For example, I need to be aware of my reactions toward dependency on me. If I have an unconscious need to keep him dependent on me, it can seriously impede therapeutic progress. If I am unaware of my feelings toward him when he responds to me in a passive/aggressive way, I can become ensnarled in my own countertransference feelings. If I have a need to be appreciated by him and instead he refuses to cooperate with me, my own unconscious reactions toward him will prove counterproductive. Thus, it is essential that I be aware of my own needs, motivations, and unresolved personal issues from my past and of how these factors are likely to intrude in our work together. Many psychoanalytically oriented therapists become aware of these countertransference issues by being a client themselves.

It is clear that the task of personality restructuring in Moe's case will take several years of intensive work, for gaining insight into the origins of his present conflicts is not sufficient. He will need to see patterns in his present behavior and, over time, learn about the connections between his past and present. It is also necessary that he integrate these insights into a fuller awareness of how he is bringing his unresolved conflicts into his relationships with people in his life today.

Follow-Up: You Continue as Moe's Therapist

When I ask you to imagine that I am referring a client to you for further therapy, my hope is that you will function as much as possible within the conceptual framework of the model under discussion in each chapter. Also, you will learn best if you think of other directions in which to move with the client and if you use techniques other than the ones I have described. Assume that you can go beyond the point I left off with the particular client, which in most of these cases is just a beginning. Build on my work and what you know about the client, as well as *your reactions* to him or her, and modify the approach I have initiated in any way that seems appropriate to you.

In Moe's case I hope that you will let yourself *think psychoanalytically,* so that you can begin to get some sense of how you might approach him from an analytic perspective and draw on its techniques. Attempting to "get the feel" of the psychoanalytic approach by staying as much as possible within its spirit will help you determine what aspects of it you might incorporate into your own style of counseling.

Some questions for you to consider as you evaluate my work with Moe and decide on the direction you might proceed with him are:

1. What clues in Moe's behavior patterns would you look for as you formulated a tentative diagnosis in his case? If you worked in an agency that expected you to diagnose a client during the intake session, would assessment present any difficulties for you? If so, what? Would you be inclined to share your diagnostic impressions with your client? Why or why not?
2. How would you work with Moe if he were from a different culture?
3. What ethical issues are involved if you accept Moe without having the background and training to deal competently with his alcoholism? Do you see any ethical considerations in working with him if you do not like him or find yourself reacting negatively to him? When might you consider a referral?
4. What are some of your reactions to Moe? Would you like to work with him as a client? Why or why not?
5. What are your reactions to the way in which I worked with Moe? How might you have used techniques differently? What themes might you have paid more attention to than I did? What different interpretations might you have made about the material that he produced?
6. To what extent do you feel a sense of empathy with Moe's struggles? Do you have a personal perspective that would enable you to identify with him to the extent that you could understand his world? If you didn't think that you could identify with him, what would you be likely to do?
7. How might you deal with Moe's feelings toward you, especially if they were hostile? How do you imagine that you would react if he were to treat you as his father? as his mother? as an all-wise authority figure?
8. How might you deal with the various manifestations of Moe's resistance? Can you see yourself becoming defensive? Can you think of ways in which you could deal with his resistance therapeutically?
9. What countertransference issues could come up for you in your relationship with Moe? Are you aware of any unresolved problems of your own that could interfere with a *therapeutic* relationship?
10. How would you proceed with Moe? Discuss some areas that you would explore with him, as well as the techniques that you might use.

RECOMMENDED SUPPLEMENTARY READINGS

Baruch, D. (1964). *One little boy.* New York: Dell (Delta). This is a fascinating account of one boy's feelings and problems. Using play therapy, it reveals how his personal conflicts originated in family dynamics. The book gives the reader a sense of appreciation for the struggles most children experience during early childhood in relating to their parents.

Erikson, E. (1963). *Childhood and society* (2nd ed.). New York: Norton. This book is based on a modified and extended version of psychoanalytic thought. The author describes a psychosocial theory of development, delineating eight stages and their critical tasks.

Linder, R. (1954). *The fifty-minute hour.* New York: Bantam. This is a collection of true psychoanalytic tales. In spite of the date of this book, it is considered a classic that presents a descriptive illustration of psychoanalysis in action.

Malcolm, J. (1982). *Psychoanalysis: The impossible profession.* New York: Random House (Vintage). Here is a popular book that captures some of the analytic process in an interesting and accurate way. Highly recommended as a nontechnical illustration of how the psychoanalytic process unfolds.

Rossner, J. (1983). *August.* New York: Warner Books. This best-selling novel provides examples of client/therapist dialogue, helping bring to life many of the concepts and techniques of psychoanalysis.

Yalom, I. D. (1989). *Love's executioner: And other tales of psychotherapy.* New York: Harper (Perennial). Yalom has done an exceptional job in capturing key lessons in therapeutic practice. The ten cases that make up this book read like a novel, and they convey more meaning than most textbooks on clinical practice.

CHAPTER THREE

Case Approach to Adlerian Therapy

AN ADLERIAN THERAPIST'S PERSPECTIVE ON RUTH, by James Robert Bitter, Ed.D.

Introduction

Jerry Corey consulted with me on the case of Ruth and asked for my help in conducting a thorough initial interview and a summary of impressions based on this initial interview. I also provided a lifestyle assessment, including a summary of the family constellation, a record of early recollections, and an interpretation of Ruth's pattern of basic convictions.

Lifestyle information is collected and interpreted by two therapists, using a technique called multiple therapy. The client is initially interviewed by one therapist, who then presents the data to a second therapist. The client experiences social interest in the very structure of therapy. The model of two therapists cooperating in a single effort is often therapeutic in and of itself.

As mentioned in the first chapter, this section is longer than those in most other chapters in order to provide you with a detailed and comprehensive assessment of Ruth's early background and her current functioning so that you can use this material as you work with her case in this book. This section begins with a general diagnosis and an initial interview using the *Individual Psychology Client Workbook*, which was developed by Robert L. Powers and Jane Griffith.*

The Individual Psychology Client Workbook, by Robert L. Powers and Jane Griffith. © 1986 by The Americas Institute of Adlerian Studies, Ltd., 600 North McClurg Court, Suite 2502A, Chicago IL 60611-3027.

GENERAL DIAGNOSIS: INITIAL INTERVIEW

The Life Situation (Items 1–20)

1. Date: February 20, 1995
2. **Present Age:** 39
3. **Date of Birth:** January 15, 1956
4. Name, address, home phone, maiden name; full name of spouse:
   Name: Ruth Walton; maiden name: Dowell; spouse's name: John
   All other information deleted.
5. Occupation, position, address, work phone; occupation of spouse:
   Homemaker, mother, student seeking certification as elementary schoolteacher; spouse is a sales manager.
6. Preferred phone and mailing address (home or work):
   Information deleted.
7. Marital status (age of spouse, how long married, anniversary, previous marriages); or current love relationship (how long, level of relationship):
   Married to John, age 45; wedding was on June 17, 1974; no previous marriage.
8. Children (names, ages, sex; deceased children and other pregnancies; adoptions, difficulties of conception; from other marriages):
   Rob, age 19 (male); Jennifer, age 18 (female); Susan, age 17 (female); and Adam, age 16 (male); no other children or pregnancies.
9. Level of education; military service; religion:
   Finished college; seeking teacher certification; no military service; childhood religion: fundamentalist Christian.
10. Parents (intact marriage, divorced, or separated; remarriages of parents; if parents deceased, date and cause; CL's age at time of any family disruption; parents' current life situation and state of health; other adults present in preadolescent household):
    Parents are still married. Marriage seems to work for them. It seems stiff and formal to client, but they stand by each other. Their general state of health is satisfactory.
11. Siblings (list by first names from oldest to youngest, placing CL, deceased siblings, and mother's other known pregnancies in their ordinal positions; using CL's age as a baseline, note the difference in years between CL and siblings; in parallel column note stepsiblings and CL's age when they entered the family; note present whereabouts and occupations of all siblings):

Ruth, age 39	Living with husband in California
Jill (-4), age 35	Architect in Chicago
Amy (-6), age 33	Social worker and homemaker in California
Steve (-9), age 30	Clerk in shipping office; still lives at home with mom and dad

12. When you were a child, if anything could have been different, what would you have wanted it to be?

Client wishes she wouldn't have had to work so hard at everything just to achieve at an acceptable level; she wishes things had come as easy for her as they seemed to come for Jill. And mostly, she wishes her father and mother had been proud of her.

13. Are you currently under a physician's care? What for? (Note type of problem; if the "presenting problem" which brought CL in to see you is a physical symptom, see item 21; note signs):
    Yes. General physician. For sleep disturbance, anxiety, dizziness, heart palpitations, and headaches.

14. Are you taking medication? (purpose, name, dosage, how long, effects and side effects):
    None.

15. Date of last physical examination:
    August 11, 1994.

16. Name, address, and specialty of physician(s) being consulted, if any:
    Information deleted.

17. General health (energy level; appetite; sleep; exercise; level of sexual activity; use of alcohol and drugs, including "recreational drugs"; tobacco; caffeine; note physical signs):
    Energy varies, but mostly low; appetite is constant; she eats a lot of food and has a problem with weight; sleep is often interrupted—she wakes up, finds it difficult to breathe, her heart is pounding, and she sweats; gets little exercise, sometimes does not leave house for days; sexual activity is seldom and often not desired; no alcohol, drugs, tobacco; caffeine from soft drinks. Client looks tired and is 20+ pounds overweight.

18. Previous counseling or therapy (when, reason, type, with whom, how long, outcome):
    Participated in a self-awareness group at college and had a few individual sessions with a college counselor she does not remember. The experience was mostly stimulating and motivated her to seek more. She sees therapy as a way to extend her current knowledge of self.

19. Referral source: Course instructor: (name deleted)

20. Emergency contact (name, address, phone, relationship):
    Husband: John (all other information deleted)

The Presenting Problem (Items 21–28)

21. What brought you in to see us? If a physical symptom, describe location, sensations, intensity, frequency.
    Client reports general dissatisfaction. She says her life is rather uneventful and predictable, and she feels some panic over reaching the age of 39, wondering where the years have gone. For two years she has been troubled by a range of psychosomatic complaints, including sleep disturbances, anxiety, dizziness, heart palpitations, and headaches. At times she has to push herself to leave the house. Client complains that she cries easily over trivial matters, often feels depressed, and has a weight problem.

22. **When did it start? What else was going on in your life at that time?**

About two years ago. Nothing particular was happening when these general symptoms started. Her kids were teenagers and gone much of the time, and she found herself getting older but "not better."

23. **Have you noticed a pattern?**

Only that she is not very active, eats a lot, and feels that she is not doing what she should be doing with her life.

24. **What happens as a consequence of having this problem? Who is most affected by it?**

Client says she guesses that she is. Family is mostly kind and understanding. She seems to be the only one who is unhappy with her life at the moment.

25. **What have you done about it until now?**

Sought a physician's help. Physician recommended therapy.

26. **How do you explain this situation to yourself?**

Client made a major career as a housewife and mother until her children became adolescents. She then entered college part time and obtained a bachelor's degree. Through her contacts with others at the university she has become aware of how she has limited herself, how she has fostered her family's dependence on her, and how frightened she is of branching out from her roles as mother and wife.

27. **How would your life be different if you did not have this problem?**

She would be happy at home and at work. She would have a job as an elementary schoolteacher and would work with a third-grade class. She would have energy for her children's activities and those of her husband, and she would see her family more often.

28. **What do you expect will come out of our work together?**

She is seeking therapy for the following reasons: (a) to handle the anxiety and depression she feels; (b) to explore what else might be added to her life beyond the structured existence she feels she lives as a wife and mother; although she would like to get more involved professionally, the thought of doing it does frighten her; she worries that she might be selfish in pursuing her goals, that she might not succeed, and that she might threaten her family; (c) she needs help at home handling Jennifer's rebellion, and she is worried about losing all of the children; (d) she is also concerned about who she is (an identity for herself) and what she should be doing with her life—she's 39, is getting older, and is losing her looks.

NOTE: If the presenting problem reveals an acute difficulty requiring immediate counseling, defer the remainder of the Initial Interview (the Life Tasks) until a subsequent session.

The Life Tasks (Items 29–34)

Love

29. *Situation.* Tell me about your love relationships. (If CL lacks relationships of emotional or sexual closeness, ask: How do you account for this?)

Key prompting questions: What makes a man a "masculine" man to you? What makes a woman a "feminine" woman? How do you compare yourself to your list of associations for your own sex? Do you experience difficulty in expressing love and affection for others? difficulty in receiving such expressions from others? What does your partner complain about in you? What do you complain about in your partner? Describe your first encounter with your partner. What was there about him or her that impressed you at that time?

"I have had only one relationship. John and I started going out after I graduated from high school. We got married, and we've been together ever since. John says he had been interested in me for a long time before we went out. He had seen me in church. We met formally at a church social. He stayed with me for a whole day. We talked, and he listened to everything I said. He was very attentive. When he walked me home, he asked if we could go to a movie. I said yes, and my parents didn't object. John was strong minded, knew what he wanted, and had goals and dreams. I liked his dreams, especially since they included me. He was always calm and never seemed to get angry. He's still very patient, the way I think men should be. He's the only man I ever dated, but he was good for me.

"I think being feminine means that you are caring and nurturing and give a great deal of yourself to others. You have to be able to balance family, which is your responsibility, and community. There is always a lot to do. I think being feminine also means that you're attractive to men. I do really well at the first part, but I doubt that I'm attractive to men, especially with the weight I've put on.

"John hardly ever complains. He would probably like to have sexual relations more often, but I have never enjoyed sex that much. It's OK, I mean, but I don't get in the mood as often as John. If I have any complaint, it's that I would like to make more decisions in the family and even for myself, but I would probably botch it up."

30. *Goals.* What do you want to improve or change in this area of your life?

"I would like to feel more feminine and appreciated and loved. I would like to feel comfortable doing things for myself without feeling as if I'm letting John down or, worse, losing him."

Work

31. *Situation.* Tell me about your work. (If CL has no occupation or is currently unemployed, ask: How do you account for this? Explore interests and ambitions in this area.)

Key prompting questions: What has been most satisfying to you in the jobs you have held? least satisfying? What other work have you done? Why have you left those jobs? Are you aware of anything about the way you work that causes trouble for you (for example, procrastination)? Do you feel appreciated at work? How do you evaluate your relationships with others at these levels: superiors, peers, and subordinates? Members of the opposite sex?

"I have worked all my life in the home: first my father's home and now my own home. I have taken care of children and a home since I was a young teenager. I have occasionally done some volunteer work, but very little really. There's so much to do with the children and John. What I like most about being a homemaker, or housewife, is when people like what I do for them. Sometimes, though, it feels as if the kids don't even notice. They just expect everything. John notices more. I notice all the things that never get done, especially now that I'm getting my teaching credential. I guess school is my work for the moment. It's still hard, but I like it more than I liked high school. I'm learning a lot, but it takes a lot of time and energy, and I'm way behind at home."

32. *Goals.* What do you want to improve or change in this area of your life?

"I want very much to finish my certification as a teacher and to teach in an elementary school, third grade. I want to help students who have a hard time."

Friendship and community

33. *Situation.* Tell me about your friends and your life in the community. (If CL reports few or no connections with others, ask: How do you account for this?)

Key prompting questions: From where do you draw your friends? How many close friends do you have? How often are you together? What do you do? Do you have friends of the other sex? How do your friendships end? How much do you feel you are able to confide in your friends? What sort of impression do you think you make on people the first time they meet you? Does this impression change over time? If I were to call one of your close friends and ask, "What do you value in (CL)?" what would he or she say? What kind of connections do you have in your community?

"I have developed some good friends recently at school. I feel that school is really a turning point for me, both for work and for having people I can talk to. My classes have helped me meet people who really seem to like me and whom I feel comfortable talking to.

"Most of my friends are women, and I don't have very many. I maybe have one or two long-term friends, but I have shared more with college friends than I have with my long-term friends. I guess people like it that I listen real well. I'm interested in what people have to say. I'm not a leader by any stretch of the imagination, but I like to be a part of things.

"I think when people first meet me, they think I'm not much; but after they get to know me, they know that I'm dependable and that I care about people. I think I make a good friend, but this is new for me.

"I also know people who work around John, but we don't socialize with them much, and I don't know what they think of me. I'm not nearly as community oriented as my mother was."

34. *Goals.* What do you want to improve or change in this area of your life?

"I would like to see the friendships I have started at school really grow and develop. I would like to have some of them as fellow teachers and get to work in the same school. That would be great, to have a friend just down the hall."

Date: February 20, 1995

Summary of Impressions Derived from the Initial Interview

The first therapist (FT) dictates the *Summary of Impressions Derived from the Initial Interview* to the second therapist (ST) in the presence of CL at the conclusion of the review and interpretation of the *Initial Interview*.

[In the following summary, Ruth is referred to in the third person to allow her to stand back from her experience and see her difficulties through a narrative that puts her life in context and shows its dynamic movement.]

Ruth has presented herself for therapy at a turning point in her life. She has spent many years doing what she began preparing to do early in life. Ruth, the oldest of four children, was drafted into caring for her brother and two sisters at a young age. She used her mother as a role model of a "good homemaker" and continued her work when she married her husband, John. John and Ruth have four children, who are now adolescents. When her children became teenagers, she decided to seek work where she would continue to feel needed. Returning to school, she completed a bachelor's degree and is seeking a teacher's certificate. College and her fellow students opened a whole new world to Ruth. She began to see many new possibilities for herself, including a place in the world as a professional teacher and as a person with many more friends than she has been used to having. She is feeling both excited by the new possibilities and worried about losing the people and world she has known all her life.

Ruth feels pulled by both worlds. In one world (school) the opportunities seem limitless and exciting and full of opportunity, if new and somewhat overwhelming and risky. In the other world (home) her life is safe, known, familiar, and predictable, and she knows exactly what she needs to do in order to succeed. She wants both worlds to fit together, but she is not always sure how to make that happen. She also wants to perform *perfectly* in both worlds. Even though part of her knows that the demand for perfection at both home and school is impossible, she has not let herself off the hook. Mostly, she wants everyone involved to be happy with her: she wants John to be happy; she wants her children to be happy; she wants her instructors to be happy; she wants her new friends to be happy; and, last and least, she wants herself to be happy. When she cannot figure out how to make it all happen, she often finds herself becoming worried, anxious, and depressed. When she doesn't have time to become worried, anxious, or depressed, she settles for dizziness, headaches, heart palpitations, sleeplessness, and other physical disturbances, which act as a message to her family and herself that she needs some rest and needs some care.

Ruth has put everyone else in life first. She comes from a family in which at least one other child achieved success easily, and she found it hard to please her mother and father. She could not guess what would make them happy, and she feared their disapproval and rejection. The family atmosphere was strict and controlled, and she found her place by caring for children and others in the way that she believed women are supposed to do. It is hard for her to put herself first at this point in life without fearing that she will lose everything.

She has a well-defined set of goals for therapy. They include dealing with the physical and emotional symptoms that express the conflict and demands she feels in her life; finding a balance between seeking what she wants and maintaining what she has; getting help with at least one daughter, whose rebellion acts as a constant reminder of "what can happen if Mom is not ever-present and vigilant"; and, mostly, discovering what she can make of herself and her life with the opportunities opening up and time running out. She is, after all, 39 years of age and "losing it" . . . fast!

SPECIAL DIAGNOSIS: LIFESTYLE ASSESSMENT

CL's present age: 39   Date: February 27, 1995

Family Constellation, Part I: Parents, Other Adults, and Milieu

1. **Father's name:** Patrick   Occupation: Minister
   Age at CL's birth: 25   Age, if living: 64   Or, at death:
   Yr & cause of death: CL's age at death:
2. What kind of a man was your father when you were a child, up to age 10 or 11, in the preschool and grammar school years? Consider activities, personality, health, level of education, and values (that is, what was important to father):
   He was devoted to his work. He was stern, and he was the authority figure in the community. He was respected and righteous. He was also cool and detached. With Ruth, he was often distant, strict, and ungiving.
3. How did he relate to you and the other children?
   "He was rather aloof from all of us and insisted on respect."
   Favorite child: Jill—he liked her accomplishments.
   Discipline and how you felt about it:
   He would yell at children. He would withdraw from a misbehaving child totally and not talk to the child for weeks on end. Client felt scared and, at times, disowned.
   Expectations regarding your behavior and achievement:
   He wanted his children to be God-fearing and grow up to be righteous adults who did what was right.
4. How do you see yourself now as like father? unlike father?
   "Both of us have high standards; both of us are critical. I'm much closer to my children than he was to us. I'm a good wife and mother."

5. Tell me briefly about father's background and family of origin.

Client doesn't know what nationality her dad was, but he was the oldest of four boys, and he came from a religious family. It was assumed early in his life that he would be a minister, and he prepared for it all his life. His family was poor but always got by, and they were always proud.

6. Mother's name: Edith   Occupation: Homemaker
Age at CL's birth: 20   Age, if living: 59   Or, at death:
Yr & cause of death: CL's age at death:

7. What kind of a woman was your mother when you were a child, up to age 10 or 11, in the preschool and grammar school years? Consider activities, personality, health, level of education, and values (that is, what was important to mother):

Ruth's mother was a hard worker; she rarely complained out loud. She was very proper, always did the right thing, and was quite dignified. She was proud of her role as a minister's wife. She was self-sacrificing. She would go without so that her husband or the kids could have the things they needed. She would even give up things for herself so that people in the church could have food or clothing or shelter.

It was very important to mother that the children maintain a good image in the church and the community. As unselfish as she could be, she was emotionally ungiving, very serious, not very happy (or so it appeared), and very strict with children.

8. How did she relate to you and the other children?

She was devoted to seeing that the children grew up right, but she was not personally involved in their lives unless they got in trouble.

Favorite child: Steve—he could do no wrong in her eyes.

Discipline and how you felt about it:

Scoldings or withdrawal. Not much more.

Expectations regarding your behavior and achievement:

She did not want any of the children to bring shame on the family, and she wanted all of them to be hard workers.

9. How do you see yourself now as like mother? unlike mother?

Both are hard workers: "I guess we both sacrifice a lot for others, too." Client sees herself as more emotional and more emotionally giving.

10. Tell me briefly about mother's background and family of origin.

Ruth's mother was Scotch-Irish. She was also poor when she was little. She was the youngest of three girls, and she was the only one to marry. "She always told us how lucky we were to have a Christian life."

11. Parents' relationship. Tell me about how your parents got along with each other when you were a child. (Were they affectionate? Was one of them "the boss"? If they argued, what about? Who seemed to initiate the trouble, and what was the outcome? Did you take sides, openly or covertly? How did you feel about the trouble? Did you feel sorry for one of them?)

They had a stiff and formal relationship. Very little affection was demonstrated, and they rarely laughed. They did not argue; mother stood behind whatever father said or did. Ruth mostly took her own side. She wanted to make them happy, but it was not an easy task.

12. Other significant adults. Tell me about any other adults who were important to you when you were a child. (If not already clear, describe the character and role of any other adults living in the preadolescent household. Describe other adults who impressed you as a child, either positively or negatively.)

   Her grandmother on her father's side took an interest in her. She seemed to understand her, and she would often talk to Ruth and give her good advice. She was the one who first approved of John.

13. Family milieu. If not already clear, inquire into socioeconomic, ethnic, religious, and cultural characteristics of the family and into the family's standards and values.

   "We were a middle-class family, I guess." Client reports that their life centered on the church. They were fundamentalist Christians, and their family values included doing right, working hard, and reflecting well on the family. What stands out most is how scared Ruth was of her father and yet how much she wanted him to like her and think well of her: "That's what happens in a God-fearing family."

Date: February 27, 1995

Family Constellation, Part II: Situation of the Child

Sibling array

Using the following page, array the siblings' names from oldest to youngest, across the page from left to right. Include CL, and any siblings deceased or separated from the family and living in institutions or elsewhere. Also note mother's other known pregnancies terminated by abortion, miscarriage, or stillbirth, entering them in the appropriate ordinal positions. Using CL's age as baseline, note the difference in years, plus or minus, between each of them and CL. Include stepsiblings, and note CL's age at any time they entered the family. Use the following items to guide the discussion with CL, placing appropriate information in the boxes on the following page.

14. Describe each of the children, beginning with yourself, with respect to personality, health, and activities.

15. Note any subgroupings among the children: who played with whom; who fought and argued with whom; who looked after and took care of whom; who taught and guided whom.

16. Note how each of the children distinguished him- or herself from the others—for example, by taking the place of the one who was:

academic	the problem child
athletic	religious
artistic	socially successful

entrepreneurial   handicapped
the good child   sickly

17. If any of the children was handicapped or sickly, note the child's and family's attitudes toward the difficulty.
18. Which sibling were you most like? least like? In what ways?
19. To what extent did each of the children accept, reject, or modify the family's standards and values?
20. Childhood chronology. If not already clear, note any changes in the course of CL's childhood and adolescent development experienced by CL as major events or turning points (for example, divorce, a move to another community), and CL's age at those times.

Sibling Array

Ruth (39)	Jill (-4)	Amy (-6)	Steve (-9)
Responsible, hard-working, organized, dedicated, capable, trustworthy, self-critical, un-demanding, scared, unable to please either parent. I was lonely; I felt useful and needed; I wanted approval from my folks; I was a good girl, and I took care of my sisters and brother.	Bright, pretty, accomplished, conforming, well-behaved. Got along with Dad; got along fairly well with Mom. Jill was the most like me; she was good and was successful at life. Things came more easily to her. She won honors at school.	Immature, de-manding, the family "trouble-maker"; admir-ing of me, hard-working, independent. In trouble with Dad, and tried to please Mom, without success. Amy was the most different from me; she seemed irre-sponsible by comparison.	Pampered, over-protected, in trouble with Dad but pro-tected by Mom. Got Mom's affection. Sensi-tive, argumenta-tive with me, not too accom-plished. Steve was also different from me; in Mom he found a shelter from life.

Family Constellation: Situation of the Child (continued)

21. What were your favorite stories, TV shows, fictitious or historical characters? What was there about them that you liked?
    Cinderella. "I liked it that she gets the prince in the end."
22. Did you daydream? What about?
    No. Ruth wasn't allowed to daydream and doesn't remember doing it much.
23. Do you remember any night dreams? Describe. How did you feel when you woke up?

"I had dreams about being chased, and I would wake up scared. Or I had dreams about doing stupid things, and I would wake up with my heart pounding. Once in a while, I would dream about flying and being up above everyone. I loved to fly in my dreams."

24. Did you have any particular fears as a child? How did others respond?
Being alone, not being liked, doing something wrong, being yelled at by her father or disappointing her mother. Fear was not addressed in her family.

25. Was food and eating an issue in the household? In what way?
Ruth was told to eat everything on her plate, and she couldn't leave the table until she did. Same for the other children.

26. What were you good at? What did you most enjoy?
Taking care of sisters and brothers, reading, taking care of the house.

27. Was there anything you did not enjoy? anything that was particularly hard for you?
School was a challenge. She always had to work hard at school. She didn't do particularly well at math or the sciences.

28. Did you experience difficulty in your mental or emotional development? How was this addressed in the family? in school? How did you feel about it?
Nothing stronger than childhood fears and worries. No one paid much attention.

29. Think back to your early years, up to age 6 or 7. What did you want to be when you grew up? What was there about that that appealed to you? How and when did this change?
"I wanted to become a minister and have people look up to me."

Family Constellation: Situation of the Child (conclusion)

30. Describe how you got along in the world of the neighborhood. How would you characterize your role among the children (for example, leader, follower, jester, outsider?). Did you have friends of the other sex?
Client didn't play much. Children from church were sometimes invited to the house, but mostly siblings worked or played with one another, if at all. She didn't have any real friends of either sex. Just her brother and sisters.

31. Describe how you got along in the world of the school. Was your role in this setting different from your role in the neighborhood? If so, in what ways, and how do you account for it? Did you have friends of the other sex? How did you get along with teachers? What were your favorite and least favorite subjects, and what was there about them that you liked or disliked?
Ruth was expected to do well in school. It was hard for her. She had to work at it all the time. Even when she worked hard, she sometimes didn't do very well. Math and sciences were the hardest for her. English and history were her best subjects. She liked to read, and that helped. She would get so nervous when she was doing math or science that she couldn't concentrate. The teachers generally liked her (with

one or two exceptions), but they always felt that she was not living up to her potential, and that's what they told her parents. She didn't socialize with other kids much. She was quiet and kept to herself. Other kids thought she was "weird."

32. Describe your bodily development in childhood and how you felt about it. How did it compare with that of your peers? Consider height, weight, strength, speed, coordination, vision, hearing, anomalies. Did you have any special difficulties (for example, bed wetting)?

"I developed like everyone else, I guess. I wasn't much different from other girls. But I didn't get to talk with kids my age very much, and my mother wouldn't tell me anything." No special difficulties.

33. Describe your sexual development and your sexual experience and initiation. How did you learn about sex? How did you feel about the bodily changes that took place at puberty? (Females: How old were you at menarche? Describe what happened. Did you understand what was happening? How did you feel about it?) Describe your experience as a sexual person during adolescence and young adulthood and your evaluation of yourself at that time.

When client was 6 years old, she reports: "My father caught me 'playing doctor' with an 8-year-old boy. He lectured me and refused to speak to me for weeks. I felt guilty and ashamed." Ruth reached adolescence with minimal information from her mother, father, or peers. She remembers being scared at 12 when menarche occurred. "I didn't know what was happening. My mother gave me the things I needed and a booklet to read." She was not allowed to date until she completed high school; at the age of 19 she married the first person she dated. "I was lucky to find a good man. All I knew was my mother's version of how to be a homemaker."

Date: February 27, 1995

Summary of the Family Constellation

FT dictates the *Summary of the Family Constellation* to ST in the presence of CL at the conclusion of the review and interpretations of the family material.

Ruth is the oldest of four children, raised in a family where hard work and perfection were the expected standard; unfortunately, as she learned early in life, hard work was no guarantee that perfection could be achieved. Even after a huge effort, the slightest mistake could lead to a rebuke or a rejection that was deeply felt, leaving her lonely, cautious, and scared.

Her father set a masculine guiding line that was characterized by a harsh, strict, stern, and angry persona; his every stance was authoritarian, critical, and religiously perfectionistic. Indeed, her father was such a dominant authority in her life that it was easy for her to confuse God-fearing with father-fearing. Like a female version of Cain in the Bible, she was locked in a struggle for approval in which she would never be good enough and her sister Jill could do no wrong. The struggle to please her father gradually settled into strategies for avoiding his displeasure, and fear became the operative motivator in her life.

Ruth's mother set a feminine guiding line that was characterized by a serious devotion to principle, righteousness, duty, and her husband. Her behavior suggested that life was filled with hard work and sacrifice, a burden that women should suffer quietly, with dignity, and without complaint. Although she provided for the children's physical and spiritual needs, she did little to provide relief from the harsh stance that her husband took in the world.

Only Ruth's grandmother provided her with a different role model for womanhood. She demonstrated that it was possible for women to be interested in, involved with, and caring toward young children.

The family atmosphere was characterized by formality and stiffness, a rigid consistency and discipline in which frivolity and, indeed, happiness were out of place. The family values included hard work, perfectionism, and a belief that appearances were extremely important. No crack in the architecture could be tolerated.

Under her father's regime it was impossible for Ruth to match the privilege and talent that was extended to Jill, her younger sister by four years. Jill was born to be accomplished, approved of, and rewarded; the combination of Ruth's mistakes and Jill's favored position rendered mythical the notion that hard work was its own reward—or even that it would ultimately pay off. Ruth formed an alliance with Amy, an equally disfavored and hard-working sibling; they were the children who would struggle through a hard life together. Amy looked up to Ruth, but she was not about to suffer her father's tyranny quietly or respectfully. Her rebellion became the only sure way she had to establish her independence.

In her father's kingdom the subservient queen birthed a prince, who stole her heart. Because no mere boy could hope to compete with the stature of the king, Steve entered into and accepted the protection of the queen. He became both spoiled and helpless in her care. In this way he avoided the family demands for hard work and perfectionism while putting the most powerful of family members in his service.

Like Cinderella, Ruth hoped that hard work, a pleasing personality, and patience would one day be rewarded with a prince who would discover her true beauty behind the ashes of a hard life. She lived in fear and captivity but longed to be free to fly. When the first prince came along, Ruth slipped on the slipper and moved out. Leaving with a prince is not the same as flying free, however, and she is still searching for a way to get off the ground.

In a world where men are powerful and women serve, her hope of becoming a minister, strong and powerful like her father, seems an unrealistic fantasy. To teach in an elementary school, however, offers her a position of significance in the lives of young people entrusted to her care and her own special world not too far from the safety of the castle of the "good" prince. Even a good prince can become displeased: Ruth's approval rating has always been and is now only as good as her last accomplished deed and as fleeting as her next discovered error. Entry into a new and different world must be balanced with the needs and demands of the old; she senses that it would not do for her to risk what is known and familiar in pursuit of what is unknown, risky, and possibly reserved only for men or the women favored by them.

Date: February 27, 1995

Record of Early Recollections

Ask for CL's early recollections (ERs). After recording the account of the recollection, narrow its range to the moment most vividly recalled, as if in a snapshot capturing a moment in the action, and ask how CL felt at that moment.

Prompting questions: How far back can you remember? What is the first incident or moment you remember in your life? Tell me about it. How old were you at the time? What is the most vivid moment in the action of the story? How did you feel about that moment?

Note that the first ER to be recorded is to be the first incident of memory. ERs recorded after the first need not be in chronological order. After recording the first ER, ask, "What is the next thing you are able to recall from before age 9 or 10?" Or, "What comes up next from your childhood before age 9 or 10?"

1. Age: 3
   I remember my father yelling at me and then putting me in another room, because I was crying. I don't remember why I was crying, but I know I was scared, and after he shouted, I was petrified.
   Most vivid moment: father yelling
   Feeling: scared, petrified.

2. Age: 4½
   I was in church, talking with a boy. My mother gave me dirty looks, and my father, who was conducting the service, gave me a stern lecture when we got home.
   Most vivid moment: the looks parents gave me.
   Feeling: scared and confused.

3. Age: 6
   An 8-year-old neighbor boy and I had our clothes off and were "playing doctor" when my father caught us in my bedroom. He sent the boy home and then told me in a cold and solemn voice that what I had done was very wrong. He did not speak to me for weeks, and I remember feeling very dirty and guilty.
   Most vivid moment: being caught by my father.
   Feeling: scared, "bad," and guilty.

4. Age: 7
   I remember my second-grade teacher saying that I was not doing well in school and that I was going to get a bad report card. I tried so hard to do well because I didn't want to bring home bad grades. This teacher didn't like me very much, and I couldn't understand what I had done wrong. I thought I was trying my best. I was scared.
   Most vivid moment: the teacher telling me I was getting a bad report card.
   Feeling: scared.

5. Age: 8
   I was in a church play, and I worked for months at memorizing my lines. I thought I had them down perfectly. My parents came to the play, and for a time I was doing

fine, and I was hoping they would like my performance. Then toward the end I forgot to come in when I was supposed to, and the director had to cue me. My mistake was apparent to my father, who later commented that I had spoiled a rather good performance by my lack of attention. I remember feeling sad and disappointed, because I had so hoped that they would be pleased. And I don't recall my mother saying anything about the play.

Most vivid moment: father commenting on my mistake.

Feeling: embarrassed.

After recording eight ERs, ask CL if there is any other recollection that is important to him or her that has not been recorded in the Life-Style Inquiry to this point. If another ER is forthcoming, record it here:

Age: _____

Nothing reported.

Most vivid moment:

Feeling:

Date: February 27, 1995

ER Summary: Pattern of Basic Convictions

FT dictates the summary of the *Pattern of Basic Convictions* to ST in the presence of CL at the conclusion of the review and interpretations of the ERs.

"I live in a man's world that is often harsh, uncaring, and frightening. Helplessness and emotion will not be tolerated in this world and will lead to being separated from it. In a man's world women must not speak, not even to other men. The rebuke of authority is both immediate and frightening. Men and their world are never available to women. A woman is wrong to want to know about men or explore them. Dabbling in a man's world can lead to banishment and total exile.

"Only achievement counts in the real world. No amount of hard work can make up for a lack of performance. No amount of pleasing can win over someone who is against you. Significant people always find out about mistakes: the most important people always seem to be present when a lack of attention leads to an error that ruins even a good effort. To err in the real world is embarrassingly human; to forgive is against policy."

Date: February 27, 1995

ER Summary: Interfering Ideas

This summary is also dictated in the presence of CL, immediately after the presentation of the *Pattern of Basic Convictions*.

The power and importance of men are exaggerated, as is her fear of their disapproval. Pleasing seems to her the best route to safety in a man's world, but it leaves her unsure of her own identity and in constant fear of rejection.

The inevitability of mistakes and failure is exaggerated and feared; the slightest human errors are to be avoided; 100% is passing; 99% is the start of creeping failure.

Doing the right thing, being "good," is required just to survive; doing the wrong thing signals impending doom: caution is always warranted in an unpredictable world.

Murphy's Law governs: What can go wrong will go wrong.

Hard work is always demanded but will not necessarily produce the desired results or achievements sought.

Adlerian Counseling with Ruth

Adlerian counselors tend to see counseling as a four-stage process that starts with *forming a relationship* based on professional interest, mutual respect, and a partnership in discovery. After this initial interview it is common to make a lifestyle assessment of the person in relation to the difficulties that must be faced. The preceding material and summaries are examples of what might be generated through such a *psychological investigation* of Ruth. Adlerians use the third stage of counseling to reach a *shared understanding* of the client's cognitions, motivations, and personal process. The final stage of counseling, *reorientation and reeducation*, suggests two approaches to change. The first approach, reorientation, is based on the notion that all people have the resources to live on the useful side of life and simply need to be oriented toward the employing of these personal abilities and resources. We think of this process as empowerment with social interest, and it is facilitated through encouragement. The second approach, reeducation, presumes that we have either learned or created some mistaken ideas, convictions, or notions in life and that it is possible to learn more functional ways of knowing (perceiving) self, others, and life. New learning leads to new meaning, and new meaning is the foundation for change.

When possible, many Adlerians use multiple therapy, or the use of two therapists with one client. There are many advantages to this approach: (a) Therapists demonstrate a cooperative relationship based on mutual respect; (b) clients receive multiple points of view in a relationship of intensified therapeutic interest; and (c) therapists are demystified, and the dependency that may occur in many single-therapist approaches is reduced. Perhaps the most important advantage of multiple therapy is that it allows the client to assume the role of participant/observer. In this role, the client can disengage periodically from the give-and-take of the therapy session and listen as two therapists discuss the meaning of the data that has been collected. Because multiple therapy is somewhat costly in time and effort, it is seldom used 100% of the time with clients. Rather, most clients have a designated primary therapist and a second therapist who meets with them on a regular, but intermittent, basis. Multiple-therapy sessions are indicated at times when two therapists can make a meaningful difference (for example, after lifestyle-assessment data are collected, when the primary therapist and the client reach an impasse or sessions become repetitious, or when it is appropriate to note or celebrate progress).

In the case of Ruth, the data for the initial interview and the lifestyle assessment (as designed by Powers and Griffith) were collected by the primary therapist. Those data were then presented to and discussed with a second therapist while Ruth listened and acted as a collaborating or clarifying agent to the discussion. The two therapists then generated the initial summaries presented above, including *the pattern of basic convictions* and *the interfering ideas*. The session ends with the two therapists listening to Ruth give her initial impressions of the ideas and information contained in the summaries. Written copies of the summaries are sent to her the following day, so that she can read them again before the next session.

Reviewing the previous session.   Following the last multiple-therapy session, Ruth meets with her primary therapist. She brings her written lifestyle summaries with her. After they greet each other:

THERAPIST: What was the last session like for you?

RUTH: I was really amazed. The summaries that you came up with seemed just like me. Then when they came in the mail, I read them, and I wondered if my family knew me as well as I feel the two of you do. I sort of left them lying around for two days to see if anyone would ask me about them or if they would read them. I think one of the kids may have read them, but I know John didn't.

THERAPIST: But you wanted him to read them.

RUTH: Yes, I would really like to know what he thinks. I think they are wonderful . . . like having a picture of myself that I actually like to look at.

THERAPIST: Yes, that's a nice way of putting it. [pause] So what was it like for you to have two therapists instead of just one?

RUTH: It was very interesting. I was surprised that the two of you disagree sometimes.

THERAPIST: Yes, we do.

RUTH: You didn't seem to get very upset when he thought you had missed an important point. I was watching you, and you didn't blush or anything. I would have, but you just asked him to explain it more.

THERAPIST [smiling]: I remember. I didn't think he was right even after he explained it more clearly, so we asked you. And you thought that his idea was very important to understanding your development from childhood to motherhood to, now, becoming a teacher.

RUTH: It was important to me. It was like a thread running through everything.

THERAPIST: I think that's true. I'm glad Bob [the second therapist] was here. We might have missed it otherwise.

RUTH: I liked the way you disagreed and stayed friends and didn't get mad or anything. That's hard for me. I don't like to disagree with John. [pause] I think I'm afraid he'll get mad at me.

THERAPIST: What does he get mad at you about?

RUTH: I know John pretty well, I guess, and there's not much we disagree about—except my schooling.

THERAPIST: If I were to hazard a guess based on what we learned in the lifestyle assessment, I would guess that there may be quite a lot you have not directly asked your husband—or even your children—because you were concerned about displeasing them. Does that fit you? Do you find yourself "guessing," trying to read their minds so you won't upset them?

RUTH: Yes, I know I do that a lot.

THERAPIST: What did you notice when Bob and I disagreed?

RUTH: Well, the two of you were just fine. You just listened, and then you asked me what I thought.

THERAPIST: And what was that like when I checked our different perceptions with you?

RUTH: I liked being asked! You didn't look upset, so I even thought it would be OK to agree with Bob.

THERAPIST: I must tell you that my facial expressions don't always match what I'm feeling inside, but last week I wasn't upset, and I was quite pleased that you and Bob had come to an understanding that I had missed. If we were all alike in this world, there wouldn't be much use in talking, would there? Bob is a brilliant man, and I like working with him. [pause] Do you think of John as basically a good mate?

RUTH: Yeah . . . I do.

THERAPIST: Do you think he would enjoy hearing your opinion even if it was different from his?

RUTH: I don't know.

THERAPIST: Do you think he would enjoy being asked his opinion about something important to you—even if you disagreed later?

RUTH: Maybe.

THERAPIST: I think you would really like to know what John thinks about your lifestyle summaries, and no amount of guessing is going to be the same as really hearing from him. The worst that might happen is that he wouldn't agree with them, whereas you do . . . to some extent at least.

RUTH: Very much, actually.

THERAPIST: OK, so you might disagree.

RUTH: I guess you loved it when Bob disagreed with you.

THERAPIST [smiling]: Yes. Thank you for noticing. Why don't we take a look at your written summaries now. We can go through them line by line and see what it's like to reflect on the meaning in them for you.

Here, in a relatively early session, the therapist uses the cooperation and mutual respect modeled in multiple therapy to encourage Ruth to take a small chance with her husband. If she actually asks John to look at her lifestyle summaries and share his opinion with her, there will be some material for the next session whatever his response or her reaction to the response may be.

A reorientation with Ruth.   In a later session, the primary therapist and Ruth are talking about her handling of a stressful incident. An opportunity arises out of their discussion to encourage the development of a stronger sense of self.

THERAPIST: So let me get this straight. Your instructor offered you a chance to work with her on a community-education research project next weekend, and you said, yes. It's also your anniversary, and you've told your husband that you'll go away with him for the weekend.

RUTH: Oh, Lord. I'm dead!

THERAPIST: You may wish you were dead, but unfortunately, you're alive and you'll probably have to face this one.

RUTH [breathing hard]: You know, my heart's pounding, and I'm having a hard time breathing. I feel as if I'm sweating. Am I sweating?

THERAPIST: I don't notice any sweat at the moment. Do you know why your heart is pounding and you're having a hard time breathing?

RUTH: I may be getting sick again.

THERAPIST: I have another idea. Would you like to hear it?

RUTH: OK.

THERAPIST: I think you're in a bind trying to please two important people in your life at once. Pleasing, saying yes, is really the first thing that comes to mind whenever you're asked to do something. Since you can't be in two places at once, maybe you believe getting sick is the only way to get out of trouble without letting anyone down.

RUTH: I just can't do this research project. I love this teacher, but John and I have been planning this trip for months. Lord, she'll probably never ask me to do work with her again.

THERAPIST: Well, let's hold that idea as a working hypothesis for a moment. Besides the idea that you're letting her down, what else could she think?

RUTH: What do you mean?

THERAPIST: Does she think you're smart, capable, and energetic? What does she think of you?

RUTH: I don't know really.

THERAPIST: Well, let's see what *you* think of you. What are ten things about you that you think are great or wonderful?

RUTH: Ten things?

THERAPIST: Yeah. Start with the best thing about you. "I am . . ."

RUTH: I am. . . . a good mother, I guess.

THERAPIST: OK, you're a good mother. That's one [writing it down and holding up a finger]. What else? We have nine to go.

RUTH: Caring.

THERAPIST: That's two.

RUTH: Loving.

THERAPIST: That's the same as caring; we're still at two.

RUTH: I think I'm intelligent. [Therapist writes and nods.] I'm organized; you have to be to handle a home and school. I write well, and I'm friendly. How many is that?

THERAPIST: You're doing great. You're up to five. You're halfway there.

RUTH [long pause]: I don't know if there are any others. [another pause] Oh, I'm intuitive. I get hunches about things, and I'm often able to know what's going on even when no one has said anything yet. Fran asked me just the other day how I knew she was upset.

THERAPIST: That's six.

RUTH: Six? Well, I guess I'm a hard worker. I really stick with things until I get them done. Is that really two qualities?

THERAPIST: Hard-working and determined. I have them both down. Two more.

RUTH: I'm fun to be with; I like to laugh. I have a sense of humor. And I'll drop whatever I'm doing usually to help out. I'm helpful, so that's two more, right?

THERAPIST: Very good. Now, I really want you to feel these wonderful qualities, so just close your eyes for a moment. Hold up your right thumb and let yourself feel everything that goes with being a good mother: all the work, the dedication, the thoughtfulness, the planning—whether it's verbally appreciated or not. You know it's important, and you've been good at it for a long time. Now, hold up your right index finger, and feel yourself being caring. Try to imagine something recently that represents a caring act. We'll go through them all slowly, one finger at a time. [pause] Next is intelligent . . . Now, organized . . . friendly . . . intuitive . . . hard-working . . . determined . . . a sense of humor . . . and last, for now, helpful. Just stay with the image of those ten qualities, as if they were close friends of yours. See if they have any information for you about how to handle a discussion with your instructor.

RUTH [after a while]: I think I can tell her that in my excitement to do work with her I said I would go with her, but I really need to spend this weekend with John. It's our anniversary, and we can't afford to miss special times. I want her to know that I think she's a great teacher, and if there is ever another chance, I would be happy to work for her.

THERAPIST: Where did these wonderful words come from?

RUTH: From my heart. I want her to know I really mean them.

THERAPIST: Yes, they came from a heart informed by caring, intelligence, hard work, determination, and helpfulness—just to name a few. How is your heart doing now? Is it still pounding?

RUTH: No. I feel calm.

THERAPIST: I have the idea that if you were to put those ten qualities on a poster—maybe on your refrigerator—and added one more quality every day for a year, you would never again doubt for a moment your worth to yourself or others.

A small reeducation during multiple therapy. Near the end of Ruth's counseling experience, she is again involved in a multiple-therapy session. This time the focus is on her value when she is engaged in meaningful work and when she is not. An early recollection is used to mark change and growth in her therapy.

THERAPIST #2: Ruth, it's good to see you again. How long has it been? About five weeks since I last sat in with the two of you? How have things been going?

RUTH: I think our work together has been very good. We had some sessions that included John, and I really feel that he's supporting me in all of the transitions I'm making. In recent weeks, I walk away from here, and I sometimes wonder if I am doing enough in therapy. Much of what we talk about now seems so easy to me. I'm not leaving as I used to—practically exhausted and sure that I was working through a lot of stuff.

THERAPIST #1: This is interesting. We haven't really talked about this before. How was it for you when you left here last time?

RUTH: Well, I think we did some good work together in that I learned something about staying with change in my life even when the going gets tough, but it was not actually hard to learn that. I used to leave here wondering if I would ever figure myself out. Last time, I felt, well, I can do what I need to do. You must feel it too. It's not much of a struggle anymore.

THERAPIST #1: I agree. We're not struggling at all. And you seem to be at a point of high integration in your life. I guess I look at that change with a sense of celebration. I don't mind at all that we're not struggling.

THERAPIST #2: When I listen to Ruth, Jim, there's an idea that is repeated over and over. It is not so much about struggle, although that's part of it. It's something like "Anything worth doing requires very hard work. Without the hard work, Ruth may doubt whether she is doing anything worthwhile." Did I get that right, Ruth?

RUTH [with a look of recognition on her face]: I think you did. That's been one of my beliefs since childhood.

THERAPIST #2: Yes, it may have been, but I think we're inviting you to reconsider that notion. It may be a mistaken notion, especially now that you're older and more competent. Things do come easier to people as they gain competence.

RUTH: Maybe I have this therapy thing figured out.

THERAPIST #1: My experience of you is that you have a lot of things figured out. There's been a lot of progress since you started about nine months ago.

THERAPIST #2: Let's try something—another early recollection. Ruth, see if you can think back to a time when you were very young. Something happened one time . . .

RUTH: Very young? Well, I remember something in second grade. Is that OK?

THERAPIST #2: Yes, fine. You were about 7 or 8?

RUTH: Seven, I think. I was asked by a neighbor to help her little girl learn colors, because she was in kindergarten. Her mother had colored four squares in the driveway with chalk. I think her name was Jan, the little girl, and we played all afternoon, bouncing a ball from one color to another. Her mother later told my mother that I had made all the difference in the world.

THERAPIST #2: What stands out about that story, and how did you feel?

RUTH: The look of pride on my mother's face when she told me what Jan's mother had said. I like making a difference in someone's life.

THERAPIST #1: It's a great memory! There's not an ounce of hard work in it. And it's a great early recollection for a future teacher to have. Can you sense how different this memory is from the ones you reported when you first came to see us?

RUTH: I don't actually even remember the early recollections I gave you originally. Is this one different?

THERAPIST #2: Very different. I was just looking at them here in your file. I think the next time you get together with us, we should go back and review where you were when you started and where you are now.

A change in one's early recollections is not uncommon when change has also happened in one's life. The change may not be dramatic, as in a completely new memory. Sometimes, it is a shift in emphasis: Something new stands out, or the client's reaction is different than originally reported. In Ruth's new memory above, she is "making a difference" in someone's life (social interest), and she is also experiencing the appreciation of others for her work. This is a significant change in her sense of belonging and a great place for a new teacher to start.

JERRY COREY'S WORK WITH RUTH FROM AN ADLERIAN PERSPECTIVE

With the detailed information about Ruth derived from the initial interview, the lifestyle assessment, and the sample therapy sessions provided by Bitter, I will continue counseling Ruth from an Adlerian orientation.

Basic Assumptions

As an Adlerian therapist I view my work with Ruth as teaching her better ways of meeting the challenges of *life tasks*. One assumption that will guide my interventions with her is that although she has been influenced by her past, she is not necessarily molded by it. This premise of self-determination leaves little room for a client to take the role of a passive victim. I assume that Ruth has the capacity to influence and create events. What is crucial is not what she was born with but what she is making of her natural endowment.

Ruth's childhood experiences are of therapeutic interest to me. They are the foundation and early context for the social factors that contributed to her psychological development. True to the Adlerian spirit, I function as a therapist on the belief that it is not her childhood experiences in themselves that are crucial; rather, it is her *attitude* toward these events. Since these early influences may have led to the development of a *faulty style of life*, I will explore with her what it was like at home as she was growing up. Our focus will be on understanding and assessing the structure of her family life, known as the family constellation, and her earliest recollections (both of which were reported in detail in the previous section by Bitter).

Because I operate from a phenomenological stance (dealing with the client's subjective perception of reality), I will want to find out how she views the major events and turning points of her life. I assume that she has created a unique style of life that helps to explain the patterns of her behavior. My attention will be on how she has developed her distinctive behaviors in the pursuit of her life goals.

Assessment of Ruth

Adlerian therapists typically use the lifestyle questionnaire in making an initial assessment of the client and in formulating the goals and directions for therapy. This questionnaire gathers information about the client's childhood experiences, especially as they relate to family influences, birth order, relationships of each of the other family members, early memories, and other relevant material that will provide clues about the social forces influencing the client's personality formation. (In his assessment Bitter drew heavily from the framework of Adlerian lifestyle assessment as presented by Powers and Griffith in their 1987 book *Understanding Life Style: The Psycho-Clarity Process*.) Thus, I will not repeat this discussion here.

Goals of Therapy

There are four major goals of an Adlerian approach to therapy with Ruth, which correspond to the four phases of the therapeutic process. These goals are (1) to establish and maintain a good working relationship be-tween Ruth and me as equals, (2) to provide a therapeutic climate in which she can come to understand her basic beliefs and feelings about herself and discover how she acquired these faulty beliefs, (3) to help her reach insight into her mistaken goals and self-defeating behaviors through a process of confrontation and interpretation, and (4) to assist her in developing alternative ways of thinking, feeling, and behaving by encouraging her to translate her insights into action.

Therapeutic Procedures

One of the aims of Ruth's therapy is to challenge her to take risks and make changes. Throughout the entire process *encouragement* is of the utmost importance. My assumption is that with encouragement Ruth will begin to experience her own inner resources and the power to choose for herself and to direct her own life. By now she will ideally have challenged her self-limiting assumptions and will be ready to put plans into action. Even though she may regress to old patterns at times, I will ask her to "catch herself" in this process and then continue to experiment with and practice new behavior. Throughout her therapy I will use a variety of techniques aimed primarily at challenging her cognitions (beliefs and thinking pro-cesses). Adlerians contend that first comes thinking, then feeling, and then behaving. So if we want to change behavior and feelings, the best way is to focus on Ruth's mistaken perceptions and faulty beliefs about life and herself. Drawing on a variety of techniques, some borrowed from other modalities, I will use confrontation, questioning, encouragement, assign-ing of homework, interpretation, giving of appropriate advice, and any other methods that can help her begin to change her vision of herself and her ability to behave in different ways.

The Therapeutic Process

In many ways the process of Adlerian therapy can be understood by recalling some basic ideas from contemporary psychoanalytic therapy. There is a link between these two approaches, especially on the issue of looking at how early patterns are related to our present personality functioning.

Elements of the process

Uncovering a mistaken belief.   Ruth and I have been working together for some time, and she is beginning to see striking parallels between the role she assumed as an adolescent, by becoming the caretaker of her sisters and brother, and her contemporary role as "supermother" to her own children.

She has discovered that for all of her life she has been laboring under the assumption that if she gave of herself unselfishly, she would be rewarded by being acknowledged and feeling a sense of personal fulfillment. As a child she wanted to be loved, accepted, and taken care of emotionally by her father, and she worked very hard at being the "good girl." As a married woman she has outdone herself in being the perfect wife and the devoted mother to their children. In this way she hopes to relate to her husband so he will love and accept her. Still, she has never really felt appreciated or emotionally nurtured by him, and now she is realizing that she has built her life on a personal mythology: If people loved her, she would be worthwhile and would find happiness through her personal sacrifices.

Helping Ruth reach her goals.   At this time in Ruth's therapy we are exploring some other options open to her. Lately we have been talking a lot about her goals and about her vision of herself in the years to come.

RUTH: I'm hoping to get a teaching credential, but I keep telling myself that I don't have a right to do this for myself. It seems so selfish. School is very demanding of my time and energies, and it means that I have that much less to give at home. If only I could throw myself more fully into my studies and at the same time feel good about that choice!

JERRY: And what stops you from doing what you say you want to do?

RUTH: I guess it's my guilt! I keep feeling I shouldn't be at school and should be at home. John keeps telling me how much he and the kids miss me. If only I could stop feeling that I should be the dedicated mother and wife! But then I wouldn't be sure of my place in the family, either, and everything would be up in the air.

JERRY: It's probably not guilt that keeps you from what you want. My guess is that guilt is one of your ways of being "good." After all, a really rotten person would "desert" her family and not even have the common decency to feel bad. At least, you're kind enough to feel bad about it.

RUTH [smiling and giving a little chuckle]: This is not a laughing matter.

JERRY: You say that John keeps telling you how much he and the kids miss you. It's really very nice to be missed; but you interpret his meaning to be "Ruth, you should stay home. You're displeasing everyone."

RUTH: That's true. That's what I think he believes.

JERRY: Well, it's an old, but mistaken, notion you have. You could check it out. You could ask John what *he* means when he says he misses you. Maybe all he means is that he loves you [pause], and believes that the kids love you too. You could ask.

RUTH: Asking John how he really feels about my school and career and what I'm doing is extremely hard. [pause] He could tell me that he hates my school and career goals and that they're threatening our relationship.

JERRY: Oh, it could be *much* worse than that. If John said all of that, he would be giving you a very clear, direct message that you could address just as clearly. But what if John said, "Being without you while you're in school is extremely hard, a real sacrifice for me and for the kids, but we're willing to suffer that hardship for you." Now, this would really hurt, wouldn't it? Have you been good enough to accept such a gift from your family? Are you worth their sacrifices for you?

RUTH [pausing and then beginning slowly]: Yes. Yes, I am. You're right. I need to know what everyone is really thinking and stop guessing. I need to face this with John. I really do believe that he loves me.

I am hoping that Ruth, by confronting a mistaken notion, will find the courage to check a lifelong idea against a current reality. She will be scared to be sure. Without some fear there is no need for courage. A week passes, and Ruth returns.

RUTH: Guess what? John and I talked. A long, wonderful talk. We both cried. He was afraid that I wouldn't need him anymore. Afraid of losing *me*! Can you believe it? But he didn't want me to stop school. "Not for anything in the world," he said.

JERRY: Ruth, that's wonderful. I'm very happy for you. What a treat to have a real risk work out so well for you.

RUTH: When John talked about the kids wanting their mother home, I started to feel guilty all over again. But a couple of hours later, I remembered what you had said about "guilt" being what a "good" person does. I still felt guilty, but I also felt a little silly feeling the guilt.

JERRY [laughing]: Good! At this point in your life, guilt is a habit. Like any habit, it takes time to change it. For now you're catching yourself after the fact, after the guilt. Soon you'll catch yourself in the middle of it and just stop. And someday you'll know you don't need guilt to be a good person, and you'll skip it altogether. So stick to it, but give yourself time.

RUTH: The thing is, I miss time with my kids as much as they miss me. When I'm studying, I can't help wondering what they're doing and what I'm missing by not being with them.

JERRY: Maybe we can spend some time looking at how you could build guaranteed "husband time" and "children time" into each week. Time that is special. Time that is not violated by school any more than "school time" can be interrupted by family.

From here we proceed to look at a week of Ruth's time and how she might balance personal needs with the needs of others. Planning special time for her family maintains (Ruth's) sense of belonging and her real need for social interest without short-circuiting the gift of time her family is giving her for school. It also provides her with a structure by which she can devote her full attention to the tasks or people at hand: quality time in both cases.

Process commentary

My major aim in our sessions is to both encourage and challenge Ruth to consider alternative attitudes, beliefs, goals, and behaviors. By seeing the link between her mistaken beliefs and her current feelings and behaviors, she is able to consider options and change. She takes some big risks in approaching her husband. Given her history with and interpretation of men, she risks a harsh, rejecting rebuke. What she gains, however, is an increased sense of her worth and value to this important man in her life. She also gains in courage and confidence.

Once Ruth has made some new decisions and modified her goals, I teach her ways in which to challenge her own thinking. At those times when she is critical of herself, I provide encouragement. Partly because of my faith in her and my encouragement, she comes closer to experiencing her inner strength. She becomes more honest about what she is doing, and she augments her power to choose for herself instead of merely following the values she uncritically accepted as a child.

A most important ingredient of the final stages of Ruth's therapy is commitment. She is finally persuaded that if she hopes to change, she will have to set specific tasks for herself and then take concrete action. Although she attempts to live up to what she believes is the role of the "good person," she eventually develops increased tolerance for learning by trial and error, and with this she becomes better at "catching herself" when she repeats ineffective behavior.

Questions for Reflection

1. As you review the lifestyle-assessment form used to gather background information on Ruth, what associations do you have with your own early childhood experiences?
2. Look at the initial interview form and the lifestyle-assessment form used by Bitter in his assessment of Ruth. Answer these questions as they apply to you. Do you see any patterns emerging?
3. As you think about your own family constellation, what most stands out for you? After reflecting on your early experiences in your family, attempt to come to some conclusions about the ways in which these experiences are operating in your life today.
4. What are three of your earliest recollections? Can you speculate on how these memories might have an impact on the person you are now and how they could be related to your future strivings?
5. List what you consider to be the major "basic mistakes" in your life. Do you have any ideas about how you developed these mistaken perceptions about yourself and about life? How do you think that they are influencing the ways in which you think, feel, and act today?

6. Compare and contrast the Adlerian and the psychoanalytic ways of working with Ruth. What are some of the major differences? Do you see any ways to combine Adlerian and psychoanalytic concepts and techniques?

7. From what you learned about Ruth through the lifestyle questionnaire, what aspects of her life might you want to give the primary focus? What themes running through her life lend themselves especially well to Adlerian therapy?

8. One of the goals of Adlerian therapy is to increase the client's social interest. Can you think of ways in which you could work with Ruth to help her attain these goals?

9. Ruth describes herself as coming from a middle-class family. They were fundamentalist Christians, and the family values involved doing right, working hard, and living in a way that would reflect well on the family. Considering this background, how well do Adlerian concepts and therapeutic procedures fit for Ruth? How would the Adlerian approach fit for her if she were an Asian American? Latino? African American? Native American?

10. What major cultural themes do you see in Ruth's case? How would you address these themes, using an Adlerian framework?

JULIE: "IT'S MY FATHER'S FAULT THAT I CAN'T TRUST MEN"

Some Background Data

Julie is interested in exploring her relationships with men. She says that she cannot trust me because I am a man and that she cannot trust men because her father was an alcoholic and was therefore untrustworthy. She recalls that he was never around when she needed him and that she would not have felt free to go to him with her problems in any case, because he was loud and gruff. She tells me of the guilt she felt over her father's drinking because of her sense that in some way she was causing him to drink. Julie, who is now 35 and unmarried, is leery of men, convinced that they will somehow let her down if she gives them the chance. She has decided in advance that she will not be a fool again, that she will not let herself need or trust men.

Although Julie seems pretty clear about not wanting to risk trusting men, she realizes that this notion is self-defeating and would like to challenge her views. Though she wants to change the way in which she perceives and feels about men, somehow she seems to have an investment in her belief about their basic untrustworthiness. She is not very willing to look at her part in keeping this assumption about men alive. Rather, she would prefer to pin the blame on her father. It was he who taught her this lesson, and now it is difficult for her to change, or so she reports.

My Way of Working with Julie as an Adlerian Therapist

I am inclined to begin my counseling of Julie with a question: "If trusting men is so hard for you, why did you choose me?" She replies that she has heard that I am "a good counselor." I note that there are many good counselors and that many of them are women. She says that she wants to work with a male counselor to learn how to trust men. I ask her if she knows why she is so angry and upset with men. If she mentions her father, I say: "He's just one man. Do you know why you react in this way to most men—even today?" If it is appropriate to her response, I may suggest: "Could it be that your beliefs against men keep you from having to test your ability to be a true friend?" Or "Could it be that you want to give your father a constant reminder that he has wrecked your life? Could you be getting your revenge for an unhappy childhood?"

Even if it is true that her father was untrustworthy and treated her unkindly, my assessment is that it is a "basic mistake" for her to have generalized what she believes to be true of her father to all men. My hope is that our relationship, based on respect and cooperation, will be a catalyst for her in challenging her assumptions about men.

As part of the assessment process I am interested in exploring her early memories, especially those pertaining to her father and mother, the guiding lines for male and female relationships. We will also explore what it was like for her as a child in her family, what interpretation she gave to events, and what meaning she gave to herself, others, and the world. Some additional questions that I will pose are:

- What do you think you get from staying angry at your father and insisting that he is the cause of your fear of men?
- What do you imagine it would be like for you if you were to act as if men were trustworthy? And what do you suppose really prevents you from doing that?
- What would happen or what would you be doing differently if you trusted men?
- If you could forgive your father, what do you imagine that would be like for you? for him? for your dealings with other men?
- If you keep the same attitudes until you die, how will that be for you?
- How would you like to be in five years?
- If you really want to change, what can you do to begin the process? What are you willing to do?

I have already indicated that my relationship with Julie is the major vehicle with which to work in the sessions. A male counselor who emphasizes listening, mutual respect, honesty, partnership, and encouragement will give her a chance to examine her mistaken notions and try on new behaviors. A lifestyle assessment will help her see the broad pattern of her life and will reveal the convictions that are leading her to safeguard herself against all male relationships. She is an adult child of a person who has had a serious problem with alcohol. She will not be alone in her tendency to generalize from this childhood experience, but she can be helped to take charge of her own life and her current relationships with men.

Julie needs to take some action if she expects to change her views toward men. Thus, we work together to determine what she can do outside of the sessions. Here is one possibility, with the follow-up that would occur within the therapy session:

Julie can write an uncensored letter to her father, explicitly airing all of her grievances. It is critical that she express her anger—that she tell him all the things she has been saying to me and other things that she has felt but kept to herself. I encourage her *not* to mail the letter, as this is only an exercise for her to symbolically work through some of her issues toward her father. At the following session we can discuss what it was like for her to write this letter and what she learned from it.

The letter writing is an avenue for Julie to examine her convictions, beliefs, and feelings. She can benefit by focusing on what she brings to her relationships and what she can learn about the humanity of others.

A major part of my work with Julie is directed at confronting her with the ways in which she is refusing to take responsibility for the things in herself that she does not like and at encouraging her to decide on some course of action to begin the process of modifying those things. A very important phase of therapy is the reorientation stage, the action-oriented process of putting one's insights to work. As an Adlerian therapist I am concerned that Julie do more than merely understand the dynamics of her behavior. My goal is that she eventually see new and more functional alternatives. This reorientation phase of her therapy consists of her considering alternative attitudes, beliefs, goals, and behaviors. She is expected to make new decisions. I encourage her to "catch herself" in the process of repeating old patterns. When she meets a man and then immediately assumes that he cannot be trusted, for example, it helps if she is able to observe what she is doing. She can then ask herself if she wants to persist in clinging to old assumptions or if she is willing to let go of them and form impressions without bias.

This phase of counseling is a time for Julie to commit to the specific ways in which she would like to be different. Encouragement during the time that she is trying new behavior and working on new goals is most useful. This encouragement can take the form of having faith in her, of support, of recognizing the changes she makes, and of continuing to be psychologically available for her during our sessions.

Follow-Up: You Continue as Julie's Therapist

1. What are some of your impressions and reactions to my work with Julie? Knowing what you know about these sessions and Julie, what might you *most* want to follow up with if you could see her for at least a couple of months?

2. How much do you imagine that your approach with Julie would be affected by your life experiences and views? How much would you want to share of yourself with her? In what ways do you think you could use yourself as a person in your work with her?
3. How might you deal with her apparent unwillingness to accept personal responsibility and her blaming of her father for her inability to trust men now?
4. What are some additional Adlerian techniques you might use with Julie?
5. Outline some of the steps in Adlerian counseling that you would expect to take for a series of sessions with Julie, showing why you are adopting that particular course of action.

RECOMMENDED SUPPLEMENTARY READINGS

Adler, A. (1979). *Superiority and social interest: A collection of later writings* (3rd rev. ed.). New York: Norton. This is an excellent source for readers who want to review some of Adler's writings. The introduction, written by H. L. Ansbacher and R. R. Ansbacher, is a clear statement on the increasing recognition of Adler's position in the development of counseling. Part VI contains a comprehensive and interesting biographical essay of Adler. Part III deals with case interpretations and treatment.

Ansbacher, H. L., & Ansbacher, R. R. (1956). *The Individual Psychology of Alfred Adler*. New York: Basic Books. Here is the classic text, organizing and annotating all of Adler's basic writings on the theory and practice of Individual Psychology. Many Adlerians consider this book to be the fundamental source for their work.

Dinkmeyer, D., Dinkmeyer, D., Jr., & Sperry, L. (1987). *Adlerian counseling and psychotherapy* (2nd ed.). Columbus, OH: Merrill. This book gives an excellent basic presentation of the theoretical foundations of Adlerian counseling. The specific focus is on stages of the counseling process, Adlerian techniques, applying Adlerian methods to a variety of populations, and working with individuals, groups, and families.

Dreikurs, R., Shulman, B. H., & Mosak, H. H. (1984). *Multiple therapy: The use of two therapists with one patient*. Chicago: Alfred Adler Institute. This is an overview of the use of multiple therapy from an Adlerian point of view. The book integrates the lifestyle-assessment process with the use of two therapists and discusses advantages and disadvantages of the approach.

Powers, R. L., & Griffith, J. (1985). *An Adlerian lexicon*. Chicago: AIAS. This is an outstanding quick reference that lists over 50 terms fundamental to basic Adlerian assumptions and theory. Each term is cross-referenced to quotations and literature that provide a conceptual context for the definition.

Powers, R. L., & Griffith, J. (1986). *Individual Psychology client workbook*. Chicago: AIAS. This is a guide for initial Adlerian interviews and lifestyle assessments. The workbook is a supplemental Adlerian approach to the authors' *Understanding Life Style: The Psycho-Clarity Process* and can be ordered from AIAS, Ltd., 600 North McClurg Court, Suite 2502A, Chicago, IL 60611; telephone: (312) 337-5066.

Powers, R. L., & Griffith, J. (1987). *Understanding life style: The psycho-clarity process.* Chicago: AIAS. This work is a thorough presentation of Adlerian theory in relation to lifestyle assessment and its therapeutic uses. The authors do an excellent job of relating process to skill development. This book is fast becoming the reference for Adlerian therapeutic practice.

CHAPTER FOUR

Case Approach to Existential Therapy

AN EXISTENTIAL THERAPIST'S PERSPECTIVE ON RUTH, by Donald Polkinghorne, Ph.D.

Introduction

Counselors who approach psychotherapy from an existential perspective emphasize the client's personal responsibility for creating his or her own existence. Existential thought holds that people are essentially different from the rest of nature in that they have the capacity for self-direction and voluntaristic behavior. People need not exist as passive objects buffeted about by instinctual needs, environmental stimuli, or social pressures. The role of the counselor working with clients in an existential crisis is to provide assistance and support for their efforts to take control of their own existence. The force of client change comes from the self's thrust toward authenticity, and the instrument of change is the client's will. The counselor is not the cause of change, nor does his or her use of techniques bring it about. Clients' primary need during this process of self-formation is a counseling relationship with an experienced person who empathetically understands their struggles and supports their efforts to claim their own lives. Such understanding and support require counselors who are skilled in helping clients move through obstructions to change and experiment with expressing their new power and freedom.

Initial Assessment

The sources of the distress that leads clients to seek counseling are varied. A clinical assessment lets the counselor and client come to an understanding of the covert source of the manifest symptoms. Ruth's symptoms include psychosomatic complaints of dizziness, hot flashes, and difficulty in breathing. Her other symptoms are feelings of depression, crying over trivial matters, occasional feelings of panic, sporadic difficulties in leaving her house, and a general dissatisfaction with her life. Because she reported that a physician could not find an organic basis for her symptoms, I will explore other possible sources.

Given the information reported in her intake form and autobiography, I tentatively explore with Ruth the possibility that the source of her distress may be an existential crisis. I initially begin with this possibility because of her general life situations: She is 39 years old; she has returned to school, has earned a bachelor's degree, and is completing graduate work on a teaching credential; and her children are in late adolescence. Her intake form reports that "she is not really sure who or what she wants to become" and that "she would like to develop a sense of herself apart from the expectations of others." Also, the variety of symptoms she is experiencing, the time she has been experiencing them, and the lack of a specific stressor lead me initially to rule out a particular life event as the source of her distress. Focusing on existential themes is not necessarily appropriate for all clients. The purpose of my assessment work with Ruth is to determine if the source of her distress is the lack of personal meaning reflecting an existential crisis. If this is the case, counseling work with her that emphasizes life's existential issues will be therapeutically the most effective and productive.

The judgment about which possible source or sources of distress should be first explored in the therapy work is a mutual project and involves collaborative decision making by Ruth and me. Also, assessment is not finished after the initial focus of therapy is chosen; rather, we return to it repeatedly. As therapy progresses, our stress on the selected source may be found unproductive or incorrect, and a reexploration of the possible source is necessary. At times, changes in the area of work may occur because the initial focus was too shallow or too deep.

Work focusing on an existential crisis as the source of manifest symptoms explores the deepest levels of Ruth's existence and requires that she reexamine the assumptions that have governed her actions and self-identity. As a result, our assessment work needs to include more than a judgment about the source of her symptoms; it also takes an inventory of her personal strengths, social supports, and willingness to undertake the rigors of self-examination. She has demonstrated personal fortitude, by enrolling in college after years away from school, and perseverance and intelligence, in completing her degree. We have to explore whether her motivation is limited to the removal of her distressing symptoms or includes a desire to take control of her self-definition and life direction. We also have to examine what social support is available to her if she undertakes the process of existential change. I try to determine if her belief that her husband and children would not support her in this change is accurate. I also explore other possible sources of support, such as close friends in whom she can confide. The purpose of this part of the assessment is to understand which areas of her personal and social strengths will be available and to tentatively determine the pace and sequence of our therapeutic work.

This collaborative activity of assessment differs from the activity of determining if the application of a DSM-IV diagnostic category is appropriate to describe Ruth's symptoms. DSM-IV definitions are reserved for "mental disorders"; that is, their use is not appropriate merely because symptoms are present, but these symptoms must be severe enough that they are associated with significant distress or dysfunction. When employed appropriately, DSM-IV descriptors serve as a shorthand vocabulary for discussing particular aggregations of symptoms. It is inappropriate to employ DSM-IV terms to classify people. Although clients seek counseling because of the distress of their symptoms, it is the *person*, with his or her unique history and interpretative meaning structure, with whom we work. Counselors working in an existential mode are not antagonistic to the use of DSM-IV descriptors to designate a symptom complex, as long as the integrity of the client's personhood is maintained.

Except in the area of organic sources of symptoms, the DSM-IV does not address the etiology of symptom complexes. It also does not support a particular theoretical orientation toward how therapists should work with clients manifesting a symptom complex. Thus, therapists holding different theoretical positions about the sources of psychological symptoms can still make use of the manual's descriptive terms.

Given these caveats about the DSM-IV, I believe that Ruth's complex of symptoms most closely fits under the designation *identity problem*. Although her distress and impairment in physical functioning, her career indecision, and the deterioration of her family relationships are painful, they do not appear severe enough to be classified as a mental disorder. Thus, her symptoms are better classified as one of the "other conditions that may be a focus of clinical attention." The focus of the clinical attention in her case will be on her uncertainty about her long-term goals, career choice, and friendship patterns. The source of an identity problem is often an existential crisis, and therapy that addresses a client's existential themes is most appropriate. I believe that this is Ruth's situation.

Goals of Therapy

The primary goal of existential therapy is for clients to lead more *authentic* lives. This means assisting them in taking charge of their lives, helping them choose for themselves the values and purposes that will define and guide their existence, and by supporting them in actions that express these values and purposes. From my initial assessment these goals seem appropriate for Ruth's therapy.

Therapeutic Procedures

The existential method shares with other psychotherapeutic approaches the use of basic counseling skills such as attending to clients' descriptions of their experience rather than assuming to know what they have experienced, reflecting rather than distorting their meaning, and reassuring rather than judging them. This approach to counseling is not technique-driven, nor can it be identified by a specific set of techniques. Different existential counselors use different procedures that they have found personally of help in enabling their clients to move through the course of authentic self-generation.

This does not mean that existential counselors are eclectic in the sense of managing a collection of techniques developed by the various theoretical schools of counseling. Also, they are not eclectic in the sense of being nontheoretical and guided by the pragmatic criterion of "doing whatever works to relieve the symptom." The various techniques that existential counselors use are chosen to serve the goals of existential therapy.

The most important therapeutic procedure in existential counseling is developing an authentic relationship in which the therapist and client are fully present to each other without the protective shields of scripted roles and social mandates. In addition to serving as a guide in establishing this special kind of relationship, the existential therapist uses a wide variety of other procedures in working with clients. Most of these fall under the rubric of *talk therapy*, including (1) questioning; (2) interpretation—for example, using an existential term to name a feeling the client is experiencing; (3) reframing—for example, redescribing a client's statement "I can't do that because a friend would not approve" as "I choose to give responsibility and control of my actions to my friend"; (4) confronting or challenging; and (5) supportive encouragement.

An array of other procedures is available to existential therapists. I sometimes ask clients to create imaginative scenarios. For example, I ask them to imagine alternative actions they could have taken in a situation and then explore what responses another person might have made and consider how they would have felt if the imagined action had been undertaken. I also ask clients to report particularly impressive dreams. In addition, I make use of rehearsals, or role playing, and homework assignments. Finally, because movement toward an authentic life can be confusing to the client's family, and because the understanding and support of family members can make an important contribution to the person's progress in therapy, I often ask clients if I could include their spouse or other loved ones in a meeting.

These examples are drawn from my work with clients and are representative only of my personal style. They are not necessarily used by other counselors who do existential therapy. The general purpose of such procedures is to help clients reflect on their experiences and achieve greater self-knowledge. The particular purpose is to help them achieve insight into the sources of authority that stand behind their self-definition and values.

A therapeutic process with Ruth

Ruth comes for counseling after two years of confusion, depression, neurotic anxiety, inability to sleep, and a range of psychosomatic complaints. An actual therapeutic process does not move smoothly through a sequence of steps to its conclusion. Rather, it has stops and starts and returns to previously worked-through areas and then forward again to further steps. Nevertheless, there is a general developmental sequence through which existential therapy advances. Sufficient progress in one area of concern lays the groundwork for developments in the next area. The sequence through which the sessions usually progress is (1) establishing a therapeutic relationship, (2) identifying the problem and setting the therapeutic goal, (3) analyzing the existential source of the symptoms, (4) developing a commitment to create an existentially authentic life, and (5) manifesting an authentic existence.

Establishing a therapeutic relationship.   The first step in existential therapy, as it is in most counseling approaches, is to establish a therapeutic alliance in which clients experience the therapist as someone who empathetically understands their distress and accepts them as a person. I work with Ruth to build a relationship of mutual trust and to establish the therapy sessions as a protective context. In the first sessions I expect her to test my responses to disclosures she offers to determine how safe it is for her to reveal "darker" fears and desires. I resist moving through this "check-out" beginning phase too quickly. She needs enough experience with me as a person to know that she can disclose the parts of her self (such as her "selfishness") that she has learned are unacceptable and that have produced withdrawal and condemnation from others. Before she can venture into the deeper layers of her self, she needs to accept that the relationship with me is different from the ones she has previously experienced; I am not her father and will not respond to her as he has. In the relationship we are creating, it will be safe for her to experiment with new behavior and self-definitions; I will not abandon her if she displeases me. I also need to convey that I support her impulse to make changes in her life and will use my experience to assist her in accomplishing these changes. During the initial sessions, I relate that her journey will be a difficult one and that there will be periods when the struggle no longer seems worth it; I am, however, committed for the long run and will see it through with her.

In existential therapy the therapeutic relationship needs to be a model of the authentic relationships Ruth will be able to establish with her family members as she takes control of her life. There are no "magic words" that I can speak to create a therapeutic relationship. I genuinely need to care about her and support her growth into authenticity. She will learn that I am trustworthy only if I am truly trustworthy. My actual feelings for her express themselves through my gestures, facial expressions, tone of voice, and statements. Ruth will pick up whether what I say about my acceptance and support is incongruent with my way of being with her. I need to reflect on my feelings about her and clear myself of doubts that I can be a therapeutic partner for her in this journey. I have to be aware of any feelings I have toward her that are leakages from my experiences with other people and might interfere with our therapeutic work. I may have to decide that these leakages are too strong and that I should refer her to another therapist.

As I have stressed, the therapeutic relationship is the prerequisite resource for work on existential issues. Attending to its development and maintenance will occupy my work with Ruth throughout our time together. It is not something that can be built and then forgotten. We will have to return repeatedly to deal with issues that might erode the special type of therapeutic encounter we have developed. I expect that my content work with her will follow the order that generally occurs in existential therapy. The work in the first phase, identifying the problem and setting the therapeutic goal, overlays the period of the initial development of the therapeutic relationship and provides the content of our discussions during the time in which the relationship is growing.

Identifying the problem and setting the therapeutic goal.   I begin by asking Ruth to recount the distress she is feeling and to describe what she hopes to accomplish in our therapeutic work. I use this time to appraise my initial assessment, which was based on her intake form and autobiographical statement. Although her subsequent life events may have pushed new concerns into the forefront, I assume that the basic issues in her life have not changed much. The concerns I expect her to report remain those of feeling lost, stuck, and confused about the direction of her life. Her hope is that therapy will help her find the right direction for her life and get her started moving in that direction. I also expect that she is continuing to experience a variety of manifest psychosomatic symptoms. I explore with her the severity of these neurotic symptoms. I want to determine whether she is so distraught or depressed that she is not able to begin the existential tasks of reflective self-exploration. If her symptoms are too severe, we will postpone the existential work until their intensity is lessened. If it is necessary to address her symptoms directly before moving on, I will instruct her in methods for anxiety reduction and, if I judge it to be necessary, will refer her for possible prescription of psychiatric medications. I use her demeanor in the sessions and her descriptions of her symptoms to judge her capacity to begin the existential therapy. If it appears that the symptoms are not so severe as to limit her performance outside therapy significantly, I do not want to suppress, disguise, deny, or mute her feelings with medications. She needs to have access to her feelings for the reflective work of existential therapy to be effective.

After hearing Ruth's description of her condition, and given that I remain confident in my understanding that her symptoms are surface manifestations of an existential crisis, we begin the existential therapeutic work proper. The first move in this portion of the therapy is for me to suggest an interpretation of the reason she is experiencing her symptoms. The context and manner in which I propose the interpretation is crucial. Before employing this interpretative move in the therapy, I wait until Ruth is signaling the question "Why am I feeling this way?" I do not say merely, "Your problem is that you're in an existential crisis and need to take charge of your life." I approach the interpretation as a process that begins as a soft and tentative suggestion from me:

THERAPIST: Other clients I've worked with, who had similar concerns and symptoms, found that they were experiencing a developmental crisis in which the ways they behaved in the past were no longer satisfying.

I listen carefully to her bodily and vocal response to this suggestion. I am looking for some genuine recognition that the interpretation describes her own situation. If the response is a simple "Yes," conveying an "OK, if you say so," I ask her if she really feels that this makes sense of her own situation. My offered interpretation makes no contribution to her therapy unless she takes it over as her own; that is, she needs to integrate this understanding into the meanings she uses to make sense of her self and her behavior. If she says that she does not experience the sense of the interpretation for her own life situation, we will stop and explore what is it in this description that doesn't fit her own understanding of what she is experiencing. We will stay with this topic until she can render in her own words that her present way of "being-in-the-world" is not working any longer for her.

Assuming that Ruth comes to the recognition that her "old" self is no longer working for her, I introduce the idea that our therapeutic task is to build a "new" self that will not produce the symptoms that are part of her present life. I explain that other clients have found that constructing a new self is a difficult task and have drawn on their reserves of strength and courage. I explain that the therapeutic journey will take up to a year of work. During this portion of the therapy we are negotiating an explicit goal for our work together. If she agrees to work with me toward this existential goal, I describe the phases through which therapy will move. I ask her to consider before our next meeting whether she wants to commit herself to this goal. This will be a crucial session, in which we make an explicit agreement to proceed with the phases of the existential work. This agreement will serve as the context and backdrop for our sessions. We will recall this commitment and the agreed-on destination many times during the succeeding sessions.

Analyzing the existential source of the symptoms. Having recognized that the old way of being is no longer working and that the goal of our work together is to build a new self, Ruth begins the specific existential portion of her therapy. I start by asking her to talk about her experience of herself. I ask her to explore what things she does that make her feel guilty and to recall when she has done things she disliked because it was proper for a person like her to do them. We gradually construct a picture of the values and rules that she has used up to this time to guide her actions:

THERAPIST: Why do you do things that you feel you don't want to do? Why did you rush home to prepare the family's meals when you wanted to stay at school and attend a special lecture?

I want Ruth to become aware of and be able to describe the content of the expectations that have controlled her life. After developing an explicit awareness of these commands, we move to a discussion of the extent of their power. Ruth recognizes that these expectations have operated in a forceful way in her life, producing compliant and obedient behavior. I ask her to consider their power to control her behavior when she continued to perform as a "good mother" and "good wife" even though this behavior was no longer consistent with what she wanted to do. In our work in this phase I emphasize that we are not judging the "goodness" or "badness" of the expectations that have been part of her self; rather, we are concentrating on becoming aware of what the expectations were and of the extent of their power over her. By making judgments at this time about her internalized commands, I may prompt Ruth into defensive diversions:

RUTH: Yes, but being a good wife is appropriate; are you saying I should be a bad wife?

After this analysis of the expectations that have guided Ruth's behavior, I ask her to consider the source of these expectations:

THERAPIST: Where do you think you got these ideas about how you should behave? How did you come to hold the idea that for you to be a good person, you had to do these things?

I propose that for most people these ideas originate with their parents. This is the occasion for us to explore her childhood relations with her parents. I ask her to link her present notions of the proper way to behave with the memories she has of edicts given by her parents. I ask her to recollect salient incidents in her childhood that were particularly formative.

We focus on the relationship with her minister father. She has described him as being especially forceful in molding her values and implanting an image of the kind of person she was to be. I ask her to consider her vulnerability as a child to her father's criticisms and her need to become the kind of person he wanted her to be. I urge her to reexperience the feelings she had when he expressed his scorn and disapproval and then withdrew from her because she hadn't done what he wanted. She is asked to return imaginatively to the situation of certain remembered events—for example, the time she was caught by her father "playing doctor" and the time she took over caring for her brothers and sisters to earn her parents' acceptance. The re-creating and reexperiencing of these powerful childhood experiences may bring forth deep emotional responses from her, and I need to be accepting and supportive of her during these sometimes painful and sorrowful moments.

The purpose of these imaginative re-creations and any cathartic experiences they bring is for Ruth to gain some emotional distance from these formative childhood experiences. This distance opens these experiences to reflective analysis, and the analysis allows her to recognize that the directives that have governed her behavior have their origin in her childhood efforts to gain her parents' acceptance. They also allow her to recognize that these directives continue to control her life and that the criteria she uses to judge her worth are powerful remnants of her parents' criteria.

We pause in the therapy to tease out the details of the ideas she uses to decide what to do and to judge her "goodness" or "badness." We consider the positive and negative ideals that motivate her behavior. On the positive side, we explore the ramifications of what it means for her to be a "good girl" and a "good wife," and we consider what is behind her drive to perform like a "superwoman." She describes a "good girl" in terms that are consistent with her father's conservative values and with her mother's belief in the appropriateness of the gender-based, socially mandated role of a housewife. On the negative side, we investigate her notion of "being selfish" and the "badness" connected to this notion:

RUTH: People who do what they want to are selfish and selfish people come to a bad end. If I do what I want, my husband and children will no longer love me, and they'll probably abandon me.

Next, the therapy moves to a discussion about Ruth's success in living up to these ideals. I ask her to recognize the advantage to her of having clear ideas about how she should behave and which directions her life should take. I want her to acknowledge that she has done well in fulfilling the expectations that have guided her life; her career choice, her parenting efforts, and her sexual behavior have all fulfilled the images she had about who she should be. I point out to her that some people lose the clarity of their life direction during the turmoil of adolescence. She, however, seems to have retained into adulthood the images she first adopted in her childhood. I ask her to reflect on any rebellious efforts during her adolescence and on her decision to marry at a relatively young age to the first boy she dated. We are looking to uncover whether she made any tentative moves toward new possibilities and different directions for her life. The purpose of this part of the therapeutic work is to deepen her understanding of the early development of her self-image and the reasons for its resiliency and potency in controlling her life. We are also looking to locate any previous attempts to question the adequacy of these controlling ideas.

In our work thus far, Ruth has gained some reflective distance from the internalized demands that have been controlling her life. She has begun to feel control over the covert assumptions that have been the source of her current tensions. She is feeling more at ease with herself and is learning how to engage in the self-reflective procedures used in existential therapy. The previous phase of this analysis has focused on helping her recognize what images she has used to control her life and how she came to form them. This phase will focus on the more contemporary events in her life and the crisis she has been experiencing. I offer the interpretation that she is undergoing new growth as a person and that the ideals that have controlled her life are becoming constricting and suffocating. I suggest that these ideals have served her as a protective garment sheltering her from the uncertainty of what she should do with her life. In recent years the garment has started to unravel, and it is no longer sufficient to protect her. The process of unraveling was begun through the pull of the inevitable events of her personal existence: The esteem she had received from her children was disrupted by their adolescence, her role of mother was ending as the children were soon to leave home, her physical attractiveness was waning, and her 39th birthday brought her to a stage of life in which she recognized her vulnerability to death. I introduce the terms *old self* and *new self* at this time to provide a language for us to distinguish the self she has been from the self she can become.

I ask her to describe her decision to go to college and to consider a career as a teacher. I want to learn if this decision was merely a continuation of her old self-directions and was an instance of being a "good girl" or if it was the beginning of the move to break away from the constraints of her old self-images. Because of the significance she gave in her intake interview to her experience in her counseling course, I ask her to describe the insights she gained in the course. I suspect that this course was a catalyst in beginning or accelerating the unraveling of her old self. At this time I suggest to her that in her present condition her old self is no longer intact and powerful enough to give clear direction to her life, and she has no new vision of self to replace the old. She is in between selves.

We move on to discuss the experience of the "in-between." I believe this is Ruth's current position, and understanding this condition provides her with an explanation for why she feels the way she does. Being in the in-between is very distressful; one is adrift with no purpose or direction to life. There are no sure guidelines for action, so that decisions cannot be made, and nothing can be accomplished. One feels off center, depressed, and anxious; the body expresses these feelings through psychosomatic symptoms. The self is a void, and there is a strong desire to fill it with some content to restore a sense of direction and control. I ask Ruth to reflect on this description and determine if it matches her present situation. If it does, I ask her to describe the possibilities that have come to her that would fill her void of the in-between. She mentioned two possibilities in her intake: either that she fill it with her old self and learn to settle for the nice and comfortable, though boring and stale, life she used to have; or that I fill it by telling her "what to do" and pushing her to do it. I suggest a third possibility: that she create a new self to fill the void.

We spend time considering these various options. I introduce the idea of existential guilt, proposing that the feelings of emptiness she is experiencing in the in-between are a call to take charge of her life and to choose a new self that incorporates what she wants to be. I concede the powerful pull she is experiencing to put things back together as they were before—that is, to reinstate the stable relationship she had with her old self before her life events called this relationship into question. She seems, however, to accept that she cannot easily return to her old self; that is, she can't put the broken old self back together. I also admit the attractiveness of having me provide her with a substitute set of directions. I propose that these choices will not eliminate her feelings of lack of control; that is, she will continue to experience existential guilt. I help her understand that her existential guilt is a reminder that she cannot continue to avoid the obligation to decide what a worthy life will be for her and to begin to form her life in that direction.

I do not pass over the difficulty of change and grant that fear accompanies any attempt at personal change. I ask Ruth to share her fears about moving on to a new self. She has expressed various concerns about making changes in her life. For example, she is concerned that if she undertakes a teaching career, she may not succeed; that if she stops being the "good mother," she may lose her children; that if she changes from being the "good wife," her husband may leave her and she will end up alone; and that if she starts to do what she wants, she will consider herself selfish. She has also said that she is afraid she will make the wrong decisions and that she may discover there is nothing inside her. I need to communicate that I understand the power and reality of these fears but that I am also aware of her strengths and the courage that she has shown in returning to school and in the reflective work of therapy. I need her to accept that I will be with her and provide support if she decides to continue with our journey. This is a time to review and renew the therapeutic goal of self-creation that we decided on at the beginning of therapy.

Up to this point in our work together, Ruth has achieved some clarity about the reasons for her present condition and a readiness to move to the constructive work of the therapy—the construction of her new self. What previously operated covertly in her life has been brought into awareness, and she has gained some freedom from the control of the old self. In addition, the reasons for continuing to the next phases of work have been specified.

Reconstruction of the self.   The task for this phase of the therapy will be for Ruth to begin deciding what kind of life she will live in the future. Existential thought maintains that the authentic self is the consequence of a process of creativity, not of discovery. The authentic self is a personal construction that is the result of a person's conscious choice of values and purposes. Existentialism holds that living authentically means being true to one's own evaluation of what is a worthy existence.

In moving into this phase of the therapy, I have to help Ruth recognize and understand the feelings of existential anxiety that appear when she becomes aware that she is responsible for deciding who she will be. When she fully realizes that she need not continue to be her old self and is free to decide what she wants to become, she begins to experience the unease of floating without being tied down by the guidelines of parental expectations and social requirements. I need to help her recognize the difference between these new feelings, which accompany her experience of open possibilities, and her previous feelings, which accompanied her experience of closed possibilities. Before, she felt tied down and afraid of not beginning "to live before it is too late." Now, she feels responsible to act without required guidelines. I help her accept the light-headedness of existential anxiety and support her in not prematurely shutting down her self-creative process. A method for avoiding responsibility for one's own existence is to give control over it to some other person or to adopt a mandated social script. I have to be alert to turn our attention back to the operation of existential anxiety when the temptation to close it off comes to the fore.

The next step for Ruth and me is the actual work of self-reconstruction. I ask her to imagine herself on her deathbed, looking back at what she has done with her life, to assist her in discerning what kind of life she considers worthwhile and meaningful for her. I ask her to create several scenarios of what she wants to be like and wants to be doing in five years, and I ask her to decide which ones she most wants to have happen. We examine the implied values of the choices, to develop options for her consideration. These exercises lead to asking her to decide tentatively what direction she wants to pursue in her life and whether such a direction will be vital and ultimately valuable for her. I remind her that one of the options she can consider is a life direction that retains the values that are part of her old self. The difference, however, is that these values will now be ones she has freely chosen, not ones she adopted out of fear of rejection and abandonment. Whatever directions she chooses, they need to be those to which she can commit herself and devote her life.

After Ruth makes some first attempts at deciding the values and purposes that will define her new self, we begin an exploration of the implications of these choices. Because her choices will change the way she lives her life, we develop thought-experiments of what it will be like to live as her new self. Although these reflective exercises begin to affect the actual choices she is making in the world, we attempt to keep the therapy discussions ahead of the changes she is acting out in the world outside the therapy environment.

Existentialist thought emphasizes that we are beings-in-the-world. We do not exist as disconnected and encapsulated beings; instead, we are engaged with and relate to our selves, to others, and to the physical environment. We have the capacity to "stand out" from these relationships and to choose how we will engage in them, but we cannot avoid the engagement. In our therapeutic work Ruth has been "standing out" from her engagement with the world and has been reflecting on the values she wants to have guide her future relations. We now move the therapy to considerations of how her tentatively chosen values will affect her relations with her own self, with her body, and with other people.

I ask Ruth to focus first on what it will be like for her to relate to her self as a person responsible for her own actions. She will have to consult her own values to decide what she should do. She will no longer act or perform simply because it is what others expect of her or because that is what someone of her sex and age does in this society. We explore her readiness to take on the burden of being the source of her own behavior. I ask her to create scenarios in which the newly chosen convictions guide her actions. We explore the feelings that arise in the imaginative playing out of the new behavior. She also brings examples of her experiments at self-direction outside the therapy. We explore these efforts by reflecting on the kinds of feelings—for example, pride or shame—she has about herself when she asserts her chosen values in her actions. I continue the reflective work on the developing authentic self-relationship until she is feeling comfortable with what she will be like as a new self.

Because of the importance that religion has had in Ruth's life and because of the continuing pressures her father exerts, I ask her to consider what she will decide about the religious dimension of her self. In the process of her self-creation, the source of her religious beliefs has to be transferred from her father to her own self. I ask her to distance herself from her father's beliefs and to reflect on what, given the freedoms of her self-creation project, she will choose as her own beliefs. We take time to examine how her chosen religious beliefs will relate to and complement the values and purposes she is choosing for her new self. I ask her to consider whether there are inconsistencies between the values and religious beliefs she is proposing. For her new self to serve as her source of personal power and authority, its values and purposes need to be integrated. It is possible that she will need to spend time on harmonizing her chosen religious beliefs and her chosen life directions. If so, we will work through any tensions between these two dimensions of her self.

Our next area in considering the implications of Ruth's decisions about her new self is her relationship to her body. She reported that she was "not very proud of her body," was overweight and unable to control her eating, and experienced her body as aging and no longer attractive. I ask her if she still feels this way, and if she does, how much of this evaluation is left over from the social images of beauty that she incorporated into her old self. I ask her to go through a reevaluation of her body using the values she has chosen for her new self as criteria. We reflect on the possibility that her lack of control in her eating was a symptom of her existential crisis. I ask her to describe the body she will need to carry out the life purposes she has chosen for her new self. I expect that her emphasis will be on bodily health rather than conformity to a youthful and thin advertising model's image. We spend time planning what behavioral changes she will need to undertake if she conceives of her body as the vehicle through which she will accomplish her new purposes. I also ask Ruth to reflect on her manner of dress and whether it expresses her new self-understanding. I will be alert to modifications in her dress as possible indications of her movement to feeling at one with her new self. As part of our work in the area of her relationship to her body, I may consider asking her how her sexuality fits into her new self; if this topic doesn't come up as part of these discussions, I will bring it up as part of the considerations of her relation to her husband.

The next area for exploration with Ruth will be the implications of her newly chosen direction for her relationships with her family. As in the previous explorations, I ask her to tease out the controls that are leftover parts of her old self. We again use imaginative exercises in considering how becoming her new self will affect her relationship with her family. I ask her to imagine what she would do if she were free from having to conform to the stereotypical social roles of wife and mother. I also ask her to imagine what relationships she would have with her family members if she were in charge and could begin to develop them from scratch. We examine these scenarios for the values she would like to have guide her relations with her family. We also consider how these family values fit with the emerging choices she is making about the purpose and direction she wants for her life. I ask her to consider what changes in her relations to her family members are implied by the new self she is creating. I suggest that she concentrate on changes in her own behavior instead of on how she would like the other family members' behavior to be different. I remind her that her authority extends only to re-creating her own self, not the selves of others. We focus extended attention on her relationship to her husband and their marriage. The marriage bond can be threatened during a period of personal change in one of the partners. This is the time I ask Ruth if she would like to bring her husband to one of our sessions. She has expressed concern that if she changes, he may leave her. I ask her to share with him her vision of what their marriage will be like if her relationship to him is guided by the ideals of her new self. She and I explore what she might do to contribute to making this vision of her marriage a reality in her newly forming life.

I ask Ruth to concentrate on the implications of her emerging self for her career. She has trained to be a teacher and yet has expressed that she is afraid to begin because she might fail. We review these feelings, and if they are still present, we reflect on their source. I remind her that in her self-creation she is free to choose her career, whether it be a homemaker, teacher, or something else. I ask her to examine the implications of her emerging values for her career choice.

In this step of therapy Ruth has begun the constructive process of self-creation. She has examined the implications of her decisions for the purposes and values that she is choosing to guide her existence. We have examined how these choices may bring about changes in her various relations. She has started to actualize her possibility for living an authentic existence. She has begun to change her actions to reflect her newly chosen values. Up to this point, the therapy has focused on having her gain insight into her situation and on having her choose the values that will guide her life. She and I are only halfway on the journey to having her existence become an expression of authenticity. The next phase will change the focus from gaining insight and making choices to changing her life activities. We will now focus on manifesting her authenticity in her daily life.

Manifesting an authentic existence.   Deciding to change in a therapy setting and actually changing how one is in the world are different processes. The previous phases of therapy have been preparatory. Ruth's determination of what it is that has ultimate value for her is not an end in itself; it is only a prelude for her living these new values and engaging in the life process of creating her authentic existence. Our goal in this phase is to enable her to find ways to implement her chosen life purposes in practice.

This final phase of Ruth's therapy concentrates on helping her put into practice behaviors that express the values she has chosen for her new self. Manifesting the self she has decided to become in the previous parts of the therapeutic work is not a simple task. She has accumulated thought and response habits over the 39 years of her life, and these habits will continue to influence her behavior and feelings even though she has decided she wants to relate to the world in a new way. Because she is not all-powerful, is not perfect, and does not control all the consequences of her actions, not all of what she decides to do will come to fruition. I tell her that implementing her desired changes will not be without adversity. I try to communicate that none of us are able to actualize completely the goals we set for ourselves. Eventually, even the most determined of us will have to acknowledge our failures and limitations to become what we have envisioned. I ask Ruth to be compassionate and forgiving to herself when she does not always manifest what she has judged to be a worthy existence. At the same time, I advise her that she needs to exercise her courage in continuing to strive to be true to her chosen values.

During this phase of the therapy, we use the sessions to review the attempts Ruth has made during the week to enact her new values. We also decide on specific actions that represent further steps in authenticity and assign them as homework to be done during the following week. I ask her to report on her successes and failures in meeting the challenge to become what she has determined she wants to be. This is a time of experimentation with new behaviors, and at times these new actions will be awkward and will not appropriately reflect the values they were meant to express. At other times circumstances and social forces will interfere with her resolve and produce results she didn't intend.

As Ruth gains experience in acting out her values, she better understands the practical consequences of the initial choices she made in envisioning her new self. This new understanding leads her to change some of her decisions. We review changes in the initial decisions she made and how she intends to be in the world.

Through the course of this part of the therapy, Ruth's confidence grows. She has settled into the new definition of her life and has learned how to manifest this definition in practice. The therapy work has accomplished its goal, and she is ready to live a life based on directions she has chosen for herself. It is time to draw our sessions to an end. Because of the intensity and depth of our work, we express the realization that it is to end soon by feelings of sadness and loss. I need to anticipate the coming separation and use part of our final sessions to recognize and acknowledge the appropriateness of the alarm she may feel about continuing her growth toward authenticity without our regular meetings. I have to be aware of my own feelings of sadness over the loss of our times together, times in which she has opened her self to me and has shared the despair and joy of her struggle. My task is to let go, and hers is to move away.

Process commentary

By the time the therapeutic process outlined above has ended, Ruth and I have been working together for a year. She has made significant changes in her life, gaining control of her existence and setting the directions that will guide her future. The fears, indecisiveness, and neurotic symptoms with which she began therapy have receded, and she is actively engaged in life tasks that are consistent with the directions she has chosen. I have noticed significant differences in her. She is more vibrant and animated; she is more sure of herself and has taken a more assertive role in our interactions.

I have accompanied Ruth on her difficult journey to a more authentic existence. During the journey we have experienced times of despair as well as times of joy. There have been times when it seemed that progress had stopped and we could not go on, and other times of breakthrough and rapid advancement. She has come to trust me enough to share her deepest fears and embarrassments as well as her pride and happiness in her achievements. Our relationship has deepened, and my care and concern for her have intensified. I have grown in my appreciation of her courage and tenacity.

During our work together Ruth has aimed her life in newly chosen directions and has begun to act in accord with these directions; she has also begun to feel at home in her new self. Although she will continue to make adjustments in her life direction, I believe she will stay on the path of self-creation. Living her new life, however, will be a continuous struggle.

She will have to make compromises and agonize over decisions, but these will now be in the context of a personal commitment to her own values. She will continue to have life projects that require her attention: the quality of her relationship with her husband and the productivity of her occupational involvement. She will have episodes when she doubts her personal authority to be the creator of her life purpose, and she will experience the untethered feelings of existential anxiety. I believe her response to these episodes will be to accept these feelings as attendant experiences of personal freedom. I do not believe that she will revert to her old way of being by turning over the decisions about who she will be to the voices and commands of others.

I invite Ruth to continue to meet with me on a less frequent basis, perhaps every other month. These meetings will be occasions for checking in and talking about the challenges she is confronting in her continuing work toward authenticity. I expect us to suspend these meetings after about a year.

JERRY COREY'S WORK WITH RUTH FROM AN EXISTENTIAL PERSPECTIVE

Basic Assumptions

The existential approach to counseling assumes that the relationship the therapist establishes with the client is of the utmost importance in determining how successful therapy will be. Therapy is not something that I do *to* the person (in this case, Ruth); I am not a technical expert who acts on a passive client. I view therapy as a dialogue in the deepest and most genuine sense, an honest exchange between Ruth and me. We will be partners traveling on a journey, and neither of us knows where it will end. At times we will not even have a clear idea of where we are heading. She and I may both be changed by the encounter, and I expect that she will touch off powerful associations, feelings, memories, and reactions within me. My hope is to understand her world from a subjective viewpoint and, at the same time, to let her know my personal reactions to her in our relationship.

Initial Assessment of Ruth

Ruth appears to be a good candidate for existential therapy. She is courageous enough to question the meaning of life and to challenge some of her comfortable, but dull, patterns. She is facing a number of developmental crises, such as wondering what life is about now that her children are getting ready to leave home. As she begins to expand her vision of the choices open to her, her anxiety is increasing. The process of raising questions has led to more questions, yet her answers are few. She is grappling with what she wants for herself, apart from her long-standing definition of herself as wife and mother. A major theme is posed by the question "How well am I living life?" One of Ruth's strengths is her willingness to ask such anxiety-producing questions. Another of her assets is that she has already made some choices and taken some significant steps. She did diverge from her fundamentalist religion, which she no longer found personally meaningful; she is motivated to change her life; and she has sought out therapy as a way to help her find the paths she wants to travel.

Goals of Therapy

The purpose of existential therapy is not to "cure" people of disorders; rather, it is to help them become aware of what they are doing and to prod them out of the stance of a victim. It is aimed at helping people like Ruth get out of their rigid roles and see more clearly the ways in which they have been leading a narrow and restricted existence. The basic purpose of her therapy is to provide her with the insights necessary to discover, establish, and use the freedom that she possesses. In many ways she is blocking her own freedom. My function is to help her recognize her part in creating her life situation, including the distress she feels. I assume that as she sees the ways in which her existence is limited, she will take steps toward her liberation. My hope is that she can create a more responsible and meaningful existence.

Therapeutic Procedures

As an existential therapist I do not rely on a well-developed set of techniques. Instead, I focus on certain themes that I consider to be part of the human condition, and I emphasize my ability to be fully present with Ruth by challenging her and by reacting to her. My role is to help her clarify what it is that brought her to me, where she is right now, what it is she wants to change, and what she can do to make these changes happen. I will borrow techniques from several therapies as we explore her current thoughts, feelings, and behaviors within the current situations and events of her life. When we deal with her past, I will encourage her to relate her feelings and thoughts about past events to her present situation. To get some idea of the questions I might pursue with her, consider the following, any of which we might eventually explore in therapy sessions:

- "In what ways are you living as fully as you might? And how are you living a limited existence?"
- "To what degree are you living by your own choices, as opposed to living a life outlined by others?"

- "What choices have you made so far, and how have these choices affected you?"
- "What are some of the choices you are faced with now? How do you deal with the anxiety that is a part of making choices for yourself and accepting personal freedom?"
- "What are some of the changes that you most want to make, and what is preventing you from making them?"

In essence, Ruth is about to engage in a process of opening doors to herself. The experience may be frightening, exciting, joyful, depressing, or all of these at times. As she wedges open the closed doors, she will also begin to loosen the deterministic shackles that have kept her psychologically bound. Gradually, as she becomes aware of what she has been and who she is now, she will be better able to decide what kind of future she wants to carve out for herself. Through her therapy she can explore alternatives for making her visions become real.

The Therapeutic Process

At this point in her therapy Ruth is coming to grips more directly with her midlife crisis. She has been talking about values by which she lived in the past that now hold little meaning for her, about her feelings of emptiness, and about her fears of making "wrong" choices. Below are some excerpts from several of our sessions.

Elements of the process

Examining Ruth's marital problems.   One of the areas that I explore with Ruth is her relationship with John:

RUTH: At 39 I'm just now agonizing over who I am. Perhaps it's too late.
JERRY: Well, I don't know that there's a given time when we should ask such questions. I feel excited for you and respect you for asking these questions now.
RUTH: What I know is that my life has been very structured up to this point, and now all this questioning is unsettling to me and is making me anxious. I wonder if I want to give up my predictable life and face the unknown. Sometimes I feel more powerful, and there are moments when I believe I can change some things about my life. But I wonder if it's worth the risk!
JERRY: I'm touched by what you're saying, and I remember some of my own struggles in facing uncertainty. When you say you're anxious, it would help me to understand you better if you could tell me some of the times or situations in which you feel this anxiety.
RUTH: Sometimes I feel anxious when I think about my relationship with

John. I'm beginning to see many things I don't like, but I'm afraid to tell him about my dissatisfactions.

JERRY: Would you be willing to tell me some of the specific dissatisfactions you have with John?

Ruth then proceeds to talk about some of the difficulties she is experiencing with her husband. I also encourage her to share with me some of the impulses that frighten her. I am providing a safe atmosphere for her to express some new awarenesses without reacting judgmentally to her. I also give her some of my personal reactions to what she is telling me. Then I ask her if she talks very often with John in the way she is talking with me. I am receptive to her and wonder out loud whether he could also be open to her if she spoke this way with him. We end the session with my encouraging her to approach him and say some of the things to him that she has discussed in this session.

Helping Ruth find new values.   In a later session Ruth initiates her struggles with religion:

RUTH: I left my religion years ago, but I haven't found anything to replace it. I'm hoping you can help me find some new values. You have so much more experience, and you seem happy with who you are and what you believe in. On my own I'm afraid I might make the wrong decisions, and then I'd really be messed up.

JERRY: If I were to give you answers, that wouldn't be fair to you. It would be a way of saying that I don't see you as capable of finding your own way. Maybe a way for you to begin is to ask some questions. I know, for me, one way of getting answers is to raise questions.

RUTH: I know that the religion I was brought up in told me very clearly what was right and wrong. I was taught that once married, always married—and you make the best of the situation. Well, I'm not so willing to accept that now.

JERRY: How is that so?

RUTH: Sometimes I'm afraid that if I stay in therapy, I'll change so much that I'll have little in common with John, and I may eventually break up our marriage.

JERRY: You know, I'm aware that you've somehow decided that your changes will cause the breakup of your marriage. Could it be that your changes might have a positive effect on your relationship?

RUTH: You're right, I haven't thought about it in that way. And I guess I've made the assumption that John won't like my changes. I more often worry that what I'm doing in therapy will eventually make me want to leave him, or he might want to leave me. Sometimes I have an impulse to walk away from my marriage, but I get scared thinking about who I'd be without John in my life.

JERRY: Why not imagine that this did happen, and for a few minutes talk about who you would be if John weren't a part of your life. Just let out whatever thoughts or images come to your mind, and try not to worry about how they sound.

RUTH: All my life I've had others tell me who and what I should be, and John has picked up where my parents and church left off. I don't know what my life is about apart from being a wife and a mother. What would our kids think if John and I split up? How would it affect them? Would they hate me for what I'd done to the family? I know I'm tired of living the way I am, but I'm not sure what I want. And I'm scared to death of making any more changes for fear that it will lead to even more turmoil. John and the kids liked the "old me" just fine, and they seem upset by the things I've been saying lately.

JERRY: In all that you just said, you didn't allow yourself to really express how you might be different if they were not in your life. It's easier for you to tune in to how the people in your life might be affected by your changes than for you to allow yourself to imagine how you'd be different. It does seem difficult for you to fantasize being different. Why not give it another try? Keep the focus on how you want to be different, rather than the reactions your family would have to your changing.

Dealing with Ruth's anxiety. Ruth has trouble changing. There is immediate anxiety whenever she thinks of being different. She is beginning to see that she has choices, that she does not have to wait around until John gives her permission to change, and that others do not have to make her choices for her. Yet she is terrified by this realization, and for a long time it appears that she is immobilized in her therapy. She will not act on the choices available to her. So I go with her feelings of being stuck and explore her anxiety with her. Here is how she describes these feelings:

RUTH: I often wake up in the middle of the night with terrible feelings that the walls are closing in on me! I break out in cold sweats, I have trouble breathing, and I can feel my heart pounding. At times I worry that I'll die. I can't sleep, and I get up and pace around and feel horrible.

JERRY: Ruth, as unpleasant as these feelings are, I hope you learn to pay attention to these signals. They're warning you that all is not well in your life and that you're ready for change.

I know that Ruth sees anxiety as a negative thing, something she would like to get rid of once and for all. I see her anxiety as the possibility of a new starting point for her. Rather than simply getting rid of these symptoms, she can go deeply into their meaning. I see her anxiety as the result of her increased awareness of her freedom along with her growing sense of responsibility for deciding what kind of life she wants and then taking action to make these changes a reality.

Exploring the meaning of death. Eventually we get onto the topic of death and explore its meaning to Ruth:

RUTH: I've been thinking about what we talked about before—about what I want from life before I die. You know, for so many years I lived in dread of death because I thought I'd die a sinner and go to hell for eternity. I suppose that fear has kept me from looking at death. It has always seemed so morbid.

JERRY: Why don't you talk about areas of your life where you don't feel really alive. How often do you feel a sense of excitement about living?

RUTH: It would be easier for me to tell you of the times I feel half dead! I'm dead to having fun. Sexually I'm dead.

JERRY: Can you think of some other ways you might be dead?

I am trying to get Ruth to evaluate the quality of her life and to begin to experience her deadness. After some time she admits that she has allowed her spirit to die. Old values have died, and she has not acquired new ones. She is gaining some dim awareness that there is more to living than breathing. It is important that she allow herself to recognize her deadness and feel it as a precondition for her rebirth. I operate under the assumption that by really experiencing and expressing the ways in which she feels dead, she can begin to focus on how she wants to be alive, if at all. Only then is there hope that she can learn new ways to live.

Process commentary

Ruth's experience in therapy accentuates the basic assumption that there are no absolute answers outside of herself. She learns that therapy is a process of opening up doors bit by bit, giving her more potential for choices. This process happens largely because of the relationship between us. She becomes well aware that she cannot evade responsibility for choosing for herself. She learns that she is constantly creating herself by the choices she is making, as well as by the choices she is failing to make. As her therapist I support her attempts at experimenting with new behaviors in our sessions. Our open discussions, in which we talk about how we are experiencing each other, are a new behavior for her. These sessions provide a safe situation for her to extend new dimensions of her being. At the same time, I teach her how she might use what she is learning in her everyday life. She risks getting angry at me, being direct with me, and telling me how I affect her. We work on ways in which she might continue this behavior with selected people in her environment.

One of my aims is to show Ruth the connection between the choices she is making or failing to make and the anxiety she is experiencing. I do this by asking her to observe herself in various situations throughout the week. In what situations does she "turn the other cheek" when she feels discounted? When does she put her own needs last and choose to be the giver to others? In what specific instances does she fail to be assertive? Through this self-observation process she gradually sees some specific ways in which her choices are directly contributing to her anxiety.

My goal in working with Ruth is not to eliminate her anxiety; rather, it is to help her understand what it means. From my perspective, anxiety is a signal that all is not well, that a person is ready for some change in life. Ruth does learn that how she deals with her anxiety will have a lot to do with the type of new identity she creates. She sees that she can either take Valium to dissipate the anxiety or listen to the message that her anxiety is conveying.

Perhaps the critical aspect of Ruth's therapy is her recognition that she has a choice to make: She can continue to cling to the known and the familiar, even deciding to settle for what she has in life and quitting therapy. She can also accept the fact that in life there are no guarantees, that in spite of this uncertainty and the accompanying anxiety, she will still have to *act* by making choices and then living with the consequences. She chooses to commit herself to therapy.

Questions for Reflection

1. What are some critical choices that you have made? Can you think of any turning points in your life? How have some of your choices affected the life you now experience?

2. What does freedom mean to you? Do you believe that you are the author of your life? that you are now largely the result of your choices? How do you suppose that your personal view of freedom would influence the way you worked with Ruth?

3. Apply the themes explored with Ruth to your own life. Can you recall any periods in your life when you experienced anxiety over the necessity of making choices? To what degree has your freedom led you to assume responsibility for your choices? In what ways have you experienced anxiety over the realization of your freedom and responsibility? In what ways are your answers to these questions relevant to the way you would approach Ruth?

4. What life experiences have you had that could help you identify with Ruth? Have you shared any of her struggles? Have you faced similar issues? How have you dealt with these personal struggles and issues? How are your answers to these questions related to your potential effectiveness as her therapist?

5. What are your general reactions to the ways in which Polkinghorne and I have worked with Ruth? What aspects of both of these styles of counseling might you carry out in somewhat the same manner? What different themes might you focus on? What different techniques might you use?

6. Compare this approach to working with Ruth with the previous approaches, psychoanalytic therapy and Adlerian therapy. What major differences do you see?

7. How might you work with Ruth's fears associated with opening doors

in her life? Part of her wants to remain as she is, and the other part yearns for a fresh life. How would you work with this conflict?

8. Using this approach, how would you deal with her fears related to dying? Do you see any connection between her anxieties and her view of death?

9. What are your thoughts and feelings about death and dying as they apply to you and to those you love? To what extent do you think that you have explored your own anxieties pertaining to death and loss? How would your answer to this question largely determine your effectiveness in counseling a person such as Ruth?

10. What are some of the other existential themes mentioned in this chapter that have personal relevance to your life? How do you react to the question "Can therapists inspire their clients to deal with their existential concerns if they have not been willing to do this in their own lives?"

WALT: "WHAT IS THERE TO LIVE FOR?"

Some Background Data

The question of meaning in life is especially critical to Walt, a 74-year-old retiree who has lived with his son and daughter-in-law in Wisconsin for four years since his wife, Rose Ann, died. Walt lived in Honolulu from his birth until shortly after Rose Ann lost a long battle with cancer. The couple were married for 50 years. As a Pacific Islander he has experienced a great deal of loneliness and dislocation since he moved away from his home. Although he admits that the people in his new community near Green Bay are friendly, it has just not been the same for him. Not only has a huge gap been created in his life with the loss of Rose Ann, but he also must contend with feelings of being cut off from his roots in Hawaii.

During the last few months of Rose Ann's life a number of people in the community helped Walt care for her at home. He says that he is surprised by how much he was able to do for her when she was so sick. However, he does feel guilty for having let her down in some ways. Shortly before she died, she wanted to talk with him about her impending death. However, he felt that he could not handle the reality of her death, and he kept hoping that somehow she would be cured or would live several more years. Even though she has been dead for four years, Walt still suffers from guilt and regret over not having talked with her more. He feels that there were so many things left unsaid between the two of them, and now he ruminates over what he wishes he had done differently. He reports that he sleeps terribly, and when he is awake he simply cannot find enough things to keep him busy and to distract him from his endless rumination. He says that he misses all the friends they had for so many years in Honolulu and that he fears making new friends because "they'll all die anyway." He often wishes that he had died instead of Rose Ann, for she would have been better able to cope with his death than he has managed to do.

During this last four-year period he spent some time in a mental-health facility because of prolonged periods of depression, disorientation, and suicidal tendencies. As a part of his recovery he participates in a day-treatment program. As an outpatient he is involved in individual therapy a couple of times each week, and this therapy has continued for several months.

Walt has discussed a number of current life issues with me, including the following:

- He feels depressed most of the time and often wishes that he could die so that he would not have to feel such loneliness, emptiness, and hopelessness. He says that he does not have much to look forward to in his life; there is only a past that is filled with mistakes and regrets.
- Walt was very dependent emotionally on Rose Ann, and when she died of cancer, a big part of him died. He continues to feel lost and like a child in so many ways. He does not feel close to anyone, and he is convinced that his presence in his son's home is a burden to all.
- He has never made the adjustment from Hawaii to Wisconsin, saying that he feels out of his element. He loved the sense of community that he and his wife enjoyed for almost 50 years. Although he has tried to make a new home, he says that he just cannot forget everything and start a new life now.
- Before he was forced to retire, Walt taught in a high school. As a teacher he felt good, because he had some measure of worth. He enjoyed working with young people, especially encouraging them to think about the direction of their lives. He was a fantastic teacher, well-liked by his students. After Rose Ann died, he went into a long and deep depression; coupled with his age, this resulted in the beginning of his retirement years.
- For Walt retirement is next to death. He feels "put out to pasture," simply passing time without getting in people's way. His major problem is this lack of purpose in life. He is searching for something to take the place of his wife, his home, and his job, yet he sees little chance that he will find a substitute that will bring any meaning to his life. The losses are simply too great.

My Way of Working with Walt as an Existential Therapist

My goal in working with Walt is to provide adequate support for him at a very difficult time in his life. What I see him as needing is an opportunity to talk about his regrets and how it feels to be depressed; he needs to feel that he is being heard and cared for. At the same time, I must challenge him to begin to create his own meaning, even though most of his support systems are gone. To accomplish this goal, I encourage Walt to talk, recounting things about his past that he regrets and wishes had been different. I urge him to talk about the losses he feels with Rose Ann gone, with his island community far away, and with his teaching career over. Early in his therapy he needs to talk freely and to be listened to, and he needs to express his feelings of guilt, regret, sorrow, and separation.

Walt's weaknesses and strengths.   Where do I proceed with Walt? I do not ignore his depression, for this is a symptom that carries a message. By beginning with his full recognition and acceptance of his hopelessness, I may be able to help him change. I am especially interested in how he derived meaning through his work. I want to know the ways in which the school contributed to his feeling that he had something to offer people. So we talk of all the things that he got from teaching adolescents and what he learned about life from them. In many ways Walt, who did not have much of an adolescence, tried to make up for this gap in his youth through his work with young people. He found them floundering and lost, in search of who they were. He derived a great deal of personal meaning from seeing his students get excited about literature and in seeing them relate the struggles of the characters they were reading about to their own search for meaning in life.

Although Walt does need this opportunity to relive times from his past, I see a danger that we could stop here. In that case our sessions would be little more than "talks" and remembrances of days gone by. I want more for him. This desire may be part of my own need to see him move in other directions. I may be fearful of getting lost in his depression with him. And if he does not find new hope and a will to continue to live, I could be threatened in many ways. For one thing, it might jar me into seeing that I could someday be faced with the same search for hope. For another, if he does not move beyond his depression, I will look at myself as a therapist and wonder if I have given him enough. Would he find a meaning for living if I were more of a person to him or more skilled in helping him at this juncture in his life?

Our therapeutic relationship.   Let me proceed by saying more about how I see Walt and what is being generated within me as I work with him. Because the existential therapist assumes that therapy is an I/thou encounter and that what happens between the two people is central to determining outcomes, I will focus on this relationship. Questions that I will explore are: How do I see Walt at this time in his life? Where does he want to go? What does he want from me? How can I be instrumental in his life?

In some ways Walt is telling me that he is a *victim*—that his choices have mostly been taken from him, that there is little he can do to change the situation he finds himself in, and that he is for the most part doomed to live out a sterile future. He continually tells me that there is nothing that either of us can do to bring back his wife; he feels almost as hopeless when it comes to getting some kind of work; and he sees no way of being able to return to Hawaii to live out his remaining years. Although I think that it is necessary for me to perceive his world as he does, I find it hard to accept his conclusions. I want to provide a supportive atmosphere, so that he can communicate to me what it is like for him to be in his world; yet at the same time I want to challenge his passive stance toward life. Although he cannot change some of the events of his life, he can change how he continues to look at his life situation. I surely will not tell Walt all the things that I mention below in any single session. But over the course of our time together these are some of the points I will make:

- "You're not a helpless victim. If I see you as a victim and accept the stance you present, I won't be able to help you move beyond being stuck in this place. I want you to at least challenge the assumption that there is little you can do to change. It's this very assumption that's limiting your potential for change."
- "How could you find some of what you had in Hawaii here in Wisconsin? Is there a way that you could hold on to your values and also find new values to give your life meaning?"
- "I see you leading a restricted existence. You've narrowed down the boundaries in which you can take action. I'll try to help you expand these boundaries and act in a greater range of ways."
- "You live in the past much of the time. In telling me all of your failures and dwelling on all of the missed opportunities, you *contribute* to your depression. You wanted to talk about how your life might have been different. Now it may be time to look at what you can do to make *today* different, so that tomorrow you won't look back in regret over one more lost day. Although I accept that your choices are somewhat limited, you do have possibilities for action that you're not recognizing."
- "I hope you can accept your past, even though it wasn't what you wanted, yet not be bound by it. Instead of looking back, you could look ahead and begin walking, however slowly, toward where you want to go."
- "Think about your death. You've fantasized about suicide and thought that death would put an end to a miserable life. What are some of the things you want to complete? What are some of the projects you'd like to finish before you die? What do you want to be able to say at the time of your death about how you've lived? What can you do today to begin working on these projects that have some meaning to you?"

In terms of Walt's themes of not finding meaning in life and thinking about death, especially his suicidal fantasies, I think it is important to confront him with questions such as "What are you living for? What stops you from killing yourself?" I would not want to take lightly his mention of suicide. In light of the fact that he experiences a good deal of depression, it is critical to make an assessment of how likely he is to try to take his life. To make such an assessment, I want to find out how often he thinks about suicide and with what degree of detail. Is he preoccupied with suicidal impulses, or is such a fantasy rare? Does he have a detailed plan? Has he cut off social contacts? Has he made any prior attempts on his life? It is essential to carefully consider how seriously he is considering suicide before we take up other themes in his life. This may be his cry for help or a signal that in some way he wants me to offer him hope for a better existence. His prior hospitalization for his suicidal tendencies makes it even more imperative that we explore the degree of suicidal danger. I would arrange for a referral or hospitalization if he were acutely suicidal. Moreover, I'd let him know that I was legally obliged to take action if I determined that he was likely to take his life.

Let's briefly look at what I think Walt wants from me and some of the ways in which I can be instrumental as a person for him. As I indicated earlier, working with him challenges me to look at my own life. What would it be like to be in his place? How might I deal with life if I lost my wife and felt abandoned during my later years? What would become of me if I could not work? How might I handle feelings of meaninglessness in my life? I think that it can be useful for me to explore with Walt some of these questions in our sessions. I need to take the time to reflect on these questions, for the degree to which I can face and deal with them is the degree to which I will be a significant force in encouraging him to do the same thing in his life. How can I offer him any hope if I am not willing to struggle with my own potential for depression and hopelessness? If I avoid contemplating my eventual death and what I want to accomplish and experience before that time, how can I challenge him to look to his death for some lessons in learning how to live? One of the most powerful means of understanding him lies within me and my willingness to explore what is being touched off in me as a result of our relationship.

I think that what Walt wants from me is the potential for an interchange of ideas and feelings. He does not want mere reassurance, nor does he want me to cooperate with him in perpetuating his view that there is nothing left to live for and little he can do to change his situation. He needs my honest response, my support and caring, my gentle pushing, my insistence that he begin asking how he wants to be different, and my exchanges with him as another human being. I do not know where we will end up. I am not aiming for major personality reconstruction in his case, yet I am pushing for some significant steps that will lead to new action.

So much depends ultimately on Walt and what he is willing to choose and do for himself. I must not let myself be duped into thinking that I can create a will to live in him, that I can do his changing for him, or that I will have an answer for him. Where he ends up will largely be determined by *his* willingness to begin to move himself by taking the initial steps. The best I can offer to him is the inspiration to begin taking those steps. I hope that through our relationship he will see that he can move further than he previously allowed himself to imagine.

Follow-Up: You Continue as Walt's Therapist

In what directions would you, as an existential therapist, move with Walt?

1. What are some of your main reactions to my style of working with Walt? Do you have ideas on how to proceed differently or thoughts on issues that you would pursue further?
2. How do you see Walt? What are your reactions to him? Would you be willing to accept him as a client? Why or why not?
3. Walt brings out a number of key themes: his wife's death, his forced retirement, his having to leave his home in Hawaii and coming to live with his son's family, his feeling of alienation from the sense of community he once knew, and his personal struggles. Which of these themes (or other ones) would you be most likely to encourage him to explore with you? Why?
4. If you are of a different age, gender, and ethnicity from Walt, do you think you'd be able to enter into his subjective world? How would you respond to him if he were to say: "I don't see how you can really understand what I'm going through. You're much younger than I am, you haven't lost your wife or husband, you don't really know about the culture I grew up with, and you've never felt as crazy as I sometimes do. It's just that you're too different from me to know what I have to live with every day." To what extent would you have to be like Walt to identify with his world? If you felt he was right, what would you say or do?
5. In what ways do you think that you could be a positive force in Walt's life? What life experiences or personal characteristics of yours might be instrumental in establishing a *therapeutic* relationship with him? In what ways might your own needs, problems, values, and lack of life experiences actually get in the way of forming a relationship that would be of benefit to him?
6. In what ways does Walt's depression (and feeling of utter hopelessness) affect you personally? How would you be likely to respond to him as a result? Might you tend to give him answers? or cheer him up? or agree that his life is hopeless? or reassure him that he *can* find a new meaning in life?
7. I spent time in Walt's sessions allowing him to talk about his past mistakes, regrets, and losses as well as his memories of what gave his life meaning. For an older person such as Walt, what potential value do you see in reminiscing? Or do you think that you might steer him away

from such discussion about his past by encouraging him to talk about his life *now* or the future he hopes for?

8. The existential approach is based on the therapist's seeing the world through the perspective of the client. In Walt's view he is a victim with little chance of changing his destiny. He feels that he is doomed to a meaningless existence, and he has resigned himself to simply marking time. What are the implications if you accept and respond to him from his vantage point? How might you help him open up to other possibilities for a different future?

9. How might you respond to Walt's talking about his suicidal fantasies? What would you feel (and probably do) if he told you that he was going to kill himself because he saw no real hope for his future?

10. What would you see as your main function as Walt's therapist? Would you want mainly to support him? confront him? guide him into specific activities? teach him skills? be his friend?

RECOMMENDED SUPPLEMENTARY READINGS

Bugental, J. F. T. (1987). *The art of the psychotherapist.* New York: Norton. Here is an outstanding book that bridges the art and science of psychotherapy, making places for both. The author is an insightful and sensitive clinician who writes from an existential perspective about the journey undertaken by the psychotherapist and the client. The book contains a number of case studies, and the author illustrates the therapeutic process through dialogue between client and therapist.

Bugental, J. F. T. (1990). *Intimate journeys: Stories from life-changing therapy.* San Francisco: Jossey-Bass. The author's intention is to convey the subjective experience of his clients in describing his cases. Bugental has done a superb job of teaching important lessons about therapy by capturing lessons that his clients have taught him about their struggles in living.

Corey, G., & Corey, M. (1993). *I never knew I had a choice* (5th ed.). Pacific Grove, CA: Brooks/Cole. This book is written from an existential perspective and deals with existential themes. It contains many exercises and activities that both counselors and clients can use, especially as "homework assignments" between sessions. The topics covered include our struggle to achieve autonomy; the roles that work, love, sexuality, intimacy, and solitude play in our lives; the meaning of loneliness, death, and loss; and the ways in which we choose our values and philosophies of life. Each chapter is followed by numerous annotated suggestions for further reading.

Deurzen-Smith, E. van (1988). *Existential counselling in practice.* London: Sage Publications. This is an exceptionally useful and well-written book that develops a practical method of counseling based on the application of concepts of existential philosophy. The author clearly puts into perspective topics such as anxiety, authentic living, clarifying one's worldview, determining values, discovering meaning, and coming to terms with life. She draws upon her experience as an existential psychotherapist in describing numerous case illustrations to highlight the value of focusing on existential themes.

Frankl, V. (1975). *Man's search for meaning*. New York: Pocket Books. In describing his experiences in a concentration camp, Frankl shows how it is possible to find meaning in life through suffering. His thesis is that we all have a need to discover meaning.

Yalom, I. D. (1980). *Existential psychotherapy*. New York: Basic Books. Here is a superb treatment of the ultimate human concerns of death, freedom, isolation, and meaninglessness as these issues relate to therapy. This book has depth and clarity, and it is rich with clinical examples that illustrate existential themes. If you were to select just one book on existential therapy, this would be my recommendation as a comprehensive and interesting discussion of the topic.

CHAPTER FIVE

Case Approach to Person-Centered Therapy

A PERSON-CENTERED THERAPIST'S PERSPECTIVE ON RUTH, by David J. Cain, Ph.D., A.B.P.P.

Assessment of Ruth

The person-centered therapist views assessment and diagnosis as ongoing processes, not as formal procedures undertaken at the beginning of psychotherapy. The word *diagnose* is derived from a Greek word that means "to know" or "to discover." In my view, therapy is basically a process of intrapersonal and interpersonal learning. The therapist's primary function is to facilitate learning in the client. Thus, the client's discovery of personal knowledge about self is much more relevant than what the therapist knows about the client or how the client is identified with a psychiatric disorder.

As a person-centered therapist, I would not undertake any formal assessment with Ruth unless she requested it, nor would I attempt to establish a DSM-IV diagnosis for her. In over 20 years as a practicing psychotherapist, I have found the practice of formal diagnosis to be fraught with more liabilities than assets.

Although an extensive discussion of the pros and cons of diagnosis is beyond the scope of this book, I will mention what I believe to be some of the most significant limitations. First, I have not found that establishing a diagnosis helps much with treatment. Neither the DSM-IV nor the ICD-9 system of diagnosis provides treatment guidelines. With few exceptions (for example, exposure and cognitive restructuring for anxiety problems), the bulk of psychotherapeutic research has shown that all established approaches have roughly equivalent success with a wide variety of problems. Second, all diagnostic categories are inevitably reductionistic, in that they reduce clients and their experiences to a list of symptoms. The reality is that there is considerable variability among individuals with the same diagnosis. Third, the uniqueness of each person tends to be lost in the diagnostic process, because the emphasis is placed on common characteristics. The act of categorizing tends to constrict the therapist's conceptual understanding of the client and deemphasizes the importance of individual differences and the complexity of the person. Fourth, diagnosis overly emphasizes what is wrong with clients and gives relatively little attention to their resources. Fifth, a diagnosis is made primarily from an external point of view, that of the clinician, rather than from the internal frame of reference of the client. Clients generally have relatively limited participation in the determination of their diagnosis, even though they are the best authorities on their experience.

I find that dimensions of the person other than diagnostic symptoms are more important in understanding and responding therapeutically to my client. Among the most relevant dimensions are the client's self-concept and worldview; incongruencies between the self-concept and experience; the capacity to attend to and process experience, especially affect; learning style and ability to learn from experience; characteristic manner of living, or comportment; and implicit and explicit personal goals and strivings.

In my experience, a critical endeavor of the client is the definition and redefinition of the self. This process is facilitated by the therapist's and client's openness to the client's experience and its personal meaning. It is hindered by limited diagnostic formulations of the client's psychopathology. In the optimal case, diagnosis is a continuous process of self-learning in which the client remains receptive to all sources of experience and relevant information. In contrast, diagnostic categorization on the part of therapists may create a false sense of security about what they "know" about the client and limit their creativity and adaptivity in responding therapeutically. The danger here is that therapists may begin to interact with a static category rather than an evolving being, thus limiting their range of perceptions and variety of therapeutic responses and, consequently, the client's potential for change.

The essential purpose of assessment, as mentioned above, is to enable the client to develop relevant and meaningful personal knowledge, especially knowledge about the "self" and how the self-concept affects behavior. One of the major factors that makes therapy "person-centered" is the responsibility placed on the client for self-direction. Although I may play a significant role in helping Ruth explore herself, she is more likely to be affected by, and to put to use, personal experiences and learning that are self-discovered. The excitement and deep satisfaction that come from self-exploration and self-discovery are potent factors that engage the client in the therapeutic process.

In working with Ruth, I will be especially attentive to how she views her *self*, including both aspects of her that are evident and those that are implicit and unclear but forming. Several components of her self-concept emerge from her autobiography. In her own words, she identifies herself as the "good wife" and the "good mother" that "*he* [husband] expects me to be." Thus, she strongly identifies herself with the roles of wife and mother, but she has defined and attempted to fulfill these roles in the image her husband wishes. By allowing her husband to define what she is and should be (if she is to be accepted), she has abdicated her role and power in defining the person she is and in making personal choices about her life. She has allowed her husband to determine her conditions of worth, and she lives in fear that if she does not live up to his conditions, "he might leave me." Her tendency to mold herself for others is a pervasive aspect of her functioning. As she says, "I've pretty much lived for others so far. . . . I've been the superwoman who gives and gives."

Until she was 30, Ruth's identity and value system were strongly influenced by the fundamentalist religion of her parents, especially her father. She feared that she would be rejected by her parents if she did not live up to their expectations of who she should be. "They haven't formally disowned me," she says, "but in many ways I think they have. I know I'll never win their approval as long as I remain away from the religion that's so dear to them." Ruth is intent on pleasing others, even at the cost of sacrificing her own needs and identity. In a real sense she is self*less*, without a clear sense of who she is or can become. Some of the basic questions she is likely to address in therapy are "What do I want?" "What kind of person do I want to be?" and "How do I want to live?"

Other aspects of Ruth's self-concept are more peripheral. An important clue to her self-concept is the view she has of her body and its many symptoms. However she defines herself, it is always important to realize that the self is embodied, that it is contained in and functions through a body. Thus, an essential part of her sense of herself has to do with how she sees and feels about her body. At present she views her physical self as overweight and unattractive. In her words: "I don't like what I see. I don't like who I am, and I certainly don't feel proud of my body." Ruth experiences many disturbing bodily symptoms, which adversely affect her body image.

A potential aspect of her identity is that of a teacher, but she has not yet incorporated this role into her self-structure. Other aspects of Ruth surely remain undeveloped but may manifest themselves in the future.

A large part of Ruth's manner of being is dominated by fear, anxiety, panic, and a sense that many daily events and ongoing issues are overwhelming. She is afraid that she will die. These fears and anxieties seem to manifest themselves in various forms of bodily symptoms (namely, insomnia, heart palpitations, headaches, dizziness, and crying spells). Quite literally, much of her life is *sickening*—depressed, fearful, constricted, and avoidant.

Although Ruth feels some pride and satisfaction in being a caretaker, this role also results in ambivalence and dissatisfaction. She experiences considerable conflict over who she is, what she believes, and how she is living. By her own admission, she doesn't like who she is, her overweight body, and the fact that her life is devoid of any joyful or meaningful activity apart from her roles as wife and mother. She imagines that teaching will be fulfilling, but as yet she places her own desires behind those of her family. Her religious beliefs and values are changing and are in conflict with her earlier fundamentalist views.

Ruth's future is vague and tentative. She is dimly aware of the person she might become, yet she is fearful that pursuing her interests and needs and developing her own identity will result in her losing her husband and family. But she has not given up. In recent years she has become a "questioner" and holds on to the glimmer of hope that she can "begin to live before it's too late." There is a yearning in Ruth to be more than she is—to expand herself and her life possibilities. She is entering a transitional phase in her life with considerable trepidation.

Key Issues

A key issue with Ruth is the *incongruence* between the person she is and the selves that are "trying" to emerge, though hesitantly and cautiously. Her incongruence manifests itself in a variety of ways: as cognitive dissonance, in her many physical symptoms, and in anxiety and stress—all of which have the tendency to impel her toward the resolution of her discomfort. Her depression and physical symptoms tell her that something is wrong with her life; her main obstacle to becoming a more autonomous, fuller, and more gratified person is fear. Fear of the loss of her husband's and children's support and love render her hesitant to move from the safety of her current life, but her dissatisfaction with it and herself are drawing her forward.

The person-centered therapist assumes that the human organism has a natural tendency to manifest its potential. Carl Rogers described the *actualizing tendency* as people's inherent inclination to develop all of their capacities, to differentiate, to expand, and to become more autonomous. This tendency for people to move in directions that maintain and enhance themselves can be deterred, however, by motives that interfere with their ability to manifest their growth needs. At such times they may fail to differentiate between actions that are gratifying (such as being liked) and those that develop their potential (namely, standing up for their values).

Ruth feels somewhat secure in her present life, though it is boring and unfulfilling in terms of personal growth and meaning. Her capacity to move forward is limited by her lack of trust in her judgment ("I'm scared I'll make the wrong decisions") and resourcefulness ("I'm trapped and don't see a way out"). As a consequence, she is inclined to look to others (God, husband, her therapist) for guidance and direction.

Paradoxically, Ruth is as much afraid of living as she is of dying. The anticipation of change terrifies her, because it threatens the limited security and stability she experiences in her family and current lifestyle. Yet there are hopeful signs. Ruth is restless, dissatisfied, and afraid that her life is slipping by. She has a fragile desire for a better life and a tenuous vision of what she might become. She is "excited and afraid at the same time." If she can listen to the inner voices of her feelings and attend to the distress signals of her body, Ruth will begin to see more clearly who she is and what she wants and, in the process, will begin to find her own voice and path.

Therapeutic Process and Techniques

As I anticipate working with Ruth, my primary focus is on the quality of the relationship I hope to provide for her. My desire is to allow myself to be curious about her and receptive to anything she would like to share about herself and her life. To the best of my ability, I will be fully present and listen carefully to what she says while being sensitive to how she presents herself, including her nonverbal and implicit messages. As much as possible, I hope to leave any preconceptions and hypotheses I may have about her behind and to attend to her with fresh ears and eyes. I aim to create a trusting, supportive, safe, and encouraging atmosphere. If I am successful in creating the relationship I would like, Ruth will experience me as genuinely interested in her, sensitive to her feelings, and accurately understanding of her expressed and intended meanings. I hope to communicate my belief in her resourcefulness and my optimism about her capacity to learn what she needs to learn and move forward in her life. If I am successful in these endeavors, she will listen to herself, learn from her experiences, and effectively apply her learning.

Any specific techniques, methods, or responses I may use will be dictated by Ruth's therapeutic needs. Since I view her as a collaborator in the therapeutic process, I will at times ask her to "help me help you," trusting that she knows best how I can serve her at a given time. I may employ a variety of therapeutic techniques, and she will participate in choosing the approaches that she feels might be most helpful. Careful listening and accurate understanding of my client's overt and tacit meanings always precede the introduction of therapeutic techniques or exercises. My basic question in employing any technique is "Does it fit?"

One important aspect of my role is as a facilitator of learning. In my view, life is constantly teaching us important lessons about ourselves, about others, and about life in general. I view my role as helping my client "learn how to learn." My style of responding to Ruth will reflect my attempt to adapt to her personal learning style.

Finally, I will be myself in the relationship. Thus, Ruth will have a good sense of who I am as a person. Consequently, she will experience my sense of humor, my openness and directness, and my serious and playful sides. She will find that I can be provocative and challenging as well as quietly attentive and gentle as she undertakes her personal journey. She will also see the pleasure I feel in working with her and seeing her become the person she wishes to be.

I anticipate that Ruth will tend to be tentative at first in therapy, perhaps starting with her general sense of dissatisfaction with her life, herself, and her physical symptoms. She may find the nondirective nature of our interaction somewhat disturbing at first, preferring that I lead her in the "right" direction, advise her on what she "should" do, and "push" her to do it. However, I believe that she will gradually perceive that my reluctance to direct or advise her is based on my trust in her ability to determine her own directions and find a course of action that fits her. My message is "This is your life, and you are the author of its future." I am confident that Ruth will discover that she has more personal strengths and resources than she is aware of at present.

The beginning phase of therapy goes as follows:

THERAPIST: I'm interested in hearing anything you would like to share about yourself—anything that's troubling you—whatever is on your mind.

RUTH: Right now the thing that's bothering me the most is my weight. Whenever I get anxious or depressed, I tend to overeat. Lately I've gained about ten pounds. I feel fat, and I hate the way I look.

THERAPIST: You're unhappy with yourself for your eating and your appearance.

RUTH: So is my husband. He likes me better when I'm thinner. I've been trying to diet, but I just can't seem to stick with it.

THERAPIST: You're not pleasing your husband or yourself. And I guess you're getting discouraged about whether you're able to lose weight.

RUTH: It's not just losing weight. It's accomplishing anything I set out to do. I just can't seem to follow through. Usually I get off to a good start, but as soon as something goes wrong, I get discouraged and put things off. Maybe I need to join one of those weight-loss groups, where they weigh you in every week. I'd be too embarrassed not to lose weight if the leader and everyone else saw me weigh in. I guess I need someone to push me.

THERAPIST: You don't trust yourself to stick to something you want to accomplish. And when you have a setback, you get discouraged and say to yourself, "I need someone else to get me to stick to my goals." You haven't learned to depend on yourself.

What quickly emerges is Ruth's tendency to evaluate herself based on whether she is pleasing to others and her belief that she needs others to help her control her behavior. She does not yet view herself as self-sufficient or acceptable just as she is. My comment to her that she hasn't learned to depend on herself is an example of what might be called inferential empathy, because it goes a bit beyond what she has said. As I hope is clear, person-centered therapy is not simply saying back to the client what he or she has just said.

RUTH: I guess I do tend to rely on others to tell me what I should do or how I should do something. I've always depended on my parents or John for guidance. I did break away from my church several years ago, but I don't think my parents will ever understand that or accept my beliefs about religion. John couldn't understand why I wanted to finish college and be a teacher. He thinks I should be happy being a homemaker and a mother.

THERAPIST: When you take a course of action based on what you believe and want to do, you don't feel that John or your parents even think you're capable of making a good decision. It sounds as if you're afraid you won't be approved of unless you do what others believe is best for you.

RUTH: I'm such a wimp. Sometimes I think I'll never be able to do what I believe in without worrying about what someone else thinks.

THERAPIST: You feel like a wimp when you let others' opinions of you become more important than your own. But you did change your religious convictions, and you did finish college. You can take a stand.

RUTH: Well, I do feel good about those things. It took me forever to finish college, but I did. And I think I did a pretty good job in my student teaching. Maybe I don't always give myself enough credit.

Ruth's dissatisfaction with her need for approval is becoming evident. When I acknowledge and affirm her self-initiated religious changes and completion of college, she begins to see herself more positively apart from the views of others and to recognize that *she* can give herself the credit she deserves for her accomplishments.

As therapy progresses, Ruth becomes increasingly aware of the incongruence she experiences between the person she is and the person she yearns to be. She feels guilty about what she perceives as selfishness when she attends more to her own needs and is fearful that her marriage and family will be disrupted. As she expands and modifies her perceptual field, however, she comes to believe that her desires and goals are as deserving of attention as those of her family.

Ruth may, at some point, wish to bring her husband into her therapy sessions in order to address the conflict she feels over taking a course of action that displeases him or her children. Whether John is supportive of her change or not, she will have to wrestle with her own conflict about doing what she wants and becoming a more separate, independent person. Her marriage will probably go through a dramatic transition if she pursues her hopes. It may improve as she becomes a fuller person or become more conflicted if her husband is threatened by her development.

The middle phase of therapy has the following dialogue:

RUTH: John and I had another fight last night. He wants me to spend more time with him and the kids and less time with my friends and at the new church I've been attending. I feel a little guilty about being away from home more, but I really like some of the new people I've met.

THERAPIST: You feel torn between allegiances to your family and yourself.

RUTH: Yes. I love my kids, and John and I like taking care of them. But there's more that I want to do. And besides, the kids are old enough now to take care of themselves more. In fact, Rob just moved out last week, and Jennifer has started in a community college. Susan and Adam are involved in lots of activities at the high school. And John is involved in his bowling two nights a week. So it's not as if they need me around all the time.

THERAPIST: As you see that they have lives of their own, it seems that your family needs you less than they did. Or maybe you need them less as you have begun to do more things that are important to you.

RUTH: I think it's a little of both. I got a lot of satisfaction from making sure they were happy—you know, being a good mother and wife. But I realize that sometimes I got too involved and didn't let them do more for themselves because I wanted them to need me. Now I kind of like taking more time for myself. The kids are basically OK. Even Jennifer has begun to settle down. She just had to realize that when I said no I meant no, not maybe. She doesn't always like some of my rules, but she's more accepting of limits.

THERAPIST: It sounds as if you've become clearer about the kind of mother you want to be and also clearer about the kind of relationship you want with your kids. And you're less worried about how they'll ever survive without you.

RUTH [laughs]: Yeah, I must have thought I was supposed to be Mother Teresa or something. Actually, the kids aren't the problem. John is. He's having a hard time accepting the ways I've changed. He's used to having me spend more time with him and doing little things for him that I don't have as much time to do now. Sometimes he complains that I'm not as interested in him as I used to be, or he just sulks. I think I've spoiled him, and he's having a hard time adjusting.

THERAPIST: Having a life of your own is risky to you and threatening to John, it seems.

Ruth is beginning to become more separate from her family, though she remains involved with them and concerned about their well-being. She is more accepting and tolerant of the reality that taking care of her needs and desires may, at times, displease other family members. She is also learning to allow her husband and her kids to take care of themselves more.

RUTH: I feel bad about taking more time for myself and worried that John will leave me. But he has things to do on his own. And we still spend a lot of time together. It's just that he doesn't think I need him as much as I used to, and I think he feels insecure about it.

THERAPIST: Maybe you don't need him as much as you used to?

RUTH: Hmm. Well, I'm not sure. I think maybe I needed him to need me more than I do now. And now he seems to want me to need him the way I used to. I think he doesn't feel as important to me as he did. He *is* important. But for different reasons. Now, I want us to be friends and more like equal partners. Before, he was more like my father—more controlling and demanding. It was as if he didn't think I could do anything without having him to guide me. And I guess I did let him take charge more then. In my mind he was more the head of the house. Now I'm a little more confident and . . . well, I guess I don't *need* him the way a little girl needs her parents. It's more as if I want his advice when I ask. What I really want is his *support*.

THERAPIST: You've changed and grown quite a bit. Earlier in your marriage you wanted and allowed John to take charge more. You felt then that you needed his guidance because you weren't able to make decisions for yourself. Now, as your confidence has grown, you want someone who will support you in your choices. Instead of a father, you want an equal partner.

RUTH: Yes! That's what I want. I want John to see that I'm different from him and to appreciate me for the person I am. When I want his input on something, I want him to understand that I may or may not do what he suggests. I think he still thinks that when I ask his opinion, it means I'll do things his way. No wonder he gets frustrated or hurt sometimes. I think I need to make it clear that his ideas do matter to me but that if I don't follow his suggestion, it doesn't mean that I don't value him. I just want to do things my own way sometimes.

Ruth is growing stronger and more independent and becoming clearer about the kind of relationship she wants with her husband. If therapy is successful, she will come to see herself in a more positive and differentiated way. She will feel more power and control in her life and will probably become more assertive. More of her satisfaction will be derived from her work and interests apart from, but not excluding, her roles of mother and wife. As she learns to listen to the messages of her feelings and her body, she will identify her needs more clearly and draw on her resources more effectively to satisfy them. Her depression, anxiety, and physical symptoms should diminish as she learns to identify and address effectively the sources of her conflicts. Gradually, she will learn that there is someone in her life on whom she can always depend—herself.

The final phase of therapy goes as follows:

RUTH: Things have settled down a lot with John. Although it's been a difficult adjustment for him, he seems to accept me more the way I am now.

THERAPIST: And how are you now?

RUTH: I think the main thing is that I feel a lot more independent. I still want my family and friends to like me and approve of what I do, but it's OK if they don't. The main thing is that I feel good about me, at least most of the time.

THERAPIST: You sure look better—more confident and settled.

RUTH: I am. And I feel pretty good most of the time. Once in a while I'll get a panicky feeling, but I've learned to pay attention to it and try to understand what the problem is. Last week I was real anxious about my younger daughter, Susan. When I tried to understand my fear, I realized that I didn't like the guy she's going out with. So I told her how I felt and why. Well, she insisted on seeing him, and I didn't know what to do. I talked it over with John, and we decided to let her continue to see this guy as long as we knew where she was and she made curfew. I think the main thing that helped me was realizing that she has pretty good judgment.

THERAPIST: It sounds as if you've learned to trust your feelings and your judgment and to tolerate your anxiety about Susan because you trust her judgment. Maybe you haven't done such a bad job as a parent. You and John also seem to be working together more as parents—more as partners.

RUTH: Believe me, it hasn't been easy. It's still hard to sleep until I hear that door open when she comes home, but nothing awful has happened so far. As for John and me, most of the time we work out our differences. We still fight occasionally, but I don't worry anymore that he'll leave me. Even when I get stubborn about something he disagrees with, he tries to see my point of view.

THERAPIST: You've found that you can tolerate your anxieties much better than you thought you could. It seems, too, that you and John can deal with your differences without their becoming fatal.

RUTH: You know, I actually think he likes me better the way I am now. I may be harder to live with in some ways, but I'm not so dependent and scared. I'm more fun now, and John likes that. I like me a lot better too.

THERAPIST: There's a lot to like in you.

Ruth now views others' acceptance and liking as desirable though not necessary to her well-being. More importantly, she has learned to like herself and feel at peace with who she is. She is more confident about herself as a wife and mother and is more able to tolerate the inevitable anxieties of parenting.

Process commentary

The process of person-centered therapy can be conceived of as a rebirth of the self, with the therapist serving as midwife. Many clients who seek therapy, like Ruth, are conflicted about who they are and how they are living. Their sense of self lacks clarity and is often viewed in terms of important roles (namely, daughter, mother, wife, student) that are largely defined by their culture and significant others. To the degree that we buy into these roles, we tend to move away from and lose a sense of our natural inclinations and tendency to actualize our potential in a manner consistent with our true selves. In an attempt to find acceptance and approval and avoid conflict with others, especially with those most important to us, we try to bend and shape ourselves in a manner that often leaves us feeling incongruent, dissatisfied, conflicted, and at odds with ourselves and with others.

Person-centered therapy, as is evident in Ruth's case, provides the client with an opportunity to experience one's self and life in a clearer, more differentiated, and personal manner. This process is assisted enormously by the therapist's ability to capture the essence of the client's experience, especially the person's current view of self, worldview, and explicit and implicit needs, goals, and strivings. The therapist helps the client recognize that his or her experiences are the basis for critical learning and the creation of personal knowledge, meaning, and choice about how one might live and who one might become. One of the critical processes of therapy is enabling clients to develop confidence in their perceptions, judgments, and sense of knowing. Because both affective and rational ways of knowing have strengths and limitations, a goal of person-centered therapy, as I conceive it, is to enable clients to draw effectively from both ways of knowing. When their knowledge of feelings is congruent with their rational knowledge, they will usually experience a sense of clarity, peace, and confidence in their learning. They will often respond to such moments with comments like "Yes, that's it" or "I've got it." The cognitive and affective realms have been integrated, and they feel freer to act on their learning.

As Ruth became clearer about what she wanted in her life—as mother, wife, and individual—and began to recreate her *self*, she also realized that this choice required that she stand up for herself and sometimes take a position that not all others would like, support, or approve of. My genuine acceptance and affirmation helped her free herself from her beliefs and feelings about how she "should" live. I believe that she learned to face life's most basic challenge: to be oneself and find a way to live with others that allows one to maintain self-respect and integrity while accepting the reality that being oneself will sometimes bring one into conflict with others.

JERRY COREY'S WORK WITH RUTH FROM A PERSON-CENTERED PERSPECTIVE

Basic Assumptions

From a person-centered perspective I view counseling as being directed at more than merely solving problems and giving information. It is primarily aimed at helping clients tap their inner resources, so that they can better deal with their problems, both current and future. In Ruth's case I think that I can best accomplish this goal by creating a climate that is threat-free, one in which she will feel fully accepted by me. I work on the assumption that my clients have the capacity to lead the way in our sessions and that they can profit without my active and directive intervention. I assume that three attributes on my part are necessary and sufficient to release her growth force:

1. *Genuineness.* I am real, without a false front, during the therapy sessions. In other words, I am congruent: My outer expression matches my internal experience.
2. *Unconditional positive regard and acceptance.* My caring for Ruth is not contaminated by evaluation or judgment of her thoughts, feelings, and behaviors.
3. *Accurate empathic understanding.* I can sensitively and accurately comprehend her present experiencing and can convey this understanding to her.

If I genuinely experience these attitudes toward Ruth and successfully communicate them to her, she will decrease her defensive ways and move toward becoming her true self, the person whom she is capable of becoming. Therapy is not so much a matter of my doing something to her; rather, it is establishing a relationship that she can use to engage in self-exploration and ultimately find her own way.

Assessment of Ruth

In talking to Ruth, I can see that she is disappointed with where she is in life and that she is not being herself around her friends or family. Her therapy is based on this concern.

As I review Ruth's autobiography, I see her as asking "How can I discover my real self? How can I become the person I would like to become? How can I shed my phony roles and become myself?" My aim is to create an atmosphere in which she can freely, without judgment and evaluation, express whatever she is feeling. If she can experience this freedom to be whatever she is in this moment, she will begin to drop the masks and roles that she now lives by. In order for her to discover her sense of self, she needs a place where she can look nondefensively at the way she is now.

Goals of Therapy

My basic goal is to create a therapeutic climate that will help Ruth discover the kind of person she is, apart from being what others have expected her to be. When her facades come down as a result of the therapeutic process, four of her characteristics should be enhanced: (1) her openness to experience, (2) a greater degree of trust in herself, (3) her internal source of evaluation, and (4) her willingness to live more spontaneously. These characteristics constitute the basic goals of person-centered therapy.

Therapeutic Procedures

When clients begin therapy, they tend to look to me to provide direction and magical answers. They often have rigid beliefs and attitudes, an internal blockage, a sense of being out of touch with their feelings, a basic sense of distrust in themselves, and a tendency to externalize problems. As therapy progresses, I find, they are generally able to express fears, anxiety, guilt, shame, anger, and other feelings that they have deemed too negative to incorporate into their self-structure. Eventually, they are able to distort less, express more feelings that were previously out of awareness, and move in a direction of being more open to all of their experience. They can be in contact, moment by moment, with what they are feeling, with less need to distort or deny this experience.

The Therapeutic Process

Elements of the process

During the early stages of her therapy Ruth does not share her feelings but talks instead about externals. To a large degree she perceives her problems as outside of herself. Somehow, if her father would change, if her husband's attitude would change, and if her children would present fewer problems, she would be all right. During one of our early sessions she wonders whether I will be able to really understand her and help her if she does share her feelings.

Exploring our relationship.   Ruth lets me know how difficult it is for her to talk personally to me, and she tells me that it's especially uncomfortable for her to talk with me because I'm a man. I feel encouraged because she is willing to talk to me about her reservations and brings some of her feelings toward me out in the open.

RUTH: I've become aware that I'm careful about what I say around you. It's important that I feel understood, and sometimes I wonder if you can really understand the struggles I'm having as a woman.

JERRY: Well, I like it that you're willing to let me know what it's like for you to attempt to trust me. I would hope that you don't censor what you say around me, and I very much want to understand you. Perhaps you could tell me more about your doubts about my ability to understand you as a woman.

RUTH: It's not what you've said so far, but I'm fearful that I have to be careful around you. I'm not sure how you might judge me or react to me.

JERRY: I'd like the chance to relate to you as a person, so I hope you'll let me know when you feel judged or not understood by me.

RUTH: It's not easy for me to talk about myself to any man; all of this is so new to me.

JERRY: What is it that you think I'd have a hard time understanding about you as a woman? And you might want to talk more about what makes it difficult to talk to me.

RUTH: So far, no man has ever been willing to *really* listen to me. I've tried so hard to please my father and then to please John. I suppose I wonder if you can understand how I depended so much on my father, and now on John, to give me a feeling that I'm worthwhile as a woman.

JERRY: Even though I'm not a woman, I still know what it feels like to want to be understood and accepted, and I know what it's like to look to others to get this kind of confirmation.

It is important that we pursue what might get in the way of Ruth's trust in me. As long as she is willing to talk about what she is thinking and feeling while we are together in the sessions, there is a direction that we can follow. Staying with the immediacy of the relationship will inevitably open up other channels of fruitful exploration.

Getting in touch with Ruth's feelings.   In a later session Ruth talks about how hard it is for her to really experience her feelings. She is not very aware of the nature of her feelings, for she blocks off any that she deems inappropriate. She does not permit herself to freely accept the flow of whatever she might be feeling. Notice how she puts it:

RUTH: It's hard for me to feel. Sometimes I'm not sure what it is that I feel.

JERRY: From moment to moment you're not aware of what feelings are flowing inside of you.

RUTH: Yeah, it's difficult enough for me to know what I'm feeling, let alone express it to someone else.

JERRY: So it's also hard for you to let others know how they affect you.

RUTH: Well, I've had lots of practice in sealing off feelings. They're scary.

JERRY: It's scary not knowing what you're feeling, and it's also scary if you know.

RUTH: Sort of . . . When I was a child, I was punished when I was angry. When I cried, I was sent to my room and told to stop crying. Sometimes I remember being happy and playful, only to be told to settle down.

JERRY: So you learned early that your feelings got you in trouble.

RUTH: Just about the time I start to feel something, I go blank or get confused. It's just that I've always thought that I had no right to feel angry, sexual, joyful, sad—or whatever. I just did my work and went on without complaining.

JERRY: You still believe it's better to keep what you feel inside and not express feelings.

RUTH: Right! And I do that especially with my husband and my children.

JERRY: It sounds as if you don't let them know what's going on with you.

RUTH: Well, I'm not so sure they're really that interested in my feelings.

JERRY: It's as if they really don't care about how you feel. [At that point Ruth begins to cry.] Right now you're feeling something. [Ruth continues crying, and there is a period of silence.]

RUTH: I'm feeling sad and hopeless.

JERRY: Yet now you're able to feel, and you can tell me about it.

In this interchange it is important for Ruth to recognize that she can feel and that she is able to express feelings to others. My acceptance of her encourages her to come in contact with her emotions. This is a first step for her. The more difficult task is for her to begin to recognize and share her emotions with the significant people in her life.

Exploring Ruth's marital problems.   In another session Ruth brings up her marital difficulties. She explores her mistrust of her own decisions and her search outside of herself for the answers to her problems:

RUTH: I wonder what I should do about my marriage. I'd like to have some time to myself, but what might happen to our family if I made major changes and nobody liked those changes?

JERRY: You wonder what would happen if you expressed your true feelings, especially if your family didn't appreciate your changes.

RUTH: Yes, I guess I do stop myself because I don't want to hurt my family.

JERRY: If you ask for what you want, others are liable to get hurt, and there's no room in your life to think both about what's good for others and what's good for yourself.

RUTH: Yes, I didn't realize I was saying that it has to be either me or them. I do wonder if they'll be angry if I start doing some things for me.

Process commentary

We proceed with how Ruth's fear of others' anger keeps her from asking for what she really wants in her life. She then begins to seek answers from me. Not trusting that she knows what is best for herself, she thinks I have the experience and wisdom to provide her with at least some answers. She continues to press for answers to what she should do about her marriage. It is as though she is treating me as an authority who has the power to fix things in her life. She grows very impatient with my unwillingness to give her answers. As she puts it, she is convinced that she needs my "validation and approval" if she is to move ahead.

We return to an exploration of Ruth's feelings toward me for not giving her more confirmation and not providing reassurance that she will make correct decisions. She tells me that if I really cared about her, I would give her more direction and do more for her than I am doing. She tells me that all I ever do is listen, that she wants and expects more, and that I am not doing my job properly. I let her know that I do not like her telling me what I am feeling about her. I also tell her that I do care about her struggle but that I refuse to give her answers because of my conviction that she will be able to find answers within herself. I hope she will learn that I can be annoyed with her at times yet not reject her.

Ruth continues to risk sharing more of her feelings with me, and with my encouragement she also begins to be more open with her family. Gradually, she becomes more willing to think about her own approval. She demands less of herself by way of being a fixed product, such as the "perfect person," and allows herself to open up to new experiences, including challenging some of her beliefs and perceptions. Slowly she is showing signs of accepting that the answers to her life situation are not to be found in some outside authority but inside of herself.

Although it is not easy for me to refuse to provide answers and direction for Ruth, I believe that to do so would imply a lack of faith in her capacity to find her own way. Therefore, I do not rely on techniques, nor do I fall into the trap of being the guru. We focus on Ruth's feelings about not trusting herself, and she explores in depth the ways in which she is discounting her ability to take a stand in many situations. At times I become angry with her when I feel set up by her. I think it is important for her to learn that I can express my anger toward her and at the same time not feel disapproving of her. She learns that she can evoke feelings in others and that she can express her own feelings.

I do value support, acceptance, and personal warmth; yet at the same time I try to challenge Ruth to look at what she is saying and doing. If I am to be an influence in her life, I have to be more than a mirror that simply reflects back what she is projecting. Thus, I attempt to give of myself in our sessions. By relating to Ruth personally, I allow her to feel an increased freedom to express whatever she is thinking and feeling. This encourages her to explore the ways in which she feels judged by her parents, the feelings that she has denied or distorted, and her lack of confidence in being able to find her own answers. She can actually use our relationship as the basis for her growth. As she grows, she can learn to be more accepting of herself, with both strengths and limitations.

Questions for Reflection

1. To what degree have you been willing to struggle with finding your own answers to life? Are there ways in which you have avoided this responsibility by looking to others to provide you with answers? How would your personal experiences with searching within yourself for answers affect how you worked with Ruth?
2. Knowing what you do of Ruth, how would it be for you to develop a therapeutic relationship with her? Is there anything that might get in your way? If so, how do you think you would deal with this obstacle? To what degree do you think you could understand her subjective world?

3. In his assessment of Ruth, Cain indicates that he would not undertake any formal assessment or attempt to establish a DSM-IV diagnosis for her unless she requested it. Instead, he places emphasis on her self-assessment and her own definition of her problems. What are your thoughts about excluding formal assessment strategies before engaging in a therapeutic relationship? Do you see Ruth as able to make a valid self-assessment?

4. Cain says, "If she can listen to the inner voices of her feelings and attend to the distress signals of her body, Ruth will begin to see more clearly who she is and what she wants and, in the process, will begin to find her own voice and path." To what degree do you agree with this assumption? How does your answer influence the way you would work with Ruth?

5. In the therapeutic relationship with Ruth, Cain's interventions were based mainly on listening and accurately responding to what she says. He did not make directive interventions but attempted to stay with her subjective experiencing. What kind of progress do you see her making with this approach?

6. Ruth confronted me with her doubts about my ability to understand her as a woman. Do you think that she would do better to see a female therapist? Would you recommend that I suggest a referral to a woman, especially since she brought up her concerns about my being a man? Do you think that a male therapist would have a difficult time understanding her world and her struggles as a woman?

7. Ruth mentioned that it was especially difficult to trust a man and that she felt judged by men. How could you work with this theme therapeutically from a person-centered perspective?

8. What are some of your general reactions to the way that I approached and worked with Ruth? What do you particularly like? What do you like least? What aspects of her therapy would you have duplicated? What would you have done differently? Staying within this model, show how you would continue to work with Ruth and what general direction you would expect your sessions to take.

9. With both this approach and the previous one (existential therapy) the client/therapist relationship is central, and the focus is on clients' choosing their way in life. Do you agree that Ruth has this potential for directing her life and making wise choices? Would you be inclined to let her select the topics for exploration, or might you suggest topics? Would you be more directive than either Cain or I was?

10. Cain's message to Ruth is "This is your life, and you are the author of its future." This particular approach assumes that if the therapist is genuine, accepts the client fully and unconditionally, and respects, cares for, and deeply understands the client, constructive change will occur. To what degree do you agree with this assumption that a client such as Ruth is the author of her future?

DON: FEELING PRESSURE TO PROVE HIMSELF

Some Background Data

Don, a major in the U.S. Air Force, comes to see me on the basis of a referral from a military doctor. He is of Latino background, is married, and has two daughters and two sons. As a member of a minority group, he feels under tremendous pressure to prove himself as an exceptional leader. He has encountered many obstacles in his attempt to rise through the military ranks. He is doing everything possible to get a promotion to lieutenant colonel, and ultimately he would like to be at least a "bird" colonel.

Don consulted with his physician because of continuing chest pains. Even though he is only in his mid-30s, he has had two mild heart attacks. These resulted in his being hospitalized and having to take a leave of absence. He is about ten pounds overweight, has high blood pressure, has a high cholesterol level, smokes cigarettes, suffers at times from angina, and develops severe headaches that are chronic under stressful situations. His physician insisted that if he wanted to live, he would have to learn to relax and deal with stress more constructively. Because his doctor was convinced that Don needed psychological as well as medical treatment, he was referred to me.

Our First Session

At our first meeting Don fills me in on his medical problems. He also talks of his feelings about being sent to see a psychologist and of how he hopes to benefit from our contact. He lets me know how unusual it is for him to ask for help with his personal life. He cannot remember a time that he felt a need to talk about personal matters. As he puts it, "If there is a job to be done, you get to it and do it." It appears that the more challenging the task, the more merit he sees in its accomplishment. But meeting continual challenges is certainly taking a toll on Don. It could literally kill him.

To give a flavor of his view of himself, as well as the manner in which I might work with him from the person-centered perspective, I present the following dialogue. I emphasize that this is my own style of working with this approach; I do not want to give the impression that it is necessarily characteristic of all those who identify themselves as person-centered counselors.

DON: Well, Doctor, it's really hard for me to admit that I have to ask for outside help. I mean, no offense or anything, but I don't need a shrink.

JERRY: I'd like to hear how it feels for you to be here now. Could you tell me in what ways seeing me is hard for you?

DON: Sure. I thought I'd never die, until I had my first heart attack, and then I realized that I might kick over long before my time. It's hard enough for me to admit that my body can't take it. Now to be told that I have mental problems that I also have to learn to deal with—that's too much.

JERRY: It seems easier to do something about your physical problems than to do something about your feelings.

DON: The physician I've been seeing says there's not much more he can do for me, besides giving me the medication. I know my job has stress. I'm under constant pressure from the upper brass to produce and keep my outfit in order. I'm responsible for a lot of other men in my unit, and that's what's hard to handle. I can handle my own responsibilities, but being expected to make sure that the other men under me follow through almost does me in. I worry constantly about whether they'll pull their end.

JERRY: As you talk, I hear how unsupported you feel, as well as how difficult it is for you to carry the weight for the rest of your men. You have all this burden on your shoulders.

DON: It's part of my job. I'm the top man in my unit, and I've gotta make sure that nobody under me messes up, because our unit is a vital unit in a chain. If we're a weak link, the rest of the chain will be useless. And it's my job to make sure that we're effective at all times and that there aren't any slipups! If I don't keep a close watch on the entire operation, everything is liable to go to pot. I can't live with myself knowing that I haven't done all that was expected of me—and then some. If I want to get that promotion I've been angling for, I can't afford any mistakes. It's so important that I get my promotion. I really want the recognition that comes with being at the top.

JERRY: As I look at you, I see the weariness in your face. You look *very* tired and extremely tense. Sitting with you here I can feel your tension. It seems that you don't see any way out of assuming all this responsibility.

DON: Not really. That's why I'm coming to see you. I hope you can teach me some relaxation methods and some better ways of living with this stress that's a part of my job.

JERRY: Maybe you can tell me more about what this stress is like for you. Is it mainly at work or in other areas of your life?

DON: I carry my work home with me. I have so much to do that I have to bring hours of paperwork home every night. In the military filling out papers is what counts. I can't get behind in the paperwork whatever I do. Besides, even when I'm at home, I always get calls from my subordinates asking me my opinion on this or that matter that needs immediate attention.

JERRY: So you're on constant call. I feel the sense of how overwhelming all this is to you. No matter how hard you try to keep up, there are always other decisions to be made, more papers waiting for you to complete, and more responsibility than you can handle. There's no place you can go to escape those who depend on you.

DON: You hit on a good point. I do feel exhausted and very tight. That's just the way I am—and that's the way it has always been. But I don't know how to change that. I look at the other officers who have positions of command, and they seem to be able to deal with the stress far better than I do. It doesn't get to them. Most of the guys are much older, and they don't have heart problems.

JERRY: You say that it has always been that way. Has it been this way even before you entered the military?

DON: For sure. I came from a large family. I was the oldest son. We all had to work hard, and my father expected a lot from all of us kids. He was tough on me and never gave me any recognition. But I kept on trying to do what he expected so that he'd be proud of me.

JERRY: It's difficult to work so hard and then still not get the recognition you want.

DON [a long pause and then a sigh]: I just keep asking myself what's wrong with me that I can't take this stress more in stride. I *should* be able to get the job done without my body giving out on me. This is a hard one for me to take!

JERRY: It's hard for you to accept that your body has its limits and that you can push yourself only so far.

DON: Yeah. Why can't I be like the rest of the guys and handle things? Not only do I have trouble handling stress on the job, but I have a heck of a time dealing with stress at home.

JERRY: It's just the same at home?

DON: Yeah. I feel that I've got to be the one in charge there, too. I've got to plan for laying aside money to send my kids through college. I've got to be the one who keeps peace in the family. It's really important that I don't break down. I've *got* to be strong, and there's no room for weakness. If I'm not strong, everything in my life will fall apart. I've got to make sure that Millie, my wife, feels important and special. I've got to be the counselor for my kids and give them answers when they come to me with problems. I've got to ride herd on my teenage boys to do their chores properly, and I've got to keep nagging at my daughters to keep the house in order. Sure, I'm the one who's the head of the house, and it's up to me to see that our family functions smoothly. When there's a fight in the house between the kids, I can't stand the arguing. I feel it's *my* job to get them to resolve their differences. So I can't relax at home either.

JERRY: I'm struck with all the responsibility you take on yourself. You've got to do everything, or it won't get done right. There's no one you can trust to take responsibility. And all these responsibilities are weighing you down and creating trouble for you.

DON: Well, it's true! When I do trust others in the family to do something, inevitably things go sour. Then I've got to get involved and clean up the mess that others made. I don't like being in that position either. I'd like to change it, but I know it's easier said than done. But I tell you, I hate having to be the strong one *all the time!*

JERRY: Even though you'd like to change the way you are, you're at a loss to know where to begin. You hate being this superstrong person all the time, but you *have* to be this way. How would it be for you if you weren't so strong *some* of the time?

DON: I don't think you can understand. In my head I say to myself that a man is strong and doesn't buckle under with burdens. I'm the kind of guy who can't show feelings of weakness. I'm supposed to be able to meet these challenges of life. I can't afford to be weak and let down. I have to hang in there and make it.

JERRY: You have to hang in there at all costs?

DON: At all costs. Even if it kills me. I'm the kind of guy who can't stop running. Once I set out to do something, I'm determined to succeed. I can't let my body get the best of me.

JERRY: Your body is speaking a loud message, and yet you're not willing to listen to what it's telling you. I sense how hard it is for you to accept that you can't manage everything in life by yourself. And I see you as willing to hang onto the notion that somehow you'll find a way to be superhuman.

DON: You're hearing me! I don't mind being superman *some* of the time, but I don't like being superman *all* of the time.

Some Observations on Our Sessions

During this first session I'm interested in seeing the world through Don's eyes. I want to understand what it's like for him to feel driven to prove himself, to be consistently strong, to meet all his obligations (and then some), to take on the responsibilities of everyone, and to keep moving ahead even if it kills him. At the same time, I want him to know I have some understanding of how his life is. But I want to do more than merely reflect what I hear him saying.

In one of his sessions Don tells me something about his cultural background and his upbringing as a child that will be important in our work. Being Latino, he feels that he must play clear roles if he is to preserve his sense of being a man. Growing up in a family with several brothers, he learned to compete and to be tough in all situations. He is convinced that he should be able to handle any challenges, and his body's resistance is hard for him to accept. Apparently, he learned his lessons well, for he now has great difficulty in accepting or expressing feelings, which are manifestations of weakness in his eyes. He also learned that it was the man's place to take care of his wife and children by making a good living. His self-concept involves the notion that he needs to be on top of all of his responsibilities, that he cannot let down, and that there is no room for errors. I certainly do not want to challenge his assumptions quickly, but I want to find out which of his cultural values, if any, he is interested in modifying. He may not be interested in becoming more emotionally expressive. And he may decide that he wants to remain the strong and dependable man that he sees himself as being. My first task is to listen to him and to understand the meanings he puts on aspects of living such as "being strong" and "always being capable in every situation."

Yet I do want to get Don to begin to look at the obvious signs that his body is sending him. I hope that he can allow himself to tune in to his own tiredness and his own pain at always having to be strong. Without pushing my values on him and encouraging him to assume goals that are mine, I hope that he can pay attention to what he is experiencing and the price he is paying for living in certain ways.

I do not think that Don will change merely from my telling him that he *should* be different—that he should allow himself to be "weak," should delegate responsibilities, or should slow down and take it easy. He has heard this from his physician, and he *knows* (intellectually) that this is what he should do; yet he *feels* (emotionally) that he has to stay together at all costs. My assumption is that he will be more open to change if I encourage him to share openly with me what it feels like for him to live the way he does. Without directly insisting that he be different from the way he is, I want to encourage him to talk more about his striving for the top, to express his frustrations over his body's failure to stand up under the pressure, and to express his need to be strong and capable. At the same time, I am hoping that he will eventually consider whether he really does need to assume the responsibility for everyone else. I hope that he will begin to question how hard he is on himself and that he may eventually challenge himself on the necessity of maintaining such standards. He may decide to give up some of his burdens and to stop putting himself in the position of being completely responsible for the functioning of his family. It is possible for me to be respectful of his cultural framework yet also invite him to look at which attitudes and values are working for him and which are not serving him.

In getting Don to take this look at himself, I will share what is being evoked in me, especially my tenseness and tiredness as I try to be with him. If I am myself with him, he is more likely to be himself with me. He may be willing to reveal whatever he is attempting to cover up by a show of strength. I do not need to give him answers, even though on some level he would like to know "the way" to cope with stress. If I can stay with him and encourage him to express whatever he is feeling, this expression will provide the needed direction for us to move in future sessions. He is giving plenty of clues to pursue, if I will listen and follow them. I do not need to rely on techniques to get him to open up or techniques to resolve his problems. The best I can offer to him is the relationship that we develop, regardless of how brief it may be. If I am able to accept him in a nonjudgmental way, I see a good chance that he will begin to listen to himself (including his body) and that he will grow toward self-acceptance, which can be the beginning of real change for him.

Follow-Up: You Continue as Don's Therapist

1. How do you see Don? What are the major themes of his life that need to be focused on and explored more fully? How do you personally respond to him?
2. Assume that I were to refer Don to you for continued therapy (in the person-centered style). How do you imagine that it would be for you to work with him? How might a person such as Don relate to you?
3. Assuming that you will be seeing Don for at least six more sessions, what are some specific issues that you most want to explore? How might you go about doing this with him?
4. Coming from a Latino cultural background, Don has certain notions of what it means to be a man. His self-concept and his masculine definition of self include being strong at all times, being able to handle his responsibilities, providing well for his family, not showing signs of weakness, and being able to keep up with the other men he knows. If you were working with him, how might you separate his self-destructive beliefs and behaviors from certain messages he has received from his cultural upbringing? Would you expect to have any difficulty in respecting his cultural differences and at the same time challenging him to examine his beliefs? What other cultural variables would you want to consider in your counseling with him?
5. If you have a different cultural background from Don's, would you initiate a discussion of your cultural differences? Would you ask him if he feels willing to confide in you, especially if he has let it be known how strange it is for him to ask for help in dealing with his personal life? How would you feel, and what would you say to him, if he confronted you with your not being able to understand him because of your differences?
6. Given the data that you have on Don, do you think he would do better with a female or a male therapist? Or does it make any difference?
7. This approach was characterized by my listening and responding to him rather than by my active intervention with therapeutic procedures and techniques. Do you think you would feel comfortable in staying in such a role in your work with Don? Why or why not? Are there other techniques that you might want to introduce?
8. Don is driving himself relentlessly, and his body is telling him that he will probably kill himself if he does not change. Can you think of anything you might do or say to him to increase the probability that he will pay attention to the messages his body is sending him?

RECOMMENDED SUPPLEMENTARY READINGS

Alxine, V. (1976). *Dibs: In search of self.* New York: Ballantine. This book gives a touching account of a boy's journey from isolation toward self-awareness and self-expression. It emphasizes the crucial effects of the parent/child relationship on the development of a child's personality. It also describes how play therapy can be a tool for developing an autonomous individual.

Gendlin, E. T. (1981). *Focusing* (2nd ed.). New York: Bantam Books. This is a step-by-step approach to identifying and experiencing feelings by a person-centered therapist formerly associated with Carl Rogers.

Levant, R. F., & Shlien, J. M. (Eds.). (1984). *Client-centered therapy and the person-centered approach.* New York: Praeger. With chapters by many significant contributors, this text offers a number of provocative papers on the theory and range of applications of the person-centered approach, including experiential focusing, family therapy, supervision, marital enhancement, administration, health care, the search for world peace, research, and pastoral counseling.

Lietaer, G., Rombauts, J., & Van Balen, R. (Eds.). (1990). *Client-centered and experiential therapy in the nineties.* Leuven, Belgium: Leuven University Press. This text has a distinctly international flavor, because many of its authors are from outside the United States. The topics are far-ranging and give the reader a good idea of the breadth of conceptual and applied developments in person-centered therapy and its variations.

Rogers, C. (1961). *On becoming a person.* Boston: Houghton Mifflin. This is a compilation of many of Rogers's significant essays on education, therapy, communication, family life, and the healthy personality. Case examples illustrate the process of person-centered therapy in action.

Rogers, C. (1981). *A way of being.* Boston: Houghton Mifflin. This book contains a series of updated writings on Rogers's personal experiences and perspectives, as well as chapters on the foundations and applications of a person-centered approach.

CHAPTER SIX

Case Approach to Gestalt Therapy

A GESTALT THERAPIST'S PERSPECTIVE ON RUTH, by Rainette Eden Fantz, Ph.D.

Assessment of Ruth

It is fairly simple to give Ruth a diagnosis by addressing her case through her presenting problems, their history, her psychosocial history, and her "autobiography." Based on this information, I would classify her according to the DSM-IV as 309.9, which is adjustment disorder, unspecified type. However, if we regard all of the above factors through the lens of the Gestalt cycle of experience—namely, the need-fulfillment cycle—we become aware that her poor adjustment and the symptomatology accompanying it apply not only to Ruth's current situation but also to her entire life patterning. Examining the cycle and noting where her internal and external behavior interrupts the smooth progression of the cycle, so that her needs are never actually met and contact never actually made, we find the situation depicted in Figure 6-1.

We begin with unpleasant *sensations*, largely somatic in nature (10 o'clock on the figure), and an absence of pleasant sensations such as sensuality, warmth, pleasure, or fullness. These unpleasant sensations do move into *awareness*, but it is a very partial awareness inasmuch as Ruth's introjections and projections prevent her from knowing herself as other than a reification of her parents' and church's values. Consequently, she cannot look at her own "wants" and "wishes" because of the guilt they engender.

Ruth shows *excitement* over the possibility of teaching. Whenever this excitement begins to emerge, however, she becomes anxious and worries about her right to think and act selfishly. Her fear of losing her husband and her secure, though mundane, life prevent her from taking *action*. Whatever action she does begin to take is interrupted by her retroflection, turning her actions back on herself, so that her anger is *not* directed to her children, her husband, or her parents but to Ruth herself, with self-

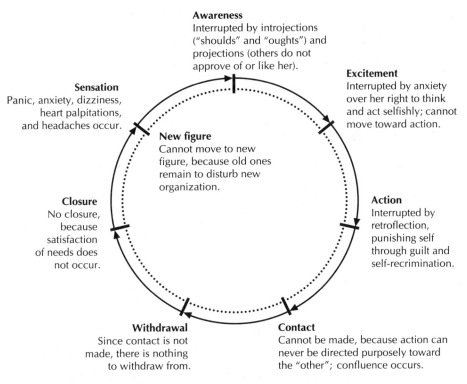

Awareness
Interrupted by introjections
("shoulds" and "oughts") and
projections (others do not
approve of or like her).

Excitement
Interrupted by anxiety
over her right to think
and act selfishly; cannot
move toward action.

Sensation
Panic, anxiety, dizziness,
heart palpitations,
and headaches occur.

New figure
Cannot move to new
figure, because old ones
remain to disturb new
organization.

Closure
No closure,
because
satisfaction
of needs does
not occur.

Action
Interrupted by
retroflection,
punishing self
through guilt and
self-recrimination.

Withdrawal
Since contact is not
made, there is nothing
to withdraw from.

Contact
Cannot be made, because action can
never be directed purposely toward
the "other"; confluence occurs.

FIGURE 6-1   The Gestalt need-fulfillment cycle

recrimination, self-deprecation, and guilt. Because she cannot make eye contact with the people she addresses, possibly out of the fear that they might actually know what she is harboring against them, she merely becomes confluent and goes along with them, or placates. No *contact* is made.

Needless to say, since contact does not occur, there is no way Ruth can complete the cycle, inasmuch as there is nothing there to *withdraw* from. She is plagued by numerous unfinished situations, which, in turn, prevent *closure* and the possibility of developing a fresh figure and starting a new cycle. (If both awareness and excitement are present and working together, the object of awareness becomes a sharper figure against an unnoticed background. This form of unified figure is called a "good Gestalt.")

Life Themes and Key Issues

In light of Ruth's lack of progress around the cycle and the reasons for her many interruptions, numerous major life themes and key issues present themselves. Among these life themes are:

- trying to please others and rarely succeeding
- overeating to the point of discomfort (which might stem from a need for rebellion and a need for an armoring of herself)
- always giving, yet never taking (no nourishment is derived; the well is empty)

Some of Ruth's key issues that we would be likely to explore in therapy are:

- her unsatisfactory relationship with her husband
- her lack of sexuality
- her distant, authoritarian father
- her largely critical and never-satisfied mother
- the little affection displayed between her father and mother
- her practice of caring for her younger siblings to gain approval
- her long-term guilt generated by playing "doctor" at age 6 and being caught by her father
- the fact that people see her as "weird"
- her fear of eternal punishment

Therapeutic Techniques and Interventions

Clearly, we have a plethora of major themes and key issues on which to concentrate in Ruth's psychotherapy. Given that Gestalt is an existential therapy, it behooves us to begin by attending to her *current process*, starting with attention and awareness. How and what does she see, hear, smell, taste, and feel in the present moment? For example, we can focus on the difference between seeing (passive) and looking (active):

THERAPIST: What is it like to allow your eyes to glaze over and let objects and people infringe on you, rather than choosing things in the room to actively look at? What is it like to make eye contact with me? What do you see? How am I different from you? What is it like to close your eyes and allow the sounds from inside and outside to encroach on you, rather than attending only to my voice? What is it like to actually experience the support of the chair under you rather than sitting on its edge with your feet not planted and your body not centered?

These are techniques we can use with *all* the senses.

Certainly it is incumbent to attend to her sensations: her dizziness, her palpitations, her headaches, her depression. One way to work with these is to have her *become* her palpitations and her other physical symptoms and discover what these symptoms are saying to her:

RUTH [speaking as her palpitations]: You don't allow me to breathe. I'm suffocating.

The suggestion to breathe is certainly in order; this allays her panic.

RUTH [speaking as her headache]: I'm going to continue to pound away at you until you stop giving yourself a hard time and allow yourself some choices.

When she speaks as her depression, we move into polarities and discover the anger that underlies it.

Polarities, indeed, are a tool par excellence to use with Ruth, inasmuch as they tap the shadow side of her personality: anger rather than depression, resentment rather than guilt, being spontaneous rather than being controlled, taking rather than giving, and speaking forthrightly from her own needs rather than always appeasing and considering those of others.

In addition to polarities we use other empty-chair work in which she can indulge in dialogues both with different facets of herself and with the different characters in her life—father, mother, husband, daughters, former peers—changing chairs and playing out each role.

All of these are important, but perhaps paramount is the side of Ruth that chooses to eat rather than allow herself to be slim and attractive and perhaps sexy. That part of the therapy is fun (as well as threatening, since she is so armored against that part of herself). Some homework I give her is to eat *very* slowly so that she can experience the satisfaction of tasting and the sensation of fullness. She does not appear to have achieved satisfaction in any area of her life.

I notice how Ruth fidgets with her clothes and wonder, out loud, what else she might like (or not like) to do with her hands. For example, would she like to stroke, tear, hit, or clutch with her hands? I encourage her to move into the area of retroflections and try to discover how to undo them. I certainly expect resistance here.

It is extremely interesting to move into the area of dreams or directed fantasy and find there her present existence, her exciting potential, and those elements she will not touch with a ten-foot pole. These are the missing parts of her *self*, which may prove to be the most important aspect that we explore in her therapy.

Over time we work extensively on Ruth's various life themes and her key issues, always exploring her sensations, her awareness, her beginning excitements, and her approach to action. I hope, in time, to enable her to make better contact so that she can complete her unfinished situations, whether in fantasy or reality. I share parts of myself with her when doing so is pertinent and not intrusive, so that she can learn to share. I am active and set up experiments, adjusting the risks so that they are tolerable yet at the growing edge. I hope that we can approach our sessions with a focus on a particular "figure," so that we can develop themes and experiments and have a beginning, a middle, and an end.

Ruth impresses me as being very capable of growth, having both intelligence and feelings ready to emerge. It is a delight to work with her.

JERRY COREY'S WORK WITH RUTH FROM A GESTALT PERSPECTIVE

Basic Assumptions

Approaching Ruth as a Gestalt therapist, I assume that she can deal effectively with her life problems, especially if she becomes fully aware of what is happening in and around her. My central task as her therapist is to help her fully experience her being in the here and now by first realizing how she is preventing herself from feeling and experiencing in the present. My approach is basically noninterpretive; instead, I will ask her to provide her own interpretations of her experiences. I expect her to participate in experiments, which consist of trying new ways of relating and responding.

I will encourage Ruth to experience directly in the present her "unfinished business" from the past. (Unfinished business involves unexpressed feelings such as resentment, rage, hatred, pain, anxiety, grief, guilt, abandonment, and so on. Because these feelings are not fully expressed in awareness, they linger in the background and are carried into present life in ways that interfere with effective contact with oneself and others.) A basic premise of Gestalt therapy is that by experiencing conflicts directly, instead of merely talking about them, clients will expand their own level of awareness and integrate the fragmented and unknown parts of their personality.

Assessment of Ruth

Viewing Ruth from a Gestalt perspective, I see her as having the capacity to assume personal responsibility and to live fully as an integrated person. Because of certain difficulties in her development, she devised various ways of avoiding problems, and she has therefore reached impasses in her quest for personal growth.

There are a number of ways in which Ruth is presently stuck. She has never learned that it is acceptable to have and to express feelings. True, she does feel a good deal of guilt, but she rarely expresses the resentment that she must feel. Any person who is as devoted to others as she is must feel some resentment at not having received the appreciation that she believes is due her. She does not allow herself to get angry at her father, who has punished her by withholding his affection and approval. She does not experience much anger toward John, despite the fact that here again she does not feel recognized. The same is true for both of her sons and both of her daughters. Ruth has made a lifetime career out of giving and doing for her family. She maintains that she gets little in return, yet she rarely expresses how this arrangement affects her. I think that keeping all of these feelings locked inside of her is getting in her way of feeling free. Therefore, I believe that she needs to embrace feelings that she is now excluding. A lot of her energy is going into blocking her experience of threatening feelings, sensations, and thoughts. Our therapy will encourage her to express her moment-by-moment experience so that her energy is freed up for creative pursuits instead of being spent on growth-inhibiting defenses.

Goals of Therapy

My goal is to challenge Ruth to move from environmental support to self-support and to assist her in gaining awareness of her present experience. With awareness she will be able to recognize denied aspects of herself and thus proceed toward the reintegration of all her dimensions. Therapy will provide the necessary intervention and challenge to help her gain awareness of what she is thinking, feeling, and doing now. As she comes to recognize and experience blocks to maturity, she can begin experimenting with different ways of being.

Therapeutic Procedures

As a Gestalt therapist I work to foster clients' ability to stand on their own two feet. Thus, in my work with Ruth I do not do her seeing, nor do I listen for her, because she has eyes and ears. Although philosophically I accept the existential view of the human condition, I draw heavily on experiential techniques that are aimed at intensifying here-and-now experiencing. These techniques are designed to help clients focus on what is going on within their body and to accentuate whatever they may be feeling. In this sense I am directive in my sessions with Ruth. I take my cues from her, but I also pay attention to what she is saying both verbally and nonverbally. From the cues I pick up, I invent action-oriented techniques that enable her to heighten whatever she is experiencing.

In my sessions with Ruth, we work with some of the emotional polarities that she generally does not express. For example, she tends to be critical and judgmental, so we focus on her dimension of self-acceptance, which does not get recognized or expressed. In this way she will find sides of herself that can be developed and integrated.

Along this line I ask Ruth to carry out some experiments. These may entail giving expression to unexpressed body movements or gestures, or they may involve talking in a different tone of voice. I may ask her to experiment with rehearsing out loud those thoughts that are racing through her, ones that she usually keeps to herself. My style is to invite clients to try new behavior and see what these experiments can teach them. I assume that if clients learn how to pay attention to whatever it is that they are experiencing at any moment, this awareness itself can lead to change.

JERRY: Ruth, rather than telling me about how guilty you feel over not having been the mother you think you should have been to Jennifer, would you simply list all the ways that you feel this guilt?

RUTH: Oh, that's not hard—there are so many ways! I feel guilty because I haven't been understanding enough, because I've been too easy on her and haven't set limits, because I haven't touched her enough, because I've been away at college when she needed me during her difficult years. And in some ways I feel responsible for her getting kicked out of school, for her drug problem—I could go on!

JERRY: So go on. Say more. Make the list as long as you can. [I am encouraging her to say aloud and unrehearsed many of the things that I assume she tells herself endlessly in her head. She continues to speak of her guilt.]

RUTH [letting out a deep sigh]: There! That's it!

JERRY: And what is that sigh about?

RUTH: Just relief, I suppose. I feel a little better, but I still have a sense that I've done wrong by Jennifer.

I am aware that Ruth is not going to rid herself forever of her guilt. If she does not let her guilt control her, however, she can make room for other feelings. Based on my hunch that behind guilt is usually resentment, I propose the following experiment:

JERRY: If you're willing to go further, I'd like you to repeat your list of guilts, only this time say "I resent you for . . ." instead of "I feel guilty over . . ."

RUTH: But I don't feel resentment—it's the guilt!

JERRY: I know, but would you be willing to go ahead with the experiment and see what happens?

RUTH [after some hesitation and discussion of the value of doing this]: I resent you for expecting me to always be understanding of you. I resent you for demanding so much of my time. I resent you for all the trouble you got yourself into and the nights of sleep I lost over this. I resent you for making me feel guilty. I resent you for not understanding me. I resent you for expecting affection but not giving me any.

My rationale for asking Ruth to convert her list of guilts into a list of resentments is that doing so may help her direct her anger to the sources where it belongs, rather than inward. She has so much guilt because she directs her anger toward herself, and this keeps her distant from some people who are significant to her. Ruth becomes more and more energetic with her expression of resentments.

JERRY: Ruth, let me sit in for Jennifer for a bit. Continue talking to me, and tell me the ways in which you resent me.

RUTH [becoming more emotional and expressive]: It's hard for me to talk to you. You and I haven't really talked in such a long time. [Tears well up in her eyes.] I give and give, and all you do is take and take. There's no end to it!

JERRY: Tell Jennifer what you want from her.

RUTH [pausing and then, with a burst of energy, shouting]: I want to be more like you! I'm envious of you. I wish I could be as daring and as alive as you . . . Wow, I'm surprised at what just came out of me.

JERRY: Keep talking to Jennifer, and tell her more how you're feeling right now.

With Ruth's heightened emotionality she is able to say some things to Jennifer that she has never said but has wished she could. She leaves this session with some new insights: Her feelings of guilt are more often feelings of resentment; her anger toward Jennifer is based on envy and jealousy; and the things that she dislikes about Jennifer are some of the things that she would like for herself.

Exploring the polarities within Ruth.   In later sessions we continue working with some of the splits within Ruth's personality. My aim is not to get rid of her feelings but to let her experience them and learn to integrate all the factions of her personality. She will not get rid of one side of her personality that she does not like by attempting to deny it, but she can learn to recognize the side that controls her by expressing it.

RUTH: For so many years I had to be the perfect minister's daughter. I lost myself in always being the proper "good girl." I'd like to be more spontaneous and playful and not worry constantly about what other people would think. Sometimes when I'm being silly, I hear this voice in my head that tells me to be proper. It's as if there are two of me, one that's all proper and prim and the other that wants to be footloose and free.

JERRY: Which side do you feel most right now, the proper side or the uninhibited side?

RUTH: Well, the proper and conservative side is surely the stronger in me.

JERRY: Here are a couple of chairs. I'd like you to sit in this chair here and be the proper side of you. Talk to the uninhibited side, which is sitting in this other chair.

RUTH: I wish you would grow up! You should act like an adult and stop being a silly kid. If I listened to you, I'd really be in trouble now. You're so impulsive and demanding.

JERRY: OK, how about changing and sitting in the chair over here and speaking from your daring side? What does she have to say to the proper side over there?

RUTH: It's about time you let your hair down and had some fun. You're so cautious! Sure, you're safe, but you're also a very, very dull person. I know you'd like to be me more often.

JERRY: Change chairs again, talking back to the daring side.

RUTH: Well I'd rather be safe than sorry! [Her face flushes.]

JERRY: And what do you want to say back to your proper side?

RUTH: That's just your trouble. Always be safe! And where is this getting you? You'll die being safe and secure.

This exchange of chairs goes on for some time. Becoming her daring side is much more uncomfortable for Ruth. After a while she lets herself get into the daring side and chides that old prude sitting across from her. She accuses her of letting life slip by, points out how she is just like her mother, and tells her how her being so proper stops her from having any fun. This experiment shows Ruth the difference between thinking about conflicts and actually letting herself experience those conflicts. She sees more clearly that she is being pulled in many directions, that she is a complex person, and that she will not get rid of feelings by pretending that they are not inside of her. Gradually, she experiences more freedom in accepting the different parts within her, with less need to cut out certain parts of her.

A dialogue with Ruth's father.   In another session Ruth brings up how it was for her as a child, especially in relation to a cold and ungiving father. I direct her not merely to report what happened but also to bring her father into the room now and talk to him as she did as a child. She goes back to a past event and relives it—the time at 6 years old when she was repri- manded by her father in the bedroom. She begins by saying how scared she was then and how she did not know what to say to him after he had caught her in sexual play. So I encourage her to stay with her scared feelings and to tell her father all the things that she was feeling then but did not say. Then I say to Ruth:

JERRY: Tell your father how you wish he had acted with you. [She proceeds to talk to her father. At a later point I hand her a pillow.] Let yourself be the father you wished you had, and talk to little Ruth. The pillow is you, and you are your father. Talk to little Ruth.

RUTH [This brings up intense feelings, and for a long time she says noth- ing. She sits silently, holding "Ruth" and caressing her lovingly. Even- tually, some words follow.]: Ruth, I have always loved you, and you have always been special to me. It has just been hard for me to show what I feel. I wanted to let you know how much you mattered to me, but I didn't know how.

Process commentary

During the time that Ruth is doing her work, I pay attention to what she is communicating nonverbally. When she asks why I "make so much fuss over the nonverbals," I let her know that I assume that she communicates at least as much nonverbally as through her words. As she is engaged in carrying on dialogues with different parts of herself, with her daughter, and with her father, she feels a variety of physical symptoms in her body. For example, she describes her heart, saying it feels as if it wants to break; the knots in her stomach; the tension in her neck and shoulders; the tightness in her head; her clenched fists; the tears in her eyes; and the smile across her lips. At appropriate moments I call her attention to her body and teach her how to pay attention to what she is experiencing in her body. At different times I ask her to try the experiment of "becoming" her breaking heart (or any other bodily sensation) and giving that part of her body "voice."

When she allows herself to speak for her tears, her clenched fists, or her shaking hands, Ruth is typically surprised by what her body can teach her. She gradually develops more respect for the messages of her body. In the same manner, we work with a number of her dreams. When she feels free enough to become each part of a dream and then act out her dreams, she begins to understand the message contained in them.

Ruth exhibits some resistance to letting herself get involved in these Gestalt experiments, but after challenging herself and overcoming her feelings of looking foolish, she is generally amazed at what comes out of these procedures. Without my interpretations she begins to discover for herself how some of her past experiences are related to her present feelings of being stuck in so many ways.

A theme that emerges over and over in Ruth's work is how alive material becomes when she brings an experience into the present. She does not merely intellectualize about her problems, nor does she engage in much talking about events. The emphasis is on trying out action-oriented techniques and experiments to intensify whatever she is experiencing. In most cases when she does bring a past event into the present by actually allowing herself to reexperience that event, it provides her with valuable insights. She does not need interpretations from me as her therapist, because by paying attention on a moment-to-moment basis to whatever she is experiencing, she is able to see the meaning for herself.

Ruth's awareness is by itself a powerful catalyst for her change. Before she can hope to be different in any respect, she first has to be aware of how she is. The focus of much of her work is on *what* she is experiencing at any given moment, as well as *how*. Thus, when she mentions being anxious, she focuses on *how* this anxiety is manifested in a knot in her stomach or a headache. I focus her on here-and-now experiencing and away from thinking about *why*. Asking why would remove Ruth from her feelings. Another key focus is on dealing with unfinished business. This case shows that business from the past does seek completion. It persists in her present until she faces and deals with feelings that she has not previously expressed.

Questions for Reflection

1. What do you think of Fantz's diagnosis of *adjustment disorder, unspecified type*? What behavior and personality patterns of Ruth's either lend support to or negate this diagnosis? At this point what diagnosis do you think best fits Ruth? Why?

2. Fantz indicates that she would tend to focus on the following life themes and key issues: pleasing others, giving to the point that the well is dry, overeating, unsatisfactory marital and sexual relationship, and problems with parents. If you were to work with Ruth as a Gestalt therapist, what techniques might you use in working with these themes?

3. Gestalt techniques are useful in working with the splits and polarities within a person. As you can see, Ruth has problems because she is not able to reconcile or integrate polarities: good versus bad, child versus adult, dependent versus independent, giving to others versus asking and receiving, feelings versus rational ideas, and the need for security versus the need to leave secure ways and create new ways of being. Are you aware of struggling with any of Ruth's polarities in your life now?

4. Knowing what you do of Gestalt therapy, what kind of client do you imagine you'd be in this type of therapy? How free would you be to try experiments? Do you see any connection between the type of client you'd be and the type of therapist you'd be within a Gestalt framework?

5. Can you think of some ways to blend the cognitive focus of Adlerian therapy with the emotional focus of Gestalt therapy in working with Ruth? Provide a few examples of how you could work with her feelings and cognitions by combining techniques and concepts from the two approaches.

6. How does the Gestalt approach work with Ruth's past differently from the psychoanalytic approach? Which style of dealing with the past do you prefer? Why?

7. What main differences do you see between the way in which Fantz worked with Ruth as a Gestalt therapist and the way in which Cain worked with her as a person-centered therapist? What about the differences in the way I counseled Ruth from these two perspectives? Which approach do you prefer? Why?

8. What do you particularly like and not like about the way in which I worked with Ruth as a Gestalt counselor? What are some other possibilities you see for working with her?

9. Think about Ruth as being from each of the following ethnic and cultural backgrounds: Native American, African-American, Latino, and Asian-American. How might you modify Gestalt techniques in working with her if she were a member of each of these groups? What are some of the advantages and disadvantages of drawing on concepts and techniques from Gestalt therapy in working with cultural themes in her life?

10. What are the specific areas of unfinished business that are most evident to you as you read about Ruth? Do any of her unexpressed feelings ignite any of your own business from the past? Are there any unresolved areas in your own life or any feelings that might interfere

with your ability to work effectively with her? If so, what are they? How might you deal with these feelings if they came up as you were counseling her?

CHRISTINA: A STUDENT WORKS WITH HER FEELINGS TOWARD HER SUPERVISOR AND HER FATHER

To demonstrate the flavor of my personal style of working with a client, I will dramatize a group session in which a client begins by saying she wants to work on her feelings toward me. I will use a dialogue to show how I draw on Gestalt concepts and employ Gestalt techniques. At the same time, I will give a running commentary on the process and my rationale for using the techniques I am using.

Some Background Data

Christina is a former student in my counseling practicum class. She says that she was constantly uncomfortable in the class, that the course and I threatened her, and that she would like to deal with some of the feelings she sat on during that entire semester. She has taken the initiative to ask for an individual counseling session to work on these feelings and on her relationship with me. The following imaginary dialogue is a sample of a typical way I would work if I were to stay within a Gestalt framework.

A Dialogue with Christina

JERRY: What would you like to get from this session, Christina?

CHRISTINA: I just get so down on myself for the way I let other people make me feel unimportant. I really became aware of this in your class. So I want to work on the feelings I had toward you then.

JERRY: Feelings you *had?* If you still have any of those feelings now, I'd like to hear more about them.

CHRISTINA: Oh, I suppose I still have those feelings, or at least it wouldn't be too difficult to get them back again. I just don't like the way you make me feel, Jerry.

JERRY: I still don't know what *those feelings* are, but I do know you're making me responsible for them. I *make* you feel? I don't like being put in that position.

CHRISTINA: Well, you *do* make me feel inadequate when I'm around you. I'm afraid to approach you, because you seem so busy, and I think you'll just brush me off. I don't want to give you the chance *not* to listen to me. I'm afraid you won't have time to hear my feelings, so that's why I stayed away from you that semester I had your class.

Without getting defensive, I want to let Christina know that *I* would like to be allowed to decide whether I have the time or the willingness to listen to her. I do not like being written off in advance or being told *who* I am and *how* I am without being given the chance to speak for myself. I let her know this directly, because I think my honest reactions toward what she is saying will be a vital component to building the kind of relationship between us that is needed to deal effectively with her feelings. Further, I call her on her unwillingness to accept responsibility for her own feelings, as expressed in her statements of "You make me feel . . ."

JERRY: If you're willing, I'd like to try an experiment. Would you just rattle off all the ways that you can think of that you feel around me, and after listing each of them, I'd like you to add *"and you make me feel that way!"* OK?

CHRISTINA: Sure, now I get my chance. This could be fun! Are you ready for this? When I'm around you, I feel so small and so inadequate—and you make me feel this way! When I'm around you, I feel judged. I feel that whatever I do isn't what you expect, and that whatever I do it won't be enough to please you—and you *make* me feel that way! [She seems more excited and is getting into the exercise with her voice and her postures and gestures.] I have to read all those damn books for the course. And then I feel I'll never be able to write papers that are clear enough for you and I'll feel stupid and inferior. And it's *your* fault that I feel this way—you *make* me feel this way! You're always rushing around doing so many things that I can't catch you long enough to get you to listen to me. Then I feel unimportant, and you *make* me feel this way.

I want Christina to say out loud many of the things that I imagine she has said silently to herself. As she lists all the ways she feels around me, as well as restating over and over that I make her feel those ways, I listen and encourage her to continue. I want her to become aware of her resentments and *experience her feelings,* not just to talk abstractly about them. I see this awareness as essential before any change can occur. While she is doing this, I pay attention to *how* she is delivering her message, because her body provides excellent leads to follow up on. I listen for changes in the tone and pitch of her voice. I notice any discrepancies between her words and facial expressions. I pay attention to her pointed finger or to her clenched fist. I notice her tapping foot. I also notice her blushing, her moist eyes, and any changes in her posture. All of these provide rich possibilities for exploring in this session, and there are any number of possibilities that I can follow through on. All the while I frequently check in with her on what she is feeling right now. This determines the direction we take next.

JERRY: What are you experiencing now?
CHRISTINA: I'm afraid you're judging me.
JERRY: What do you imagine I'm saying about you?

CHRISTINA: You're thinking I'm really immature and stupid. I'm feeling small again. And I'm also feeling vulnerable . . . weak . . . helpless . . . but mostly as if you're up there and I'm down here looking up at you. And I don't like feeling little and making you that important.

JERRY: What would your "littleness" say to me now?

CHRISTINA: I'm feeling hopeless. As if I'll never be able to touch you or really reach you. [A long pause follows.]

JERRY: What are you experiencing now?

CHRISTINA: I'm thinking about my father.

JERRY: What about your father? Let me be him, and you talk to me.

CHRISTINA: I'll never be able to touch you or really reach you. I feel so dumb with you. [another long pause]

JERRY: And what else do you want to say to your father right now?

CHRISTINA: I'd love to really be able to talk to you.

JERRY: You're talking to him right now. He's listening. Tell him more.

CHRISTINA: I've always been scared of you. I'd so much like to spend time with you and tell you about my pains and joys. I like that you're listening to me now. It feels so good.

JERRY: It feels good . . . What is it?

CHRISTINA [smilingly]: I feel good. [another pause]

JERRY: What do you want to do next?

CHRISTINA: I'd like to give you a hug, Dad. [She gives Dad a hug, sits down.]

JERRY: You look different now than you looked earlier.

CHRISTINA: I feel more at peace with myself.

JERRY: Anything else you'd like to say?

CHRISTINA: To my Dad or to you?

JERRY: To either or both of us?

CHRISTINA: You know, Jerry, right now you don't seem as much *up there* as you did. I think I could actually talk to you now and feel straight across with you—in fact, I'm feeling that way now. It feels good to me not to give you all that power, and the more I talk, the less scared I feel. Right now I'm feeling a real strength. I think you can see me for what I am, and I *am* worth something! I *am* important! And looking at you now, I feel that you're with me, and that you're *not* judging me and putting me down. I'm feeling good saying all this.

JERRY: Sitting across from you and looking at your face now and hearing you, I'm feeling good too. I don't like being put in unreachable places and then told how distant I am. I feel good sensing a quiet power in you, and I really like the way you are with me.

I continue by telling her some of the observations I had of her work and sharing what I was feeling at different points in our dialogue. I also tell her how I experience her very differently when she is soft, yet direct and powerful, instead of whining and giving me critical glances. I again offer her support and recognize the difficulty of her work.

Commentary on the Session

I think Gestalt techniques are powerful ways to help bring feelings out and also into focus. There is a vitality to Christina's work as she lets herself assume the identities of various objects. She can begin to reclaim disowned sides of herself and to integrate parts within herself. She is doing far more than reporting in an abstract fashion details from the past. She is bringing this unfinished business from her past into the present and dealing with whatever feelings arise in her.

Although I value Gestalt techniques as a way to take Christina further into whatever she is experiencing, I want to stress that these techniques cannot be used as a substitute for an honest exchange and dialogue between us. I can use myself and my own feelings to enhance the work of the session. Even though I will be departing from "pure" Gestalt, I want to integrate some cognitive work by asking Christina to put into words the meaning of what she has experienced and encourage her to talk about any associations between her work in our session and other aspects of her life. She may continue to talk about her awareness of how she puts *all* authority figures up high and what this is like for her. In my view blending this cognitive work with her affective work seems to result in longer-lasting learning.

Follow-Up: You Continue as Christina's Therapist

Assume that Christina and I decide that it is best that she continue her counseling with another therapist, one with a Gestalt orientation. I refer her to you.

1. Overall, what are your general impressions of Christina? Does she evoke any reactions in you? Knowing what you know of yourself and of Christina, how do you imagine that she would respond to you?
2. How comfortable would you be using Gestalt techniques similar to the ones I demonstrated in my work with Christina? Are there any techniques I used that you would *not* use? Why? Are there other Gestalt techniques you would like to try in your sessions with her?
3. I put a lot of emphasis on helping Christina pay attention to whatever she was feeling or experiencing at the moment. Why do you think I did this? What value, if any, do you see in this?
4. Does my work with Christina bring to the foreground any unfinished business in yourself that you recognize? How might any of your own conflicts affect your work with her?
5. Where would you go from here with her? How?

RECOMMENDED SUPPLEMENTARY READINGS

Fagan, J., & Shepherd, I. (1970). *Gestalt therapy now.* New York: Harper & Row. This book contains excellent readings dealing with the theory, techniques, and applications of Gestalt therapy.

Passons, W. (1975). *Gestalt approaches in counseling.* New York: Holt, Rinehart & Winston. Here is a useful resource for learning how Gestalt techniques can come alive in individual counseling sessions. The chapters contain many clear examples of dealing with fantasy, bringing the past or the future into the present, working with both verbal and nonverbal messages, and using techniques appropriately.

Perls, F. (1969). *Gestalt therapy verbatim.* Moab, UT: Real People Press. This is a useful book to get a flavor of Gestalt concepts and a firsthand account of the style in which Fritz Perls worked. Many examples of clients working with him provide a sense of how Gestalt techniques bring the past into the here and now.

Rainwater, J. (1979). *You're in charge: A guide to becoming your own therapist.* Los Angeles: Guild of Tutors Press. This is an excellent self-help book based on principles and techniques of Gestalt therapy. The author suggests exercises to increase self-awareness. She has useful ideas for keeping a journal, using autobiography, working with dreams, constructively using fantasy, and living in the here and now.

Yontef, G. M. (1993). *Awareness dialogue and process: Essays on Gestalt therapy.* Highland, NY: Gestalt Journal Press. This volume is a collection of significant essays that review the theory and practice of Gestalt therapy and identify recent trends in the field.

Zinker, J. (1978). *Creative process in Gestalt therapy.* New York: Vintage. Here is an exceptionally good book that captures the essence of Gestalt therapy as a combination of phenomenology and behavior modification. The author provides many excerpts from therapeutic sessions to show how the therapist functions much like an artist. He shows how Gestalt therapy can be practiced in a creative and eclectic style.

Zinker, J. (1994). *In search of good form: Gestalt therapy with couples and families.* San Francisco: Jossey-Bass. The author draws on a wealth of detailed clinical examples in making Gestalt therapy come alive with couples and families. His book deals with both theory and practice.

CHAPTER SEVEN

Case Approach to Reality Therapy

A REALITY THERAPIST'S PERSPECTIVE ON RUTH, by William Glasser, M.D.

Introduction

It is not possible to practice reality therapy without a clear understanding of the control theory on which it is based. I believe that all we do is behave and that all purposeful behavior, which means all client behavior, is chosen. Therefore, what are usually called psychological problems are, in fact, the ways we choose to behave when we find it particularly difficult to satisfy our needs. The task of the therapist is to help the client learn and then put into practice more responsible or more need-satisfying behavioral choices. Everything I suggest below should be the product of a dialogue in which my various points are brought up through the process of good reality-therapy questioning. From experience I know that it all can be done, but I can't teach the actual techniques here except to say that Ruth is asked to evaluate these suggestions.

Assessment of Ruth

Because psychological symptoms are chosen behaviors, in the description of my therapy with Ruth I use verb forms rather than nouns to describe how she chooses to behave. For example, you will see that I use *panicking* instead of *panic* to describe her symptoms. A panic disorder would be a consistent choosing of panicking behaviors as exemplified by Ruth. She will be taught to say, "I am choosing to depress" or "I am depressing" instead of saying, "I am depressed" or "I am suffering from depression." This new way of describing symptoms or disorders makes sense when you understand control theory.

As Ruth presents herself, it is obvious that she has never been able to satisfy her needs. In terms of the basic needs, the only one that she is satisfying now is her need for survival. She does not feel that she has love, power, fun, or freedom in her life, and her *anxieting, panicking,* and *psychosomaticizing* are her ways of expressing her extreme frustration. These symptoms keep her anger from bursting forth, and they "scream," Help me!

Ruth hasn't the strength to come out and say what she wants: a life far different from the one she has. So her symptoms and her complaints are her only way to express her intense dissatisfaction with her life. If she does not get the counseling she needs, she will choose more and more symptoms and will ultimately become disabled by them. She will also grow fat because eating (a survival need) is her only satisfaction, and she will choose *phobicking* to the point where she will say she is not able to leave the house alone.

Key Issues and Themes

First of all, Ruth needs someone who will listen to her and not criticize her for what she says. She has never had this, and she needs it desperately. She will, however, present her story and continually ask for criticism by saying things like "It's wrong for me to complain; I have so much; I'm acting like a baby." She will make a whole family of comments like this. She knows how to "guilt," and the counselor must not get involved in the process. My most important task as her therapist is to listen to her and tell her that she has a right to express herself, that she does not deserve to be criticized, and that I will never criticize her no matter what she does or fails to do.

Then, it is important for Ruth to learn about her basic needs. It is essential that she learn how to satisfy these needs and that she recognize that she can do this without hurting her husband or children. If her parents disapprove of what she does and say they are hurt, this is their choice, and she can do nothing about it. I can ask over and over "How does your being miserable help you or anyone else?" Although Ruth can be kind to her parents and others when she talks to them, it is important that she tell them firmly that she is going to do what she believes is right for her life.

Ruth should be encouraged in her choice to go to work, although it would be a good idea to discuss with her the choice to become an elementary schoolteacher. This is a very giving role, and she may not do well at this now. She may need to work among adults and to be appreciated for her adult qualities by her peers. She needs a job where she does not have to be a "good" person to be appreciated. It would be good for her to survey the job market.

Ruth's weight, diet, or symptoms should not be discussed in detail. If she wants to talk about them, I will listen but not encourage her. Talking about her problems or failures will lead her to choose to guilt, because she will not be able to solve them quickly. My approach will be to focus on her getting out of the house and finding a satisfying place in the adult world. When she does this, her complaints and symptoms will disappear, and her weight will be possible to control.

Ruth's finances will be discussed. What she earns for the first several years might be spent on herself and on doing things with her husband and children that are especially enjoyable to her. She should be encouraged not to save her money, give it to charity, or spend it on necessities unless that is what she really wants to do. It would be helpful to constantly encourage her to do what is right for her, not what is right for others or "good" for the world. She needs to learn to be a little selfish; she does not have to worry about becoming too selfish.

Finally, when Ruth has made progress, her marriage should be discussed, and her husband could be encouraged to be a part of this discussion. There is every reason to believe that she has little love in her marriage, but through marriage encounter or some such help this lack may be remedied. It may be that she will divorce, as she fears, but this is not an immediate issue.

Every session will end in a concrete plan for her to do something that will get her some love, power, fun, or freedom. What she plans need not be a big deal, but she has to learn, through doing things that satisfy her, that she is in control of her life and can use this control for her benefit.

Therapeutic Techniques

It is important that I be warm and uncritical and teach Ruth to be accepting of herself. In fact, I may say to her, "In here we will not criticize anyone and will focus only on what you can do for yourself, first, and then what you can do for the others around you."

It would be useful for Ruth to carefully read my book *Control Theory*, and we could discuss it in each session until she is well aware of these concepts and how they apply to the life she has and is still choosing to live.

It is best that plans be discussed, written out, and checked off. Ruth is competent, but her competence is never used for herself. She can be asked over and over "How will your satisfying your needs hurt anyone else?" and "How may doing this actually help others? Let's talk about this, because the answers to these questions are important for your life."

As much as possible, humor in the sessions will be helpful. Ruth is overdue for a laugh or two, and laughter will allow her to let go of her psychosomatic symptoms more quickly than anything else she can do.

There can be an emphasis on her good points, which are many, and at each session she can be encouraged to tell what she did that was good for her and what she accomplished that she never thought she would be able to.

It will be good for Ruth to consider the idea of inviting friends in and making a social life. She needs people. If her husband does not want to help, she can be encouraged to do this by herself. If she has a job, she might get hired help in to do the housework, which is something that this woman probably has never done or even dreamed of doing. The idea of spending money for enjoyment is worth a lot of therapy time.

Ruth can be encouraged to talk about her children and apply the ideas of control theory to them. I will ask her what she thinks she needs to do to get along with her daughter Jennifer, and I will advise her to stop telling her daughter what to do. Also, Ruth can be challenged to stop criticizing Jennifer completely, no matter what Jennifer or any of her other children say or do. Instead, Ruth might go out with her daughter for a good time, tell her she likes her the way she is, and say, jokingly, that she should not model herself after an unhappy mother, only a happy mother.

I can teach Ruth that it is her life and that it is up to her, not anyone else, to make what she wants of it. Whenever she says that she can't do something, I can ask her why she can't, ask her to give all the reasons why she could do it, and then compare the two sets of reasons.

What Ruth needs is freedom. She has locked herself in a prison of her own making for most of her life, and there should be a discussion of who can let her out. My job is to persuade her through good reality-therapy questioning to throw away the key. If she is locked in, it is because she won't open the door.

A Sample Session with Ruth

I keep the sessions as light as I can. Ruth needs to learn to take her problems less seriously so it will be easier for her to convince herself that she can make better choices. Here is how I guide the therapy after about a month, enough time for her to get to trust me and to begin to doubt that she is doomed to a life of panicking:

RUTH: It was really bad last night, all horrible feelings.

THERAPIST [interrupting]: The sweats, the palpitations, the fear of impending doom, the whole kit and kaboodle of your midnight misery. I'll grant you this, if you've learned anything in your 39 years, it's how to panic. Don't you think it's time to learn something better to do at night?

RUTH: How can you talk like that? Do you really believe I'm choosing this panic, that I enjoy these attacks? How can I possibly be choosing them? They come on while I'm sleeping, and they wake me up.

THERAPIST: Tell me, if you're not choosing them, who is? You've read about control theory. You choose all you do, just as I do and just as everyone does. Of course, you're not enjoying this choice, but—I know this is hard to believe—to you it's better than anything else you could choose in the middle of the night.

RUTH: You're crazy! It's not better or worse, it's what I do as I sleep. Don't you listen to me? I'm asleep; it wakes me up.

THERAPIST [not rising to the bait of arguing with her but continuing on]:

Suppose I called you in the middle of the night and woke you up before you woke up with your choice to panic. In fact, let's do it right now. Pretend you're sleeping and I give you a call. You do sleep, don't you? You don't panic all night every night, do you?

RUTH: Of course I sleep, but I'm getting afraid to go to sleep, even to go to bed. The attacks are excruciating. You don't have any idea of how bad they are. You've never had one. If you had, you wouldn't be sitting there so smugly telling me I'm choosing this misery.

THERAPIST: If you want to be able to make better choices while you're asleep at night, you've got to learn to make better choices in the daytime. But, c'mon, let me call you and wake you up. Will you do it, or do you have a better idea?

RUTH: Of course I don't have a better idea. If I did would I be here listening to this nonsense? Go ahead and call me.

THERAPIST: OK, ring, ring!

RUTH: Hello, who is it? What time is it?

THERAPIST: It's me, Dr. Glasser. I got to thinking about you and your problems, and I decided to call you. Can we talk for a few minutes?

RUTH: I'm sleepy. Couldn't it wait until morning?

THERAPIST: Just one question—one, OK?

RUTH: OK, OK, I'm up now, so I might as well talk. What do you want to know?

THERAPIST: I want to know what you were thinking about tonight when you went to bed. Tell me as much as you remember.

RUTH: What I always think about—that my life is all messed up, and it's not getting better. I'm in a rut. There's nothing going on in my marriage, my body looks just awful, and my whole day is horrible. I can understand why people drink and take drugs if they feel the way I do all the time. What more is there to tell you? It's what I tell you every time we talk. That's what I think about, my awful day and my miserable life. What's the sense of repeating it now? What good will it do?

THERAPIST: If I call you tomorrow night do you think the story will be the same?

RUTH: Of course it'll be the same. It's been the same for the last ten years.

THERAPIST: No, it hasn't. It's different now.

RUTH: What are you talking about? How is it different?

THERAPIST: The panicking is new, and seeing me is even newer. That's different, a lot different.

RUTH: Yeah, it's even worse than it was. At least I didn't have the panic. And you're no bargain either. I never thought of it that way. Maybe if I get rid of you I'll get rid of the panic.

THERAPIST: If you want to quit, I won't try to stop you.

RUTH: Well, you don't seem to be doing me much good.

THERAPIST: You don't seem to be doing yourself much good either. Why don't you choose to do something for yourself? We've talked about your doing some things for yourself, but all you want to do is tell me how miserable you are and how incompetent I am. Maybe it's time to stop complaining about me—maybe to stop complaining altogether. Do you want to keep going to bed afraid you're going to wake up scared to death and then come here and blame me because I'm not doing anything to help you? How's that going to help you?

RUTH [in helpless-little-girl tone of voice]: What can I do?

THERAPIST: You do a lot all day long, but you just don't do anything for *yourself*. Believe me, you'll get through the rest of the night no matter what happens. But tomorrow, even if you have what you call a panic attack, don't tell me about it. It's your choice, and I can't do a thing about it. All I can help you do is have a better day and *do* some different things than you've been doing. Do you want to start tomorrow, start changing the way you live, or do you want to choose to go on as you are?

RUTH [Softening now. She's been listening. The middle-of-the-night-call technique is getting her attention.]: But how can I?

THERAPIST [with emphasis]: How can you *not?* Why keep waiting? I know you're afraid. We're all afraid to try new things, because they might not work out. But this is different. You're not trying by yourself. I'm here, and I'll help you. I've been through this with a lot of people, and almost all of them were able to do what you find so frightening. So, I say let's get going. We're not on the phone—we're here in the office. Let's stop wasting time and start right now to make a plan for you to do something for *you*. You won't hurt anyone if you start to take care of yourself. If you begin feeling better, you'll be doing your whole family a favor.

After this, we make a plan to do something that, for a change, will satisfy her needs, and we're on our way.

Process commentary

I dare not wait much longer than a month to confront Ruth's resistance. She's not a weakling; it takes a lot of strength to panic as she has. But if I don't do this, and if I let her control me with her panicking as she has been trying to control everyone else, she won't change. To gain a sense of control, she has been willing to choose the suffering she complains about. We all do it once in a while, it's just that she does it a lot. I need to intervene, for that's my job as a therapist. There is no other way. As I told her, I've seen a lot of Ruths, and they have all changed. From my experience, her prognosis is very good if she's treated this way. Once she begins to put the energy into taking effective control of her life that she puts into panicking, she will make rapid progress.

This woman will need at least a year of one counseling session a week, but she will emerge as a vastly different and happier person. Group counseling with others like her would be a helpful supplement. I would say that the chances of her achieving a better life through the use of reality therapy is about 100%. People like her are a delight to counsel.

ANOTHER REALITY THERAPIST'S PERSPECTIVE ON RUTH, *by Robert E. Wubbolding, Ed.D.*

Introduction

I will present several examples of interventions that typify the practice of reality therapy. These dialogues include specific questions that can be asked when using reality therapy. It is not my intention to imply that if the therapist merely asks a few questions, the client will automatically make a rapid or dramatic change. The dialogues represent samples of the most important interventions, which are made repeatedly and rephrased in dozens of ways throughout the process of counseling.

Setting the stage for therapy. Because of the importance of informed consent, at the beginning of the first session or as soon as is appropriate, I review with Ruth all pertinent details related to professional disclosure: my credentials, the nature and principles of reality therapy, confidentiality and its limits, her rights and responsibilities, and the general goals of counseling. I emphasize the common formulation used in reality therapy: "my job, your job, our job." "My job" is to function as an ethical professional who recognizes his limitations. "Your job" is to keep the scheduled appointments and to disclose as much as you choose. "Our job" is to work for changes in your life that will result in increased happiness (need satisfaction).

Exploring Ruth's expectations. I then ask Ruth what thoughts she had when she decided to come for counseling and what thoughts she had today before her first visit. She describes her uncertainties, her hesitancy, and her sense of failure. I encourage her to discuss her fears about counseling and about "opening Pandora's box" and becoming overwhelmed with what she might find. By my listening in a nonjudgmental way to her anxieties, she comes to realize that they aren't overwhelming. With empathic listening I begin to form a relationship with her. I show confidence that she can make progress, on one condition; that she is willing to work at feeling better. If she will expend some effort, she can gain a sense of control, which is now lacking. But I point out that this effort may mean "working smarter, not harder." The goal of the first session is to communicate that I am trustworthy and that there is hope for a better tomorrow.

In the initial session and in subsequent sessions, we spend a lot of time on exploring her "mental picture album," or "quality world," as it relates to counseling. In other words, she goes into detail about the statement that what she wants most from therapy is to be told "what I have to do and be pushed to do it, so that I can begin to live before it's too late." I again make a significant point that she already has a tremendous advantage. Even now she believes that she can do something and that she wants to begin to live. I ask her to define what it means for her to "live." She describes her feeling of being a doormat at home, being overweight, being lonely and isolated, and being spiritually alienated. As she describes her pain, I express excitement that she is able to put it into words and point out that being able to articulate this pain is a major step.

THERAPIST: What thoughts went through your mind when you came here today?

RUTH: I was afraid and apprehensive. I wondered what would happen. Perhaps I'm afraid that I might have to change. I feel like such a failure.

THERAPIST: I would be surprised if you weren't upset about seeking outside help. It's a very normal and healthy way to feel. But actually, you deserve to be congratulated for taking this first big step. It must have taken courage.

RUTH: Well, I never thought of it as a big step.

THERAPIST: As you sit here now, do you believe that counseling can help you?

RUTH: I came because I think it will help.

THERAPIST: I've read your history, and we've talked here for a while, and I believe you could feel better. I make no guarantees, but I think a better life is possible. And I base that thought not on an idle wish, but on four pieces of specific information: You have taken a step by coming here, and you also have at least some belief that your life can be better. Moreover, you've already set a goal: to keep living. And finally, you're very open about what hurts. In other words, you can describe your pain.

RUTH: So there's hope?

THERAPIST: What do you think?

RUTH: That's why I'm here.

THERAPIST: I agree. There *is* hope. I also believe that you can feel at least a little better quickly, on one condition.

RUTH: What is that condition?

THERAPIST: That you're willing to put forth some effort.

RUTH: I'm willing to do that.

THERAPIST: How hard do you want to work at it?

RUTH: I want to work hard.

THERAPIST: I'd like to ask you not to feel that you have to do more or put a lot of pressure on yourself. Instead, let's try to figure out some ways for you to use your time more effectively without adding work. OK?

RUTH: OK.

Working with Ruth's Depression

Ruth at times resists my optimistic attitude and my emphasis on her positive steps, insisting that they are minor successes and that she sometimes feels depressed. Because of her insistence, I determine how depressed she has become. I ask her the five most important suicide assessment questions:

1. "Are you thinking about killing yourself?"
2. "Have you tried it previously?"
3. "Do you have a plan?"
4. "Do you have the means available to kill yourself?"
5. "Will you make a no-suicide contract with yourself [not merely for me, the counselor] not to kill yourself accidentally or intentionally?"

She tells me that the thought of suicide has occurred to her but that she has never tried it, has no plan, and has no effective means accessible to her. She readily makes a unilateral agreement to stay alive and healthy for at least two months.

Having assessed that the risk of suicide is absent, I decide to use paradoxical techniques with Ruth. At first she schedules some time for choosing to depress herself, perhaps ten minutes every other day. I ask her to describe in detail what she can do to make the situation worse. She enjoys this discussion and laughs heartily as she goes into detail about how she can criticize herself publicly, procrastinate even more over her plans, increase her guilt, and exaggerate her fear of death. She comes to see how such ineffective thinking holds her back from a happier and need-satisfying life. But most importantly, she learns through this upside-down logic that if she can make her life more miserable, she can also make it more enjoyable. It is important to reemphasize that I have determined early on that she is not suicidal or depressed to the point of being incapacitated. In such cases, paradoxical techniques are to be avoided.

I then encourage Ruth to describe what she wants that she is not getting and to say what she actually is getting from her husband, from each of her children, from her religion, from school, and, most importantly, from herself. (She has already described what she wants from me.) This exploration takes more than one session. She gradually develops more specific goals or wants related to her family, social life, self (for example, weight), professional life, and the spiritual aspect of her life (a much-neglected area in the counseling profession).

Exploring What Ruth Wants

An exploration of one aspect of Ruth's wants as they relate to her family—more specifically, her husband—is described below:

THERAPIST: You've described your relationship with your husband. Describe how you would like the relationship to be. To put the question another way, what do you want from him that you're not getting?

RUTH: I want him to be understanding.

THERAPIST: Could you be more specific about what you want that you're not getting?

RUTH: He takes me for granted. He only wants me to be a mother for his children. He's always busy at work and doesn't think of me as an independent person. And, you know, sometimes I think he's right.

THERAPIST: What do you want him to feel toward you?

RUTH: I would like him to appreciate me, to like me, to be friendly.

THERAPIST: And if he appreciated you, what would he do differently?

RUTH: He would show me more attention.

THERAPIST: Ruth, if he showed you attention tonight, what would you do?

RUTH: I'd be friendly. If he would share something about himself, I'd realize that he has confidence in me and has some feelings for me.

THERAPIST: Would you be interested in working toward having a better relationship with him?

RUTH: Of course.

THERAPIST: I think you've established a goal for your counseling. We'll be talking about what you can do to make the situation better for yourself. But first let's define a little more clearly what you would be like if the marriage were better.

RUTH: What do you mean?

THERAPIST: What are some adjectives that would describe you in a satisfying relationship with your husband?

RUTH: I'd be comfortable with him, confident, more assertive, able to stand up for myself, not so guilty if I have to say no to him, and I'd definitely be more attractive to him.

THERAPIST: Would you feel more control in your life if you reached these goals?

RUTH: I definitely would.

THERAPIST: You're certainly clear about what you want!

In this dialogue, Ruth has defined one want or goal. Using similar questioning, I help her clarify her wants as they relate to her children, religion, school, and other aspects of her life. The emphasis in formulating such goals is on helping her state her own role in the desired outcome.

Part of my initial sessions with Ruth are devoted to helping her examine her perception of how much control she has in her life. She defines what she can control and what she cannot control. I ask her to evaluate whether she can "force" others to change and how much control she can exert over her past history. I gradually help her come to believe that her life will be happier if she focuses on changing her own behavior in small increments. She comes to this conclusion without feeling added guilt about her past ineffective behaviors.

THERAPIST: You've defined what you want for yourself regarding your husband, children, and school. You've said that you want to feel that your life has some spiritual purpose—that it has lasting value. Would you describe the components of your life process that you have control of and what is beyond your control?

RUTH: I've tried hard to get my husband to change, and I've also tried to lose weight, to see some purpose to my life, to get rid of the night terrors, cold sweats, and all the pain I feel, and to get a professional identity and a life of my own.

THERAPIST: Can you really change any of these—the people or things on the list?

RUTH: I'm not sure. I'm so confused.

THERAPIST: Let's take them one by one. Can you force your husband to be the kind of person you want him to be?

RUTH: No, I've tried for years.

THERAPIST: Have your efforts gotten the result you wanted?

RUTH: No.

THERAPIST: Can you control your weight?

RUTH: I've lost and gained it back so many times.

THERAPIST: You have lost weight! So you know how to reduce your pounds, and you've succeeded many times.

RUTH: Well, I haven't looked at it as a success. It seems to me that regaining weight is a failure.

THERAPIST: But you have succeeded many times. You've taken charge of your eating for extended periods.

RUTH: I suppose you're right.

THERAPIST: What about gaining a sense of purpose—what I would call a sense of importance—that you are somebody, that you are worthwhile? How much control do you have over specific plans to formulate this ideal and to work toward it?

RUTH: Well, the way you put it makes it sound as if I could do it and as if I do have some control.

THERAPIST: Ruth, in my counseling I try to translate my clients' ideas into actions—actions that they can take to fulfill their needs. Now what about the night fears, the cold sweats? Can you simply make them vanish?

RUTH: They haven't disappeared yet.

THERAPIST: And they won't leave immediately. But I believe when you feel better about your daytime hours, you won't have nearly as much pain and upset at night.

RUTH: In other words, the night problems are symptoms of my daytime frustration?

THERAPIST: Exactly.

RUTH: What about the guilt about my childhood, when I was caught playing doctor?

THERAPIST: Same thing. When you're doing things that you feel good about and when you have the relationships you feel good about, you won't feel as guilty about the past.

RUTH: So how do I begin?

THERAPIST: By taking small steps—one at a time. But let's not rush. In fact, I'd suggest that you not make any radical or extensive changes until we talk some more.

Process commentary

As is clear from the above dialogue, I also ask Ruth to decide on her level of commitment. She is obviously not at the basic level: "I don't want to be here." For some parts of her life such as her weight, she may be at the second level: "I would like the outcome, but not the effort." "I'll try," the third level, is probably characteristic of much of her life. But I want to help her see her efforts to lose weight as successes. And so I lead her to the fourth and fifth levels: "I'll do my best" and "I'll do whatever it takes."

The real benefit in utilizing this system is not "the words" but "the music." This questioning format, often discouraged in counselor-training programs, helps Ruth develop an internal perceived locus of control. She restructures her belief system from the perception that she is powerless to the belief that she has control of many aspects of her life. Thus, when she is asked the above questions in a variety of ways, she describes her "internal music." As she explores her beliefs and perceptions, she is able to assess her underlying beliefs about the direction of her life, which increases the degree of effective control she can gain. She then gains a profound belief that life can be better, that she can feel better, and that she has more control than she ever dreamed of. It should be clear that reality therapy involves more than superficial planning and problem solving.

Along with the above issues she would describe specifically how she spends her time via-à-vis her husband, children, and career; what she thinks about when she is going to class or coming home; and what she tells herself about the amount of control she perceives she has.

Helping Ruth Evaluate What She Is Doing

Interspersed with the entire process above are dozens of questions related to self-evaluation: "Did your specific activities yesterday help you to the degree that you had hoped for?" "Are your wants realistically attainable?" "Is what you want really good for you?" More specifically, "Is your boring but comfortable life what you truly want?" "Is it good for you now?" "Are you spiritually the kind of person you want to be?" And the key question, "What would you be doing differently if you were the type of person you wanted to be?" We pick up the dialogue in a subsequent session:

THERAPIST: Let's focus on one aspect of what you have referred to as a source of great pain, your relationship with your husband. You mentioned in previous sessions that he ignores you, takes you for granted, and talks only minimally to you. And so I gather that you want this situation to change?

RUTH: I sure do.

THERAPIST: And you've also decided that your own actions are the only ones that are within your control.

RUTH: Yes.

THERAPIST: Now I want to ask you some important questions about the choices you've been making and what you've been doing in the relationship.

RUTH: OK.

THERAPIST: What happened last night? Describe exactly what you did last night from the time your husband came in to the time you went to bed.

RUTH [She describes the entire evening in detail. I help her to be precise.]: I arrived home just before he did. While I was changing my clothes, he came home. The first thing he did was to read the mail. He mumbled "Hello" and then ignored me. I mumbled, "Oh, you're home" and walked past him and into the kitchen to get supper ready. He propped himself in front of the TV and read the paper.

THERAPIST: What did you want from him at that time?

RUTH: I wish he would have said: "It's good to be home with you. Let's both look at the mail and then fix supper together."

THERAPIST: When was the last time anything like that happened?

RUTH: Are you kidding? It's been years.

THERAPIST: Ruth, we've discussed whose actions you can control . . .

RUTH: Yes, yes, I know. I can only change my choices, not his actions.

THERAPIST: Right. Now, let's discuss tonight. If you don't act on what you want, if you do the same thing you did last night, if you change nothing, will you get a different or a better result?

RUTH: I guess not.

THERAPIST: Right. So what will you change tonight?

RUTH: I'll try something different.

THERAPIST: Like what?

RUTH: I'll tell him what I want from him. I'll take the initiative.

THERAPIST: Sounds as if you have two ideas. How would you take the initiative?

RUTH: I could approach him first with a greeting that would be unusual. I could say something affectionate.

THERAPIST: What would you say that's different from what you said last night?

RUTH: I'll say, "Hello, how was your day?" and give him a hug. Then I'll say, "Let's read the mail and then fix supper together."

THERAPIST: Sounds good. So you'll take charge of the only part of the relationship that's within your ability to control?

RUTH: Yes, my own actions.

THERAPIST: Now let's suppose he doesn't respond the way you would like. What then?

RUTH: I'll feel bad.

THERAPIST: But what will you tell yourself internally that is based on the counseling you've received so far?

RUTH: All right, all right . . . I'll tell myself: "I've done what I can do, and there's no guarantee that he'll change. I choose to feel satisfaction at having made better choices than those I've made in the past."

Process commentary

In this session, I put emphasis on helping Ruth evaluate her own behavior rather than her husband's actions. By questioning her, I indirectly reminded her that she has control only of her own actions and that if she takes action, she will feel that she is doing her part. She was then helped to make short-range, attainable plans that have a high likelihood of success. In subsequent sessions she explores the other aspects of her control system—that is, her other unmet needs and their accompanying ineffective and effective behaviors as well as her perceptions regarding the inner sense of control that she has gained and still wants to gain.

I encourage Ruth to make more attainable special plans to fulfill her need for fun. I select fun because it is the most obvious unmet need, the one she is most likely to be able to meet more effectively, and the easiest to work on. In view of the fact that she has said she wants to lose weight permanently, I encourage her to join a support group such as Weight Watchers. I suggest that she get to know the students in her classes and organize study groups. This will give her a sense of belonging and help her fulfill her need for power or achievement. Such planning will, of course, be subsequent to her expressing that such actions will be need-satisfying.

I ask Ruth to read ten minutes a day (if she wants to) on a topic that is spiritually uplifting. To be avoided is anything that encourages guilt, fear, or self-deprecation. She has expressed a deep need for "an anchor," and to neglect this part of her life would be unfortunate. She can at least be referred to a sensible clergyman who understands reality therapy.

Overall, I help her fulfill her needs for belonging and power and fun more effectively. This is accomplished by use of the "WDEP" system: determining *wants*, including level of commitment and perceived locus of control; examining the total behavior; her *direction* and what she is *doing* as well as her thinking and feelings; assisting her to make her own inner self-*evaluations*, especially regarding her wants and behaviors; and finally by helping her develop positive and realistic *plans* aimed at fulfilling her needs in ways that are different from previous choices.

I feel confident in applying reality therapy to Ruth. And though I also feel challenged by the multitude of problems, knowledge of control theory helps me to see that when she changes any behavior, the good feeling and success generalize. Thus, I am confident that picking any symptom to work on will lead her to increased satisfaction with her entire life. Her obvious high level of motivation and minimal resistance facilitate relatively steady and visible progress toward the fulfillment of her wants (goals).

JERRY COREY'S WORK WITH RUTH FROM A REALITY-THERAPY PERSPECTIVE

Basic Assumptions

Reality therapy is active, directive, practical, and cognitive-behavioral. As a reality therapist I see my task as helping clients clarify their wants and perceptions, evaluate them, and then make plans to bring about change. My basic job is establishing a personal relationship with my clients that will give them the impetus to make an honest evaluation of how well their current behavior is working for them. Reality therapy concentrates on total behavior (which includes doing, thinking, feeling, and physiological components).

A basic premise underlying the practice of reality therapy is that *behavior* controls our perceptions. Although we may not be able to control what actually is in the real world, we do attempt to control our perceptions to meet our own needs. Applied to Ruth, this means that she creates her own perceived world. Her behavior has four components: acting, thinking, feeling, and physiology. Because I make the assumption that controlling feelings and thoughts is more difficult than controlling actions, the focus of therapy is on what she is doing—behaviors that are observable. She will find that it is typically easier to force herself to *do* something different than to feel something different. Although it is acceptable to discuss feelings, this is always done by relating them to what she is doing and thinking.

Assessment of Ruth

Rather than merely focusing on Ruth's deficits, problems, and failures, I am interested in looking at her assets, accomplishments, and successes. Initially I ask her questions such as these: "What do you want? How might your life be different if you had what you wanted now? What do you consider to be your major strengths? What are the qualities that you most like about yourself? What have you done that you are proud of? What resources can you build on?" From Ruth's autobiography and intake form, I know that she has several strengths. She has graduated from college and is in a teacher-education program at the graduate level. She has done this against many odds. Her parents could see no real reason why she should get a college degree. In her current situation her husband and children have not been supportive of her efforts to complete her education. She has been involved in numerous community groups and made some contributions there, she has managed to keep up her family life and still have time for her education, and she has set some career goals that are meaningful to her. Now she needs to develop a clear plan for attaining her *personal* objectives.

Goals of Therapy

Ruth's present behavior is not working as well as it might. She is unproductively dwelling on unfortunate events from her past, and she is paying too much attention to feelings of guilt and anxiety and not enough to those things that she is doing to actually create these feelings. In short, she is making herself anxious and guilty by what she is doing and not doing in everyday life. I try to direct her attention toward these actions, because they are the most easily controlled part of her life. I continue challenging her to make an honest assessment of how well her current behavior is getting her what she wants. Then I help her make plans to bring about change.

Therapeutic Procedures

I will expect Ruth to make a commitment to carry out her plans, for if she hopes to change, *action* is necessary. It is essential that she stick with her commitment to change and not blame others for the way she is or give excuses for not meeting her commitments. Thus, we will work with a therapeutic contract, one that spells out what she wants from therapy as well as the means by which she will attain her goals.

   If Ruth says that she is depressed, I will not ask *why* she is depressed, nor will I ask her to dwell on feelings of depression. Instead, I will ask what she has *done* that day to contribute to her experience of *depressing*. Changes in behavior do not depend on changing one's attitudes or gaining insights. On the contrary, attitudes may change, as well as feelings, once clients begin to change their behavior. I am also concerned about Ruth's *present*, not her past. Why should I dwell on the unsuccessful person that she has been? I would rather focus on the successful person that she can be. Also, I do not pay heed to psychoanalytic factors such as transference, unconscious dynamics, dreams, and early memories. Through my real involvement with Ruth I hope to help her to choose more effective behaviors aimed at fulfilling her realistic wants, thereby satisfying her needs for belonging, power, fun, and freedom.

The Therapeutic Process

Ruth's therapeutic journey consists of my applying the procedures of reality therapy to help her meet her goals. Although the principles may sound simple, they must be adapted creatively to the therapeutic process. It should be noted that although these principles are applied progressively in stages, they should not be thought of as discrete and rigid categories. Each phase builds on the previous stage, there is a considerable degree of interdependence among these principles, and taken together they contribute to the total process that is reality therapy. This process weaves together two components, the counseling environment and specific procedures that lead to changes in behavior. We will now look at a few of the highlights and turning points in Ruth's therapy.

Elements of the process

Establishing the relationship.   During our initial sessions my main concern is to create a climate that will be conducive to Ruth's learning about herself. The core of the counseling environment consists of a personal involvement with the client, which must be woven into the fabric of the therapeutic process from beginning to end. I convey this involvement through a combined process of listening to Ruth's story and skillful questioning. This process increases the chances that she will evaluate her life and move in the direction of getting what she wants.

In some of our early sessions Ruth wants to talk about occasions when she experienced failure in her childhood and youth. She quickly wants to blame past negative experiences for her fears. She seems a bit stunned when I tell her that I do not want to go over her past failures and that if we are going to talk about the past at all, I am more interested in hearing what went right for her. From that topic she jumps to complaining about feeling anxiety, depression, and some physical symptoms. I ask her to describe what she would be doing if she were not depressing. This focus begins a process of redirection and gets her to think about other alternatives besides depressing. I do not encourage her to focus on feelings related to negative experiences. Part of her present problem is that she is already stuck in some negative feelings, and I do not want to reinforce her in continuing this pattern.

Challenging Ruth to evaluate her behavior.   After getting a picture of how Ruth sees her world, I encourage her to try something different: to take a hard look at the things she is doing and see if they are working for her. After some debating she agrees with my suggestion that she is depressing herself by what she is doing. Questions that I pose to her are: "What are the things you've done today? What did you do this past week? Do you like what you're doing now? Are there some things you would like to be doing differently? What are some of the things that stop you from doing what you say you want to do? What do you intend to do tomorrow?" Let me stress that I do not bombard her with these questions one after another. The early sessions are, however, geared to getting her to consider this line of questioning. Rather than looking at her past or focusing on her attitudes, beliefs, thoughts, and feelings, I want her to know that we will be zeroing in on what she is doing today and what she will do tomorrow.

I believe that Ruth will not change unless she makes some assessment of the constructiveness or destructiveness of what she is doing. I assume that if she comes to realize that her behavior is not working for her and that she is not getting what she wants, there is a real possibility that she might choose other alternatives. Here is a brief excerpt of a session:

RUTH: So what do you think I'm doing wrong? There are times I want to give up, because I don't know what to do differently. [She is very much wanting me to make a value judgment for her.]

JERRY: You know how important it is for you to be the one who makes a judgment about your own behavior. It's your job to decide for yourself what is and isn't working. I can't tell you what you "should" do. [For me to simply tell her that some of her present ways are ineffective will not be of much value to her.]

RUTH: Well, I do want to go out and get some practice with interviews for part-time or substitute teaching. I often find lots of reasons to keep me from doing that. I keep telling myself that I'm so busy I just don't have time to set up these interviews.

JERRY: And is that something you'd like to change? [My line of questioning is to ascertain how much she wants what she says she wants. I am attempting to assess her level of commitment.]

RUTH: Yeah, sure I want to change it. I want to be able to arrange for these interviews and then feel confident enough to have what it takes to get a part-time job.

We look at how Ruth stops herself (not why) and explore ways in which she might begin to change behavior that she calls "sitting back and waiting to see what happens." She says that she does not like her passivity and that she would like to do more initiating. One of the factors we talk about is how she lets her family get in the way of her doing some of these things she says she wants to do.

Planning and action.   We devote a number of sessions to identifying specific behaviors that Ruth decides are not working for her. A few of these ineffective behaviors are procrastinating in arranging for job interviews; sitting at home feeling depressed and anxious and then increasing these feelings by not doing anything different; allowing her 19-year-old son, Rob, to come home after squandering money and then taking care of him; allowing her daughter Jennifer to control her life by her acting out; and continually taking on projects that she does not want to get involved in. Knowing that we cannot work on all fronts at once, I ask her what areas she wants to do something about.

Ruth decides first to line up some interviews for jobs. She makes it clear that her life is boring, stale, and without much challenge. Then she tries to convince me that everything she has to do for her family makes it next to impossible for her to get out of her boring rut. I reply, "If things are as bad as you say, do you expect them to change if you keep doing what you have been doing?" We gradually work out some realistic plans, which include her filing applications with school districts and setting up interviews. Interestingly enough, after taking these beginning steps, she reports that she is already feeling much better.

We also develop some plans to set clear limits with Ruth's family. She has a pattern of doing things for her children and then resenting them and winding up feeling taken advantage of. Part of her plan calls for sitting down with each of her sons and each of her daughters and redefining their relationships. I suggest that it would be a good idea to have at least one session with her family. The idea both excites and frightens her. Yet she actually surprises herself when she is successful in getting John and her four children to come in for a two-hour session of family therapy. At this session we mainly negotiate some changes in roles after Ruth has told each family member specific changes that she would like and has been striving for. One of her sons and one of her daughters is not at all excited about some of the proposed changes, and they want to know what is wrong with the way things are. What I had in mind when I suggested this family session was to give Ruth an opportunity to ask for what she wants and to witness her negotiating for these changes. The session helps me see how she relates to her family, and it helps her ask for what is important to her.

Other phases of Ruth's therapy.   Most of our work together consists of developing realistic and specific plans and then talking about how Ruth might carry them out in everyday life. When she does not stick with a subgoal or carry out a plan for the week, I am not likely to listen to any excuses. In a few cases in which she persistently does not follow through with an agreed-on plan, we then discuss whether what she has planned is something she really wants or something she thinks she should want. Several times she returns looking sheepish, almost expecting to be punished or yelled at. I try to get across that as long as she keeps coming in, I do not intend to give up on her, nor will I get into a punishing stance with her. Instead, I want her to deal with the consequences of her actions and then be her own judge.

Eventually, Ruth gets better at setting smaller goals and makes more realistic plans. She stops and says, "Now I wonder if I really want to do this, or am I hearing someone else tell me that I should want it?" Before finishing her therapy, she fills out a form evaluating her progress over the months. Her comments are reproduced below:

> After two months of weekly visits with a reality therapist, I have a better idea of what I can do to get out of the boring rut I've been in for so long. I've gotten a lot of miles out of complaining and feeling helpless, but I must say this is something that Jerry just would not tolerate. He quickly told me when I whined that if I was really interested in being different, I'd be taking steps to see that I became different.

I remember the time I agreed to begin a daily exercise and jogging program as one way of losing weight. For several weeks I had complained to Jerry that I couldn't stand the way I looked. He worked with me to develop a realistic program for losing weight—and then I didn't follow through with the plans. Jerry said he didn't want to listen to my rationalizations for having failed. I tried to convince him that I had gone on another eating binge because my husband had been ignoring me and I had gotten depressed. I said to myself, "Why should I lose weight for John if he's going to treat me so badly?" When I told Jerry this, he countered with: "Whom are you losing weight for, *yourself* or John? Whom are you hurting with your eating behavior?" That got me to thinking about how I so often make others responsible instead of putting the responsibility on me, where it belongs. I do see that if I don't like my weight, or anything else in my life, matters won't be different until I get in there and take action.

By the way, I interviewed for the job, and I did get part-time work as a substitute. This shows me that I'll get nothing unless I make an attempt.

Process commentary

As a reality therapist I do not tell Ruth what she should change but encourage her to examine her wants and determine her level of commitment to change. It is up to her to decide how well her current behavior is working for her. Once she makes a value judgment about what she is actually *doing*, she can take some significant steps toward making changes for herself. She has a tendency to complain of feeling victimized and controlled, and my intention is to help her see how her behavior actually contributes to this perceived helplessness. Rather than focusing on her feelings of depression and anxiety, I choose to focus on what she does from the time she wakes up to the time she goes to bed. Through a self-observational process she gradually assumes more responsibility for her actions. She sees that what she does has a lot to do with the way she feels.

After Ruth becomes clearer about certain patterns of her behavior, I encourage her to develop a specific plan of action that can lead to the changes she desires. Broad and idealistic plans are bound to fail, so we work on a concrete plan for change that she is willing to commit herself to. Once she makes a commitment to a certain course of action, I do not accept excuses if she does not follow through with her program. I simply ask her to look at her plans again to determine what has gone wrong. Through this process she learns how to evaluate her own behavior to see ways in which she might adjust her plans and experience success.

Questions for Reflection

1. In Glasser's assessment of Ruth, he says, "If she does not get the counseling she needs, which will lead to a more satisfying life, she will choose more and more symptoms and will ultimately become disabled by them." What are the main symptoms that Ruth presents? What

are your thoughts about the manner in which Glasser deals with her symptoms and the key themes that she presents?

2. In Glasser's commentary on Ruth, he suggests asking over and over, "How does your being miserable help you or anyone else?" To what extent do you think that she is choosing her misery? How would you be inclined to work with her on this score?

3. Both Glasser and Wubbolding seemed very directive in pointing out the themes that Ruth should explore, and they were also fairly directive in suggesting what she should do outside of the sessions. What are your reactions to this stance? Would you be inclined to bring up topics for Ruth to explore if she did not specifically mention them?

4. Do you have any concerns that reality therapy could be practiced in such a way that the therapist imposed his or her values on the client? Do you see this as potentially happening with the way Glasser, Wubbolding, or I worked with Ruth?

5. Because of Ruth's depression, Wubbolding asked five key questions to assess her potential for suicide. What are your thoughts about his intervention?

6. Wubbolding made use of frequent questioning to help Ruth clarify what she wanted and evaluate the degree to which her behavior was moving her in the direction of meeting her goals. What are some of his questions that you most like? What are some specific things you might do differently from this therapist?

7. What are your reactions to the lack of focus on matters such as Ruth's early childhood experiences? her unconscious dynamics? her dreams? her feelings of being bound by her parents' teachings? her feelings of guilt? Do these have a place in reality therapy? If so, what is it? What are the major differences you see between reality therapy and psychoanalysis? Which do you think is more appropriate for Ruth?

8. Assume that you are Ruth's therapist and she wants to present you with the reasons that she has failed at a particular plan for action. How might you respond? What do you think of the reality therapist's view of *not accepting excuses* and of *not blaming the past* for the way one is today?

9. Apply the procedures of reality therapy to what you know of Ruth. Systematically show how you would get her to focus on what she is doing, on making an evaluation of her behavior, and on helping her formulate realistic plans.

10. Assume that you are a client in reality therapy. What do you think this experience would be like for you? How would you describe your current behavior? Can you come up with a plan for changing a particular behavior you really want to change?

MANNY: A LOSER FOR LIFE?

The scene is a U.S. Army base in Germany. The army has a mandatory counseling program for drug and alcohol rehabilitation of personnel with addictive personalities. I am called in as a consultant to train the counselors who are a part of this program. I mention that I would like to get some feel for the clients they work with, and I am quickly given an opportunity. They know that my theoretical orientation is reality therapy, and because the army is very supportive of this approach to rehabilitation programs, I am sent a client to interview for one session.

My Approach with Manny

Manny, at 27, has made the military his career. He approaches the session in a high state of anxiety and displays many nervous bodily mannerisms. After we briefly introduce ourselves, our exchange goes this way:

MANNY: I really don't want to be here, you know. The only reason I'm here is because my commanding officer told me "You will report to Dr. Corey at 1600 hours on 7 July at the health clinic."

JERRY: If you don't want to be here, how come you're here?

MANNY: What do you mean, man? I *had* to show up. The commanding officer didn't give me any choice!

JERRY: Well, you walked through the door by yourself. Nobody brought you here. What would have happened if you hadn't shown up?

MANNY: They gave me one more chance, and then they're booting me out.

JERRY: So you *did* decide to come and see me rather than get kicked out.

MANNY: Yeah, I don't know what good this will do, but it's better than getting my walking papers.

JERRY: Well, I'm not sure how much good counseling will do unless we both agree to do what's needed to make it work. But you're here, and how you use this time is largely up to you.

MANNY: I don't want them to discharge me, especially since I have all those years in toward retirement.

JERRY: So I'd like to hear more about what might be the consequences if they do discharge you and about what you see that you can do to prevent this from happening.

Initially, Manny does not want to be in the office. Rather than fighting his resistance, I go with it by engaging him in a discussion of the possible consequences of both seeing me and not seeing me. My hope is that he will find it easy enough to talk with me, that I will not appear overly threatening to him, and that I will be able to lay the foundations for more meaningful *involvement* with him. Note that even though he sees himself as an involuntary client, I challenge him a bit on the fact that he indeed chose to come and see me rather than suffering the consequences of not keeping his appointment. He could have been more difficult and more resistant by simply saying: "Hey, why am I talking to you? I don't want to talk to you." Examples of facilitative remarks would be: "And who would you rather talk to?" "Where would you rather be right now?" Maybe we can talk more about what is likely to happen if you don't come for counseling." "Are you willing to say why you are here?" Again, if I let him lead the way and go with his resistance, he can provide me with useful information about himself that will help me understand his current situation. My aim is to help him acquire a new perspective about a situation in which he sees himself as an involuntary client, so that he might perceive some payoffs in choosing to participate in counseling.

At another point Manny reminds me that he does not want to attend therapy sessions. I tell him then what we will be doing in the sessions and what he can expect of me. But I also tell him what I expect of him. I am not willing to see him unconditionally, nor am I willing to sit with him silently or try to pry things out of him. I suggest that I see him three times to explore the possibilities of what counseling can offer him. He agrees to come in for three sessions, the time mainly to teach him about the counseling process, to get him to look at what he is *doing* now, and to decide how well it is working for him. Notice that I am not determining what he will talk about, but I insist that on some level he address his present behavior. We then proceed in the first session as follows:

JERRY: I'd like to talk more about why you were sent here and what you might get from this one session today. Are you willing?

MANNY: You're calling the shots. Whatever you say. I'm here because the army thinks I have a big problem with drugs—Big H and all that stuff—and they think you're supposed to put my head on straight. My problem isn't the drugs. It's the army and all those Mickey Mouse rules.

JERRY: What about the army and its rules?

I want to give Manny some slack in saying what problems he has, if any. Unless *he* sees that he has a problem, one that is getting in the way of living, he may do nothing to change any of his behavior. It is one thing for his commanding officer to order him to seek counseling for a problem he sees with Manny and quite another matter for Manny to accept that he does indeed have a problem. At this point he sees his locus of control as being outside of himself. Part of creating the involvement process consists of helping him find ways of gaining more effective control of his life. My aim is to help him look at what specific areas he has control over and what areas are outside of his control. I facilitate this process by encouraging him to explore his wants, needs, and perceptions.

MANNY: Sure, I've got my share of problems. You'd have some problems if you grew up the way I did. My old man kicked me out of the house when I was a kid, and I had to go and live with an uncle in East Los Angeles. I got in with a gang and started being a loser then. I got kicked out of school for peddling dope and gang activity. Never was able to hold a job. I mean, man, I've had a rough life. If you had all the things happen to you that I've had to go through, you might not have made it as far as I have. I'm a loser, but at least I'm still alive. I mean,

Doc, you don't look like the type who's been with gangs and had to put up with the kind of life that I did. How can you understand what I'm going through?

I need to exert some caution here not to become defensive. Also, I do not want this to become a session in which Manny tells me that he is not to blame for all his woes. In reality therapy we do not want to encourage a pattern of blaming, in which clients absolve themselves of any personal responsibility for the way they are, nor do we want to encourage a recitation of past history as an explanation of current behavior. But another issue is that Manny is again trying to take the focus off of himself and telling me that I am not able to understand what he has been through. I must deal directly with the question of my ability to understand him.

JERRY: You're right, I haven't been through all that you have. I'm not sure I'd have survived. That doesn't necessarily mean that I can't understand you. I'd like for you to give me that chance. Even though I've had different life experiences from yours, I may still be able to have some of your feelings and see things the way you do. I'd like an opportunity to make contact with you, even for this single meeting.
MANNY: Well, before you can understand the way I am, you need to know about what I've lived through. My old man was never there, I got beat up all the time, I failed at everything I tried—I was a real loser. A loser from the word go. And it's mostly because I never had the things in life most normal kids have.

Again, there are some rich leads here. I can get some idea of what it is like to be Manny if I let him talk in more detail of what his life was like, as well as what he is facing now. But there is the danger that we can lose sight of his *present behavior*—what he is doing now—if we dwell on the adversity he has faced and the loser that he has been in the past. I want to focus him on the present by beginning to examine if what he is doing is working for him. If he does not like what he has in his life, the doors are open for counseling to proceed.

JERRY: You know, the way I work, I prefer to look at what you're doing *right now* in your life and what this behavior is actually getting you. I think we can easily get sidetracked if we go back into your past with all the details of the negative things that happened to you. I'm not so much interested in hearing about the loser you've been all your life as I am in getting you to think about the winner you can be in your future. I'd like to hear you talk about what you can have *some* control over *now*.
MANNY: But I want to figure out why my head is all messed up the way it is. Don't you need to know about my childhood to help me? Don't I need to know what's caused my problems before I can straighten them out?
JERRY: I don't think that talking about the past is important or that it will help you much, *unless* we discuss how your past relates to what you

see as being a problem for you currently. What I'm after is to get you to look at your life to see in what ways it is or isn't working for you now. With what time we have left today, I'd be very willing to discuss with you what your present behavior is getting you. Are you willing to take this look?

MANNY: Well, it's not getting me much except heaps of trouble. I've spent time in the military jail because of my drug trip, and things don't look too rosy for the future. There are times when I'd like to be different, but I don't know how to do it.

Where I'd Proceed with Manny from Here

Assuming that Manny is willing to at least take a look at the results of his behavior, I ask him if he is committed to a better life for himself and how much he really wants change in his life. I ask him to talk more about some of the ways in which he has been a failure, and I challenge him to see if there are any ways in which he has contributed to his setbacks. However, my focus is on helping him see what steps he can now take toward becoming a successful person. Thus, our work together is grounded on the assumption that his behavior is an attempt to fulfill his basic needs for belonging, power, freedom, and fun. It is crucial that I do not judge his present behavior for him but that I continue to challenge *him* to do this. Thus, my attempts will be directed toward getting him to realistically appraise his behavior.

My main concern at this point is for Manny to simply see that nothing in his life will change unless he sees the need for change. He says that although there are times when he would like to be different, he does not know how to go about it. This provides an excellent lead for a discussion of specific plans that could lead to constructive changes for him. Therefore, I will at least begin by exploring with him some of the things he can do well, some of the things he likes, and some of the ways he would like to be different. This includes encouraging him to talk about the mental pictures he has about the life he would like. My hope is that he will begin to consider possibilities for himself that he has previously ruled out. For example, in our discussion I find out that he would like to specialize in electronics, and he even admits to having some talent in this area. So I talk with him about the chances of enrolling in the army's electronics program. If he agrees to look into the program, this will be a responsible action, for he will not just be moaning about his ill fate but doing something about changing this fate.

My job is to help him make plans that are immediate and realistic. Such plans can even begin during the session. I hope that before our session ends, he will at least have some plan for checking out the electronics program. This could even involve his making a phone call during the session to inquire about it. It is a good idea to write these plans down. If he agrees to short-range plans, we can discuss how he can best carry them out and what he might do if he encounters difficulties in doing what he says he would like to do. It would also be a good idea to ask him to consider what he might get from some further counseling sessions.

Follow-Up: You Continue as Manny's Therapist

Assume that Manny does do something about his life and decides to give short-term counseling a try. He consults you and asks you to continue where he and I left off, using reality therapy as a base. How might you proceed with him?

1. First of all, how do you perceive Manny? What are your personal reactions to him? Does it make any difference that he has sought counseling with you voluntarily, rather than being sent by his commanding officer? How might you be affected by him differently if he were an involuntary client? Would you want to work with him? Why or why not?

2. What are your general impressions of the way I worked with Manny? What would you do to further this work? What differences can you see between your style and mine in dealing with him (still staying in the reality-therapy perspective)?

3. From what was presented, what kinds of "pictures," or perceptions, does Manny have about his life now? What might you do or say to increase the chances that he would look at his behavior and make a value judgment about it?

4. To what degree have you had life experiences that would allow you to identify with Manny's drug problem and his failures? If you have not had similar feelings of being a "loser," do you think you could be effective with him?

5. How might you respond to Manny as your client if he reacted to you in a flip and sarcastic manner?

6. Manny wants to talk about his past and the experiences that he thinks contributed to the person he is today. I keep focusing him on the present and on what he might do about his future. What do you think of such an approach? What are its possible merits and demerits?

7. This approach stresses the importance of a concrete plan of action and a commitment from the client to follow the plan. What might you say and do if Manny neither developed a concrete plan for change nor committed himself to the process of behavioral change?

8. In my session with Manny I make it clear that I am interested mainly in his actions, not in his feelings, not in changing his attitudes and beliefs, and not in helping him to acquire insight. What do you think of an approach that focuses so directly on one domain—in his case, what he is doing today?

9. Manny was not identified with respect to cultural and ethnic back-

ground or to his race. Consider how you might work with him differently depending on his specific cultural and ethnic background. What variables might you attend to if his background were different from yours? How might you proceed with him if he were African-American? White? Native American? Latino? Asian-American?

RECOMMENDED SUPPLEMENTARY READINGS

Glasser, N. (Ed.). (1989). *Control theory in the practice of reality therapy: Case studies.* New York: Harper & Row. This is a book of cases showing how control theory is applied to the practice of reality therapy with a diverse range of clients. This casebook brings the concepts of reality therapy up to date by showing how therapists integrate the concepts of control theory into their practice. These cases demonstrate how the key ideas of control theory actually work in helping clients ask themselves the question "Is what I am choosing to do now getting me what I want?"

Glasser, W. (1985). *Control theory.* New York: Harper & Row. The author develops the thesis that we always have control over what we do and that if we come to understand how our behavior is an attempt to meet our needs, we can then find ways of taking control of our life. He explores such topics as choosing misery, craziness and responsibility, psychosomatic illness as a creative process, addictive drugs, taking control of your health, and how to start using control theory.

Wubbolding, R. (1988). *Using reality therapy.* New York: Harper & Row. The author extends the principles of reality therapy by presenting case studies that can be applied to marital and family counseling as well as individual counseling. He has summarized control theory in five clear principles. This book offers practical guidelines for implementing the principles of reality therapy in practice. Many excellent questions and brief examples clarify ways of using its concepts. There are chapters on guidelines for creating an effective counseling relationship, as well as on specific procedures used by the reality therapist to facilitate change. The author has extended the scope of practicing reality therapy by describing other procedures such as paradoxical techniques, humor, skillful questioning, supervision, and self-help. He presents reality therapy as a philosophy of life rather than a doctrinaire theory or set of prescriptions.

Wubbolding, R. (1991). *Understanding reality therapy.* New York: Harper & Row. This book utilizes a metaphorical approach as a way to explain the basic components in the practice of reality therapy. Drawing on his therapeutic practice, the author explains how metaphors and analogies can illuminate the ways in which we view the world.

CHAPTER EIGHT

Case Approach to Behavior Therapy

A MULTIMODAL-BEHAVIOR THERAPIST'S PERSPECTIVE ON RUTH, by Arnold A. Lazarus, Ph.D., A.B.P.P.

Introduction

Multimodal therapy is a broad-based, systematic, and comprehensive approach to behavior therapy, which calls for technical eclecticism. The multimodal orientation assumes that clients are usually troubled by a multitude of specific problems that should be dealt with by a wide range of specific techniques. Its comprehensive assessment, or therapeutic modus operandi, attends to each area of a client's BASIC I.D. (B = behavior, A = affect, S = sensation, I = imagery, C = cognition, I = interpersonal relationships, and D = drugs and biological factors). Discrete and interactive problems throughout each of the foregoing modalities are identified, and appropriate techniques are selected to deal with each difficulty. A genuine and empathic client/therapist relationship provides the soil that enables the techniques to take root.

Multimodal Assessment of Ruth

In Ruth's case, more than three dozen specific and interrelated problems can be identified by using the following diagnostic, treatment-oriented BASIC I.D. methodology:

Behavior
> fidgeting, avoidance of eye contact, and rapid speaking
> poor sleep pattern
> tendency to cry easily
> overeating
> various avoidance behaviors

Affect
> anxiety
> panic (especially in class and at night when trying to sleep)
> depression
> fears of criticism and rejection

pangs of religious guilt
trapped feelings
self-abnegation
Sensation
dizziness
palpitations
fatigue and boredom
headaches
tendency to deny, reject, or suppress her sexuality
overeating to the point of nausea
Imagery
ongoing negative parental messages
residual images of hellfire and brimstone
unfavorable body image and poor self-image
view of herself as aging and losing her looks
inability to visualize herself in a professional role
Cognition
self-identity questions ("Who and what am I?")
worrying thoughts (death and dying)
doubts about her right to succeed professionally
categorical imperatives ("shoulds," "oughts," and "musts")
search for new values
self-denigration
Interpersonal relationships
unassertiveness (especially putting the needs of others before her own)
fostering her family's dependence on her
limited pleasure outside her role as mother and wife
problems with children
unsatisfactory relationship with her husband (yet fear of losing him)
looking to the therapist for direction
still seeking parental approval
Drugs and biological factors
overweight
lack of an exercise program
various physical complaints for which medical examinations reveal no
organic pathology

Like Jerry Corey, I typically don't think in diagnostic terms. Indeed, a multimodal clinician sees the range of problems across the BASIC I.D. as the "diagnosis." Many of the labels contained in the DSM-IV would seem to apply to Ruth. These include:

300.4: dysthymic disorder
300.01: panic disorder
309.28: adjustment disorder with mixed anxiety and depressed mood
V61.1: partner relational problem
313.82: identity problem

If I had to pick one of the labels, I would say that adjustment disorder with mixed anxiety and depressed mood comes closest to covering her main difficulties.

Selecting Techniques and Strategies

The goal of multimodal therapy is not to eliminate each and every identified problem. Rather, after establishing rapport with Ruth and developing a sound therapeutic alliance, I would select several key issues in concert with her. Given the fact that she is generally tense, agitated, restless, and anxious, one of the first antidotes might be the use of relaxation training. Some people respond with paradoxical increases in tension when practicing relaxation, and it is necessary to determine what particular type of relaxation will suit an individual client (for example, direct muscular tension/relaxation contrasts, autogenic training, meditation, positive mental imagery, diaphragmatic breathing, or a combination of methods). I have no reason to believe that Ruth would not respond to deep muscle relaxation, positive imagery, and self-calming statements.

The next pivotal area is her unassertiveness and self-entitlements. I will employ behavior rehearsal and role playing. Our sessions will also explore her right to be professional and successful. Cognitive restructuring will address her categorical imperatives and will endeavor to reduce the "shoulds," "oughts," and "musts" she inflicts upon herself. Imagery techniques may be given prominence. For example, I may ask her to picture herself going back in a time machine so that she can meet herself as a little girl and provide her alter ego with reassurance about the religious guilts her father imposed. One of her homework assignments may be the use of this image over and over until she feels in control of the situation.

If Ruth and her husband agree to it, some marital counseling (and possibly some sex therapy) may be recommended, followed by some family-therapy sessions aimed at enhancing the interpersonal climate in the home. Indeed, if she becomes a more relaxed, confident, assertive person, John and her children may need help to cope with her new behaviors. Moreover, I can try to circumvent any attempts at "sabotage" by him or the children.

If Ruth feels up to it, I will teach her sensible eating habits and will embark on a weight-reduction and exercise regimen. Referral to a local diet center may be a useful adjunct.

As a part of the assessment process, I ask Ruth to fill out the 15-page Multimodal Life History Inventory, which has been designed by A. Lazarus and and C. Lazarus (1991).* This process enables me to detect a wide range of problems throughout the BASIC I.D. The following dialogue ensues:

---

*See the Recommended Supplementary Readings.

THERAPIST: On page 12 of the questionnaire, you wrote "no" to the question "Do you eat three well-balanced meals each day?" and also to the question "Do you get regular physical exercise?" And on page 15, you wrote that you frequently drink coffee, overeat, eat junk foods, and have weight problems.

RUTH: Maybe I should go on a diet again.

THERAPIST: Well, the problem with going on a diet is that people soon come off it and gain weight, perhaps even more weight than they lost. I think the goal is to develop sensible eating patterns. To begin with, I have a list of foods that a nutritionist gave me, stuff that we should avoid eating or cut down on. [The list contains mainly foods with a high fat content, especially those with saturated fats, as well as foods with a high sugar content.] For starters, would you be willing to take it home and see how many of these items you can cut out of your diet?

RUTH: Certainly.

THERAPIST: I wonder if we could make a pact?

RUTH: About what?

THERAPIST: That you would agree to take a brisk 1- to 2-mile walk at least three times a week.

RUTH: I can do that.

THERAPIST: By the way, there's an excellent diet center in your neighborhood. They have a program in which they train people to understand food contents and to easily calculate the amount of fiber and calories you require. They also run support groups. It's often easier to develop new eating habits when you're part of a group instead of trying to do it on your own.

RUTH: Yes, I know the place you mean. I've often thought of going there. Do you really think it would be a good idea?

THERAPIST: Yes, I really do.

Therapy Sessions with Ruth

After I draw up Ruth's Modality Profile (BASIC I.D. chart), the clinical dialogue proceeds as follows:

THERAPIST: I've made up a list, under seven separate headings, of what your main problems seem to be. For example, under *behavior* I have the following: fidgeting, avoidance of eye contact, rapid speaking, poor sleep pattern, tendency to cry easily, overeating, and various avoidance behaviors.

RUTH: That's what I do; they're all correct. [pause] But I'm not exactly sure what you mean by "various avoidance behaviors."

THERAPIST: Well, it seems to me that you often avoid doing things that you'd like to do; instead, you do what you think others expect of you. You avoid following through on your plans to exercise and to observe good eating habits. You avoid making certain decisions . . .

RUTH: I see what you mean. I guess I'm a pretty hopeless case. I'm so weak and panicky, such a basic coward, that I can't seem to make up my mind about anything these days.

THERAPIST: One thing you seem to be very good at and never avoid is putting yourself down. You sure won't feel helpless if you start taking emotional risks and if you're willing to speak your mind. What does that sound like to you?

RUTH: Are you asking me if I'd like to be more outgoing and less afraid?

THERAPIST: That's a good way of putting it. What do you think would happen if you changed in that regard?

RUTH: I'm not sure, but I certainly don't think my father would approve.

THERAPIST: And how about your husband?

RUTH [looking downcast]: I see what you're getting at.

THERAPIST: Would you agree that you first tended to march to your father's drum and then handed most of the control over to your husband? [Ruth is nodding affirmatively.] Well, I think it's high time you become the architect and designer of your own life.

Ruth does not feel overwhelmed, so I discuss the other items on her Modality Profile. If she had showed signs of concern ("Oh my God! I have so many problems!") I would have targeted only the most salient items and helped her work toward their mitigation or elimination.

Whenever feasible, I select data-based methods of treatment. Thus, in dealing with her panic attacks, I first explain the physiology of panic and the fight-or-flight response. Emphasis is placed on the distinction between adaptive and maladaptive anxiety. For example, anxiety is helpful when it prompts Ruth to study for an exam, but it is maladaptive when its intensity undermines her performance. Her anxiety reactions are examined in terms of their behavioral consequences; secondary affective responses (such as fear of fear); sensory reactions; the images, or mental pictures, they generate; their cognitive components; and their interpersonal effects. In each instance, I apply specific strategies. Behaviorally, for example, I encourage her to stop avoiding situations and instead to confront them. In the cognitive modality, she is enjoined to challenge thoughts like "I must be going crazy!" or "I'm going to die!" and to replace them with the following self-statements: "My doctor confirmed that I'm physically healthy." "Being anxious won't make me crazy!" Because so many people who suffer from panic tend to overbreathe (hyperventilate), I teach Ruth how to breathe more slowly and use her diaphragm, thereby dampening her physical symptoms. The adjunctive use of drug therapy such as the new generation of antidepressants may also be considered, especially if her progress is unduly slow.

It is usually important to deal with "pivotal events"—critical incidents or significant memories that seem to play a central role. Thus, in an effort to extinguish the guilt and proscriptions associated with her father's general remonstrations, especially the way he berated her for "playing doctor," the following procedure is helpful:

THERAPIST: Would you mind doing a little imagery exercise that will help counteract certain painful memories?

RUTH: What do you mean?

THERAPIST: It's very easy. Would you mind relaxing in the chair for a few moments? [pause] Just let your body feel pleasant and at ease. [pause] Can you close your eyes and imagine that we have a time machine that will take you back to visit yourself at the age of 6? [pause] You step into the device, and you step out and see the 6-year-old little Ruth. The 39-year-old Ruth, you at present, looks at the 6-year-old Ruth, 33 years into the past. [pause] Can you picture that?

RUTH [nods affirmatively]: Oh yes, I see her allright.

THERAPIST: What is she doing?

RUTH: She's holding a rag doll in her right hand and sucking two fingers of her other hand.

THERAPIST: Can you tell if your visit to her has come before or after her father caught her playing doctor?

RUTH [pausing]: Judging by the guilty look in her eyes, it must be after.

THERAPIST: Now little Ruth, the 6-year-old child, looks at you, at 39-year-old Ruth. She doesn't realize that you really are *her*, 33 years into the future, a grown woman, a wife, a mother, little Ruth all grown up. But she senses something special about you, and she feels very close to you and trusts you. Can you get into that image?

RUTH [softly]: Yes.

THERAPIST: Good. Now what do you want to say to the 6-year-old Ruth?

RUTH: First I want to tell her not to buy into all that stuff about religion, the gospel, and all that guilt [pause].

THERAPIST: Talk to her, explain it to her. She'll hear you. She'll listen to you.

As this dialogue continues, Ruth is encouraged to offer her 6-year-old alter ego some good advice, encouragement, and nonjudgmental insights. Often, when performing this exercise, clients become deeply involved and grow very emotional, especially when challenging the painful notions and events that have tended to haunt them. At the end of the exercise, the client is asked to step into the time machine again and to travel forward into the present. A detailed discussion then ensues, and many clients experience reparative effects. The active mechanism behind this procedure is presumed to be a form of desensitization and cognitive restructuring.

A Conjoint Session with Ruth and John

The treatment trajectory depends mainly on Ruth's readiness for change (for example, her willingness to take risks, be assertive, and challenge her dysfunctional thoughts) and the extent to which her husband is invested in keeping her subservient. John feels threatened by Ruth when she starts expressing and fulfilling herself, and conjoint sessions are essential to persuade him that he will be better off in the long run with a wife who feels personally satisfied rather than bitter, frustrated, and bored. Thus, I suggest to her that she encourage him to attend at least one therapy session with her. I tell her that I intend to go out of my way to bond with John, so as to gain his compliance. In this connection, I have the following dialogue with Ruth and John:

THERAPIST [addressing John]: Thank you for agreeing to meet with me. As you know, I've been trying to help Ruth overcome various fears and anxieties, and I believe she has made considerable headway. But now we're at a point where I need your input and assistance. I wonder if we can start by hearing your views on the subject.

JOHN [glancing at Ruth]: What do you want to know?

THERAPIST: Quite a number of things. I'd like to know how you view her therapy, whether you think it was or is necessary, and if you think she has been helped. I'd like to hear your complaints about Ruth—after all, no marriage is perfect.

JOHN [addressing Ruth]: Can I be perfectly honest?

RUTH: Honey, that's why we're here.

THERAPIST: Please be completely frank and aboveboard.

JOHN: What do I call you?

THERAPIST: Let's not be formal or stuffy. Call me Arnold.

JOHN: Well, Arnold, the way I see it is that Ruth has bitten off more than she can chew. Things were pretty good until she decided to go to college. I don't think she can manage a career and a home. It's putting too much pressure on her. I mean, you know, I think if you take things away from the family, everyone suffers. It's not as if she needs to work for the money. Heck, I've always made enough to support my family.

THERAPIST: That's very important. Have things changed for the worse inside the family since Ruth started studying? Has she neglected you and the kids? Is the family suffering?

JOHN: Well, not exactly. I mean, Ruth's always been a good wife and a devoted mother. But [pause] I don't quite know how to put it. [pause]

THERAPIST: Perhaps you're reacting to a feeling inside of yourself that there's the potential for some sort of penalty or withdrawal . . . that something will be taken away from you.

JOHN: Yeah, maybe.

THERAPIST: You're facing a turning point that many families encounter. The job of mothering is virtually done. Let's see. Your four children are now 19, 18, 17, and 16 years old. So the energy that Ruth had to expend in taking care of them in the past must be replaced by something else. Now that the kids are almost grown up, she has more time on her hands. Her full-time homemaking has now become a part-time activity. As Ruth approaches 40, it seems that she needs to become more than a wife and mother. Not less, but more. It would be a mistake for her to do anything that would damage or undermine her relationship with you and the children. Let's say she aspired to become an executive who would spend 60 hours a week at work. Then there would be big trouble.

JOHN [smiling]: You can say that again!

THERAPIST: Well, if she works as an elementary schoolteacher, the time that she used to devote to caring for your kids would be put to constructive use. But if she just hung around at home, you'd soon have a bitter, resentful, and frustrated woman on your hands. What would she do with all that free time except become a royal pain in the neck? Does that make sense?

JOHN: I guess I see what you're getting at.

THERAPIST: Besides, let's face it. Even though you make good money, with four kids to put through college, a bit of extra cash won't hurt. [talking to Ruth] I hope you don't mind too much that John and I have been talking about you as if you weren't in the room. I meant no disrespect, but I really wanted to touch base with him.

RUTH: No, I understand. May I ask something?

THERAPIST [paradoxically]: Only if you get down on bended knee.

RUTH [smiling]: The 6-year-old strikes again! [turning to John]: Honey, have I ever neglected you or the children?

JOHN: Like I said, you've been a good wife and mother.

THERAPIST: Now the question is whether you can continue being a good wife and mother and also become a good teacher.

A follow-up session with Ruth after the conjoint meeting commences as follows:

THERAPIST: I'm curious to know if our threesome meeting seemed to have any positive effects. What do you think we accomplished?

RUTH: It's hard to tell. I mean John came away saying that you made sense, which I think is a very good sign. He seemed quite comfortable with you.

THERAPIST: Well, I hope that the "sense" I made adds up to getting him to realize that if you don't work but function as a full-time homemaker now that the children have grown up, it will be to *everyone's* detriment. I want you, from time to time, to underscore that point. We need John to become fully aware that there's a positive payoff, a definite advantage for him if you work, and that it's in no way a reflection of his earning capacity. As I told him, the extra money will be useful, but it's not essential. Can you gently but firmly make those points over and over?

RUTH: I think that's what's needed for John to feel OK about it.

THERAPIST: And you? Do you feel OK about it? You've expressed quite a bit of conflict over this issue.

RUTH: I'm still afraid of many things, and I'm still not entirely confident that I can succeed.

THERAPIST: Well, should we look into this now?

RUTH: Susan—she's my 17-year-old—has me a little upset over an incident that occurred. Can we discuss this first?

THERAPIST: Sure.

Concluding Comments

The initial objective was to gain permission from "Big Daddy John" for Ruth to pursue a career. If John seemed motivated to enter couples therapy with a view to improving their marriage—really getting to know and appreciate each other, enhancing their levels of general and sexual communication—this would be all to the good. It would not surprise me if he also elected to seek personal therapy for some of his insecurities. As a multimodal therapist, I would expect to encounter no difficulties in treating Ruth individually, Ruth and John as a couple, and John as an individual.

The multimodal approach assumes that lasting treatment outcomes require one to combine various techniques, strategies, and modalities. A multimodal therapist works with individuals, couples, and families as needed. The approach is pragmatic and empirical. It offers a consistent framework for diagnosing problems within and among each vector of personality. The overall emphasis is on fitting the treatment to the client by addressing factors such as the client's expectancies, readiness for change, and motivation. The therapist's style (for example, degree of directiveness and supportiveness) varies according to the needs of the client and situation. Above all, flexibility and thoroughness are strongly emphasized.

Most therapists would probably find Ruth capable of being helped and relatively easy to treat. Unlike some clients with severe personality disturbances, she displays no excessive hostility, no intense self-destructive tendencies, and no undue "resistance," and her interpersonal style appears to be collaborative rather than belligerent or contentious. Nevertheless, if one treats only two or three modalities (which is what most nonmultimodal counselors address), several important problems and deficits may be glossed over or ignored, thereby leaving her with untreated complaints that could have been resolved and with a propensity to relapse (for example, revert back to her timid, conflicted, anxious, depressed, and unfulfilled modus vivendi).

In this era, when *brief therapy* is the order of the day, the multimodal clinician, instead of focusing or dwelling on one or two so-called pivotal issues (which is what many time-limited counselors attempt to do), would rather address one major problem from each dimension of the BASIC I.D. Thus, in Ruth's case, if we had only six to ten sessions within which to work, the following issues might be selected:

Behavior: Address her avoidance response.

Affect: Implement anxiety-management techniques.

Sensation: Teach her self-calming relaxation methods.

Imagery: Use positive self-visualizations.

Cognition: Try to eliminate categorical imperatives ("shoulds," "oughts," and "musts").

Interpersonal relationships: Administer assertiveness training.

Drugs and biology: Recommend a sensible nutrition and exercise program.

The multimodal maxim is that *breadth is often more important than depth.* The clinician who sinks one or two deep shafts is likely to bypass a host of other issues. It is wiser to address as broad an array of problems as time permits. Through a "ripple effect," a change in one modality tends to generalize to others, but the greater the number of discrete problems that can be overcome, the more profound the eventual outcome is likely to be.

ANOTHER BEHAVIOR THERAPIST'S PERSPECTIVE ON RUTH, by Barbara Brownell D'Angelo, Ph.D.

Introduction

Behavior therapy encompasses a wide variety of specific techniques, including biofeedback training, assertiveness training, desensitization, operant conditioning, modeling, and role playing. The common thread running through these techniques is a focus on finding solutions to current behavioral problems and complaints. The client identifies a specific complaint and, together with the therapist, devises a plan to address it. There is little mystery in the behavioral approach. In addition, since the treatment goals are well defined, it becomes clear early in the therapeutic process how well the therapy is progressing. The therapist's task is to fine-tune the program with constant attention to whether it is working. The behaviorist asks "what," "when," and "how" questions rather than "why" questions.

Basic Assumptions and Their Application

Behavior therapists make six basic assumptions. After listing them, I will show how I apply them in counseling Ruth.

1. Assessment is an ongoing process in behavioral therapy. It begins with the client's complaint, which is then analyzed to determine its antecedents and consequences. The client keeps a record of the frequency and intensity of occurrences, and this becomes the tool in devising a therapeutic plan and in deciding whether the therapy is working.

2. The therapeutic relationship is a powerful reinforcer and is very important if treatment is to succeed. The therapist must be supportive and attentive and must engender a feeling of confidence and trust in the client.
3. The major focus is on the present rather than the past. When the past is discussed, the emphasis is on discovering how it applies to the current situation.
4. Attention is directed toward observable behavior, although this can include not only actions but also feelings and thoughts. Anything that is identifiable, discernible, and quantifiable is fair game.
5. The therapist and client together conduct a careful evaluation of the antecedents and consequences of a behavior in order to determine how best to set up a program of behavioral change. Creativity is crucial because each person presents a unique challenge, and the most effective combination of techniques must be fine-tuned for each individual.
6. The client is encouraged to try new behaviors and, together with the therapist, to devise plans to put the program into effect. During the sessions, the therapist may model the desired behavior, role-playing with the client, and may ask the client to practice the new behavior in the neutral office setting prior to trying it out in real life.

Assessment.   Traditional diagnostic categories are rarely useful to the behavior therapist, because there is no direct relationship between the diagnosis and a specific treatment. However, the therapist may be required to submit a diagnosis in order for the client to qualify for insurance to defray part of the cost of therapy. In such cases, the diagnosis is made but is not a factor in decisions on treatment. There may also be unintended ramifications for clients should they be pinned with a diagnosis of mental disorder. The ethical issues involved with such diagnoses should be fully studied and understood to preclude clients from suffering future consequences. For example, disability, life, and health insurance plans may consider such diagnoses as negative factors in determining future eligibility for insurance.

Given these cautions, if Ruth chooses to participate in a third-party reimbursement process and if a formal diagnosis is required by her insurance carrier, I think that an *adjustment disorder* is most fitting in her case. She evidences clinically significant emotional or behavioral symptoms in response to stressors such as having her children leave home, completing graduate school, and securing a teaching position.

As a behavior therapist, I rely on Ruth for direction by asking what is motivating her to seek therapy. I want to know from her which of her issues are causing her the most discomfort. Rather than theorizing about hidden meanings, I directly ask her what she would like to change.

THERAPIST: Good morning, Ruth. Have a seat.
RUTH: Thank you.

THERAPIST: Would you tell me what brings you here today?

RUTH: I've been in therapy before, and it helped me a lot. I guess I had thought I could use what I'd learned and didn't need any more help.

THERAPIST: And now you're not so sure.

RUTH: Yeah, I'm just not following through on trying to get a job, and I'm feeling more and more upset with myself in general.

THERAPIST: What bothers you about this? Not having a job or the feeling of being upset?

RUTH: Both. I hate moping around, but I feel in my heart that if I got moving on a plan, I wouldn't be so depressed. Then, too, I'm afraid if I really did get a job, I couldn't be there for my family.

THERAPIST: It sounds as if you're not sure what you really want for yourself.

RUTH: You're right. I keep flip-flopping.

THERAPIST: OK. It's important that I understand how you see things. Before we look at this in more detail, could you tell me if you're concerned about any other issues?

RUTH: Well, yes. I was doing great on my weight-control program. I lost almost 12 pounds. And then I just stopped exercising and started stuffing again. I've already gained half of it back.

THERAPIST: So after initially being successful, you're finding yourself backsliding.

RUTH: Sad but true. I started to feel guilty about not getting breakfast for John and the kids. The exercise class was at eight in the morning, so I just dropped out.

THERAPIST: Your children . . .

RUTH: Four of them. They're all teenagers.

THERAPIST: And they expect you to make breakfast for them.

RUTH: Not really. But if I don't, then they'd just skip it altogether.

THERAPIST: It sounds as if you're carrying the full weight of responsibility for your family.

RUTH: I always have. I've always put their needs ahead of mine. It seems I can never find the time or energy to do anything I want to do—I mean, just for me.

Ruth touches on several specific areas she would like to target: getting a job, losing weight, and changing her role as supermom. Upon further discussion it becomes clear that most of her difficulties are a result of her relationships with her husband and children. Her continuous sacrificing for them has created in her a reservoir of resentment, which has, in turn, immobilized her.

THERAPIST: Let me try to summarize what you've been saying. You would like to start putting yourself first, for a change.

RUTH: Yes, but I don't want to feel guilty about it.

THERAPIST: I understand. That's something we'll want to work on. This week, though, I'd like you to do some record-keeping. It'll give us a good idea of what's really going on.

RUTH: You want me to write things down?

THERAPIST: Yes. We'll need some very concrete information to help us get a handle on this. Here's a small binder, divided into two sections. Let's write the day of the week at the top of each page. Now, whenever you do something for yourself, or do something that you really, truly want to do, write it down here. On the other hand, whenever you do something for your husband or your children, describe it on this page. Also, make a note next to each entry about your feelings related to each episode. OK?

RUTH: All right. I think this is going to be interesting.

Ruth has identified her major complaint, but we don't know enough about it yet. After a week of keeping track, she will have a good record of the extent of the problem, and we will be on our way toward designing a program to deal with it. A second benefit of data collection is that her motivation is being put to a test. If she returns the following week with a blank binder and a bushel of excuses, we will wonder if she is truly motivated to make changes. A final reason for asking her to record her interactions is that it will give her a feeling of accomplishment and a sense that she is taking some positive action.

The therapeutic relationship.   Regardless of the therapeutic approach, the chemistry between the therapist and client must be right if progress is to be made. Ruth has benefited from previous therapy, and she therefore has a positive expectation about seeking help. In order to comfirm this feeling, I need to communicate my interest and caring. I do this through attentive body language, reflecting her feelings and concerns, and offering encouragement. During the first session, we discuss her experiences with her previous therapist and her current expectations.

THERAPIST: You said you benefited from your previous therapy. Can you tell me what was particularly helpful?

RUTH: I felt he really cared about me . . . that he was in there pulling for me to succeed.

THERAPIST: And that made a big difference in your willingness to work at things.

RUTH: It did. One thing he did was push me into this exercise class. I really didn't want to join it, and I guess I did it just as a favor to my therapist. But it turned out to be really good for me. I actually looked forward to it. For the first time in years, I made a couple of new friends. Of course, since I stopped going, I've sort of lost touch with them.

THERAPIST: OK. Was there anything else in your previous therapy that seemed to help you?

RUTH: I've been thinking about it a lot. I came to the conclusion that going to a therapist was just about the only thing I allowed myself to do just for me. And I didn't even have to feel guilty about it, because my doctor recommended it.

THERAPIST: So you weren't going for the fun of it. Since it was a medical necessity, that made it OK.

RUTH: Yes, you're right. That made it acceptable.

THERAPIST: You said just a minute ago that your therapy was something you did "just for you." Can you tell me what you mean by that?

RUTH: It was the attention I got. I've always craved attention, but that's the one thing no one's ever given me. My sister always got the honors when we were growing up. My husband is too busy to notice how well I keep the house . . . plus he's not a talkative kind of guy. And of course, there's the kids. I'm not alone in this. I know you can't expect a whole lot of appreciation from your kids.

THERAPIST: So your therapist gave you the attention you needed.

RUTH: An hour a week. We just talked about *me*. It was a real trip.

Ruth's need to be appreciated is a strong motivation for her, and it will facilitate her willingness to make difficult changes. Social approval and attention are apparently powerful reinforcers for her, and this information is crucial when we begin to design her program.

Focus on the present.   We want to concentrate on Ruth's current life and to encourage changes in the present. However, the past contains valuable lessons for the present, and we will therefore call upon past experiences when necessary. A consistent pattern of self-denial characterizes Ruth's daily life. Even she was surprised to recognize the extent of it. At this point, we wish to determine the nature of the problem as she currently experiences it. We are not interested in searching for causative factors in her childhood. We basically want to know "what is going on."

RUTH: Well, here it is—my week in review. Maybe I should sign up to play Joan of Arc.

THERAPIST: Something tells me you were a martyr this week.

RUTH: Not just this week. I hate to say it, but this has been pretty typical. If anything, by the end of the week, I was grasping for things to do to write on the "me" page.

THERAPIST: You started on Tuesday. Let's see what you've got here.

RUTH: It started bright and early on Tuesday. Adam needed cotton balls for a school project, so I drove across town to the all-night grocery. Then I made breakfast and packed lunches for everyone but Jennifer. She snubs brown-bagging.

THERAPIST: This brought you to nine o'clock in the morning.

RUTH: Yes. I don't waste time. Then I cleaned up after everyone. I hate to say it, but I couldn't stand the messes in Susan's and Adam's rooms, so I picked up there too.

THERAPIST: And what were you feeling when you were in their rooms?

RUTH: I guess I felt disgusted . . . ticked off. I mean they're 16 and 17 years old, for heaven's sake. I felt like a servant, a totally unappreciated servant, at that.

THERAPIST: No wonder. Balanced against these 26 entries on Tuesday is one thing you did entirely for yourself. You made yourself a banana split.

RUTH: With a half a jar of maraschino cherries on top.

Now that Ruth is aware of the degree to which she sacrifices for her family and ignores her own needs, we want to begin thinking about making changes. We ask her for some ideas of what she might find enjoyable and ask her to recall activities from her past that gave her pleasure.

THERAPIST: This is a good time to do some brainstorming. Let's write down some of the things you think you might enjoy doing. Does anything come to mind?

RUTH: Well, that banana split wasn't bad.

THERAPIST: All right. Let's put down, "Treat myself to a banana split." What else?

RUTH: I like going out to eat. Let's say, "Go out with John to Sunday brunch."

THERAPIST: So far you only have pleasures that involve food. Can you think of some that don't?

RUTH: How about, "Chat with Meg and Susan during break at exercise class"?

THERAPIST: That's a good one. What else?

RUTH: I don't know. Between taking care of John and the kids and getting my degree at college, I haven't had any time.

THERAPIST: And now you're finishing with your graduate classes.

RUTH: Yes, unfortunately. One instructor in particular made the subject really interesting. I took every class she offered.

THERAPIST: And you didn't feel guilty enjoying it because it was required for your education.

RUTH: Exactly. How did you know?

THERAPIST: Just a guess. What about things in the past that you enjoyed doing?

RUTH: I used to sing in the choir. They say I have a pretty decent voice.

THERAPIST: OK, let's write, "Join the church choir."

RUTH: And right after John and I married, we went on long walks together. I remember that as having been fun.

THERAPIST: Good. Keep going. What else do you remember that was enjoyable?

RUTH: We used to go to the park and have picnics . . . but that's food again, isn't it?

THERAPIST: No problem. You have to eat. Let's get that down, too.

RUTH: Oh, I almost forgot. I used to love taking pictures and arranging them in artistic collages. Gosh, I haven't done that in years.

THERAPIST: This is a nice start. You've come up with several things, some simple to carry out and some—like joining the choir—that would take a lot of time. During the next several days, keep your mind alert to ideas you can add to the list, and jot them down. We'll go over them at our next meeting and make some selections.

RUTH: Do you want a certain number?

THERAPIST: It's entirely up to you, but the more ideas you come up with, the better.

Attention directed to observable behavior. Ruth has observed and recorded interactions with her family. In addition, she made notes on her thoughts and feelings about these interactions as they took place. Midway through the second session, we discuss some alternative behaviors she might try, but we must also address the thoughts and feelings that are causing her such discomfort.

THERAPIST: So this gives us a good idea what happened to your exercise class.

RUTH: No kidding. I obviously can't be in two places at once.

THERAPIST: That's true. But tell me, do you really want to get back into the class?

RUTH: Believe me, I do. If I thought I could leave the family to their own devices, I would.

THERAPIST: It's very important to you that your family have breakfast. But do you have to be there to serve it?

RUTH: Not really. It's more that I feel a need to supervise it so that everyone gets taken care of.

THERAPIST: As a first step, how do you feel about setting out cereal and fruit in the morning before you leave for class—maybe even displaying names at each table setting so they know which plate is for them?

RUTH: I don't know.

THERAPIST: You seem reluctant. Let's try something. Close your eyes for a minute and imagine you've just set breakfast out for your family and you're getting into the car, heading for class.

RUTH: OK. Now what?

THERAPIST: Let this image become as real possible to you, and tell me what you're saying to yourself.

RUTH: I'm saying, "What if Adam doesn't eat what I've put out for him?"

THERAPIST: Good. Keep imagining. Now, what else are you hearing yourself say?

RUTH: I'm thinking, "I'll bet John is grousing because I'm not there to wait on him."

THERAPIST: Anything else?

RUTH: No. These two thoughts just keep repeating.

THERAPIST: All right. Now, tell me what you're feeling.

RUTH: A knot in my stomach . . . kind of a constricted feeling in my chest. I hate that feeling.

THERAPIST: OK. Now, just as an experiment, I'd like you to take control of those two thoughts. Let's start with Adam. I'd like you to say— aloud—"I've done more than enough for them this morning. Adam will eat what he needs." Would you repeat that statement five times, and put some intensity into it.

Ruth repeats the statement aloud, and then I instruct her to repeat it silently until it seems natural to her. We do the same for the next statement, suggesting that she practice the thought "John can take care of himself for breakfast." After several repetitions, I ask Ruth to focus on her feelings.

THERAPIST: What do you feel now?

RUTH: The knot in my stomach is dissolving somewhat. It's still there, but it's much less intense.

THERAPIST: It sounds as if there's a pretty strong connection between your thoughts and the reaction in your stomach.

RUTH: I didn't realize that, but you're right. And you know what? I'm always talking to myself, silently, of course. But I'm always thinking these negative thoughts.

THERAPIST: It's become so habitual that you're probably not aware of them all.

RUTH: That's probably true.

THERAPIST: So it looks as if you have a couple of things to work on this week. First, I'd like you to take this wrist counter, and every time you catch yourself thinking one of those self-defeating thoughts, click it. Like this.

RUTH: So I'll keep track?

THERAPIST: Right. And then go one step further. Just as we've done here today, I'd like you to substitute a positive, self-affirming thought in its place. Do you think you can do that?

RUTH: I'll do it. I can't guarantee I'll catch every thought, but I'll definitely do it.

THERAPIST: No doubt a few of them will slip past your censorship. Just see how many you can catch and turn around.

At this point, further practice is desirable. We take turns being Ruth and substituting positive statements into her "self-talk." This practice should continue until she feels natural and comfortable with it. We may also suggest that she take a step toward trying out a new behavior.

THERAPIST: Now, how do you feel about setting out breakfast for John and the kids and going to the exercise class? Is this something you'd be willing to do maybe one time this week? You don't want to push yourself until you're ready.

RUTH: Hey, life is short. I'll tell you how it goes next week. OK?

THERAPIST: Wonderful. See you then.

Analyzing antecedents and consequences.   One of Ruth's short-term goals is to resume her morning exercise class. I want to assist her by making it easy for her to succeed and ensuring that she will feel positive about the experience. Setting the stage for success—arranging favorable antecedents—is crucial to carrying out the plan.

RUTH: I came very close this week to going back to the class.

THERAPIST: Tell me about it.

RUTH: For a starter, I've really become aware of my negative self-statements. And I pretty much clobbered them each time.

THERAPIST: And did that have any effect on the knot in your stomach?

RUTH: It must have, because I had that sensation only a couple of times this week. It happened while I was fighting with my daughter Jennifer.

THERAPIST: And that was another problem area you wanted to deal with . . .

RUTH: She's just rebelling, and she's been driving me to distraction. But I'm ready to go to the exercise class tomorrow.

THERAPIST: Good. Let's see what we can do to make it a success. There are some things you can do to set the stage. You've already got a good start on retraining your thought patterns. And why not call the two friends you made in the class and talk to them about your return.

RUTH: I could do that. And I'm going to try your idea about setting breakfast out for the family in the morning.

THERAPIST: How about telling each person about the new plan? That'll also help your resolve.

RUTH: Yes, and I thought I'd pack their lunches the evening before.

THERAPIST: I'd also suggest you keep in mind that you've been away before—like the week you spent with your father when he became ill.

RUTH: And the sky didn't fall.

THERAPIST: And it won't fall now, believe me.

We have worked together to structure Ruth's situation so that she will find it easy to attend the exercise class. A related strategy is to build in as many rewards as possible. This is done by ensuring that the consequences of a behavior are rewarding.

THERAPIST: You're going to want to congratulate yourself for your success, to start planting some self-affirmations and repeating them to yourself.

RUTH: OK. That sounds good.

THERAPIST: Can you think of doing something associated with the class? Something you'd enjoy?

RUTH: I remember Sally asked me once if I wanted to join her for a snack after class. Maybe I'll take her up on that.

THERAPIST: Do you think you'd like spending a little time with her?

RUTH: Oh, yes.

THERAPIST: Then by all means do it, and jot down your observations in your notebook. Also, how about keeping a record of the amount of time you exercise—so you can feel proud of yourself? Each time you go, give yourself a star or some other sign of recognition.

RUTH: Why not? I used to do that with the kids, and it pretty much worked for them.

THERAPIST: And then we'll hope some natural rewards will fall into place. You'll feel more fit and trim, and you'll get a few compliments from John. These things can mean a lot.

RUTH: Yes, John did notice last year after I lost those 12 pounds. That felt good.

Trying out new behaviors.   The therapy session provides a neutral setting where behaviors can be practiced without risk. Ruth needs assistance in developing a more assertive stance with her family. The following is one aspect of assertiveness training, a technique that relies heavily on role playing.

THERAPIST: Sometimes you have to ask for what you want. You've said you don't feel comfortable doing that.

RUTH: I have to admit I do a lot of hinting, and then when no one responds, I just mope around feeling sorry for myself.

THERAPIST: Let's do some role playing. First we need to get an idea of how you ask for what you want. Pretend I'm John. Go ahead, be yourself.

RUTH: I'll try. Umm. John? I've joined the exercise class again.

THERAPIST [as John]: Uh-huh.

RUTH: That's about all I get from him, too.

THERAPIST: All right. Now I'll pretend I'm you. [as Ruth]: John, you know I've joined the exercise group. I'd like your support.

RUTH [as John]: Uh-huh.

THERAPIST [as Ruth]: I need your encouragement. I'm not sure you're with me on this, and if you just tell me you support me, it would mean a lot to me.

RUTH [as John]: Like, what should I say?

THERAPIST [as Ruth]: I'd like you to say something like "Way to go" or "Hey, good for you."

THERAPIST: OK, let's break the roles for a minute. Could you see the difference?

RUTH: You seemed more persistent than I would have been, and a lot more direct, that's for sure.

THERAPIST: Right. Also, notice how I expressed my needs. I didn't criticize him or attack him. I just told him what I wanted from him.

RUTH: That hasn't been my style, but I'm willing to try.

THERAPIST: OK, let's do it again. This time, pretend I'm John.

Concluding Comments

Ruth is an exceptionally motivated client with positive expectations about the value of therapy. She shows willingness to take suggestions and follows through on homework assignments. These qualities are especially crucial if behavior therapy is to be effective, because the burden of change is squarely on the shoulders of the client.

Maladaptive behavior develops over many years, beginning in early childhood, and continues to cause problems throughout an individual's life. Therefore, we must have patience when we encounter a person like Ruth, because her behaviors are deeply entrenched. We cannot expect to erase the effects of years of maladaptive behaviors with a few suggestions. Rather, we should expect that she will cling to familiar patterns of behavior as she slowly comes to accept new ways of thinking and being.

Why did Ruth seek therapy in the first place? She was motivated by her emotional pain, of course, but she also had a tremendous need for acknowledgment and support. In order for her therapy to be successful, it is essential that I recognize the sum total of her needs. She would have been unsatisfied had I offered her only advice, directives, and suggestions. Instead, I balanced my directions with a large dose of support and understanding. I wanted her to feel special, accepted, and acknowledged. I wanted to talk "with" her, rather than "at" her.

The behavioral therapist must be somewhat eclectic in order to be effective. The focus is on overt behaviors but also includes thought patterns and emotions. All of these can be articulated and therefore manipulated by the client. Ruth was aware of the strong emotional reactions she felt when she put her own needs before her family's. Unless we address these powerful emotions, we set ourselves up for failure.

It is also important that Ruth have realistic expectations regarding therapy. Permanent change will not come immediately, and she should expect that living well is truly a lifelong process. This doesn't mean that therapy lasts forever. Therapy is seen as an aid in helping her establish more rewarding patterns of behavior. After 10 or 15 weekly sessions, I would recommend her tapering off to monthly meetings. This allows her to become increasingly self-sufficient while guaranteeing therapeutic support for as long as she truly needs it. As she begins to obtain rewards from her positive changes, she will come to depend on her own abilities. My hope for Ruth is that she will learn more effective coping skills that will translate into improved relationships and greater self-acceptance.

JERRY COREY'S WORK WITH RUTH FROM A BEHAVIORAL PERSPECTIVE

Basic Assumption

A basic assumption of the behavioral approach is that therapy is best conducted along systematic and scientific lines. Although behavior therapy represents a variety of principles and therapeutic procedures, its common denominator is a commitment to objectivity and evaluation.

Assessment of Ruth

I very much like beginning with a general assessment of a client's current functioning. This assessment begins with the intake session and continues during the next session if necessary.

Ruth and I come up with two problem areas on which she wants to focus: (1) She feels tense to the point of panic much of the time and wants to learn ways to relax. (2) From the standpoint of her interpersonal relationships, she does not have the skills to ask for what she wants from others, she has trouble in expressing her viewpoints clearly, and she often accepts projects that she does not want to get involved in.

Goals of Therapy

After making the assessment of Ruth's strengths and weaknesses, I clarify with her the behaviors that she wants to increase or decrease in frequency. She will now set specific goals in her two problem areas. Before treatment we establish *baseline data* for those behaviors that she wants to change. The baseline period is a point of reference against which her changes can be compared during and after treatment. By establishing such baseline data, we will be able to determine therapeutic progress. There is continual assessment throughout therapy to determine the degree to which her goals are being effectively met.

The general goal of behavior therapy is to create new conditions for learning. I view Ruth's problems as related to faulty learning. The assumption underlying our therapy is that learning experiences can ameliorate problem behaviors. Much of our therapy will involve correcting faulty cognitions, acquiring social and interpersonal skills, and learning techniques of self-management so that she can become her own therapist. Based on my initial assessment of her and on another session in which she and I discuss the matter of setting concrete and objective goals, we establish the following goals to guide the therapeutic process:

- to learn and practice methods of relaxation
- to learn stress-management techniques
- to learn assertion-training principles and skills

Therapeutic Procedures

Behavior therapy is a pragmatic approach, and I am concerned that the treatment procedures be effective. I will draw on various cognitive and behavioral techniques to help Ruth reach her stated goals. If she does not make progress, I must assume much of the responsibility, because it is my task to select appropriate treatment procedures and use them well. As a behavior therapist I am continually evaluating the results of the therapeutic process to determine which approaches are working. Ruth's feedback in this area is important. I will ask her to keep records of her daily behavior, and I will expect her to become active to accomplish her goals, including working outside the session.

I expect that our therapy will be relatively brief, for my main function is to teach Ruth skills that she can use in solving her problems and living more effectively. My ultimate goal is to teach her self-management techniques, so that she will not have to be dependent on me to solve her problems.

The Therapeutic Process

Elements of the process

The therapeutic process begins with gathering baseline data on the specific goals that Ruth has selected. In her case much of the therapy will consist of learning how to cope with stress and how to be assertive in situations calling for this behavior.

Learning stress-management techniques.   Ruth indicates that one of her priorities is to cope with tensions more effectively. I ask her to list all the specific areas that she finds stressful, and I discuss with her how her own expectations and her self-talk are contributing to her stress. We then develop a program to reduce unnecessary strain and to cope more effectively with the inevitable stresses of daily life.

RUTH: You asked me what I find stressful. Wow! There are so many things. I just feel as if I'm always rushing and never accomplishing what I should. I feel pressured so much of the time.

JERRY: List some specific situations that bring on stress. Then maybe we can come up with some strategies for alleviating it.

RUTH: Trying to keep up with my schoolwork and with the many demands at home at the same time. Dealing with Jennifer's anger toward me and her defiance. Trying to live up to John's expectations and at the same time doing what I want to do. Getting involved in way too many community activities and projects and then not having time to complete them. Dealing with how frazzled I feel in wearing so many hats. Feeling pressured to complete my education. Worrying that I won't be able to find a good teaching job once I get my credential . . . How's that for starters?

JERRY: That's quite a list. I can see why you feel overwhelmed. We can't address all of them at once. I'd like to hear more about what being in these stressful situations is like for you. Tell me about one of these situations, and describe what you feel in your body, what you're thinking at the time, and what you actually do in these times of stress. [I want to get a concrete sense of how she experiences her stress, what factors bring it about, and how she attempts to cope with it.]

RUTH: Well, I often feel that I wear so many hats—I just have so many roles to perform, and there's never enough time to do all that's needed. I often lie awake at night and ruminate about all the things I should be doing. It's awfully hard for me to go to sleep, and then I wake up in the morning after hours of tossing and turning feeling so tired. Then it's even harder for me to face the day.

JERRY: Earlier you mentioned that you have panic attacks, especially at night. I'd like to teach you some simple ways to use the relaxation response just before you go into a full-scale attack. You'll need to identify the cues that appear before a panic attack. I'd then like to teach you some simple and effective relaxation methods. Instead of wasting time lying there trying to sleep, you could be practicing a few exercises. It's important that you practice these self-relaxation exercises every day, for 20 minutes.

RUTH: Oh my! That's 20 minutes of one more thing I have to cram into my already busy schedule. It may add to my stress.

JERRY: Well, that depends on how you approach it.

We talk at some length, because I am afraid that she will make this practice a chore rather than something that she can do for herself and enjoy. She finally sees that it does not have to be a task that she does perfectly but a means of making life easier for her. I then teach her how to concentrate on her breathing and how to do some visualization techniques, such as imagining a very pleasant and peaceful scene. Then, following the guidelines described in Herbert Benson's book *The Relaxation Response*, I provide her with these instructions:

JERRY: Find a quiet and calm environment with as few distractions as possible. Sit comfortably in a chair, and adopt a passive attitude. Rather than worry about performing the technique, simply let go of all thoughts. Repeating a mantra, such as the word *om*, is helpful. With your eyes closed, deeply relax all your muscles, beginning with your feet and progressing up to your face. Relax and breathe.

A week later, Ruth tells me how difficult it was to let go and relax.

RUTH: Well, I didn't do well at all. I did practice every day, and it wasn't as bad as I thought. But it's hard for me to find a quiet place to relax. I was called to the phone several times, and then another time my kids wanted me to do their wash, and on and on. Even when I wasn't disturbed, I found my mind wandering, and it was hard to just get into the sensations of feeling tension and relaxation in my body.

JERRY: I hope you won't be too hard on yourself. This is a skill, and like any skill it will take some time to learn. But it's essential that you block off that 20 minutes in a quiet place without disturbances.

Ruth and I discuss how difficult it is for her to have this time for herself. I reinforce the point that this is also an opportunity to practice asking others for what she wants and seeing to it that she gets it. Thus, she can work toward another of her goals: being able to ask for what she wants.

Learning how to say no. Ruth tells me that she has been a giver all of her life. She gives to everyone but finds it difficult to ask anything for herself. We have been working on the latter issue, with some success. Ruth informs me that she does not know how to say no to people when they ask her to get involved in a project, especially if they tell her that they need her. She wants to talk about her father, especially the ways in which she thinks he has caused her lack of assertiveness. I let her know that I am not really interested in going over past experiences in childhood or in searching for reasons for her present unassertiveness. Instead, I ask her to recall a recent time when she found it difficult to say no and to describe that scene.

RUTH: Last week my son Adam came to me late at night and expected me to type his term paper. I didn't feel like it at all, because I had had a long and hard day, and besides, it was almost midnight. He begged me, saying that it was due the next day and that it would only take me an hour or so. I got irked with him for giving it to me so late, and at first I told him I wasn't going to do it. Then he got huffy and pouty, and I finally gave in. Then I didn't sleep much that night because I was mad at myself for giving in so quickly. But what could I do?

JERRY: You could have done many things. Can you come up with some alternatives?

I want Ruth to search for alternative behaviors to saying yes when it is clear that she wants to say no. She does come up with other strategies, and we talk about the possible consequences of each approach. Then I suggest some behavioral role playing. First, I play the role of Adam, and she tries several approaches other than giving in and typing the paper. Her performance is a bit weak, so I suggest that she play Adam's role, and I demonstrate at least another alternative. I want to demonstrate, by direct modeling, some behaviors that she does not use, and I hope that she will practice them.

As the weeks progress, there are many opportunities for Ruth to practice a few of the assertive skills that she is learning. Then she runs into a stumbling block. A PTA group wants her to be its president. Although she enjoys her membership in the group, she is sure that she does not have time to carry out the responsibilities involved in being the president. In her session she says she is stuck because she doesn't know how to turn the group down, especially since no one else is really available. We again work on this problem by using role-playing techniques. I play the role of the people pressuring her to accept the presidency, and I use every trick I know to tap her guilt. I tell her how efficient she is, how we are counting on her, how we know that she won't let us down, and so on. We stop at critical points and talk about the hesitation in her voice, the guilty look on her face, and her habit of giving reasons to justify her position. I also talk with her about what her body posture is communicating. Then we systematically work on each element of her presentation. Paying attention to her choice of words, her quality of voice, and her style of delivery, we study how she might persuasively say no without feeling guilty later. As a homework assignment I ask her to read selected chapters of the paperback book *Your Perfect Right*, by Alberti and Emmons. There are useful ideas and exercises in this book that she can think about and practice between our sessions.

The next week we talk about what she has learned in the book, and we do some cognitive work. I especially talk with her about what she tells herself in these situations that gets her into trouble. In addition to these cognitive techniques I continue to teach her assertive behaviors by using role playing, behavioral rehearsals, coaching, and practice.

Process commentary

In this approach Ruth is clearly the person who decides what she wants to work on and what she wants to change. She makes progress toward her self-defined goals because she is willing to become actively involved in challenging her assumptions and in carrying out behavioral exercises, both in the sessions and in her daily life. For example, she is disciplined enough to practice the relaxation exercises I have taught her. She learns how to ask for what she wants and to refuse those requests that she does not want to meet, not only by making resolutions but also by regularly keeping a record of the social situations in which she was not as assertive as she would have liked to be. She takes risks by practicing in everyday situations those assertive skills that she has acquired in our therapy sessions. Although I help her learn *how* to change, she is the one who actually chooses to apply these skills, thus making change possible.

Questions for Reflection

1. What are your thoughts about Lazarus's multimodal approach to assessment as a way to begin therapy?
2. What are some of the features that you like best about Lazarus's approach? about D'Angelo's approach? about my approach in working with Ruth? What are some of the basic similarities you see in the three

behavioral approaches? What about some basic differences in style? How might you have proceeded differently, still working within this model, in terms of what you know about Ruth?

3. This model assumes that the therapist's technical skills are essential to behavior change. What are your reactions to this assumption in light of the assumption of some other approaches that the therapeutic relationship itself is a sufficient condition for change?

4. Lazarus succeeded in getting Ruth to agree to take a brisk walk at least three times a week. As a behavior therapist, how would you deal with her if she told you that she had not kept her agreement to carry out her exercise?

5. What is your reaction to both D'Angelo's and my attempts to get Ruth out of therapy as fast as possible so that she can apply self-management skills on her own? What skills can you think of to teach her so that she can be more self-directed?

6. In what ways did Lazarus work with Ruth's past in helping her understand her present condition? What reactions do you have to my lack of interest in exploring the past? Do you think that Ruth's present personal issues can best be taken care of by focusing on learning coping skills? Do you think that for change to occur in her current situation, she must go back to her past and work out unfinished business? Explain.

7. What are your reactions to the manner in which Lazarus conducted the conjoint session with Ruth and John? If you were conducting such a behaviorally oriented session, what homework might you suggest to them as a couple? Do you have any suggestions for specific behavioral assignments for each individual?

8. Identify some specific coping skills that D'Angelo taught Ruth. Assuming that you were to teach her some new skills in dealing with her problems, how might you help her if she were to backslide by getting stuck in some old patterns?

9. Using other behavioral techniques, show how you might proceed with Ruth if you were working with her. Use whatever you know about her so far and what you know about behavior-therapy approaches to show in what directions you would move with her.

10. What specific behavioral changes do you want to make in your life? What behaviors would you like to eliminate or decrease? acquire or increase? Applying behavioral methods to yourself, which specific techniques would be most helpful to you in making these changes?

SALLY: HOPING TO CURE A SOCIAL PHOBIA

Sally is 27 years old, single, and Latina, and she comes from a family of eight children. She supervises employees at a large office of the Internal Revenue Service. She has come to a community mental-health center on the recommendation of a close friend. Although she had many reservations about admitting to herself that she had personal problems, let alone admitting it to someone else, she felt reassured after talking with her friend about her experience in counseling. Sally still has mixed feelings about seeking professional help, for this is not something that she ever saw herself doing. In her culture it is acceptable to talk about personal concerns with family members, with a priest, or perhaps with a very close friend. But it is considered a taboo to talk about such matters with outsiders.

Sally's major presenting problem could be labeled a *social phobia*. She has a persistent and exaggerated fear of being exposed to scrutiny by others in social situations. She fears that she may act in ways that will be humiliating or embarrassing, so she tends to avoid social gatherings. Another major problem is her insomnia. Even though she is tired when she goes to bed at night, she tosses and turns and becomes highly anxious because of her inability to sleep. She goes to work exhausted in the morning and then feels like nodding off when she needs to be alert.

Sally's fears and difficulties in coping with the demands of everyday living are becoming so pressing that she feels she must defy her cultural injunctions and seek professional help. When she told her parents that she wanted to go to counseling, they were offended and took it personally. They tried to persuade her to see the parish priest instead. She respectfully, but with some guilt, declined to follow their advice.

Sally's Self-Presentation

On meeting the counselor, Sally lists many of the fears that she would like to conquer and shares some key themes going on in her life:

> It seems as if I'm afraid of *everything!* I'm very afraid of being in this office now, and my fear of coming here almost kept me from doing it. A good friend who's been to counseling here gave me the push I needed. Actually, she practically forced me to come, at least for one session. I'm afraid of new situations, because I have no idea how I'll react. I'm afraid to go to work, because I have a hard time feeling good about the decisions I make. I'm afraid of speaking out in our staff meetings and expressing my opinions on an issue. I'm so afraid that I'll do some dumb thing and totally embarrass myself. When I have to tell any of the employees that I supervise that they're not doing an adequate job, it takes every bit of my courage to sit down with them. And even then, I worry about what I'll say and how it will come across. If someone at work confronts me, I begin to doubt myself and start backpedaling.
>
> Although I have this trouble at work, it's even more difficult for me to get involved in social situations. I panic at the thought of going to parties or going on a date. I just don't know how to act around people. I break out in a cold sweat just thinking about being in a social situation. Generally, I'm very quiet and unassuming in these situations, because I've been taught that it's not appropriate for a woman to be too assertive. So I keep a lot of what I feel and think to myself.

What else? I guess that I think that by 27 a woman should be married. Often I dream of how nice it would be for me to have a man in my life that I really cared for and who cared for me in return. I'd love to have a family, also. My parents are pressuring me to get engaged to a family friend, Ramon, whom they see as an eligible bachelor. They keep telling me that he's a nice Latino man with a great job. I know they would be so pleased if I got engaged to Ramon, yet I've never felt attracted to him in that way. He's a nice guy and we go out on dates once in a while, but I have a hard time feeling really close to him. Someday I really would like a close friendship with a man. Most of my fears have to do with not knowing what's appropriate or expected of me when I'm with people—especially when I'm with men.

My Way of Working with Sally as a Behavior Therapist

I view the therapeutic relationship as a collaborative one. I do not view therapy as merely a matter of my being the all-knowing expert who makes decisions for a passive client. Instead, from our first until our final session, Sally and I will work together toward goals that we have agreed will guide our sessions—if, in fact, she decides to enter counseling with me. At the outset my procedures will include the following:

- During the initial session I will explore with Sally what it is like for her to come to the center for counseling as well as her expectations, reservations, and hopes.
- I will explain the nature and purpose of counseling goals and the importance of making those goals specific and concrete.
- Sally will decide on the specific changes or goals she desires as a result of her relationship with me.
- Together we will explore the feasibility of her stated goals.
- Both of us will identify and discuss any risks associated with these goals.
- We will discuss the possible advantages of counseling as a way of meeting these stated goals.
- By the end of the initial session, I hope, Sally and I will have made one of the following decisions: to continue counseling for a specified number of sessions, to reconsider her goals, to evaluate whether counseling is appropriate at this time and whether she is willing to actively work at achieving her goals (both in the sessions and in her daily life), or to seek a referral to another therapist or another agency.

Dealing with Sally's immediate feelings and thoughts.   Some of the things that I know about Sally are important to attend to during the first session. I am aware that she comes to the office with some reluctance and only after the goading of a close friend. As a place to begin, I ask her how it was for her to call and make the appointment and what it was like for her as she walked into the waiting room. Building trust with her involves talking about her reservations about seeking counseling, about talking to a "stranger," and about the difficulties that she had to overcome simply to be in the office now. Some questions that I ask are: "What would you most hope to get from this session or from the next several sessions? What is going on in your life now that prompted you to take the action of coming here today? What expectations did you have in mind after you talked to your friend?"

After we have had a chance to talk for a time, I invite her to let me know how she feels about our exchange so far. This is especially important because I know she has difficulty in encountering men and because she said that she could never see herself talking personally to a "stranger." In several ways I could be a stranger. She is a 27-year-old, Latina administrator, and I am a 58-year-old, white, male psychologist of Italian background. The fact that we differ in age, cultural background, and gender could influence a counseling relationship. Although I do not automatically assume that she would feel more comfortable with a younger, Latina counselor, I still need to be alert to her reactions to me and my reactions to her. This certainly may not be discussed fully at the first session, but it may be introduced as a topic for discussion if it seems appropriate.

Goal setting and deciding on a course of action.   Sally and I work at narrowing down her goals. Like many other clients she is approaching her therapy with global and fuzzy aims. It is my task to help her formulate clear and concrete goals, so that she and I will know what we are working toward and will have a basis for determining how well the therapy is working. When I ask her what she wants from therapy, for example, she replies with statements such as these: "I want to learn to communicate better. I want to be able to state my opinions without being afraid. I don't do very well in social situations. I'd like to get over feeling scared all the time. I wish I could go to bed and sleep instead of just lying there." Although her goals are general, they do relate to becoming more effective in social situations. I can facilitate her moving from global to specific goals by asking her: "Whom in your life do you have trouble talking to? Are there any particular people to whom you find it difficult to say what you'd like to say? What are some situations in which you have problems in being assertive? In what social situations don't you do well? How would you like to change in these situations? Would you tell me about a few specific fears you experience? When you are frightened, what do you tell yourself? And what do you do at these times? What would you like to do differently? When you are unable to sleep, what are some of the things that you feel or think? If you were able to sleep better, how do you think your life would be different?" My line of questioning is aimed at helping her translate fuzzy goals into clear statements pertaining to what she is thinking, feeling, and doing (and ways that she would like to think, feel, and behave differently).

Eventually, Sally and I draw up a contract that is geared to helping her develop a course of action to attain her goals. We determine that the basis of her contract will be the following goals: She will work on *identifying* and *lessening* (or, ideally, removing) her unrealistic fears. She will identify specific manifestations of unassertive behaviors on her part, which include her difficulty in expressing her opinions, in making contacts with people, in turning down others when that is what she wants to do, and in making her wants and needs clearly known to others. She will experiment with new behaviors, both in the therapy sessions and in daily life. Practicing these behaviors will lead to *increasing* her repertoire of social skills, especially her *assertive behavior*.

Because it will take some time to learn and practice skills related to Sally's stated goals, we discuss a realistic time frame for therapy. She decides to commit herself to a series of six one-hour individual counseling sessions. This kind of structuring will encourage her to evaluate her progress after each session and will serve to keep her focused.

Sally learns systematic desensitization.   Sally initiates a discussion about dealing with her fears relating to men. She tends to avoid men, mainly because she is frightened of them. She is both put off by them and attracted to them, and she has the dual fear of being rejected by them and being accepted. She thinks that she can handle rejection easier than acceptance; she wonders what she would do if a man actually liked and desired her and if he wanted an intimate relationship.

At this point I work with Sally on clarifying her values. Before using behavioral techniques, I believe, it is essential that she become clear about what she wants, so that she is freely deciding on her behavioral goals. After examining her values, she says that she respects her parents and that it hurts her that she does not meet their expectations. Specifically, she feels guilty that she is not engaged to Ramon, yet she knows that this is not what she wants. We discuss possible ways in which she can show regard for her family yet at the same time do what is right for her. Here, role playing is useful. I invite her to talk to me as her father, which gives us an opportunity to deal further with her self-talk about pleasing him. This role playing helps her sort out her values from what her father wants for her.

Sally also says that she would like to be free enough to go to parties, to accept dates, and to initiate social contacts with selected men. It is clear to her that initiating these contacts is particularly difficult because of her socialization, which has taught her that "proper" women do not behave in this manner. She hopes to learn how to assertively say what she wants and does not want, which is also going against her cultural conditioning.

We then proceed with systematic-desensitization procedures, which start with a behavioral analysis of situations that evoke anxiety in her. We then construct a hierarchy of her anxieties by ranking them in order, beginning with the situation that evokes the least anxiety and ending with the worst situation that she can imagine. The following is her hierarchy of fears:

1. She sees a man across the room to whom she is attracted.
2. They are sitting together in a room.

3. They are sitting together, and he initiates a conversation with her.
4. He invites her to go on a date.
5. She accepts the date.
6. She goes on a date.
7. He asks her to go to his apartment after a party.
8. They express a mutual attraction toward each other and plan to go on another date.
9. They have an intimate realtionship, which proves to be short-lived.
10. They become intimate with each other and he expresses his desire to continue developing the relationship.

I then teach Sally some basic relaxation procedures, which she practices until she is completely relaxed in the session. I ask her to select a peaceful scene where she would like to be. She picks a lake in the forest. We proceed with the relaxation exercise until she is fully relaxed, has her eyes closed, and has the peaceful scene in her mind.

I describe a series of scenes to Sally and ask her to imagine herself in each of them. I present a neutral scene first. If she remains relaxed, I ask her to imagine the *least anxiety-arousing* scene she set up in her hierarchy (seeing a man whom she found pleasant on the far side of a room). I move progressively up the hierarchy until she signals by raising her index finger that she is experiencing anxiety, at which time I ask her to switch off that scene and become very relaxed and imagine herself at her lake. We continue until we progress to the *most anxiety-arousing* scene in her hierarchy (imagining an intimate relationship with a man who wants to continue the relationship).

In our therapy sessions we continue the desensitization procedure until Sally is able to imagine this "worst" scene without experiencing anxiety. Basically this procedure consists of combining an incompatible stimulus and response. We pair the relaxation exercises and the imagining of a pleasant scene with scenes that evoke anxiety, until gradually the anxiety-provoking stimuli lose their potency. Now that we have successfully desensitized her of her fears of relating to a man she perceives as attractive on an imaginary level, we hope that she is ready to try new behavior in a real-life situation.

Sally Goes on a Date

As a behavior therapist I believe in the value of assignments. These are not activities that I pick out as good for Sally. Rather, *she* decides on some new behaviors that she would like to experiment with outside of our sessions. Then she applies what she has learned in therapy to a social situation in the hope of acquiring new social skills and overcoming her inhibitions and negative self-talk. She tells me that she has decided to ask Julio, whom she met through her friend, to the upcoming office Christmas party.

Before she actually carries out this assignment, we examine what she is telling herself before inviting him. She recognizes that she is setting herself up for failure by telling herself that he probably will not want to go and that if he does accept, it is only because he feels sorry for her. So we do some additional cognitive work that will lead to positive expectancies on her part. Before she asks Julio to the party, she practices her relaxation exercises and calms herself so that anxiety will not interfere with what she wants to do.

When Sally returns to her session the next week, she reports that all went well. She is feeling an increasing sense of confidence and is willing to tackle new social situations that are more difficult.

A Commentary

Sally's therapy began with assessment, and at our last session we assess the degree to which she has met her goals. We also review what she has learned in these sessions as well as what she has done in various situations at school, at work, and at home. Our focus now is on consolidating what she has learned and helping her translate it into future real-life situations. I suggest that she continue by reading self-help books, doing her daily relaxation exercises, giving herself behavioral assignments, monitoring and assessing her behaviors, and keeping a behavioral log in her journal. Finally, she agrees to join a ten-week assertion-training group designed to help students improve their social skills. In this way she is able to continue what we have begun in these sessions.

Follow-Up: You Continue as Sally's Therapist

After my six individual sessions with Sally, she enters the ten-week assertion-training group. Assume that she has now finished this group and consults you for further counseling.

1. What are your reactions to the very structured approach I used with Sally? To what degree would you be comfortable using such an approach, and how effective do you think you would be?
2. What are your reactions to the specific techniques that I employed with Sally? What other (behavioral) techniques can you think of that you might use? What general direction do you see yourself taking with her?
3. What cultural variables might you be alert to in this case? Some of the clues provided initially are these: Sally is reluctant to talk about her personal problems to people outside of her family; she has mixed feelings about admitting that she needs professional help; she has a desire to follow the traditions and expectations of her family; and she is struggling with a cultural injunction that says that women should not be

too direct and too assertive. How might you work with any of these themes?

4. What advantages, if any, would there be if Sally saw a female therapist? What factors would determine whether it might be best that she see a Latino therapist?

5. If you are of a different gender and have a different ethnic background from Sally, how might this be for you as a counselor? Given what you know of her case, would you anticipate any difficulties in establishing a rapport with her?

6. What factor in yourself do you see that might contribute to or detract from your effectiveness in working as Sally's therapist?

RECOMMENDED SUPPLEMENTARY READINGS

Alberti, R. E., & Emmons, M. L. (1990). *Your perfect right: A guide to assertive behavior* (6th ed.). San Luis Obispo, CA: Impact. Here is my recommendation for those who want a single book on the principles and techniques of assertion training. The book is clearly written, with many examples of ways of acquiring assertive skills.

Benson, H. (1976). *The relaxation response.* New York: Avon. This national best-seller is a readable and useful guide to developing simple meditative and other relaxation procedures. Particularly helpful are the author's summaries of the basic elements of meditation (pages 110–111) and methods of inducing the relaxation response (pages 158–166).

Lazarus, A. A. (1989). *The practice of multimodal therapy.* Baltimore: Johns Hopkins University Press. An interesting, easy-to-read, and highly informative book. The author describes a wide variety of behavioral techniques and shows how such diverse procedures can be integrated into an eclectic framework.

Lazarus, A. A., & Lazarus, C. N. (1991). *Multimodal life-history inventory.* Champaign, IL: Research Press. This is a comprehensive inventory that allows for an assessment of a wide range of problems throughout the BASIC I.D.

Spiegler, M. D., & Guevremont, D. C. (1993). *Contemporary behavior therapy* (2nd ed.). Pacific Grove, CA: Brooks/Cole. This is a comprehensive and up-to-date treatment of basic principles and applications of the behavior therapies, as well as a fine discussion of ethical issues. Specific chapters deal with behavioral assessment, modeling therapy, systematic desensitization, cognitive restructuring, and cognitive coping skills.

Watson, D. L., & Tharp, R. G. (1993). *Self-directed behavior: Self-modification for personal adjustment* (6th ed.). Pacific Grove, CA: Brooks/Cole. This book is aimed at assisting readers to achieve control over their life. Specific steps are described for setting up behavioral self-management programs.

CHAPTER NINE

Case Approach to Cognitive-Behavior Therapy

A RATIONAL EMOTIVE BEHAVIOR THERAPIST'S PERSPECTIVE ON RUTH, by Albert Ellis, Ph.D.

Assumptions

The name of rational-emotive therapy (RET) has been changed to rational emotive behavior therapy (REBT) to more clearly indicate the interactive nature of this approach, which emphasizes the unity among the cognitive, emotive, and behavioral dimensions of human functioning. REBT assumes that people like Ruth do *not* get disturbed by the unrealistic and illogical standards they learned (from their family and culture) during their childhood but that they largely disturb themselves by the dogmatic, rigid "musts" and commands that they creatively construct about these standards and values and about the unfortunate events that occur in their lives. Ruth is a good case in point, because she has not only accepted some of the fundamentalist ideas of her parents (which innumerable fundamentalist-reared children adopt without becoming disturbed) but also rigidly *insists* that she *has* to follow them while simultaneously *demanding* that she *must* be herself and *must* lead a self-fulfilling, independent existence. She could easily neuroticize herself with *either* of these contradictory commands. By devoutly holding *both* of them, she is really in trouble! As REBT shows, transmuting any legitimate goals and preferences into absolutist "musts" will usually lead to self-denigration, rage, or self-pity, and Ruth, as I show below, seems overtly or covertly to have all these neurotic feelings.

Assessment of Ruth

Ruth has a number of goals and desires that most therapies, including REBT, would consider legitimate and healthy, including the desire to have a good, stable marriage, to care for her family members, to be thinner and more attractive, to keep her parents' approval, to be a competent teacher, and to discover what she really wants to do in life and largely follow her personal bents. Even though some of these desires are somewhat contradictory, they would probably not get her into serious trouble as long as she only held them as *preferences*, because she could then make some compromises.

Thus, Ruth could choose to be *somewhat* devoted to her husband and children, and even to her parents, but *also* determined to pursue a teaching career and to follow her own nonfundamentalist religious views and practices. She would then fail to lead a *perfectly* conflict-free and happy life but would hardly be in great turmoil. However, like practically all humans (yes, whether they are reared very conservatively or liberally), she has a strong (probably innate) tendency to take some of her important values and to dogmatically "sacredize" them. From early childhood onward, she antiscientifically concluded: "Because I want my parents' approval, I completely need it!" "Because I love my children, I have to be thoroughly devoted to them!" "Because I enjoy thinking for myself and doing my own thing, I have to do so at practically all times!" "Because I'd like to be thinner and more attractive, I've got to be!"

With grandiose, perfectionist fiats like these, Ruth takes her reasonable, often achievable, goals and standards and transmutes them into absolutist "musts." She thereby almost inevitably makes herself—that's right, *makes* herself—panicked, depressed, indecisive, and often inert. Additionally, when she sees that she feels emotionally upset and is not acting in her best interests, she irrationally upsets herself about *that*. She strongly—and foolishly—tells herself, "I must not be panicked," instead of, "I wish I were not panicking myself, but I am. Now how do I *un*panic myself?" She then feels panicked about her panic. And she rigidly insists, "I have to be decisive and do my own thing." Then she feels like a worm about her worminess! This self-castigation about her neurotic symptoms makes her even more neurotic and less able to see exactly what she is thinking and doing to create these symptoms.

As a rational emotive behavior therapist, I assess Ruth's problems and her belief system about these problems as follows. She asks certain questions that lead to practical problems:

- "How much shall I do for others, and how much for myself?"
- "How can I exercise and keep on a diet?"
- "How can I be a teacher and still get along well with my husband?"
- "How can I get along with my parents and still not follow their fundamentalist views?"
- "How can I benefit from therapy and live with the things I may discover about myself when undergoing it?"
- "How can I be myself and not harm my husband and kids?"

She has certain rational beliefs that lead to healthy feelings of concern and frustration:

- "If I do more things for myself, people may not like me as much as I want them to. Too bad!"
- "Exercising and dieting are really difficult. But being fat and ugly is even more difficult."
- "If I get a teaching job, I may antagonize my husband. But I can stand that and still be happy."
- "My parents will never like my giving up fundamentalism, and that's sad. But it's not awful."
- "If I find out unpleasant things about myself in therapy, that'll be tough. But I can also benefit from that discovery."
- "Being myself at the expense of my husband and kids is selfish. But I have a right to a reasonable degree of selfishness."

She has certain irrational beliefs that lead to unhealthy feelings of anxiety and depression and to self-defeating behaviors of indecision and inertia:

- "I must not do more things for myself and dare not antagonize others."
- "Exercise and dieting are too hard and shouldn't be that hard!"
- "If my husband hates my getting a teaching job, that would be awful!"
- "I can't stand my parents criticizing me if I give up fundamentalism."
- "I would be a thoroughly rotten person if therapy revealed bad things about me!" "I must never be selfish, for if I am, I'm no good."

She has certain irrational beliefs that lead to secondary disturbances (panic about panic, depression about depression):

- "I must not be panicked!"
- "It's awful to be depressed."
- "I'm no good because I'm indecisive."

Key Issues

The key issues in most neurotic feelings and behaviors, and those that are suspected and looked for by me and other REBT practitioners, are (1) self-deprecation, stemming from the irrational belief that "*I* must perform well and be approved of by significant others"; (2) the irrational insistence that "*you* [other people] must treat me kindly and considerately"; and (3) the irrational idea that "the *conditions* under which I live have to be comfortable and easy."

Ruth seems to have the first of these disturbances, because she keeps demanding that she be giving and lovable, that she be thin and beautiful, that she be a good daughter, that her "badness" not be uncovered in therapy, and that she make only good and proper decisions. With these perfectionist commands, she leads a self-deprecating, anxious existence.

Ruth also seems to have some unacknowledged (and sometimes overt) rage, stemming from her underlying insistence that her husband not expect her to be a "good wife," that her parents not demand that she be a fundamentalist, and that everyone stop criticizing her for trying to be herself.

Finally, Ruth has low frustration tolerance and self-pity, resulting not from her desires but from her dire needs to lose weight without going to the trouble of dieting and exercising, to have a guarantee that she won't die, to have the security of marriage even though she has a boring relationship with her husband, to be sure that therapy will be comfortable, and to have a magical, God-will-take-care-of-me solution to her problems.

Because Ruth strongly holds the three basic irrational ideas (dogmatic "musts") that REBT finds at the root of neurosis and because some of her demands—like those that she be herself *and* be quite self-sacrificial—are contradictory, I imagine that she will be something of a difficult customer and will require about a year of individual therapy and perhaps some additional group therapy. But because she has already taken some big risks and worked at changing herself, I predict a good prognosis despite her strong tendency to create self-defeating beliefs.

Applying Therapeutic Techniques

REBT invariably includes a number of cognitive, emotive, and behavioral methods. As I work with Ruth, I use these main methods:

Cognitive techniques of REBT.   I show Ruth how to discover her rational preferences and distinguish them from her irrational "musts" and demands. Then I teach her how to scientifically dispute these demands and change them back into appropriate preferences. I encourage her to create some rational coping statements and inculcate them many times into her philosophy—for example, "I want to be a caring mother and wife, but I also have the right to care for myself." I help her do REBT "referenting"— that is, making a list of the disadvantages of overeating and nondieting and thinking about them several times a day. I also have her do reframing to see that her losing some of her husband's and children's love has its good as well as its bad sides. I encourage her to use some of REBT's psychoeducational adjuncts—books, pamphlets, cassettes, lectures, and workshops. I show her the advantages of teaching REBT to others, such as to her husband, children, and pupils, so that she will better learn it herself. I discuss with her the advantages of creating for herself a vital, absorbing interest in some long-range project, such as helping other people guiltlessly give up their parental fundamentalist teachings.

A specific dialogue I have with Ruth to implement the cognitive technique of helping her dispute her irrational beliefs goes as follows:

RUTH: Because I love my children, I have to be thoroughly devoted to them.

THERAPIST: That's an interesting conclusion, but how does it follow from the observation, which I assume is true, that you really do love your children?

RUTH: Well, isn't it right and ethical to be kind and helpful to one's children?

THERAPIST: Of course it is. You brought them into the world without asking them to be born, and you'd be quite unethical and irresponsible if you didn't devote considerable time and energy to them. But why *must* you be ethical? What law of the universe says you always *have* to be?

RUTH: My own law says so—and that of many other people.

THERAPIST: Fine. But why do you have to always keep your own laws? Actually, *do* you?

RUTH: Well, no. Not always.

THERAPIST: And do other people always keep their own and their culture's laws?

RUTH: No, not always.

THERAPIST: So obviously, although it's highly desirable and moral for you to care for your children, is it absolutely necessary that you do so?

RUTH: No, I guess not.

THERAPIST: But it still is highly desirable. What is the difference between something being preferable and desirable and its being utterly necessary?

RUTH: I see. Quite a difference!

THERAPIST: Right. And no matter how much you love them, do you always have to be thoroughly devoted to them?

RUTH: No, but it's still desirable.

THERAPIST: I'm not even sure of that. Do you see why?

RUTH: Mmm. You're questioning my desire to be thoroughly devoted.

THERAPIST: Yes, I am.

RUTH: Good objection. If I were thoroughly devoted to them, I wouldn't have the time and energy to love my husband or my parents. I've never thought about that.

THERAPIST: And how about yourself?

RUTH: Yes, myself, too. Completely loving them would leave little time left for me.

THERAPIST: And would be somewhat obsessive/compulsive.

RUTH: Right. It would.

THERAPIST: And how realistic would thorough devotion be?

RUTH: Thoroughly unrealistic. I need time for other important things.

THERAPIST: So your dire need to be thoroughly devoted to your children doesn't stem from your love for them, doesn't follow from any law of the universe, and is impractical and unrealistic. Right?

RUTH: I think so. But I'd better give this more thought.

THERAPIST: By all means. Don't accept my conclusions. Think out your own. I, your parents, and other authorities may well be wrong.

RUTH: Wrong for me.

THERAPIST: Exactly. Think for yourself and out of your own experience.

RUTH: My own experience?

THERAPIST: Yes. If you strongly believe that you absolutely must be completely devoted to your children, what results will you probably get?

RUTH: I'll feel very anxious about doing what I supposedly must do and depressed in case I don't.

THERAPIST: Yes, your *must*urbation probably won't work.

RUTH: It certainly hasn't up to now.

THERAPIST: No, so try to forcefully dispute it, as we've just been doing.

RUTH: By questioning its logic and realism?

THERAPIST: Yes, and by showing yourself that it just won't work. It won't help your husband, your children—or you.

RUTH: Especially me.

Emotive techniques of REBT.   I recommend that Ruth use some of the main emotive, evocative, and dramatic methods that I have found effective in REBT, such as these:

- She can forcefully and powerfully tell herself rational coping statements: "I do not (definitely *not*) need my parents' approval, though I would certainly prefer to have it!"
- She can tape a rigorous debate with herself, in which she actively disputes one of her irrational "musts." Then she can listen to her disputation to see not only if its content is good but also if its force is effective.
- She can do rational-emotive imagery, by imagining one of the worst things that could happen to her—for example, her father strongly berating her for her nonfundamentalist views. Then she can work on her feelings so that she first gets in touch with the horror and self-downing she inappropriately feels and then changes it to the healthy negative feelings of sorrow and regret.
- She can do some of the famous REBT shame-attacking exercises, whereby she publicly does something she considers shameful, foolish, or ridiculous and simultaneously works on herself not to feel ashamed while doing it.
- She can learn to receive unconditional acceptance from me, no matter how badly she is behaving in and out of therapy. I can show her how to always—yes, always—accept herself, whether or not she does well.
- We can do role playing, where I play her irate father and she plays herself, to see how she can cope with his severe criticism. In the course of it we stop the playing from time to time to see what she is telling herself to make herself anxious and depressed.
- We can practice reverse role playing, where I stick rigidly to some of her irrational beliefs and encourage her to argue me out of them.
- She can use humor to rip up her irrational beliefs, especially singing to herself some of my humorous songs.

In one session with Ruth I use one of the emotive techniques of REBT:

THERAPIST: We've been disputing your irrational belief that because you love your children, you have to be thoroughly devoted to them. You could also use one of our popular emotional techniques, rational-emotive imagery. Would you like me to show you how to use this exercise?

RUTH: Yes, I would.

THERAPIST: OK, close your eyes—just easily close them.

RUTH: All right.

THERAPIST: Now vividly imagine one of the worst things that could happen to you. Imagine that you're not thoroughly devoted to your children—in fact, that you're somewhat neglecting them. Vividly imagine that they're complaining about this and that your husband and your mother are also chiding you severely for this neglect. Can you vividly imagine this happening?

RUTH: Definitely. I can clearly picture it.

THERAPIST: Good. Now, how do you honestly feel in your gut and in your heart? What is your honest feeling?

RUTH: Very guilty. Depressed. Self-critical.

THERAPIST: Good. Really get in touch with those negative feelings. Feel them. Strongly feel them!

RUTH: I really feel them. Quite strongly.

THERAPIST: Good. Now, keeping the same image—don't change it—make yourself feel *only* sorry and disappointed about what's happening but not guilty, not depressed, not self-downing. Only sorry and disappointed, which are healthy and appropriate negative feelings, instead of guilty, depressed, and self-downing, which are unhealthy and inappropriate negative feelings. You control your feelings, so you can change them. So let me know when you're only feeling sorry and disappointed.

RUTH: I'm having a hard time getting there.

THERAPIST: Yes, I know. But you can do it. You can definitely change your feelings.

RUTH: I'll try.

THERAPIST: Fine!

RUTH [after a pause of two minutes]: I changed them.

THERAPIST: And now you feel only sorry and disappointed, not guilty or depressed?

RUTH: Yes, I do.

THERAPIST: Good! How did you change your feelings? What did you do to change them?

RUTH: I told myself: "It's too bad that my children, my husband, and my mother are chiding me for neglecting the children, but I'm not sure I *am* being neglectful. Even if I am, that's bad, that's wrong of me, but that behavior doesn't make me a rotten person. I'll try to be less neglectful, while not being overly devoted to my children. But if I'm still criticized, it's just too bad—not the end of the world. I can take this criticism and still have a good life."

THERAPIST: Excellent! Now what I'd like to see you do is to help yourself by repeating this exercise every day for the next 20 or 30 days. Remember, it only took you about two minutes to change your unhealthy feelings of guilt and depression to healthy negative feelings of sorriness and disappointment. So repeat this every day, using the same excellent coping statement that you used this time or using several other similar coping statements that will occur to you if you keep doing this rational-emotive imagery. If you keep doing this, I think you'll see at the end of 10, 20, or 30 days, when you imagine this bad event with your children happening or when some unfortunate activating event actually does occur, you'll tend to feel automatically—yes, automatically—sorry and disappointed instead of unhealthily guilty and depressed about it.

RUTH: You think that will really help me?

THERAPIST: Yes, I'm fairly sure it will. So will you try it to help yourself?

RUTH: Yes, I will.

THERAPIST: Great. Now, if you stop doing this exercise, because you think it's too hard to continue it or something like that, you can always challenge your irrational belief that it must be easy and that you shouldn't have to do it to improve. You can also use reinforcement methods to encourage you to keep doing it.

RUTH: How do I do that?

THERAPIST: Very simply. What, for example, do you enjoy doing that you do practically every day of the week?

RUTH: Really enjoy?

THERAPIST: Yes, really enjoy regularly.

RUTH: Uh, reading.

THERAPIST: Fine. No reading, then, for the next 20 or 30 days, until after you do rational-emotive imagery for the day and change your feelings of guilt and depression to those of sorriness and disappointment. Is that OK?

RUTH: Yes, that's OK.

THERAPIST: And if that doesn't work, though it probably will, you can enact a penalty when you don't practice your rational-emotive imagery.

RUTH: A penalty?

THERAPIST: Yes. For example, what do you hate doing—some task or chore that you usually avoid doing because you don't like it?

RUTH: Well—uh—cleaning the toilet.

THERAPIST: Good. If, during the next 30 days, your bedtime arrives and you haven't done your rational-emotive imagery exercise, you can make yourself clean your toilet for an hour.

RUTH: That would work! I'm sure I'll do the exercise every day.

THERAPIST: Fine!

Behavioral techniques of REBT.   As with virtually all REBT clients, I stress several behavioral methods with Ruth, including these:

- I show her how to select and perform *in vivo* desensitization assignments, like registering for education courses despite her anxiety about her family's disapproval.
- I encourage her to do what she is afraid to do—for example, to talk to her husband about her career goals many times until she thoroughly loses her irrational fears of his disapproval.
- I encourage her to reinforce herself with some enjoyable pursuits, such as reading or music, only after she has completed her difficult-to-do homework: And if she is truly lax about doing it, I urge her sometimes to penalize (but never damn) herself with an unpleasant chore, such as getting up an hour earlier than usual.
- I plan with her, and supervise her carrying out, practical goals, such as arranging for help with her household tasks.
- If she starts getting over her emotional hangups but has skill deficiencies, I help her acquire missing skills, such as assertiveness, communicating well, or decision making.

In one session I show Ruth how to use one of REBT's action-oriented techniques:

RUTH: How will I deal with my panic and—as you say—my panic about panicking?

THERAPIST: Good question. First, let's deal with your panic about your panic. Because of this secondary symptom, you often avoid situations where you might panic, even though it would be good to participate in them. Right?

RUTH: Yes. I especially avoid seeing or talking to my father, who's critical of my handling of the children and almost everything else. So I rarely call him, and when he calls, I get my family members to say I'm out when I'm really not.

THERAPIST: That's a good example. By avoiding these calls, what are you telling yourself?

RUTH: If he criticizes me, I'll panic, and that would be awful! I must not panic.

THERAPIST: Right. But every time you avoid speaking to your father, you reinforce these irrational beliefs and thereby make yourself *more* prone to panic about being panicked.

RUTH: You're right about that. Whenever I even think of talking to him, I panic.

THERAPIST: So the first thing you can do is to say to yourself, many times and very strongly: "Panicking is very uncomfortable, but it is not horrible. It's only inconvenient."

RUTH: That will cure me?

THERAPIST: Not exactly, but it will help a lot. In addition, deliberately arrange to talk to your father *more*. Do, as we say in REBT, what you're afraid of doing. Act, as well as think, against your phobia of panicking.

RUTH: But won't that make me panic more?

THERAPIST: It may, at first. But if you keep doing what you're terrifying yourself about—talking to your critical father—and convince yourself at the same time that your panic is *only* inconvenient, not awful, you will significantly decrease your panic about your panicking.

RUTH: Will my original panic about my father's criticism decrease, too?

THERAPIST: Most likely it will, and it may even disappear completely. For you were originally panicked about his criticism but then made yourself so panicked about your panic that this secondary symptom became more important than your primary one and actually helped keep it alive. So if you surrender the panic about panic, your original horror of criticism may well disappear, too. If it doesn't, just go back to the disputing, which we previously discussed, of the irrational belief that criticism makes you a rotten person and that you can't stand it.

RUTH: So I'd better think and act against my panic?

THERAPIST: Yes, think and act, think and act against it. Against your original panic and your panic about your panic.

RUTH: Sounds good. I'll try it.

Process commentary

As can be seen in these typical excerpts, rational emotive behavior therapists have collaborative, Socratic dialogues with their clients and try to help them think, feel, and behave against their disturbances and, as they do so, to try to gain positive growth and self-fulfillment in accordance with their self-chosen goals, values, and purposes.

In using any or all of these REBT techniques with Ruth, I do not merely try to help her ameliorate her presenting symptoms (panic, guilt, and indecisiveness) but also try to help her make a profound philosophical change. My goal is for her to acknowledge her own construction of her emotional problems, minimize her other related symptoms, and maintain her therapeutic progress. By the time my therapy with Ruth ends, I hope, she will have strongly internalized and kept regularly using the three main insights of REBT:

1. "I mainly emotionally and behaviorally upset myself about unfortunate conditions in my life, and I largely do so by constructing rigid 'musts' and commands about these conditions."

2. "No matter when I originally started to upset myself and no matter who helped me do so, I'm now disturbed because of my present *mus*turbatory beliefs."

3. "To change my irrational thinking, my inappropriate feelings, and my dysfunctional behaviors, I'd better give up all magical solutions and keep working and practicing—yes, keep working and practicing—for the rest of my life."

One of Ruth's main problems is learning to try to be "herself" and at the same time to resist conforming too much to social rules that tell her that she must be a "good woman," must be a "thin woman," and must be a "good fundamentalist." Although she theoretically has the right to avoid following these social rules, she will tend to feel guilty and she will tend to get in some amount of trouble with her family of origin and her current family if she decides to "truly" be herself. By using REBT and trying to follow her strong preferences without turning them into absolutist demands, she can probably determine how to largely, but not completely, be herself and at the same time largely, but not completely, avoid antagonizing her parents, her husband, and her children. REBT encourages her to lead a balanced life in these respects. But in being an individual, she will have to select the kind of balance she desires and will have to accept the consequences of her choices.

After working with Ruth for several sessions, I would say that she definitely has a panic disorder and is also definitely dysthymic. I see her as someone with a personality disorder rather than as a "nice neurotic." She is very troubled and conflicted, but she has the ability and, I hope, the determination to work through her main problems. I like working with clients like Ruth, because I find them to be quite open to help. If she is willing to keep working to uphold the antidisturbance theories and practices of REBT, I can't guarantee that she will significantly change and stay changed, but I can confidently accord her a high degree of probability. She has already chosen not to follow some of the rigid rules of her family and her culture and is appropriately sorry about the difficulties her rebellion entails. If I can help her continue to be sorry and regretful but to give up her severe guilt and self-deprecation about her rebelliousness, I think that she will keep choosing workable resolutions and that not only she but also her close family members will considerably benefit. I sincerely hope so.

ANOTHER RATIONAL EMOTIVE BEHAVIOR THERAPIST'S PERSPECTIVE ON RUTH, by Linda Gilbert, Ph.D.

Introduction

Among those of us who have been trained in rational emotive behavior therapy, there are a variety of styles and personalities. My style of doing REBT is the same as Albert Ellis's in that I am aware of the emotions my client is feeling during the sessions. Once I discover one of the emotions that we consider to be self-defeating—anger, depression, anxiety, or guilt—I work to discover the irrational beliefs the client is holding that create those emotions and then teach my client to develop rational beliefs and thus to acquire more functional emotions and behaviors.

Before being trained in REBT, I was trained in person-centered therapy, developed by Carl Rogers. This approach uses a lot of empathy and is nondirective. Due to this background, I believe, I am a bit more empathic with my clients than Ellis is. My sessions are usually 50 to 60 minutes in length, whereas his are only 30. Another difference between us is that due to my conservative, Christian upbringing I use less profanity with my clients than he does, and whereas he is an atheist, I believe in God.

The next section will focus on how I view Ruth and what I will concentrate on in my sessions with her. My original contact with her occurred after she called the Institute for Rational-Emotive Therapy in New York and inquired about an REBT therapist in her area. She had done some reading about the various approaches to therapy in her Psychology 101 class while obtaining her elementary education degree and believed that REBT would be helpful to her in sorting out the problems she was facing. Because she lived in Palm Springs, California, I was the closest REBT therapist to her. She called me after receiving the referral from the institute in New York and asked to set up an appointment. The next week when she came for her scheduled appointment, she brought her autobiography with her.

Focusing on Three Problematic Emotions

In reading through Ruth's biography, I hypothesize that she is having an ongoing struggle with the three emotions that in REBT are identified as being self-defeating. The first one is depression. She states that she often feels depressed, is overweight, has trouble sleeping, and is dissatisfied with her life.

In rational emotive behavior therapy, depression is seen as being self-defeating because when Ruth experiences this emotion, she is likely to withdraw from healthy activities in her life. While experiencing depression, she often stops doing things with her children, withdraws from her husband, and refuses to interact with her friends.

The second major problem that I see is anxiety. During sessions Ruth avoids eye contact and speaks rapidly. She reports dizziness, heart palpitations, and a general feeling of anxiety. Anxiety is seen as being self-defeating because if she feels anxious, she is likely to stop herself from doing interesting, worthwhile activities that will make her life more fulfilling.

The third emotion that I believe Ruth harbors is anger. Although she does not overtly state that she is angry, my guess is that she does have some anger toward her husband for "keeping her in the housewife role" instead of supporting her in developing a more interesting life. She may also feel some anger at herself because her life is not more fulfilling. Further, she may feel anger toward God, her parents, and her church because the spiritual beliefs with which she grew up are no longer working the way she was taught they would.

The first thing I want to do with her in session is to question whether her current life is working. I begin by asking her what she wants to work on first.

Our Initial Therapy Session

During our first session, Ruth and I have the following interchange:

RUTH: My life is just a mess. I don't know how it got to this point. When I was younger, I dreamed that I would be a good mother, that I would be with a man whom I loved and who loved me. Now I just feel depressed so much of the time. I don't know what happened to my goals, to my dreams. Sometimes I just feel as if it's no use. I might as well give up.

THERAPIST: Sounds as if you're pretty depressed that life didn't turn out the way you wanted it to. Would you like to work on your depression this session?

RUTH: Yes, I think I would. Sometimes I just don't see how things will ever change. I just feel so hopeless.

THERAPIST: First, let's look at your depression. I know there are a number of things in your life that you aren't satisfied with and that aren't going the way you'd like them to go. We won't be able to focus on all of them in one session, but over the course of the next few weeks we will. Right now what I want to do is help you break down the things that you want to work on into manageable pieces so you can start with something that will help you get more of what you want from life.

RUTH: OK. I'm still not very optimistic that this will help.

THERAPIST: There's no magic in therapy, but I've seen a number of people work hard and make some important changes that they felt good about. So I do think it's possible for you to get more of what you want from life. Do you think you've reached a point in your life where you're willing to commit yourself to some hard work in order to have your life be more satisfying to you?

RUTH: I think so. I certainly don't want things to keep going the way they have been. I can't continue to live like this.

THERAPIST: Let's begin working on your depression. What do you think causes feelings?

RUTH: I don't know. I've never really thought about it that much. I guess I'm not happy with my life, and I don't like how things are turning out for me. That's what causes my depression.

THERAPIST: Well, you're right to a certain extent. Many people would agree with you. We tend to think that our emotions are caused by external events. Certainly if you were happy with your life, were enjoying what was going on, and had stimulating, interesting activities, you would probably feel less depressed. But let's look at a possible different cause of your depression. If events we experience caused our emotions, then wouldn't it make sense that every person experiencing that event would feel the same emotion in response to that event?

RUTH: I guess so.

THERAPIST: Let's look at an example. You've probably known some people who have gone through a divorce. What emotion does divorce cause?

RUTH: Well, some people I have known felt depressed.

THERAPIST: Right. Some people do feel depressed when they're going through a divorce. But if divorce caused depression, then all divorced people would experience depression. Is that the case?

RUTH: I suppose not. My friend Sue was very angry at her husband when they split up. She couldn't believe he would have an affair with her best friend right in front of her face, especially while she was pregnant. My friend Mary, though, was relieved. She was tired of having her husband having relationships on the side and lying to her about it time after time after time. But both Sue and Mary felt depressed part of the time that their marriage was falling apart.

THERAPIST: Most of us feel a number of different emotions after any serious event. Let's look at the reasons that the same event can result in various emotions. Suppose I go through a divorce, and I'm thinking: "I'll never find anyone else to love me. I'll be alone the rest of my life. This is just horrible. I can't stand it. I'll never be happy again." How will I feel if I think that way?

RUTH: It sounds as if you'd feel depressed.

THERAPIST: Suppose I go through a divorce and I'm thinking: "That horrible idiot. He had no right to have that affair. I'll think of some way to get even with him. I've never been so hurt and humiliated in my life, and he's not going to get away with this." How will I feel if I think that way?

RUTH: That one sounds like anger.

THERAPIST: Right. What I'm driving at is that the emotion you feel to a particular event depends very much on the way you're thinking about the event. Now let's look at your depression and some of the thoughts that you have. Let's see what we can do to help you feel less depressed. We'll start by having you think of the last time you felt depressed. Can you tell me when that was?

RUTH: Yes, it was a couple of days ago. My two youngest kids, Susan and Adam, were watching TV. Susan wanted to look at one of her favorite shows, and Adam wanted to watch a baseball game. They started fighting, and it escalated. I finally had to yell at them. I called them some names that I didn't really mean. Then I felt so depressed, because I wasn't being a good mother anymore. In fact it seems as if I'm not good for anybody anymore. I make my kids miserable. My husband isn't happy with me these days, and it just seems as if there's no point in going on. My life is awful. My kids don't love one another. My husband works a lot, and I hardly ever see him. My kids would be happier if I weren't around. They certainly don't need me anymore.

THERAPIST: What happens to your relationship with your children when you feel this depressed?

RUTH: I withdraw. I don't want to be around anyone when I feel that way. I go in my bedroom and stay there.

THERAPIST: So at the times you're depressed, you're the one who pulls away from your family and doesn't want to spend time with them.

RUTH: I guess you could say that. I've never really looked at it that way before. I thought if they loved me, they would try to spend time with me. They know how much it bothers me when they fight.

THERAPIST: Do you think it helps anything when you get depressed? Does anything get better when you get depressed?

RUTH: Well, sometimes when I'm real depressed, my husband will start feeling bad. You know, he might call from work and if I'm in the middle of being really depressed, he sometimes senses it and asks if there's anything he can do. He'll ask if he can take me out to dinner and will try to cheer me up. But that doesn't always work. Lately I've noticed that he'll ignore me. He might stay late at work. When he comes home and I'm still depressed, he'll find work to do at home, or he'll watch TV or go somewhere with the kids.

THERAPIST: It sounds as if you might be getting something out of your depression. At least on occasion it gets you some attention and concern from your husband. But even that attention isn't consistent, and perhaps he gets tired of giving it to you under those circumstances. I wonder if just getting his attention is important to you? One of the things we can work on in your therapy sessions is some other ways you can get attention and care from him without making yourself depressed.

RUTH: My husband is basically a good man. I know he does care about me. I suppose there might be some other ways to get the attention I want from him.

THERAPIST: That's one of the things I want us to look at. You may find that you don't want to give up your depression if that's the only way you can get attention from your husband. If depression is getting you what you want in life, you may not want to quit depressing yourself. Now let's look at what you were probably thinking while you were feeling so depressed a couple of days ago. Based on our earlier examples of the way that thinking causes feelings, do you have any idea what you were thinking at the time that caused you to feel depressed?

RUTH: It was probably something like this: "My life is just so awful. Who would want to live the kind of life I have?"

THERAPIST: Ruth, your life might not be that interesting right now, and maybe there aren't very many people who would want to live it. But does that mean that things can't change? Does that mean you can't create a more interesting life? But right now, let's spend a little more time looking at what you were thinking when you were feeling depressed the other day.

RUTH: When my kids were fighting and I started getting depressed, I was thinking: "I must have been a rotten mom. My kids don't love one another. They probably never will. My husband doesn't love me. They don't love me." At times like this I ask myself what's the point of going on.

THERAPIST: Let's accept for the moment your belief that your kids don't love you. Are there any other things in life that you can get pleasure from and enjoy doing? Are there any other things in life that are meaningful to you?

RUTH: Not really. I've spent my whole life trying to be a good wife and mother, and now that those things aren't working out, what's the point?

THERAPIST: You can't think of anything else you ever enjoyed in your whole life up to this point?

RUTH: Well, at times I've enjoyed reading. When I was in college, I used to play tennis. I enjoyed both of those things.

THERAPIST: If your children didn't love you and they never expressed love toward you at all anymore, could you find some meaning in life and find some interesting things to do, like playing tennis or reading?

RUTH: I suppose so . . . Actually I know my kids *do* love me. It's just hard for me to believe it sometimes when they won't listen to me and are fighting. Also, they're getting more involved in their own interests and lives and hardly ever have time for me anymore. They don't need me now the way they did when they were young.

THERAPIST: You're right on that point. Would you really want them to? Would you really want to have to take intensive care of them for their entire lives as you did when they were infants? What would it mean about your children if they still required as much of your time as they did at that age?

RUTH: Well, I don't really want them to be that dependent on me. If they were, it would mean they were retarded or had something seriously wrong with them. Some parents do have to take care of their children for their entire lives. I really don't want that. I want them to be able to have their own friends and their own interests. I just wish they had more time for me.

THERAPIST: Wanting them to have more time for you is fine as a desire. But when you convince yourself that their lack of time for you means that they don't love you as they should, that's when you feel miserable. How would you feel if the next time they were fighting or didn't have time for you, you thought: "There they go, being normal kids again, not having time for their mom. Thank goodness they're no longer completely dependent on me the way they were at birth. Oh, well, I guess I'll have to entertain myself today."

RUTH: I'd probably feel a little better. I might not be quite so depressed. But I still might not like it that they weren't taking time for me.

THERAPIST: I never said you had to be happy about their not having time for you. But do you think you would feel so depressed if you thought this way?

RUTH: No, I don't think I would.

THERAPIST: Is what I just said about their being normal and your having to take responsibility for making your life enjoyable believable to you?

RUTH: Yes, but it's not the way I usually think.

THERAPIST: I know that. Would you be willing to practice saying it to yourself in front of a mirror at least three times a day this week to see what happens? Let me hear what you'll say.

RUTH: Thank goodness that my kids are normal and that they have the ability to take care of themselves and don't need me as much as they did when they were babies. I guess the fact that they're developing their own interests means that I'll be better off if I develop some interests of my own, too. It may be difficult to make some of the changes I need to, but that's why I'm in therapy and why I'm working so hard.

Process commentary

I had three main goals during this session with Ruth. The first was to show her that her depression is dysfunctional. By dysfunctional I mean that it is not helping her get what she wants in life. People who feel depression generally withdraw from family, friends, and work and expend very little effort toward helping themselves get better. I believe that once Ruth can see that the depression is hurting her, rather than helping her, she will be much more likely to work on giving it up.

The second goal that I had in this session was to show Ruth the connection between beliefs and feelings. Most people in the world believe that emotions (feelings) just happen to them. I was attempting to show her that her feelings are very closely connected to her beliefs. Once she sees that she is creating her depression by her thoughts and is willing to work hard, she will be able to change her feelings instead of being trapped in a self-defeating feeling such as depression. When she feels less depressed, she is more likely to act in ways that help her achieve her goals.

My third goal was to accept Ruth's perception of reality. At one point during the session she starts to talk about her children not loving her. One mistake that beginning therapists often make with this type of information is to attempt to convince the client that his or her view of reality is false. In Ruth's case, this means trying to convince her that her children really do love her. The difficulty with this approach is that although she may feel better during the session while she believes that her children do in fact love her, she will leave the office and go out into the real world, where her children do mean, unthoughtful, unloving acts, and will once again start thinking that her children do not love her. When she does this, she will sink into her depression again. If she can learn to accept their lack of love and unloving acts and not depress herself, she will be more content and less depressed both when they act lovingly and when they act unlovingly.

Ruth Explores Some Key Themes in Her Life

A few weeks later, Ruth wants to work on issues involving her children, her religion, and her parents' expectations:

RUTH: I've been feeling very confused about my religion. I just don't know what to believe anymore.

THERAPIST: Tell me what you mean by that.

RUTH: When I was younger, I thought I knew all the answers. I was raised in a very conservative home. In fact, my father was a minister. We were expected to be examples in our church. We couldn't wear jewelry. Movies were considered sinful. Drinking, smoking, and drugs were all considered very immoral. When miniskirts were popular, I had to wear my skirts long, and all my classmates made fun of me. But I also felt safer then. I knew that if I did what was right, I would go to heaven. I thought that at some point in my life being good would become easy, and I would know what the right answers were. Here I am ready to turn 40 in a few months, and I have more questions than answers.

THERAPIST: Tell me what some of those are.

RUTH: Well, last week my daughter Susan came home wearing a necklace that looked beautiful on her and perfectly matched the outfit she was wearing. I hit the roof. If my parents saw her wearing that, I know they'd think I was an unfit mother and would assume that Susan had lost all her morals. The worst part was when she came to me and asked what she had done that was wrong. I thought she ought to know. It's not as if she's a baby. She asked me to explain to her what I thought the issues involved were. I was stunned. It's something we just don't do, and I didn't really have an answer for her.

THERAPIST: It sounds to me as if two or three issues are bothering you. One is the anger you feel toward Susan for violating the rules of the family and your church. The second is the guilt you feel about your daughter doing something that your parents and others in your church would consider evil. And the third is the anxiety you feel about not being able to come up with an answer that made sense to you and to her. Which one of those do you want to focus on first?

RUTH: I think I'd like to focus on my anger with Susan first. It really is important to me to have a good relationship with her.

THERAPIST: In the past we've talked about the relationship between thoughts and feelings. What do you think you were thinking that made you feel so angry with her?

RUTH: John and I have been very clear with her what our family's rules are. She knows that we don't wear jewelry. She knows what I think, what her grandparents think, and what our church says about that.

THERAPIST: If you were angry with her, you were also thinking that she had no right to violate those rules. Because if those had been the rules and she had worn jewelry and you had thought, "Oh, isn't that interesting, she's becoming her own person and making up her own mind about what to do and what's right," how would you have felt?

RUTH: I probably wouldn't have been nearly so disturbed by the whole incident.

THERAPIST: Do you want to get over this anger you feel?

RUTH: Yes, I really do.

THERAPIST: So what's wrong with jewelry?

RUTH: In our church we don't believe in wearing outward adornment. We believe that what really counts is what's in a person's heart.

THERAPIST: That principle sounds fine, but let me ask you about what some of the people in the church wear. Do any of them wear scarves with their outfits?

RUTH: Well, yes they do.

THERAPIST: Is a scarf a necessity or a luxury? Would anyone in your church be upset if you wore a pretty scarf with an outfit to church?

RUTH: I think it is a luxury, and no, I don't think anyone would be upset by a scarf. It's just different.

THERAPIST: How is it different?

RUTH: The necklace probably costs more.

THERAPIST: But what if it didn't? What if you went to Saks and found a necklace that went well with one of your outfits for, say, $25 and a scarf that would also go well with the outfit for $40. Which one would you get?

RUTH: I would get the scarf.

THERAPIST: Why? You wear both of them around your neck, and the scarf is more expensive than the necklace.

RUTH: I would get the scarf because in our church it's not considered bad.

THERAPIST: Who defines what is right or wrong in a church?

RUTH: I don't know. I never really thought about it. I guess I always assumed we did things because that's what God wanted us to do.

THERAPIST: If it was what God wanted you to do, then would it make sense that all people who consider themselves Christians would be convinced of the rightness of a particular activity, such as wearing or not wearing jewelry? Why do we see diversity among churches and people from different religious backgrounds?

RUTH: I believe God helps people learn different things at different times.

So that explains why one church might think that wearing jewelry was wrong while another one would not.

THERAPIST: Might what you just said apply to people in the same church, that they might be convicted differently at different times?

RUTH: Yes, it could apply.

THERAPIST: Might that rule of thumb apply to people in the same family, too?

RUTH: I see what you're getting at. You're saying that my daughter and I may disagree and that she tends to see things differently than I do.

THERAPIST: Right. How will you feel if that is what is happening with you and Susan?

RUTH: It makes me uncomfortable. I don't like it. I know if she wears that necklace around my family and friends, they're going to think that I've lost total control of her and that she has lost all her morals.

THERAPIST: Let's suppose that what you said earlier is true. You believe that jewelry is wrong. Susan, on the other hand, doesn't feel that there is anything wrong with a necklace, any more than with a scarf. What do you suppose will happen if you demand that she not wear the necklace?

RUTH: She'll be angry with me and will think that I don't understand her.

THERAPIST: Do you?

RUTH: Honestly, there are times when I don't think I do. I was so compliant with my parents and did whatever I could to gain their approval. I would never have dreamed of challenging their rules.

THERAPIST: What were the advantages for you in doing that?

RUTH: Well, it kept us from fighting. I knew if I went against them, they'd be extremely angry with me.

THERAPIST: Might there be some advantages to the way that Susan's choosing to do things?

RUTH: Sometimes I think she's learning to think for herself at a younger age than I did. She certainly can't be controlled by her parents' opinion of her the way I could be.

THERAPIST: Do you want her to be just like you?

RUTH: No, not really. I didn't have the courage to question and challenge what my parents said. I'm having to ask myself a lot of questions now about what's right and wrong.

THERAPIST: How will you be able to tell when Susan is violating an important moral code, or committing a sin, and when she isn't? How would you answer this for yourself?

RUTH: What you're asking me is how I really know for sure what sin is versus what human rules and expectations are. I've been thinking a lot lately about sin. I think it's when someone gets hurt based on something I either do or fail to do.

THERAPIST: Let's apply what you just said to yourself. Are you hurting anyone?

RUTH: Well, in our church we think that people get hurt by someone else's influence. I might be being a bad influence on someone.

THERAPIST: Who?

RUTH: I can't think of anyone in particular, but perhaps some of my friends.

THERAPIST: Let's look at another example. When Jesus was on earth, some of the people were angry with Him because He gathered food on the Sabbath. He also healed on the Sabbath. He was violating the moral code of his day. Was He being a bad influence?

RUTH: I don't think so.

THERAPIST: But weren't there people in His day who would say He was?

RUTH: Yes, they were saying that.

THERAPIST: What was the point Jesus was trying to make by violating their code?

RUTH: He was trying to teach them that people mattered more than rules.

THERAPIST: Do you agree with that?

RUTH: Yes.

THERAPIST: How might you be able to apply this lesson to your daughter?

RUTH: I could keep in mind that she matters a lot more than wearing or not wearing a necklace. I could also remember that perhaps this is a human code, not one that God really cares about. But these things don't help me in facing my parents or the people in my church.

THERAPIST: It seems that the main problem in facing those people is that they're going to disapprove of you for being a bad mother and of your daughter for being a bad person and wearing jewelry.

RUTH: That's right.

THERAPIST: Ruth, what am I thinking about you right this moment?

RUTH: I can't tell.

THERAPIST: Right. You can't read my mind.

Process commentary

In this therapy session I had three main goals. The first was to help Ruth focus on what she wanted to accomplish in the session. Once she was focused, my goals were twofold. First, I wanted to help her get over her anger with her daughter by showing her that Susan had a right to be an individual and to make her own decisions even if some of them were wrong. Second, I wanted to help her accept the criticism she was getting from members of her church and her family. If she can get over the guilt she feels about being a fallible mother and not being able to control her children, she will be much more effective in deciding which battles and moral issues are worth fighting over with her children and which ones are merely human opinion about right and wrong.

I expect to continue to see Ruth weekly for approximately six months. During that time we will continue to work on her depression, anxiety, anger, and guilt. During that time I expect that she will increasingly change her self-defeating emotions by changing her faulty thinking. She will learn to use her emotions as flags, or warning signals. In other words, when she starts to feel depressed, she will say to herself: "I notice that I'm starting to feel depressed. Do I want to feel this way? No, I really don't, because it won't help me get what I want from my life. OK, what am I believing that's making me feel depressed? It must be that my children don't love me and that I must have their love to be happy in life. Now, let me look at that. Have I survived other times when they didn't love me? Yes, I certainly have. I'll survive this time, too. Now what am I going to do with my day? I think I'll start by riding my exercise bike for half an hour, and then I'll work on applying for that job I'm hoping to get in the school district."

If she starts to feel guilty about her daughter wearing jewelry, she will be able to process it like this: "I'm feeling guilty. My daughter wore a necklace over to my parents' house today. Will it help solve anything for me to feel guilty? No, it really won't. My daughter has made it clear she plans to wear jewelry no matter what I think. My mother has made it clear that she believes it's wrong to ever wear any type of jewelry. So am I an awful mother because my daughter is doing something that I was raised to believe was evil? I was a fallible, human mother. I loved my children. I also hurt them. But they've reached an age where they need to decide right and wrong for themselves. I was the only type of mother I knew how to be. If my mother is going to reject me for my children's choices, that's too bad. I can't control her. But I hope she won't choose that route. I guess she's being the only type of mother and grandmother she knows how to be. She doesn't know how to be accepting of choices she thinks are evil. Now what am I going to do with my day? I think I'll call my husband and see if we can have lunch, and then I'll see if my mother wants to go do some shopping with me, her only fallible, imperfect daughter."

As Ruth learns how to think more rationally, I see her prognosis for getting over her anger, anxiety, guilt, and depression as excellent. As she begins to accept personal responsibility for her life and her feelings, she will feel these emotions less frequently. She will then feel freer to pursue the personal goals that will make her life more fulfilling. She will quit blaming her emotions on her family and friends. She will also feel more freedom to pursue her goals, because she will learn that she is not responsible for causing the feelings of the people she is in relationships with, such as her husband, children, and parents. For example, just because her husband feels angry when she begins to pursue a career, it doesn't mean that she is doing something wrong. She will learn that her husband is responsible for his anger, which is caused by his thinking she has no right to leave the home to work.

My final hope for Ruth is that she will learn to take responsibility not just for her emotions but also for her life. I hope that she will assess what she wants out of life—love, fun, career, and relationships with friends, husband, parents, and children—and work hard to achieve those goals.

A TRANSACTIONAL ANALYST'S PERSPECTIVE ON RUTH, by John M. Dusay, M.D.

Assessment of Ruth

A transaction is a stimulus from one person and a related response from another.* The observation of a transaction—whether it occurs between therapist and patient in a dyadic setting, between husband and wife in couples therapy (or family members in family therapy), or between nonrelated clients in group psychotherapy—is the basic unit for analysis. The psychological assessment is an ongoing process and is not separate from treatment.

After saying hello and exchanging a few informal remarks, I beckon Ruth to choose where she wants to sit in the office. She nervously hesitates and asks me where to sit (there are several different chairs and a sofa). I tell her that it's up to her. Although seemingly insignificant, this interchange is her introduction to the attitude that she has the power to choose. She looks uncomfortable, hesitates, and looks toward me for guidance, which is not forthcoming; then she cautiously sits down.

Although Ruth's behavior during the first 45 seconds may seem to be a simple nervous attempt to find a place, I intuitively know that this is a capsule presentation of her personality and is perhaps a clue to her entire life course. She is insecure in being herself and seeks approval. She is uncomfortable in freely choosing what might be pleasant for herself, even at the superficial level of finding a suitable chair. I will reassess this initial intuitive hunch throughout the course of treatment.

Transactional analysis is a contractual treatment in which the client and the therapist agree on the goal. "How will you know—and how will I know—when you get what you are coming here for?" is a succinct expression of the contract and will suffice for Ruth's case. The development of a contract is a means not only to attain a mutual goal but also to reveal how she proceeds to set the goal. This process is very important in her evaluation.

I then tell Ruth that in this first session an important priority is to find out what she is seeking and to decide whether her goal is reasonably attainable. I tell her that she has the opportunity to find out whether she wants to work with me, and I give her permission to be candid and say whatever she wants. Some people, depending on their unique personalities, find this challenge easy to respond to. Others, like Ruth, who is not accustomed to expressing what she wants, may find that this simple opening is difficult:

---

*Although transactional analysis (TA) is generally considered a free-standing orientation to therapy, I am placing it in this chapter because of its clear emphasis on working with clients from a cognitive-behavioral perspective. John Dusay's approach is another way of working with Ruth's cognitions, the messages that she received as a child, her early decisions, and the development of her life script.

THERAPIST: Tell me what you're seeking.
RUTH: Dr. McCole [the referring physician] said that you're very good and maybe could help me.

Her statement is an attempt to portray me as a powerful helper and to represent her presence in the office as a transfer from one authority figure to another. Many other statements empowering me or my methods follow: "You must be successful" or "Transactional analysis can help me."

THERAPIST: Tell me what you're seeking for yourself.
RUTH [trying to find what she can say or do to please me]: What do you want me to say?
THERAPIST: It's OK to say what you want for yourself.
RUTH [tearfully and meekly, with a bowed head]: I really don't know what I want.

A direct assertion of what she *wants to gain* is a laborious undertaking for Ruth; it's not the nature of her personality. She is not making crisp, clear, logical assertions, like an adult, but is more like an indecisive, unsure little girl, who won't venture to say what she wants for herself. She finds it easier to tell about what she wants to go away, such as her symptoms of panic, insomnia, and obesity, than to make positive assertions. Her posture is marked by pulling in her chin and gazing upward toward me; she pulls on her dress, and her inflections end high at the end of sentences, creating an inquisitive tone. She sounds unsure as she frequently says, "You know, you know."

All transactional analysts work with ego states. I diagnose by visual observation and by listening to Ruth's tone and inflection, as well as her verbal content, that her predominant presentation of herself is as a child, not as a grown-up. Her little-girl part is labeled her Child ego state. (When referring to ego states in transactional-analysis literature, upper-case letters are used, and when referring to actual biological children, lower case is used.) An ego state is defined as a cohesive system of thoughts, feelings, and related actions. Every person has a basic trio of Parent, Adult, and Child. The Parent is the expression of values, morals, and "shoulds," which are introjected from actual parents or surrogates. The Parent is observed to use a downward eye gaze, a more erect chin, finger pointing when speaking, and an "absolute" vocabulary, such as *always, never, all,* and *none,* as opposed to more Adult words, such as *usually, probably,* and *occasionally.* Although Ruth suffered under the influence of her authoritative father, she will actually speak, feel, and act toward her own children in the same way that her father and mother acted toward her. She may be surprised, when confronted about her difficulties with her own daughter, that she is similar to her own parents. For example, when she disapproves of her daughter's wearing fashionable clothes, she is in her Parent ego state, although she infrequently expresses that state. Her Adult ego state is her logical, nonemotional, thinking state. When in her Adult ego state, she can add up her bank account (and get the correct balance), plan a menu, and perform well in school examinations. Under the stress of seeing a therapist for the first time, her Child is dominant. Under stress the most familiar, habitual part of the personality usually emerges.

The function of these basic ego states varies from one person to another. Ruth has much more energy in her Child ego state and, more specifically, in the Adapted Child function of her Child ego state. Adaptation refers to her learning how to exist with her father, how to please him, how to conform to his personality, and how to survive in her father-dominated biological family. Her mother also played an important role in her adapting to her father, as she seemed to set an example by being subservient and raising her daughter to be a good and pleasing little girl. Some children decide to rebel against authoritarian parents; Ruth chose to conform. More than 30 years later, this adapted little girl still lives in her Adapted Child ego state, as witnessed in my office. The other vital and very different function of the Child is that of freedom, autonomy, creativity, sexual pleasure, wanderlust, and growth. This is termed the Free Child ego state, and it is what every individual is born with. This ego state was severely suppressed in Ruth, so much so that she was even uncomfortable in freely choosing a chair in the therapist's office. Not only does she have different ego states, but she also has different amounts of energy in the parts. Her Adapted Child is highly charged, and her Free Child is very low in energy.

I also note that Ruth's Parent ego state, like that of all other people, has functions of both nurturing and of criticizing. She is less critical, probably because her father seems to be the critic and keeper of the morals in the family. Her Critical Parent is low, but she is able to survive by developing the nurturing part of her Parent ego state. Ruth's unique profile of energies—low Critical Parent, higher Nurturing Parent, moderate Adult, extremely low Free Child, and very high Adapted Child—is the mosaic that is her personality.

Ego-state analysis is a fundamental consideration. At some point I will have Ruth reexamine the roots of her personality. This is most frequently done by a psychoregressive technique. I sense that Ruth is exhibiting a repetitive pattern in deciding what she wants. For example, she expresses discomfort in finding a seat, she is agitated in her attempt to form a contract, and she is afraid to advance her career out of the fear that she will provoke the wrath of her husband. I have her trace the feelings that are being expressed in the here and now of the consulting room back to their original source. While talking about her husband, she exhibits her telltale somatic signs: a furrowed brow, downcast chin, upward-gazing eyes, and nervously fidgeting hands.

I tell Ruth to close her eyes, and I may enhance her discomfort by pinching her already tightened brow and squeezing her hands to reinforce her discomfort.

THERAPIST: Say how you're feeling.
RUTH: I'm frightened. I'm afraid my husband won't let me work.
THERAPIST: Let those feelings go back, back in time.

With this suggestive technique she goes further and further back in time as I offer many guiding comments. I allow several minutes for her to go back all the way to childhood, if possible.

Finally, I say, "Say where you are." Ruth, in a very emotional state, has gone back to age 6, when her father discovered her playing doctor with a friend. I encourage her to be 6, to speak in the present tense as if she were 6 years old. She sobs and appears very frightened:

RUTH [age 6]: I'm bad. I shouldn't play like this . . .
THERAPIST [allowing a full expression of her affect]: What are you deciding about yourself?
RUTH [age 6]: I'll never do this again.

Although this was not the only time that she displeased her father by playing, being herself, and doing natural and free things, this recall is very dramatic. She decided at the young age of 6 that she would not be free again. In essence, her father repeatedly gave her the injunction "Don't be yourself" and she agreed, at age 6, "I won't be myself." That decision is the "it," the "real problem," that, like a self-fulfilling prophecy, has determined her life course of suppressing her desires. Thirty-three years later, she is still hanging on to this childhood decision. It is now so habitual and reinforced that she believes that this is just the way she is. This pattern is what transactional analysts call a script.

The process of reexperiencing those decisive childhood moments reveals the nature of the decision. A transactional analyst does not utilize regressive techniques primarily to discover information but, rather, to reopen the emotion of the learning situation for renegotiation. Ruth now has more options than when she was absolutely dependent on her physiological family for survival. This process is inspirational for Ruth, who is introduced to the notion that she is responsible for her life course and that she may actually have the power to change. The transactional analyst's assumption is that anything that has been learned can be relearned. This assessment of the script is crucial, and it is usually made during the process of psychoregression rather than by historical questioning and data gathering.

Over the years Ruth has come to believe that she should please others, starting with her father when she was a little girl and culminating with a decision at age 6. From that point on she habitually proved that her self-decision was correct and reinforced it by playing psychological games. A game is an orderly series of transactions with two levels. One is an overt social level:

RUTH: Will you treat me for my problem?
THERAPIST: Yes, that is my specialty.

This is an overt Adult-to-Adult transaction. The two are discussing thera-pist/client business. The other level is a covert psychological one:

RUTH: How can I please you?
THERAPIST: Treat me as God.

This game fulfills her script needs to please the authority figure and to forgo being herself. (The therapist in this example, hopefully not a trans-actional analyst, has his or her own hidden ulterior agenda of being treated as a deity.)

The first clue to Ruth's game came when she attempted to empower me, by viewing herself as weak—"What do you want me to say?"—and by viewing me as strong—"Dr. McCole said you're very good." While on one level an Adult-to-Adult transaction revolved around getting treatment, she has a secret, hidden level of transaction: "How can I please you?" My needs are portrayed as more important than her needs.

Key Issues

The transactional analyst focuses on the three distinct facets of every patient in treatment—namely, the personality as revealed in the function of the *ego states*, the genesis of this personality as it unfolds in the *script*, and the lifelong reinforcing behaviors that have the qualities of a *game*. Like so many other innovators of the time, Eric Berne, the father of transactional analysis, was a trained Freudian analyst. From this background he de-veloped his basic theory from an intellectual, analytic route. His major objections to psychoanalysis were that it was time-consuming, complex, and poorly communicated to patients.

Transactional analysts do not apologize for being concise, and they have chalkboards in their consulting rooms. This approach is especially useful to Ruth, who seems to have a love/hate relationship with authority figures, including me as her therapist. With the concise TA symbols, she can understand what I understand—on an equal footing—allowing her to experience her own power and ability to change. Therapists, instead of being deifed and hiding behind big words, share their knowledge equally.

Three diagrams will highlight Ruth's key issues. The egogram is a bar graph showing Ruth's personality functions (see Figure 9-1). She is highly energized in the Adapted Child (AC) function and extremely low in Free Child (FC). Her seeking of treatment is a direct reflection of her desire to become more free and to raise this part of herself. She is also low in her Critical Parent (CP), the part that criticizes others, as she is more habitually comfortable in being criticized. This function is the part that stands up for her rights and desires and that is protective of her. Her Nurturing Parent (NP) and Adult (A) functions are about average.

Ruth's script matrix symbolizes from where her personality arises (see Figure 9-2). She introjects the values and morals of her father and mother

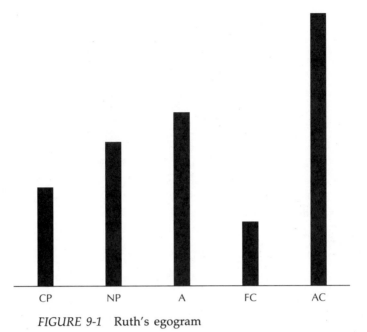

FIGURE 9-1   Ruth's egogram

into her developing Parent ego state. But on the Child level, from the Child in her father to her own Child, she receives many thousands of injunctions, both direct statements (symbolized by a solid line) such as "Don't play like that" and indirect signs (dotted lines) such as a disapproving frown saying, "Don't be yourself." At age 6 these injunctions culminated in her script decision "I won't be myself," reflected in her resolve to please her father and snuff out the free proclivities with which she was born. Her mother reinforced this suppression by showing her how to please her father. To a 6-year-old girl the father is the prototype of all men, and indeed she carried this decision into her marriage and through life, with male (and possibly female) authority figures.

Although Ruth left her biological family, this learned behavior did not become extinct, as she reinforced the phenomenon by playing games, as

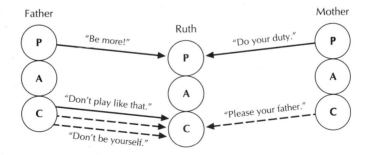

FIGURE 9-2   Ruth's script matrix

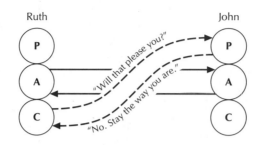

FIGURE 9-3   Ruth's game

seen in Figure 9-3. She recounts how she discussed her educational goals with her husband on the Adult-to-Adult level:

RUTH: I'd like to go to college.
JOHN: That's fine with me.

But on the Child-to-Parent level she transacts in a hidden way:

RUTH: Will that please you?
JOHN: No, stay the way you are.

Both Ruth and John might deny the existence of the hidden level if I saw them as a couple. She might glance at him and seek approval, and he might look disgusted when she talked about being absent from the home.

Therapeutic Techniques

Two major advantages of transactional analysis as a psychotherapeutic approach are (1) there is a complete, crisp, and easily communicated theory of personality and (2) because of this solid foundation the therapist is quite free to develop an innovative style of treatment utilizing his or her own strengths. Although Berne's treatment style was reminiscent of that of an intellectual analyst of the 1950s, his theories were greatly influenced by the evolving human-potential movement, especially in northern California, where he practiced in the 1960s. Following his death in 1970 these influences were rapidly incorporated into techniques for doing transactional analysis. Nowhere was this more evident than through the work of Robert and Mary Goulding at the Western Institute for Group and Family Therapy in Mt. Madonna, California. They married Berne's transactional analysis with the techniques of Fritz Perls's Gestalt therapy, along with others, and developed *redecision therapy*. This has been the predominant and major advance in transactional analysis after Berne.

Observing trained transactional analysts in action, you may see treatment styles ranging from a more "intellectual" cognitive approach to a highly emotive "feeling" display. At different times you may observe the transactional analyst using techniques such as hypnosis, psychodrama, and role playing. The same therapist may later be seen standing at a chalkboard offering a cognitive review that is so specific that the process and problems are actually being diagrammed with circles, arrows, and bar graphs. To a transactional analyst this apparent intellectual/emotional dichotomy is melded into a cohesive system in which neither thinking nor feeling is discounted or exalted as the primary vehicle.

Ruth's treatment began when she first contacted me. Her game of "How can I please you?" in which she had great difficulty in stating what she wanted for herself was gently but consistently confronted. When she became very emotional in discussing what pleased her husband, I initiated a redecision model. I asked her to close her eyes and trace the "bad" feelings back into her past. She regressed to the incident at age 6 when she was discovered having fun in normal childhood sex play—in essence, *being herself*—and was abruptly shocked by her disapproving, critical father. "I will never play again" ("I will not be myself") became her resolve.

I intervene by placing an empty chair in front of Ruth. When her sobbing subsides, I ask her to come and sit in this other (curative) chair. As I direct her to the "cure chair," I gently massage her tense shoulders, stroking her in a nurturing manner, unlike the pinching of her brow earlier to enhance the bad feelings:

THERAPIST: Take care of the little girl who is so sad.
RUTH [cure chair]: Why are you so sad?
THERAPIST: Switch back and respond.
RUTH [script chair]: I have disappointed my father.
THERAPIST: Switch back.
RUTH [cure chair, sobbing again]: It's hard to please him. You must feel bad.

After a few of these switches I observe that Ruth seems to be getting nowhere; she is at an impasse. She seems unable to overcome the negative feelings of her Adapted Child, and she has actually slipped into an Adapted Child state while sitting in the curative chair. This, unfortunately, reinforces the bad-feeling script state, and therefore I am quick to intervene. I do so by having her sit in another chair placed perpendicular to the script chair and the cure chair. She is then directed to comment on the process. This immediately allows her to cathect her observing Adult ego state. She says, "I was sad in both chairs, like the blind leading the blind."

The TA therapist is like a consultant. Ruth and I have an Adult-to-Adult conversation. This is the technique to resolve the impasse. We may decide that she needs some practice in having fun, dancing, writing poetry, taking part in sexual counseling, or the like, by which she can raise the energy in her Free Child ego state.

After weeks or, sometimes, a few months of treatment focused on the strengthening of weaker ego states, she may reapproach the redecision model. In the curative chair she may spiritedly tell the Adapted Child: "To hell with your father! Do what you want to do."

When she switches back to the original chair she responds: "That feels good—to hell with him and with my husband, too, if he wants to be a fuddy-duddy."

Then she is cured! Cure means that she has redecided her script, that she is not here to please her father, her husband, me, or anyone else. From a personality standpoint her Free Child has gained energy relative to her Adapted Child, and she will no longer look for how she can please others. Her habitual game has abated.

There is rarely a dramatic redecision in the first attempt. But by separating ego states, opposing the forces against each other, and strengthening the weaker growth forces, the client and therapist can achieve at least gradual results and, occasionally, dramatic breakthroughs. The cure is in the process itself. Note that though the transactional analyst is quite active in structuring the session, is an active catalyst for the redecision, and confronts impasses (slippages into the Adapted ego state), the client does all of the actual work. The patient has the power to change negative childhood decisions and does so by developing and then using more positive ego-state forces. The use of multiple chairs is similar to J. L. Moreno's pioneering psychodrama, done as early as 1924 in Vienna. What happens in the different chairs is that Ruth is able to utilize different forces that were always present in her head.

A final note is that John may be invited to couples therapy and may be able to have a deeper understanding of why Ruth seems rebellious toward him as she participates in her regressions and exposes her childhood decision. He is able to recognize that the problem started long before he even met her. He may also explore why he is so afraid of letting go of his tendency to control by tracing his own "fear of abandonment" back to his own childhood. Transactional analysts frequently encourage joint sessions for couples therapy, and Ruth and John can become allies rather than adversaries in a different, but growing, marriage.

JERRY COREY'S WORK WITH RUTH FROM A COGNITIVE-BEHAVIORAL PERSPECTIVE

Basic Assumptions

In this section I combine elements from Ellis's rational emotive behavior therapy (REBT), Beck's cognitive therapy (CT), and transactional analysis (TA) in my work with Ruth. Because I do not repeat too much detail about the cognitive-behavioral approaches, it would be well to review the perspectives of Ellis, Gilbert, and Dusay. It would also be useful to look at Frank Dattilio's cognitive-behavioral approach to family therapy with Ruth, in the following chapter. These sections provide a comprehensive picture of applying the cognitive-behavioral orientation to Ruth's case. In this section I focus on my own way of using an integrated cognitive and behavioral perspective.

Rational emotive behavior therapy assumes that individuals are born with the potential for rational thinking but tend to fall victim to the uncritical acceptance of irrational beliefs, which are perpetuated through self-reindoctrination. Beck's cognitive therapy shares with REBT an active, directive, time-limited, person-centered, structured approach. As an insight therapy, cognitive therapy emphasizes identifying and changing negative thoughts and maladaptive beliefs (also known as schemata). According to Beck's cognitive model of emotional disorders, to understand the nature of emotional problems, it is essential to focus on the cognitive content of a client's reaction to an upsetting event or stream of thoughts. I draw on a range of cognitive, emotive, and behavioral techniques to demonstrate to my clients that they cause their own emotional disturbances by the faulty beliefs they have acquired. As a cognitive-behavior therapist I operate on the assumption that it is not an event or a situation in life that actually causes problematic emotions such as guilt, depression, and hostility. Rather, it is mainly the evaluation of the event and the beliefs that people hold about these events that get them into trouble.

Initial Assessment of Ruth

As I review Ruth's intake form and her autobiography, it becomes evident that the majority of her problems are self-induced and self-maintained. True, as a child she was subjected to many absolutist and moralistic beliefs, some of which were irrational. Yet she is still clinging to these beliefs and living by them as though they were tested and proven values. The trouble is that she uncritically and unthinkingly accepts these values, many of which rely on guilt as a main motivation to control behavior. She probably invented or created some of her faulty thinking herself, as well as accepting some of it from her parents and culture. So she is not actually making clear decisions based on self-derived values; rather, she is listening to archaic and intimidating voices in her head that tell her what she should and ought to do. In short, she is the victim of *mus*turbatory thinking.

Ruth has an underlying dysfunctional belief that she must be perfect in all that she attempts. If she is not perfect, in her mind, there are dire results. She is continually judging her performances, and she is bound to think poorly of herself because of her unrealistically high standards. Indeed, there is a judge sitting on her shoulder and whispering in her ear. What I hope to teach Ruth are practical ways to talk back to this judge, to learn a new self-dialogue, and to help her reevaluate her experiences as she changes her behavior. This will be the focus of my therapy with her.

Goals of the Therapy

The basic goal of REBT is to eliminate a self-defeating outlook on life and acquire a rational and tolerant philosophy. The goal of CT is to change the way clients think by using their automatic thoughts to reach the core schemata (negative thoughts and faulty beliefs) and to begin to introduce the idea of cognitive restructuring. To do so, I will teach Ruth the A-B-C theory of personality. This theory is based on the premise that A (the activating event) does not cause C (the emotional consequences); rather, it is *mainly* B (her belief about the activating event) that is the source of her problems. (Ellis goes into greater detail on the goals that guide his interventions with Ruth.)

In addition to drawing on REBT and CT, I am also influenced by TA in helping Ruth formulate the goals for her therapy. Specific goals will be defined by her and stated in her contract, which is the beginning point in TA. During the initial session she indicates that she does not want to act out the rest of her life according to her parents' design. One of the points of her contract is to talk directly to her husband and to tell him specific ways in which she wants their marriage to be different. She agrees that she is willing to risk displeasing him by saying how she would like to change their family life.

Therapeutic Procedures

In working with Ruth as a cognitive-behavior therapist, I will employ a directive and action-oriented approach. Functioning as a teacher, I will focus on what she can learn that will lead to changes in the way she is thinking, feeling, and behaving. I will explore with her the early messages that she received from her parents. Once we have identified some of the major injunctions that she bought into, I will ask her to begin thinking about the decisions that she made about herself, others, and the world. I will also ask her to reflect on the direction in which her early decisions are taking her.

Drawing upon Beck's ideas from CT, I intend to focus on the inaccurate conclusions that Ruth has reached by teaching her to look for the evidence that supports or contradicts her views and hypotheses. She will frequently hear the question "Where is the evidence for———?" Through the use of open-ended questions and a Socratic dialogue, I will try to teach her ways of systematically detecting errors in her reasoning that result in faulty assumptions and misconceptions (cognitive distortions). After she has recognized her cognitive distortions, I will encourage her to carry out a range of homework activities, to keep a record of what she is doing and thinking, and to form alternative interpretations to replace her faulty assumptions. Eventually, through a process of guided discovery, I expect her to acquire insights into the link between her thinking and the ways she feels and acts. I also expect her to learn a range of specific coping skills to deal with current and future problems. It will help if she reads literature from a cognitive-behavioral perspective as an adjunct to her therapy sessions. For instance, I'll strongly recommend that she study books such as

Ellis's *How to Stubbornly Refuse to Make Yourself Feel Miserable about Anything—Yes, Anything!* Ellis and Harper's *A New Guide to Rational Living;* Burns's book *Feeling Good;* Beck's books, such as *Love Is Never Enough* and *Cognitive Therapy and the Emotional Disorders;* and Goulding and Goulding's *Changing Lives through Redecision Therapy.** Furthermore, like any other form of learning, therapy is *hard work.* This means that if Ruth hopes to successfully change her beliefs and thus change her behavior, it will be necessary to practice what she is learning in real-life situations. I will stress completing of homework assignments. And I will ask her to fill out an RET Self-Help Form, which has her analyze activating events, her beliefs about these events, the consequences of those beliefs, her disputing and debating of her faulty beliefs, and the effects of such disputing.

In working with Ruth, I attempt to integrate the cognitive and affective (feeling) dimensions. It is fair to say that I emphasize the cognitive aspects of therapy as I pull together concepts from REBT, CT, and TA. I realize that changing entails actually experiencing feelings. In my view, however, experiencing feelings alone is not enough to bring about a substantive change in behavior. Much of our therapy will focus on examining Ruth's current behavior and trying on new ways of behaving both during the therapy hour and in her daily life.

The Therapeutic Process

Elements of the process

When I first mention to Ruth that our work will be defined by a therapeutic contract, she seems resistant. She thinks it sounds so formal and legalistic, and she wonders why it is necessary.

JERRY: A contract sets the focus for therapy. As the client you decide what specific beliefs, emotions, and behaviors you plan to change in order to reach your stated goals.

RUTH: But I'm not quite sure what I want to change. I was counting on *you* to point out to me what I should work on. There's so much to change, and frankly I'm at a loss where to begin.

JERRY: Part of our work here will be for you to take increasing responsibility for your own actions.

Helping Ruth define her goals. At this point Ruth and I discuss this issue in some detail. The essence of what I let her know is that my approach to therapy is based on the expectation that clients focus on their goals and make a commitment. It emphasizes the division of responsibility and provides a point of departure for working.

RUTH [after some exploration]: I just want to be me. I want to be happy. I'm tired of taking care of everyone else, and I want to take care of me.

*See the Recommended Supplementary Readings.

JERRY: That's a start, but your statements are too global. Can we narrow them down? What would make you happy? What do you mean by taking care of yourself? How will you do this? And in what ways are you not being you?

I work with Ruth until she eventually comes up with clear statements of what she wants from therapy, what steps she will take to get what she wants, and how she will determine when her contract is fulfilled. After much discussion and a series of negotiations, she is able to come up with a list of changes she is willing to make.

RUTH: For one, I'm willing to approach my husband and tell him what I feel about our relationship. I know you say that I can't change him and that I can only change myself, so I'll tell him what I intend to do differently. And later, I would like to deal directly with my four children. They all take advantage of me, and I intend to change that. I can begin by telling them what I'm willing to do and what I'm no longer willing to do.

Although the above list is more specific than her original goals, there is still a need for greater specificity. Thus, I proceed by asking her exactly what she does want to change about each area she has mentioned, including what she intends to do differently. One part of her contract involves asking her husband to attend at least one of the sessions so that she can tell him the specific things she most wants to change in their relationship.

Role-playing Ruth's marriage.   In another session Ruth and I do some role playing in which I stand in for John. She tells me (John) how frightened she is of making demands on me, for fear that I might leave. Out of that session she begins to be aware of how intimidated she has allowed herself to become. She continues to set him up to punish her by giving him the power to make her feel scared and guilty. As a homework assignment I ask her to write a letter to him, saying all the things she really wants him to hear, but not to mail it. The writing is geared to getting her to focus on her relationship with him and what she wants to be different. (In an earlier session I gave her a similar assignment of writing a detailed letter to her father, which she agreed not to send him but to bring in for a session with me.) I make the observation to Ruth that in many ways she is looking to John for the same things she wanted from her father as a child and adolescent. Further, she assumed the role of doing whatever she thought would please each of them, yet she typically ended up feeling that no matter how hard she tried, she would never succeed in pleasing them. From here I try to show her that she will have to change her own attitudes if she expects change in her relationships, rather than waiting until her father or her husband might change. This is a discovery for her, and it represents a different direction for her life.

Holding a joint session with John.   Later I remind Ruth of her contract, and I suggest that she ask John to attend a therapy session with her so that we can deal directly with some of the issues that surface. Initially, she gives a list of reasons why she is sure that he will never come in. After some discussion with me she does agree to ask him directly and clearly to attend at least one session (which we will also role-play first). To her surprise he agrees to join her. Following are a few excerpts from this initial joint session:

RUTH: I brought John here today even thought I don't think he really wanted to be here. [Notice that she speaks for him.]

JERRY: John, I'd like to hear from you about what it's like to attend this session.

JOHN: When Ruth asked me, I agreed because I thought I might be of some help to her. I know I don't need therapy for myself, but I couldn't see any harm in giving it one shot.

RUTH: Now that he's here, I don't know what to say.

JERRY: You could begin by telling him why you wanted him here.

RUTH: It's that our marriage just can't go on this way much longer. Things are no longer satisfactory to me. I know that for many years I never complained—just did what was expected and thought that everything was fine—but the truth is that things are not fine by me.

JOHN [turning to me]: I don't know what she means. Our marriage has always seemed OK by me. I don't see the problem. If there's a problem, *she's* got it.

JERRY: How about telling Ruth this? [I want Ruth and John to talk *to* each other directly, rather than talking *about* each other. My guess is that at home they are very indirect. By having them speak to each other in this session, I get a better sense of how they interact.]

RUTH: See, *that's* the problem. Everything is fine by John—I'm the one who's crazy! Why is he so contented while I'm so discontented?

JERRY: Tell John. You're looking at me. He needs to hear from you, not me.

RUTH: Why, John, am I the only one who is complaining about our marriage? Can't you see anything wrong with the way we're living? Do you really mean that everything is just fine by you? Why is everything on me?

JERRY: Wait a minute, Ruth. I hear lots of questions. Rather than asking all these questions of John, tell him what you really want him to hear.

RUTH: [again turning to me and addressing me]: But I don't think he ever hears me! That's the trouble—I just don't think he cares or that he listens to me when I talk about our life together.

JERRY: I can understand why he might not hear you. You're not telling him what you want, and you're not giving him a chance. You know, Ruth, part of the problem I'm seeing is that you aren't telling him about you. If this is the way it is at home, I can see why you feel you're not listened to. Are you willing to hang in there with him and tell him directly what you say you'd like him to hear?

RUTH: [with raised voice and a great deal of emotion]: John, I'm tired of being the perfect wife and the perfect mother, always doing what's expected of me. I've done that for as long as I can remember, and I want a change. I feel that I'm the only one holding up our family. Everything depends on me, and all of you depend on me to keep things going. But I can't turn to any of you for emotional support. I'm the nurturer, but no one nurtures me. And there are times that I need to know that I matter to you, and that you recognize me.

JOHN: Well, sure—and I appreciate your hard work. I know you do a lot in the home, and I'm proud of you.

JERRY: How does it feel to hear John say that to you?

RUTH: But you never say that—you just don't tell me that you appreciate me. I need to hear that from you. I need to feel your emotional support.

JERRY: Ruth, you still didn't tell John how you were affected by what he said to you. [I am calling to Ruth's attention that in this brief interaction, for one short moment, her husband responded to her in a way that she says she would like him to. She does not acknowledge it and instead continues with her litany of complaints. I am letting her know that John may be more likely to change if he gets some positive comments.]

RUTH: I like it when you tell me that you're proud of me. It means a lot to me.

JOHN: I'm just not used to talking that way. Why make a lot of useless words? You know how I feel about you.

JERRY: John! That's just the problem. You don't tell Ruth how you feel about her and what she means to you, and she is not very good at asking that from you.

RUTH: Yeah, I agree. I hurts me that you think I want to hear useless words. I'm missing affection from you. It's so hard for me to talk about my life with you—about you and me—about our family—oh! [Ruth's eyes grow moist, she lets out a sigh, and then she grows quiet.]

JERRY: Don't stop now, Ruth. Keep talking to John. Tell him what your tears and that heavy sigh are about. [My hunch is that Ruth often feels defeated and stops there, seeing herself as misunderstood. I am encouraging her to stay with herself and continue to address John. Even though he is looking very uncomfortable at this point, he seems receptive.]

JOHN: Sometimes I find it hard to talk to you because I feel criticized by you. But how can I be sensitive when you don't tell me what you want?

JERRY: Sounds like a reasonable request. Will you tell him?

RUTH: You may not know how important going to college really is for me. I so much want to finish and get my credential. But I can't do that and be responsible for the complete running of our house. I need for the kids to pitch in and do their share, instead of always expecting me to do everything. I need some time to myself—time just to sit and think for a few minutes—when I'm at home. And I'd like to be able to sit down with you, John, after dinner and just talk for a bit. I miss talking to you. The times we do talk, the topic is household maintenance.

JERRY: What are you hearing, John, and how does this sound to you?

JOHN: Well, we have to talk about chores. I just don't understand what she wants me to say. [John continues for a time with a very critical voice, in many ways belittling Ruth. Yet eventually he does admit that the children don't help as much as they could and that he might be willing to do a bit more around the house.]

RUTH: Well, I'd really like your help at home. And what about spending time with me? Do you want to talk with me?

JOHN: Yes, I do, but too often I just want to relax after busting my butt at work all day. I want it to be positive at home after a long day.

JERRY: It sounds as if both of you would like to talk to each other. Would you be willing to set aside some time during the next week when you can have some uninterrupted conversation?

Together we develop a realistic contract that specifies when, where, and how long they will spend uninterrupted time with each other. John agrees to come in for another joint session. In the meantime I ask Ruth to monitor what she actually does at home for two weeks and to keep these notes in her journal. I suggest that she write down a specific list of the changes she wants at home, along with what she could do to make these changes happen.

Process commentary

Ruth and I spend several sessions working with her part in creating and maintaining the difficulties she is experiencing in her marriage. I challenge her to stop focusing on John and what he can do to change and, instead, to change her own attitudes and behaviors, which will inevitably lead to changes in her relationship with him. She begins to see how difficult it is for her to make requests of him or ask him for what she needs emotionally. Although she initially resists the idea of telling him directly what she wants with him and from him, she eventually sees some value in learning to ask for what she wants. Ruth has decided in advance that he (and others) will not take care of her emotionally, and with this expectancy she has blocked off possibilities of feeling emotionally nourished by others. She often becomes aware of slipping into old patterns, many of which were developed as a child, yet she becomes increasingly able to avoid these traps and to behave in more effective ways.

I do a fair amount of teaching with Ruth. Although her therapy does involve reliving earlier events that are associated with intense emotions, I am interested in helping her cognitively understand the nature of certain decisions that she made as a child. The majority of our sessions consist of reviewing and critically examining these early decisions, with the aim of determining the degree to which they are still functional. I continually challenge her to think about what she decided about herself and about her place in life at these moments.

Working with Ruth's faulty beliefs.   To achieve the goal of assisting Ruth in achieving a constructive set of beliefs and acquiring a self-enhancing internal dialogue, I perform several tasks as her therapist. First of all, I challenge her to evaluate the self-defeating propaganda that she originally accepted without questioning. I also urge her to give up her faulty beliefs and then to incorporate sound beliefs that will work for her. Throughout the therapeutic process my attempt is to actively teach her that self-condemnation is the basis of many of her emotional problems, that it is possible for her to stop critically judging herself, and that with hard work, including behavioral homework assignments, she can greatly reduce many of her dysfunctional notions. Self-condemnation is one of the main bases of emotional disturbance.

Ruth's *real* work, then, consists of doing homework in everyday situations and then bringing the results of these assignments into our sessions for analysis and evaluation. I am concerned that she not only recognize her self-defeating thought patterns and the resultant feelings but also take steps to challenge and change them. My main function is to caringly confront her if I see her clinging to these deeply engrained beliefs.

We explore how her fear of making a fool of herself stops her from doing so many things. She then says that she would love to square-dance but has not because she is afraid of being clumsy and looking like a jerk. She would love to ski but avoids it for fear that she will fall on the "bunny hill" and break a leg—and then really look like a fool. I explain to her that the purpose of the shame-attacking exercise is to challenge her worst fears and to test them. Chances are, she will survive the embarrassment and will not die of shame. In these shame-attacking exercises, moreover, I want her to work on herself so that she either does not feel ashamed when she does the exercises or quickly gets rid of the feeling of shame after she does it and first feels ashamed.

RUTH [next week]: I hate to say it, but I didn't follow through. I went to the elevator door and stood there for the longest time, but I just couldn't walk into the elevator and make a fool of myself.

JERRY: Couldn't? At least say, "I would not!" You could have done it, but you chose not to. Any idea why you didn't do it?

RUTH: I was just too afraid of being that far out. But I've decided to go ahead with that impromptu speech this week.

JERRY: Good, let's work on that. But let's talk some about your reactions to standing outside that elevator door.

Even though she did not do the assignment, there is plenty of therapeutic potential in what she put herself through. So we explore her thinking, her catastrophic expectations, and what she might do differently. One of her great fears, for example, was that people would think she was crazy. Finally, we begin talking about her upcoming speech:

RUTH: I'm just afraid I'll freak out or, worse yet, chicken out.

JERRY: So let's go through it right now. Close your eyes and imagine that you're giving the speech, and all the worst things you can imagine happen.

After her fantasy of catastrophic expectations we take them one by one and try to demolish them. I am working with her on her evaluation of events and her prediction that she will fail. All the time, I want her to see that even if she fails, she can still stand the outcomes. They may be unpleasant but surely not absolutely horrible.

We continue for a couple of months, with Ruth agreeing to do some reading and also carrying out increasingly difficult homework assignments. Gradually she works up to more risky homework assignments, and she does risk looking foolish several times, only to find that her fantasies were much worse than the results. She gives her speech, and it is humorous and spontaneous. This gives her an increased sense of confidence to tackle some other difficult areas she has been avoiding.

Dealing with Ruth's beliefs about herself as a mother.   Ruth is feeling very guilty about letting one of her daughters down. Jennifer is having troubles at school and, Ruth says, is "going off the deep end." Ruth partially blames herself for Jennifer's problems, telling herself that she must be a better mother than her own mother was.

RUTH: I don't want Jennifer to suffer the way I did. But in so many ways I know I'm unloving and critical of her, just as my mother was of me at that age.

JERRY: What are you telling yourself when you think of this? [Again, I want Ruth to see that her self-defeating thoughts are getting her depressed and keeping her feeling guilty. My hope is that she will see that the key to eliminating needless anxiety and guilt lies in modifying her thinking.]

RUTH: I feel guilty that I didn't help Jennifer enough with her schoolwork. If I had tutored her, she would be doing well in school. I tell myself that I'm the cause of Jennifer's problems, that I should have been a better mother, that I could have cared more, and that I've ruined her chances for a good life.

JERRY: Do you see that this absolutist thinking doesn't make sense? What about Jennifer's role in creating and maintaining her own problems?

RUTH: Yes, but I've made so many mistakes. And now I'm trying to make up for them so she can shape up and change.

JERRY: I agree that you may have made mistakes with her, but that doesn't mean it will be the ruination of her. Can you see that if you do so much for her and make yourself totally responsible for her, she doesn't have to do anything for herself? Why should she accept any responsibility for her problems if you're blaming yourself? [My attempt is to get her to dispute her own destructive thinking. She has continued this pattern for so long that she now automatically blames herself, and then the guilt follows.]

RUTH: Well, I try to think differently, but I just keep coming back to these old thoughts. What would you like me to say to myself?

JERRY: When Jennifer does something wrong, who gets the blame for it?

RUTH: Me, of course. At least most of the time.

JERRY: And those times that Jennifer does well, who gets credit?

RUTH: Not me. Anyway, I dwell so much on what she's not doing that I don't often see that she does much right.

JERRY: How is it that you're so quick to place blame on yourself and just as quick to discount any part you have in Jennifer's accomplishments?

RUTH: Because problems occupy my mind, and I keep thinking that I should have been a better influence on her.

JERRY: I'd just hope that you could stop damning yourself and *should*ing yourself to death. Do you think you can begin to be kinder to yourself? What I'd like you to consider saying to yourself is something like this: "Even though I've made mistakes in the past and will probably continue making mistakes, that doesn't mean I've ruined Jennifer or will. It doesn't mean I'm the same kind of mother to her that mine was to me. I'll lighten up on myself and be more forgiving, because if I don't, I'll drive myself crazy." What I want you to see is that even if you have acted badly toward your daughter and were pretty much the same kind of mother that your mother was to you, that still wouldn't make you a rotten person. It would merely mean that you might need to acquire mothering skills.

RUTH: That sounds pretty good . . . If only I could say those things and mean them, and feel them!

JERRY: Well, if you keep disputing your own thinking and learn to substitute constructive self-statements, you're likely to be able to say and mean these things—and you'll probably feel different, too.

Process commentary

As can be seen, my major focus with Ruth is on her thinking. Only through learning to apply rigorous self-challenging methods will she succeed in freeing herself from the defeatist thinking that led to her problems. I place value on behavioral homework assignments that put her in situations where she is forced to confront her irrational beliefs and her self-limiting behavior. I also consistently challenge her to question her basic assumption that she needs the approval of others in order to feel adequate.

Questions for Reflection

1. What are your general reactions to Ellis's and Gilbert's approaches to working with Ruth? What similarities did you notice in their concepts and techniques? What differences did you detect between them? What do you think were some of the most useful interventions they made? After reading their descriptions of Ruth's assessment and their treatment strategies, what aspects of her life would you focus on if you were to continue as her counselor?

2. Compare the way REBT therapists work with Ruth with the way the psychoanalytic therapist worked with her. Do the same for the existential therapist and the person-centered therapist. What approach do you prefer in Ruth's case? Do you see any basis for combining some aspects of REBT practice with existential and person-centered practice?

3. What are your reactions to the manner in which Ellis drew upon cognitive, emotive, and behavioral techniques in working with Ruth's dysfunctional beliefs?

4. What are your reactions to Gilbert's way of dealing with Ruth's depression? How about her style of helping Ruth examine the expectations of her children, her religion, and her parents?

5. Assume that you suggested a technique to Ruth (such as doing a shame-attacking exercise, keeping a journal, or reading self-help books) and she refused, telling you that what you were asking was too much to expect. What might you say to her?

6. What common faulty beliefs do you share with Ruth, if any? To what degree have you challenged your own irrational thinking? How do you think that this would affect your ability to work with her?

7. Working with Ruth very forcefully and in a confrontational manner could raise some ethical issues, especially if you attempted to impose your values by suggesting what she should value. As you review Ellis's, Gilbert's, Dusay's, and my work with Ruth, do you have any concerns that any of us are "pushing values"?

8. REBT assumes that by changing our beliefs about situations, we also change our emotional reactions to these events. How valid do you find this assumption to be for you? Can you come up with examples of how changing your beliefs and interpretations of events has changed your ways of feeling and acting?

9. What might you do if Ruth came from a background where her "musts," "oughts," and "shoulds" arose out of her cultural conditioning? What if she insisted that she felt guilty when she dared to question her upbringing and that in her culture doing so was frowned upon? Might you adjust your confrontational techniques? If so, how would you challenge her *must*urbatory thinking (or would you)?

10. Can you think of possibilities of using the Adlerian lifestyle questionnaire to detect basic mistakes and then working with them using a cognitive-behavioral framework?

11. In the example of my work with Ruth as a cognitive-behavior therapist, I blended some of the concepts and techniques of Ellis and Beck. What are your reactions to attempting to combine elements of REBT and CT? How comfortable would you be in employing REBT techniques in your therapy with Ruth? How about using CT strategies? Do you prefer Ellis's or Beck's approach to cognitive-behavior therapy? Do you see any basis for integrating these two perspectives in your practice?

12. What ideas do you have for using cognitive-behavioral concepts and procedures in conjunction with Gestalt techniques? Can you think of examples from Ruth's case where you could work on her feelings (with Gestalt techniques) and then proceed to work with her faulty thinking (by using cognitive-behavioral techniques)?

13. Dusay (TA) paid particular attention to Ruth's behavior patterns and mannerisms during the first few minutes of the initial session. How much importance do you place on your initial reactions to a client? How might you have interpreted Ruth's mannerisms as described by Dusay if you were meeting her for your first session?

14. In Dusay's account, Ruth had great difficulty in stating what she wanted for herself, and she was unclear in defining a therapeutic contract. How might you assist her in getting a clearer focus on what she wanted? What would you do if she put pressure on you to tell her what she *should* work on in her therapy?

15. What do you think of beginning therapy with a clear contract, one that spells out what the client wants and states the functions and responsibilities of the therapist? What differences do you think there are between working with a contract and not using one? Which is your preference? Why?

MARION: A WOMAN WHO LIVES BY "OUGHTS" AND "SHOULDS"

Some Background Data

Marion, age 37, is an African-American physician who has lived by a series of "shoulds" and "oughts" for most of her life. Among the things she is now telling herself is that she *must* succeed in her profession. From her perspective, succeeding means being *far* better than most of her colleagues in her professional specialty, family medicine. She constantly berates herself for not being able to publish more research articles, for not keeping up with all the reading in her field, and for sometimes failing to live up to the expectations her patients have for her. One of her beliefs is that she should take care of everyone: her family, her friends, her colleagues, and her patients. It is essential for her to always be in control. Even without the benefit of therapy, she is aware that a key motivating force in her life is to demonstrate her success both as an African-American and as a woman.

There is not much room in her life for making mistakes. Her perfectionistic strivings are literally making her sick. She experiences frequent migraine headaches, chronic constipation, stomach pains, and dizziness. Although her body is sending her clear messages that she is driving herself relentlessly, she keeps forging ahead, thinking that she must meet all of her standards. Unfortunately, these standards are unrealistically high, and she will never be able to attain them. No matter what her level of achievement, she persistently puts herself down for not having done better or done more. On top of all this she feels guilty about having all of her physical symptoms, because as a physician, she thinks that she should be in better control of her physical and mental state.

Marion judges herself constantly in all areas of her life. She gives herself grades for her performances, and typically her grades are low, for she demands so much of herself. Although her grades during medical school were consistently high (mostly "A"s with an occasional "B"), when she reflects on her record, she rates herself as a "C" student. In the area of being a wife she gives herself a low "C" at best. She does not cook fancy meals the way her mother or her husband's mother did. She feels that she is neglecting her husband, Byron. In her sex life she gives herself an "F." Byron complains that she is not responsive enough, not playful, way too serious, and too prudish. She almost never experiences an orgasm, because she is so worried about her performance and Byron's approval. It is next to impossible for her to relax and enjoy having sex. Of course, she sees it as her fault that she is not as sexually responsive as she thinks she ought to be. In her social life she gives herself a "C." She keeps telling herself that she ought to entertain her husband's clients more often, that she ought to have friends over for dinner more often, and that when she does, she ought to be a far better hostess than she is now. Marion struggles with feeling uncomfortable in social situations. She typically tells herself that she is not an interesting person and wonders how other people could enjoy her.

The reality is that Marion is deeply committed to her medical practice in a community health center. Both her colleagues and her patients have a great deal of respect for her. She puts in long hours and rarely takes any time off from work. When she is not working or achieving something, it is almost unbearable for her. The drive to accomplish more and more in a shorter amount of time keeps her from being able to relax. Often she says that she cannot afford the luxury of free time because there are so many important things to do.

In her family of origin Marion learned that it was not enough for African Americans to be simply good or even excellent but that they must be *outstanding* in everything they attempted. Her parents frequently told her that if she followed through with her plans to go to medical school, she would certainly encounter more than her share of discrimination on the grounds of both her race and her gender. She would have to prove herself time and again. She has accepted this view of life; moreover, she feels a great deal of pressure to live up to the high expectations of her parents and not to disappoint them.

How I Would Proceed with Marion by Using Cognitive-Behavioral Methods

Marion presents herself voluntarily for therapy, for she recognizes that her pressurized lifestyle is killing her. She would like to continue doing her best, but she does not want to feel that she always has to be the best in every aspect of her personal and professional life. It has finally come down to her feeling desperate: She feels miserable both physically and emotionally and has not been able to change her situation in spite of her most determined efforts. It is clear to her that she is driving herself in self-destructive circles. She says that she wants to break this chain, learn to modify her perfectionism, and begin accepting herself as a worthwhile person in spite of her limitations. She would like very much to be able to enjoy her work, without telling herself that she should and must do more. She has told herself that she ought to be less judgmental of herself than she is, yet this does little good. She finally seeks professional help.

Exposing Marion's self-defeating beliefs.   In essence, I want to show Marion that her dysfunctional beliefs are the partial cause of her psychological and physiological problems. Further, I will show her that *she* is the one who is feeding herself these faulty and unrealistic assumptions and that she is the one who can change her misery by learning to challenge and modify them. Together we will identify and actually write down the "musts," "shoulds," and "oughts" that keep her the driven and unhappy person she is. Finally, I will work with her to create a new set of assumptions that lead to constructive outcomes.

Drawing on some of Beck's notions in cognitive therapy, I also focus on Marion's internal communications. I assume that she monitors her thoughts, wishes, feelings, and actions. In social situations she probably keeps score of how other people are reacting to her. Her thinking is also polarized in many respects. She sees things in terms of good or bad, wonderful or horrible. Further, she engages in some "catastrophizing," in which she anticipates negative outcomes of her ventures. In sum, she is contributing to her emotional problems by what she is telling herself, by the assumptions she is making, and by her belief system.

To more clearly identify Marion's faulty cognitions, I use the RET Self-Help Form as one of the main homework assignments. First of all, I ask her to write down an activating event (A), such as one of the times she made a mistake. Next she writes down the consequence (C), which is her guilty feelings or self-defeating behavior that she would like to change. Then, using the RET form, I ask her to keep track of all of her irrational beliefs (IBs) that led to the consequence. The activating event was a situation in which one of her patients got upset and complained to her that she was not helping him and that he would be switching physicians. Initially, Marion says, she felt devastated. Although she had tried as hard as she could, her patient was a chronic complainer. Yet her beliefs about his displeasure over his medical care led her to feel depressed and inadequate. Below is a partial record of her irrational beliefs (IBs), followed by a dispute (D) for each irrational belief, which is followed by an effective rational belief (RB) to replace her irrational belief:

IB: "All of my patients should feel satisfied, and I must please all of them all of the time."

D: "Who told me this nonsense to begin with? And what's more, why must I continue telling myself that it's true?"

RB: "Although I'd like all of my patients to appreciate me, I can live with the fact that not all of them will like my care."

IB: "I must do very well."

D: "And this is the very belief that keeps me stressed out and makes me sick."

RB: "I'd like to do as well as I can, but I'm imperfect, and I can tolerate my shortcomings."

IB: "If I make a mistake, this proves that I am an incompetent person."

D: "Where is the evidence that my worth as a person hinges on being totally competent in everything I do?"

RB: "I'm a competent physician in spite of the fact that one of my patients thinks I'm incompetent. Furthermore, even if I were incompetent at times, it wouldn't mean I was incompetent as a person."

By keeping a record of the irrational beliefs that crop up, along with taking the time to dispute each one and substitute a rational belief, Marion begins to learn how to refuse to feel miserable.

A typical session.   During a typical session Marion and I follow through with a critical evaluation of one of her irrational notions. She relates several situations in which older, white, male patients have expressed doubts about her ability to help them. She believes that she has had to face and struggle with the reality of prejudice and discrimination all of her life and that she must still contend with prejudice from some of her patients. Together we explore this reality that she continues to face, and we begin to sort out realistic and unrealistic conclusions. Given the reality of prejudice and discrimination against minorities, I still challenge Marion to change her thinking when it is not possible to change her environment. After discussing the many instances of discrimination she has experienced and her reactions to these events, we proceed to explore her belief that she must be an outstanding physician largely because she is an African-American woman. I ask her to show me the evidence for her conclusion that because she is an African-American woman, she must constantly prove herself. I confront her in this way: "Who is telling you these things now? Why do you burden yourself with *having* to live up to those expectations? Do you get tired of always having to be in control and taking care of everyone? In your mind do you think there is anything you could do to prove your worth to yourself? What would be so terrible about doing a fine job without being perfect? And what would be absolutely horrible and devastating about being less than outstanding?" "I hope Marion will come to see that all the catastrophic thinking and expectations of doom are not nearly so unbearable as she thinks. It might not be pleasant for her to be imperfect, but I hope that she will learn to accept herself as a fallible human.

During this session Marion confronts me with being too hard on her and tells me that maybe her "irrational beliefs" about having to prove herself as a competent African-American female physician may be more rational than I am willing to admit. She tells me, "You are a white male psychologist, and I wonder if you can really understand the irrational world that I have had to struggle with in being a minority on two counts!" She tries to convince me that her convictions have helped her get through some difficult times and that she has to constantly fight to create her place in the professional arena. We spend some time talking about our differences, because if she does not trust me, there will be little that I can do or say to help her. She eventually accepts that I can understand her struggles and her feelings, in spite of the fact that I have not experienced the same discrimination that she has lived with.

Integrating techniques.   As our sessions continue, I draw on a variety of diverse methods of a cognitive, affective, and behavioral nature. I employ an eclectic approach suited to Marion's individual problems. If a technique does not seem to work in a session, I find alternative procedures that will work. As I mentioned earlier, Marion's progress will be determined in large part by her willingness to work hard outside of the sessions. Thus, I ask her to give herself homework assignments to practice in confronting her irrational thinking. The aim here is to learn how to deal with anxiety by resolving difficult situations that are anxiety-provoking. For example, she has said that she feels inadequate as a wife. She is burdening herself with the conviction that she has to please Byron in all respects. As a matter of fact, her work schedule is far more demanding than his, so eventually she challenges her notion that it is her duty to be a full-time housewife as well as maintaining a demanding professional life. She begins to take a critical look at her assumptions about her role as a woman in a dual-career family, and as a result she changes some of her reactions to "neglecting her husband." Instead, she begins to see that on many counts it is she who is being neglected by *him.* Marion begins to take action at home to bring about the changes that she wants. One of these changes consists of her hiring a person to clean the house, do most of the time-consuming chores, and even to cook most of the dinners. Even though Byron resists this change, she persists in restructuring her beliefs about the absolute necessity of always pleasing him. She is learning to please herself, even if she does not receive support for this change.

Employing techniques of cognitive behavior modification.   Marion continues to monitor her thoughts during a typical week by writing down specific situations that produce stress for her. She is getting better at noticing those factors, and she is also improving her ability to detect self-statements that increase her level of stress. As a part of her homework she records what she *tells* herself in problematic situations, what she then *does*, and how she *feels*. During her sessions we go over her written analysis of her thinking, behaving, and feeling patterns in various situations. We then discuss alternative statements that she could make to herself, as well as ways that she could actually behave differently.

A *bibliotherapy* program, which is a supplement to Marion's sessions, is helping her become a more astute observer of her own experience. I introduce her to the work of Donald Meichenbaum, as set forth in his book *Cognitive Behavior Modification*. I operate on the assumption that reorganizing her cognitive structures (her thoughts and self-statements) will result in a corresponding reorganization of her behavior in interpersonal situations. At the same time, I assume that forcefully and vigorously changing her behavior will change her irrational thinking.

The beginning step in Marion's changing consists of continued observation of her behavior in interpersonal situations. Thus, we go over her week as she recorded it to see what we can learn about the ways she is contributing to her fears in social situations through her negative thoughts. She reports that she has become aware of how many times in various social situations she sets herself up for failure by telling herself that people will not be interested in her.

The second step in changing Marion's cognitive processes involves my teaching her how to substitute *adaptive behavioral responses* for the maladaptive behaviors she now displays. If she hopes to change, what she says to herself must initiate a new behavioral chain, one that is incompatible with her maladaptive behaviors. Thus, we look at positive self-talk that can generate new expectations for her. She considers saying to herself: "Even though I'm nervous about meeting new people, I will challenge my assumption that people find me boring. I can learn to relax, and I can tell myself that I do having something to say." As a cognitive-behavior therapist I also try to get Marion to see that even if she didn't have anything interesting to say, she could always fully accept herself as a person and never damn or condemn herself for being inept. She is beginning to learn some new internal dialogues, and she is learning how to create positive expectations to guide new behavior.

The third phase of Marion's cognitive modification consists of learning more effective coping skills, which can be practiced in real-life situations. In this case I teach her a standard *relaxation exercise* used in the cognitive-behavioral approaches. I ask her to practice it twice a day for about 20 minutes each session. I teach her some training procedures in breathing and deep-muscle relaxation, ones that she can apply to many of the situations she encounters that bring about anxiety. As she practices more effective coping skills, she notices that she is getting different reactions from others, which reinforce her to continue with new patterns of behavior.

Follow-Up: You Continue as Marion's Therapist

Consider the concepts and techniques I drew on and the style in which I did so as you think about how you might work with Marion further. What would you do differently?

1. Do any of Marion's "shoulds," "oughts," and "musts" remind you of messages that you tell yourself? How successful do you see yourself in identifying and working through some of your major irrational beliefs?
2. How do you imagine it would be for you to work with Marion? What might you do if she persisted in clinging to certain self-defeating notions and refused to recognize some of her beliefs?
3. Are there any ways in which you might work with Marion differently than you would with a white female physician? or with a white male physician? What special issues might you want to explore with her that are related to her gender and race?
4. How might you react if Marion were to say to you: "How can you understand my problems if you are not an African-American woman who happens to be involved in a male-dominated medical profession?" What problems, if any, do you think you'd have in establishing an effective therapeutic relationship with her?
5. How comfortable would you be using cognitive-behavioral methods? How effective do you imagine you would be?
6. Most of Marion's work with me consists of identifying self-defeating notions and learning to dispute them, both in the session and through activity-oriented homework assignments. I am trying to get her to see how her faulty beliefs lead to self-defeating thoughts, feelings, and actions. What do you think of this approach? Do you think it is sufficient to produce lasting change? If not, what else do you think might be needed?
7. To what degree do you find it helpful to integrate the cognitive-behavioral perspectives of Ellis, Beck, and Meichenbaum?

RECOMMENDED SUPPLEMENTARY READINGS

Beck, A. (1976). *Cognitive therapy and the emotional disorders*. New York: New American Library (Meridian). This is a very useful book illustrating how emotional disorders often have roots in faulty thinking. Beck clearly outlines the principles and techniques of cognitive therapy, giving many clinical examples of how the internal dialogue of clients results in various emotional and behavioral problems.

Beck, A. (1988). *Love is never enough.* New York: HarperCollins. This book was designed for the layperson and provides an overview of cognitive therapy for couples in a clear and concise manner. It is used as required reading for couples in treatment as well as students and therapists using the cognitive approach with couples.

Burns, D. (1981). *Feeling good: The new mood therapy.* New York: New American Library (Signet). This is a practical self-help book based on the principles of Beck's cognitive therapy. The focus is on learning how to cope with everyday stresses and to control our feelings and actions by becoming aware of and changing our self-defeating thinking.

Ellis, A. (1973). *Growth through reason: Verbatim cases in rational-emotive therapy.* Hollywood, CA: Wilshire Books. This is a recording of actual cases. It gives the reader a good grasp of how the author works with a wide range of clients.

Ellis, A. (1988). *How to stubbornly refuse to make yourself miserable about anything— yes, anything!* Secaucus, NJ: Lyle Stuart. This is a self-help book that shows how to translate insights into action by uprooting irrational beliefs and learning functional beliefs. The book presents the basics of REBT and cognitive-behavior therapy in a simple and interesting way.

Ellis, A., & Harper, R. (1975). *A new guide to rational living* (rev. ed.). Hollywood, CA: Wilshire Books. The authors show how to apply the principles of REBT to problems of everyday living. An easy-to-read and interesting book.

Freeman, A., & Dattilio, F. M. (Eds.). (1992). *Comprehensive casebook of cognitive therapy.* New York: Plenum. This is an excellent compilation of case studies and of chapters dealing with specific treatment strategies for various clinical problems.

Goulding, M., & Goulding, R. (1979). *Changing lives through redecision therapy.* New York: Brunner/Mazel. This is a clear presentation of the major concepts of TA. The book deals with concepts such as injunctions, early decisions, and redecisions. Many examples of therapy sessions show how TA concepts can be integrated with techniques from cognitive-behavior therapy and Gestalt therapy.

Granvold, D. K. (Ed.). (1994). *Cognitive and behavioral treatment: Methods and applications.* Pacific Grove, CA: Brooks/Cole. This is a useful handbook of cognitive-behavioral methods. Especially helpful are the chapters dealing with cognitive and behavioral treatment of adults, problem-focused interventions, and stress-management techniques.

Meichenbaum, D. (1977). *Cognitive behavior modification: An integrative approach.* New York: Plenum. This is an excellent source for learning about cognitive-behavioral techniques such as cognitive restructuring, stress-inoculation training, and self-instructional training. The author does a good job of discussing how cognitive factors are related to behavior. He develops the theme that clients have the power and freedom to change by observing their behavior, telling themselves new sentences, and restructuring their belief system.

CHAPTER TEN

Case Approach to Family Therapy

A COGNITIVE-BEHAVIORAL APPROACH TO FAMILY THERAPY WITH RUTH, by Frank M. Dattilio, Ph.D., A.B.P.P.

Introduction

The cognitive-behavioral approach to families is virtually in its infancy as compared with some of the more traditional theories of marriage and family therapy. It originated in the late 1960s and early 1970s with the application to families of behavioral concepts that had been used with individuals. Principles of behavior modification were applied to the interactional patterns of family members only after their successful application to couples in distress. Behaviorists treating children soon recognized family members as a highly influential component of a child's natural environment and included them directly in the treatment process.

Behavioral family therapy focuses mainly on observable behavior or specific symptoms rather than on trying to establish any intrapsychic or interpersonal causality. It directly manipulates certain targeted behaviors through external means of reinforcement. Families are trained to monitor these reinforcements and make modifications where necessary. The cognitive component, which was added later, has proved to be effective in fostering permanent change in families in conflict.

As you saw in the last chapter, there are many subtypes of cognitive-behavioral therapy. The two major versions that will be highlighted here are those of Albert Ellis and Aaron T. Beck. Ellis's REBT emphasizes each individual's interpretation of the events that occur in the family environment. The basic theory contends that family members largely create their own world by the phenomenological view that they take of what happens to them. The focus of therapy is on how particular problems of the family members affect their well-being as a unit. Throughout the course of therapy, family members are treated as individuals, each of whom subscribes to his or her own specific set of beliefs and expectations. The role of the family therapist is to help members come to the realization that illogical or irrational beliefs and distortions serve as the foundation for their emotional distress. Beck's cognitive therapy, which also balances cognition and behavior, takes a more expansive and inclusive direction by focusing in greater depth on family interactional patterns and by remaining consistent with elements derived from a systems perspective. This theory has been elaborated on by Epstein, Dattilio, and others.

Basic Concepts and Assumptions

Consistent with systems theory, the cognitive-behavioral approach to families includes the premise that members of a family simultaneously influence one another. Consequently, a behavior of one family member leads to behaviors, cognitions, and emotions in other members, which, in turn, elicit cognitions, behaviors, and emotions in response. As this process continues to cycle, the volatility of the family dynamics escalates, rendering members vulnerable to a negative spiral of conflict. As the number of family members involved increases, so does the complexity of the dynamics, adding more fuel to the escalation process.

Some of the more recent cognitive-behavioral approaches place a heavy emphasis on the *schema*, or what has otherwise been defined as a set of core beliefs. As this concept is applied to family treatment, the therapeutic intervention is based on the assumptions with which family members interpret and evaluate one another and the emotions and behaviors that arise in response to these cognitions. Just as individuals maintain their own basic schemata about themselves, their world, and their future, they also maintain schemata about families. I have found in my clinical experience that emphasis should be placed both on these cognitions among individual family members and on what can be termed the *family schema*. This consists of beliefs held jointly by the family that have formed as a result of years of integrated interaction among members. An example of such a belief in Ruth's family of origin might be "It is unacceptable to talk about feelings and emotions openly."

Individuals actually maintain two separate schemata about families. The first is the schema related to the parents' families of origin, which comprises the beliefs that both partners learned during their upbringing and brought to the marriage. The second and more emphasized is the schema related to families in general. These schemata have a major impact on how an individual thinks, feels, and behaves within the family setting and also contribute to the development of rules and family patterns. An example in Ruth's present family is that emotions and feelings may be discussed, but selectively.

Schemata are thus the long-standing and relatively stable basic assumptions that people hold about how the world works and their place in it and are introjected into their current family constellation. In a familial situation such as Ruth's, for example, where it is understood that the father is the head of the household, all decisions regarding the family may be suspended until he has the final word. This pattern may disempower the mother in disciplining the children, and they may perceive her, in effect, as another sibling.

The family schema is very important when conducting family therapy. It also contains ideas about how spousal relationships should work, what problems should be expected in marriage and how they should be handled, what is involved in building and maintaining a healthy family, what responsibilities each family member should have, what consequences should be associated with failure to meet responsibilities or to fulfill roles, and what costs and benefits each individual should expect to have as a consequence of being in a marriage.

It is important to remember that the family schema is shaped by the family of origin of each partner in a relationship as well as by environmental influences such as the media and peer relationships. Beliefs funneled down from the family of origin may be either conscious or unconscious, and they contribute to a joint schema, or blended schema, that leads to the development of the current family schema (see Figure 10-1).

This family schema is then disseminated and applied in the rearing of the children, and, when mixed with their individual thoughts, perceptions of their environment, and life experiences, contributes to the development of the family belief system. The family schema is subject to change as major events occur during the course of family life (death, divorce) and also continues to evolve over the course of ordinary day-to-day experience.

As this schema begins to form, distortions may develop, contributing to family dysfunction. Ten of the more common distortions found with both couples and families are listed below:

1. *Arbitrary inference.* A conclusion is made by family members in the absence of supporting substantiating evidence. For example, one of Ruth's teenage children who returns home half an hour after his curfew is judged by the family as having been "up to no good."
2. *Selective abstraction.* Information is taken out of context; certain details are highlighted, and other important information is ignored. John fails to answer Adam's greeting the first thing in the morning, and Adam concludes, "Dad must be angry at me."
3. *Overgeneralization.* An isolated incident or two are allowed to serve as a representation of similar situations everywhere, related or unrelated. Because John and the kids have left food out from time to time, Ruth develops the belief that her family is wasteful and takes everything, including her, for granted.
4. *Magnification and minimization.* A case or circumstance is perceived in greater or lesser light than is appropriate. John demands that the children wash their hands before eating, but he fails to do so himself. When confronted by the children, he minimizes it by saying, "Well, I don't miss very often—so I'm excused."

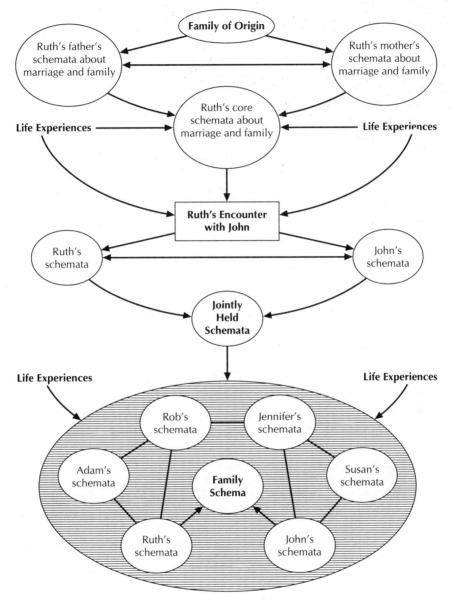

FIGURE 10-1   Ruth's family schemata

5. *Personalization.* External events are attributed to oneself when insufficient evidence exists to render a conclusion. Jennifer blames herself for her parents' repeated arguments, saying, "Maybe I should have never been born."

6. *Dichotomous thinking.* Experiences are codified as all or nothing, a complete success or a total failure. After repeated incidences in which Adam becomes involved in trouble at school, John and Ruth conclude, "We failed as disciplinarians."

7. *Labeling and mislabeling.* Imperfections and mistakes made in the past are allowed to serve as a stereotype of all future behaviors. Ruth and John failed to follow through on their word on one occasion and are consequently regarded by the children as being unreliable.

8. *Tunnel vision.* Family members sometimes see only what they want to see or what fits their current state of mind. John holds on to the rigid belief that the man is the "head of the household," because this is the way he perceived a father to be when he was growing up.

9. *Biased explanations.* In a polarized way of thinking that family members develop during times of distress, they assume that another member has an ulterior motive. John and the children distrust Ruth because she is reluctant to disclose to them what she has been discussing in her private therapy.

10. *Mind reading.* A family member has the magical gift of being able to know what others are thinking without the aid of verbal communication. Ruth anticipates that the family views her as a failure because she is unable to stand up for herself and demand what she wants.

These distortions become key targets in family therapy. Family members are oriented to the cognitive-behavioral model and are taught to identify such distortions in their own thinking as well as in the thinking of other members. Much of the intervention in therapy involves helping members identify such distortions and then gather evidence to aid in reconstructing their thinking. It may also include practicing alternative patterns of behavioral interaction and dealing with their negative attributions.

The cognitive-behavioral theory operates on a set of assumptions that Schwebel and Fine feel are central. Below is a modified version of these assumptions:*

• *Assumption 1.* All members of a family seek to maintain their environment in order to fulfill their needs and wants. They attempt to understand their environment and how they can function most effectively in it, even if it sometimes means testing the boundaries. (For example, Adam may exceed his curfew by half an hour.) As family members gather data about how the family operates, they use this information to guide their be-

*See Schwebel, A. I., & Fine, M. A. (1994). *Understanding and helping families: A cognitive-behavioral approach.* Hillsdale, NJ: Erlbaum.

haviors and to aid in building and refining family-related cognitions. This leads to the development of an individual's construct of family life and family relationships. In Adam's case, he may begin to develop the concept that he can stretch the limits and not be chastised, thus inferring that rules may be broken.

• *Assumption 2.* Individual members' cognitions affect virtually every aspect of family life. Five categories are identified as cognitive variables that determine these cognitions: (1) selective attention (John and Ruth's focus on the children's negative behaviors), (2) attributions (Ruth's explanations for why the children act up), (3) expectations (John's expectation that Ruth and the children will do as he asks without questions), (4) assumptions (Adam's view that life is not fair), and (5) standards (Jennifer's thoughts about how the world should be).

• *Assumption 3.* Certain "obstacles" to satisfaction lie within individual family members' cognitions (for example, Ruth's rigid view of the role of a wife and mother).

• *Assumption 4.* Unless family members become more aware of their family-related cognitions and how these cognitions affect them in certain situations, they will not be able to identify areas that cause distress and replace them with healthy interaction.

Assessment of Ruth

My differential DSM-IV diagnosis of Ruth would probably be the following:

Axis I: V61.1, partner relational problem; 300.40, dysthymic disorder secondary to identity problem; 300.21, panic disorder without agoraphobia.
Axis II: 301.6, dependent personality disorder; 313.82, identity problem.
Axis III: exogenous obesity.
Axis IV: problems related to social environment.
Axis V: GAF = 60 (on admission).

A family history is conducted to ascertain pertinent information about Ruth's family of origin. Although in most cases the family approach, like other modalities of family therapy, prefers to avoid "identifying a patient" and instead takes a balanced approach to dealing with family dysfunction, there are often exceptions. It appears that this case is one. Ruth has already initiated individual psychotherapy, and it was decided to include her family as well. In a sense, therefore, she has already been designated as the "identified patient," and family treatment can initially center on her issues. Given her history and background, I elect to work on gaining a better understanding of her family of origin by having her invite members in for several visits. This will certainly lead toward developing a good grasp of her core schemata about herself and family life and will possibly provide me with an insight into the development of her thinking style. Tradition-ally, this should only involve Ruth, her parents, and any siblings. No other extended family members are invited—most importantly, her husband.*

This session is exclusively designed for Ruth and the therapist to better understand the thinking styles of her origin and also to clear up any areas of conflict that remain from her past. If all were amenable, we could meet for three to five sessions of two hours each, focusing on the family schema and particularly on her emancipation from certain thinking styles that are deleterious to her. Although idealistic, such meetings are not always so successful. The following is a brief excerpt from this session.

Initial Session with Ruth's Family of Origin

THERAPIST: Ruth, my understanding is that your three siblings could not attend today because of the distance and that one of them was simply not interested in attending at all. So this is it today?

RUTH: Yes, we're it.

THERAPIST [to Ruth's parents]: Thank you for coming to this meeting. OK, as Ruth has explained to you, she has entered into psychotherapy with me in order to deal with some areas of conflict in her life more suc-cessfully. A significant part of my work with her involves examining some of the values she was exposed to during her early development as well as her patterns of thought and belief about life in general. One of the ways in which I help clients is to conduct what is referred to as a family-of-origin meeting. This may help clear up any misconceptions that she has developed about her relationship with you as well as improve her current relationship with her husband and immediate family. It will also help her understand herself better.

RUTH'S FATHER: Well, I was wondering what this was all about. I wasn't so sure why we were here.

RUTH: Dad, you know I've been struggling with some things in my life, and I've sought help for it.

FATHER: Yes, well of course I'm sure that more of this has to do with John as opposed to your mother and me. [to therapist:] You know how we feel about him?

THERAPIST: I don't, sir. Could you tell me more about your feelings about John and about Ruth's marriage to him?

FATHER: Well, we were against it from the start. He came from a broken home where the mother just left for a couple of years, and he had a brief marriage before he married Ruth. My wife and I were always concerned about how that would affect Ruth's life, not to mention their children. We're a very strong and committed family. We don't believe in that sort of stuff.

---

*For a more detailed explanation, see *Family of Origin Therapy* by J. Framo, 1993, New York: Brunner/Mazel.

THERAPIST: What sort of stuff is that, sir?

FATHER: Bustin' up families and divorce. You know, that nonsense.

THERAPIST: So this was a very strong principle emphasized in your home, and my impression is almost that, with all due respect, divorce was viewed with disdain.

FATHER: Yes, I certainly feel that way.

THERAPIST [to Ruth's mother]: Ma'am, you haven't said very much. Do you feel the same way?

RUTH'S MOTHER: Yes, for the most part, but . . . I . . . well, I'll let my husband do the talking. He's the spokesman in our family.

THERAPIST: So, it sounds as though you have some concerns about Ruth's marriage to John.

FATHER: Yes, we just feel that it's not a strong marriage and that the entire family atmosphere is no good.

THERAPIST: What is your opinion about what constitutes a good family atmosphere? Can you elaborate a bit on your philosophy?

FATHER: Well, certainly I view a strong traditional family as being one where the father and mother are the head of the household and, of course, what they say goes. Needless to say, I'm a bit disturbed by this business of John siding with Rob against Ruth.

RUTH: Dad, it's not just John—some of it's me, too. I have some of my own conflicts with Rob.

FATHER: Nonsense! If your husband and son had any respect, the boy wouldn't be treating you the way he does, and John wouldn't allow it. And Jennifer, she's completely out of control.

THERAPIST [to Ruth's father]: This troubles you greatly.

FATHER: Oh! I can't stand it. Ruthie knows that this is not the way we raised her, and certainly it's not what we want for our daughter. John has to buck up and start acting like a man and take control.

RUTH: But Dad, those were your rules. And if you don't mind my saying so, they were too strict. I can't be that rigid.

FATHER: Nonsense. It's not rigid. It's respect and rules. Discipline is a key virtue in a strong, traditional family. If there's no discipline, there's no love. That's the way Mother and I were raised, and that's the value system we instilled in our children.

THERAPIST: Ruth, what's your response to all of this?

RUTH: I don't know. I'm just confused, I guess.

In just this short dialogue, you can see the dynamics that existed in the home in which Ruth was raised. Her father was clearly the patriarch, whose word was rarely challenged. Ruth's mother clearly empowers her husband and acquiesces to his demands, even though he tries to give the impression that he shares his role equally with her. Hence, the wife and mother's role in Ruth's schema development was one of a passive/dependent disposition that heeds to the role of the man. When she attempts to challenge this, she meets with an even greater opposition, which causes her to question her motives and to fall back on her notion of living for others. Her mother only reinforces this pattern through her continued silence and passivity. This is a rather rigid family structure that leaves little room for emotional expression or autonomy. You can understand how Ruth would be somewhat inhibited emotionally and resist change. What's more, as a safeguard, she married someone who is resistant to change, locking her into the old mode that has been safe for so many years yet continues to produce inner conflict for her. No wonder she is experiencing panic attacks.

THERAPIST [to Ruth's parents]: I sense that you're angry with your daughter, not only about her marriage to John but for other reasons.

FATHER: Yes, quite frankly we are.

THERAPIST [to Ruth's mother]: Could you tell me personally how you feel toward your daughter?

MOTHER [looking to her husband almost as if asking permission to speak]: Well, of course we love her very much, but she's broken our hearts. [She begins to sob. Ruth's father hands her his handkerchief. Ruth also begins to cry at this point.] She left our church, which just devastated us. Now she's on this idea about becoming a teacher and is going to leave her family to be off teaching all day. This has got us beside ourselves. [She turns to Ruth.] This is not what we wanted for you. You were not raised this way!

FATHER: Yes, and then this.

THERAPIST: This what?

FATHER: Well, these meetings. We don't believe in them much.

THERAPIST: Oh?

FATHER: Yes, I'm sorry, doctor, but this is not part of our belief. This is nothing against you personally, but we've conveyed to Ruth that we think this is a bunch of foolishness and that she knows where the answers in life come from.

RUTH: Yes, father, the Bible. The Bible has all the answers!

FATHER: That's correct, and don't ever forget it. All is within the power of the Lord. Seek and you shall find!

THERAPIST: Sir, I respect your faith and your strong religious convictions, and obviously this has worked well for you and your wife in raising your family. But it appears to me that because Ruth has begun to question some of the principles of your particular denomination, in your view she's abandoning her faith in God completely, and I don't know if this is true. All that I see her doing is . . .

FATHER [interrupting]: Look, young man. I don't really know who you are or what your beliefs are, but don't tell me what my daughter is doing. She's questioning the teachings of the church, and in my book, that's heresy. Furthermore, I happen to view what you do as witchery and against our beliefs, and this little charade is over. I'm sorry, but I'm not going to sit here and listen to this!

THERAPIST: Well, I'm sorry you feel that way, sir. This was certainly not intended to be offensive to you.

FATHER: Well, the whole damn thing is offensive to me. We're leaving! Good-bye, Ruth, we'll see you later. [The parents leave.]

THERAPIST [to Ruth]: I'm sorry things turned out this way. Your father is pretty stern.

RUTH [crying]: Yes, I know. I've lived with that my entire life.

THERAPIST: OK, but you do know you have a choice in how you desire to live and govern your life.

RUTH: Yes, I know, but the cost is a lot to bear.

Unfortunately, things did not go as planned, and the family-of-origin visits have ended abruptly. This certainly puts Ruth on the spot to make a choice. Perhaps this is good, in a way, because now more than ever she knows that she must live for herself and no one else. This session also helped me obtain a firsthand flavor for the dynamics that existed in her household during her upbringing and to see that her perceptions were indeed accurate. In fact, it is obvious that these patterns are reinforced each time she visits her parents. This visit sets the stage nicely for me to begin to work directly with her current family and to aid her in restructuring her schemata as well as inadvertently changing some of the family schema as well.

Initial Session with Ruth's Current Family

Because cognitive-behavior family therapists attempt to identify both distorted schemata and maladaptive behavior patterns in family interaction, the next order of business in Ruth's case is to meet with her entire (immediate) family. As a result of what has been gathered from her family of origin and a separate interview with John, I now have a firm foundation for understanding the diverse philosophies that exist in each of their family backgrounds and can develop some insight into what schemata may have trickled down into the immediate family dynamics and family schema.

During the initial family therapy session, I may ask the various members of the family to describe their perceptions of the family and how things operate at home. It is often best to start with the youngest child and work up to the parents, so that the younger children are not influenced by what is said by their older siblings. As you will see in the following excerpt from the initial session, I aim directly at ascertaining a solid understanding of the individual perceptions of the family and then attempt to conceptualize a joint consensus of the family schema. Once this is accomplished, the next step is to begin to educate the family in how the cognitive-behavioral model of therapy works and then to begin to collaboratively identify cognitive distortions and erroneous thinking patterns that lead to maladaptive behavior patterns and dysfunction in the family.

THERAPIST: Well, first of all, I want to thank everyone for attending this meeting today, since I know that you all have your own schedules and this may not be everyone's top priority. Ruth, have you explained to the family what these meetings are all about and the intention behind family therapy?

RUTH: Well no, not really. I simply told them that we needed to meet together and that you had wanted to address some of the problems in the family in order to help me in my individual therapy.

THERAPIST: OK. Well, in essence that's what this is designed to do in part, but it's also my intention to address some of the problems that exist in the family for the family's sake as well. Does that sound reasonable to everyone?

FAMILY: [Three members nod reticently in affirmation.]

JENNIFER: It doesn't to me! I think this is bogus, and I don't want to be here.

THERAPIST: So why did you agree to come?

JENNIFER: I didn't. I was brutally forced.

RUTH: Oh, Jennifer, come on!

JOHN: You weren't "brutally forced." Knock that stuff off. This is serious business here. The doctor needs to see us.

JENNIFER: I don't care. I don't want to be here—it's not fair.

THERAPIST: I hear you, Jennifer, and I want you to know that I never expect people to come here against their will. So if you feel that strongly, you can leave, provided that your parents and the rest of the family agree. [silent pause]

JENNIFER: Well, so what do I do? Just leave now?

THERAPIST: Yes, I suppose you could.

JENNIFER: So where do I go?

THERAPIST: I don't know. That's for you to decide.

JENNIFER: Well that's dumb. I'm not going to just sit outside in the car—bored!

THERAPIST: OK, you're certainly welcome to stay if you wish, but I'm actually interested in hearing why you don't want to be here, particularly if being here would help the family.

JENNIFER: Because this is all bull, and it's not my problem—it's Mom's. She just makes it everyone else's problem.

THERAPIST: Ah, interesting. Does anyone else view things the same way Jennifer does? [brief pause]

JOHN: No, I don't, totally. I think we all have some issues here that need to be discussed besides Mom, but Mom does have problems.

THERAPIST: Anyone else have an opinion?

ROB: Yes, I'd like to say something. I think our family definitely has some problems in the way we think. Everyone is, like, all over the place, and there's no sense of . . . how would you say . . .

THERAPIST: Family unity?

ROB: Yeah! Sort of. I mean, like, Dad is sort of off in his own world—no offense, Dad—and Mom is doing her thing and trying to do for everyone else. It's sort of crazy.

THERAPIST: So, I'm hearing you say that things at home are somewhat chaotic at times, and you're uncomfortable with it?

ROB: Yes, but not at times. A lot of the time.

THERAPIST: OK, but I want to get back to Jennifer's statement about how Mom makes her problems everyone else's. Does that seem to be true for everyone here? Are we all in agreement with Jen's statement?

JOHN: No, I'm having a problem with Jennifer's statement. You know, Ruth and Jennifer really lock horns, and Jennifer will often take every opportunity she can to blame her mother, or anyone else for that matter—except, of course, herself.

THERAPIST: John, in addition to your concerns about Jennifer, you sound as though you're a bit protective of your wife.

JOHN: Well sure, but that's also the way I really see it.

THERAPIST: OK, but is there any agreement with any of what the kids are saying?

JOHN: Yeah, maybe some. I mean, look, Ruth has some problems. She's had a really rough upbringing, so I sort of see our roles as being to support her and not to give her a hard time.

THERAPIST: It seems to me that this is somewhat how your family has functioned for a long time until recently.

JENNIFER: Yeah! Until I screwed everything up, right? Right, Mom? That's it—say it!

RUTH [begins to sob]: Oh, Jennifer, stop!

ADAM: I think Jennifer's problem is that she wants to grow up, and Mom won't let her, and that's why she's mad at Mom.

SUSAN: I sort of agree. I can see Mom starting to do a little of the same with me.

JOHN: What? Do what?

SUSAN: Uh-oh! I opened my big mouth. [Everyone chuckles.]

THERAPIST: No, that's OK, Susan. Say what you feel.

SUSAN: Well, she's starting to be kind of overprotective with me the way she has with Jen.

JENNIFER: Yeah, and it's only with the girls. She's not like that so much with Adam and Rob.

THERAPIST: Ruth, how do you respond to everything you're hearing here today?

RUTH: Well, it's true, I guess, if I have to be honest, but it's also hard to listen to.

THERAPIST: OK, so you're protective of the girls, John is protective of you, and who is protective of Rob, Adam, and Dad?

ROB: Rob, Adam, and Dad. [Everyone laughs.]

THERAPIST: Ah-ha! So the men take care of the men. That's interesting!

Protecting one another appears to be a very important theme in your family.

JOHN: Well sure, you've seen that with both mine and Ruth's family.*

THERAPIST: So I guess it would be fair to say, in a way, that it was carried down to your family here. [Everyone agrees.]

THERAPIST: We've just identified what's called a family schema—that we protect each other in certain ways that sometimes differ. So what's the core belief governing why we do this? In other words, what belief exists in your family that calls for this behavior as opposed to the idea of everyone protecting themselves? [silent pause]

SUSAN: Is it bad that we do this?

THERAPIST: Well, not necessarily, but the way it has evolved in your family patterns here has caused some trouble. What you need to do is begin to change or modify this so that you get along with one another better. But let me get an answer to my question, because I think this is very important. Again, where does this core belief of protectiveness stem from? [silent pause]

JOHN: Well, I guess as the father, I feel the blame for some of it. While I support Ruth, I've kind of dumped on her by not taking more of an active role with the kids.

THERAPIST: Yes, and as a result of Ruth's upbringing, she has felt compelled to assume all of the responsibility for the family, perhaps in part to compensate for you. So there are several family-held distortions, as well as individual distortions about ourselves.

ADAM: What do you mean, distortions?

THERAPIST: Good question, Adam. Let me explain. [The therapist explains and reviews the cognitive distortions listed on pages 284–286 in a clear manner that the family members can understand, often using specific examples from their family.] So let's try to identify some of the distortions together.

ROB: I have one that Mom does big-time.

THERAPIST: OK, let's hear it.

ROB: Well, it's the arbitration thing you said . . .

THERAPIST: Arbitrary inference?

ROB: Yeah, I guess that's it. Well, like if we're out past curfew, she freaks and starts accusing us of being up to no good, like we're guilty until proven innocent.

THERAPIST: Well, that's one that you may perceive Mom as doing, but do any of the other family members engage in the same distortion?

ADAM: Yeah, Jen does!

JENNIFER: Do not!

ADAM: Yes, you do.

SUSAN: Yes, you do, Jen. You're just like Mom in that way.

---

*John is referring to a meeting that I had with him and Ruth alone to sum up our understanding of the respective families of origin.

THERAPIST: Look, guys, you're just trying to identify cognitive distortions that you all engage in from time to time. This is not meant to be an antagonizing session. Also, you want to identify those distortions that you engage in yourselves as well as those that you witness with other family members.

JOHN: OK, I have one about myself. I sometimes find myself thinking much the way Ruth's father does, and I get annoyed when my decisions are questioned—as much as I hate to admit it. I guess I view compliance by the other members of my family as respect, yet I tend to dump a lot onto Ruth.

At this point, the therapist has attempted to uncover some of the family's schemata and also identify cognitive distortions. At the same time, the family members are being oriented to the cognitive model in a subtle but clear way in which they will eventually be able to apply some of the techniques to themselves. The next step after identifying these distortions will be to teach them to begin to question and weigh the evidence that supports the internal statements that they make to themselves and to challenge any erroneously based assumptions.

THERAPIST: All right, that's a good one, John. So one of your beliefs that you're choosing to identify as being based on a distortion is that "the boss is never questioned, or it's disrespectful." In a sense, it's a matter of "do as I say, not as I do."

JOHN: Yeah, I guess. Boy, that sounds horrible when someone else actually says it in those terms.

THERAPIST: Well, don't worry so much about that, John. Let's just analyze it for a moment and see if we can challenge some of the basic tenets of that belief. Now, do you have any idea why you believe in that manner—that the man should be the boss and his requests or decisions should go unquestioned?

JOHN: Well, I know that I was closer to my father than I was to my mother. I also think that Ruthie's father had something to do with it early on. When we were first married he used to . . . sort of . . . drill me.

THERAPIST: Drill you?

JOHN: Yeah, you know, like take me aside and give me his lecture about how I need to act as the man of the house and family. Also, well, this may sound odd, but I kind of get the impression that this was sort of the way Ruthie was more comfortable with also, you know—like she kind of . . . oh, I forget the word that you guys use all of the time. It's a popular term . . .

THERAPIST: Enabled it?

JOHN: Yeah, yeah, enabled. That's it. She enabled me to be that way, subtly, I guess.

THERAPIST: I see. So, do you believe that you may enable Ruth as well with certain things, and perhaps you both enable the children?

RUTH AND JOHN [in unison]: Yes! Definitely.

THERAPIST: Might this be tied to the schema of taking care of one another? How does this all relate?

ROB: Well, I was thinking about that for a while when you were talking to Dad, and I think we're like a pack of wolves that sort of just look out for one another casually, and if one of us is in need, somebody will step in. But we never talk about it openly otherwise.

THERAPIST: OK, but how does this cause conflict?

ROB: I'm not sure.

SUSAN: I think that maybe the conflict comes when one person has one expectation and the other has a different expectation and it's never communicated. We just sort of . . . uh . . .

THERAPIST: Mind-read.

SUSAN: Yeah.

THERAPIST: OK, that's another distortion.

ADAM: Wow, we're one distorted family—cool! [Everyone laughs.]

THERAPIST: Well, yes, you have your distortions, but all families do. It's not so bad!

RUTH [in jest]: I don't know. When I listen to it all, it makes us sound as if we're the Addams family. [Everyone laughs.]

THERAPIST: Good, Ruth! That was funny!

Here the therapist is attempting to bolster some family cohesion through levity at the same time as trying to understand the family dynamics and how each member thinks and perceives various situations. Next, the therapist will attempt to introduce slowly the idea of restructuring some of the thinking styles in order to bring about change.

THERAPIST: I think that it might be important for us to take a look at some of the distortions that you frequently engage in, now that you have identified a few of them, and see whether we may be able to challenge them, particularly those that interfere the most with your family dynamics. For example, John, would you be willing to volunteer so that I can demonstrate?

JOHN: Sure.

THERAPIST: You said, as I recall, that one of your beliefs is that as the father and one of the heads of the household, "the boss is never questioned, or it would demonstrate disrespect"—something to that effect.

JOHN: Right.

THERAPIST: OK, now how well do you believe that this statement can be substantiated? In other words, is it based on any sound rule of thumb or theory of parenting?

JOHN: I don't know. It's just something that I've come to know.

THERAPIST: So there's no substantiating evidence that renders it a sound principle. It's merely conjecture. So is it possible that it might be based on erroneous information?

JOHN: Possibly.

THERAPIST: Well, what do you know about the effect of this principle? In other words, what results have you received from it thus far?

JOHN: Well, not too good. In fact, no one obeys it, and I'm sort of scoffed at by my kids for believing it.

THERAPIST: All right, so perhaps you're seeing more evidence that says that it's not so effective than evidence supporting its use. So maybe it needs some modification, and you don't have to abandon the principle completely. I mean, respect is important, but to expect that no one will ever question what you say or do may be a bit unreasonable.

JOHN: Yeah, I see your point. But then how do I get it out of my head? I mean, it's ingrained there pretty heavily.

THERAPIST: Good question. Cognitive therapy utilizes a great deal of homework assignments. The basic theory contends that you must practice challenging negative self-statements, or what we call automatic thoughts, just as much as you have been using them in the past. One way to do this is by writing the corrected statement out each time you experience a negative self-statement, or in this case, a cognitive distortion. So, I'd like you to take a piece of paper and write across the top several headings, drawing a vertical line down the side of each to make columns like this:

Situation or Event	Automatic Thought	Cognitive Distortion	Emotion	Challenging Self-Statement	Alternative Response

Then, each time a situation occurs when you have a negative automatic thought, write it down. Starting with the left-hand column, record the situation or event in which you had the thought, and in the next column put exactly what the thought was. Next, attempt to identify what type of distortion you are engaging in and the emotional response that accompanies it. Then try to challenge that thought or belief by weighing the evidence that exists in favor of it. After that, write down an alternative response, using any new information that you may have gathered. Does that make sense to you?

JOHN: Yes, but could we run through it once so that I'm sure I have it right?

THERAPIST: Certainly. Let's try an example.

JOHN: Something happened last week with Adam when he came in a little past curfew, and I said something about his being five minutes late. He started to, well, what I call challenge my authority by attempting to minimize what he had done, saying it had only been five minutes and was no big deal.

THERAPIST: So let's get everything down on paper.

Situation or Event	Automatic Thought	Cognitive Distortion
Adam arrives home five minutes late for curfew.	"He's defying me. He doesn't respect my position. If I don't chastise him, I'll be a lousy father."	Arbitrary inference Dichotomous thinking Personalization
Emotion	Challenging Self-Statement	Alternative Response
Upset Angry	"Just because he comes home five minutes beyond his curfew doesn't mean that it's aimed directly at me. It also doesn't mean that he's intending to defy me."	"I could talk to him about it rather than jumping to conclusions and punishing him. Perhaps he just honestly lost track of time."

THERAPIST: That's excellent. Do you all see how we attempt to restructure some of our thinking?

ROB: Yeah, but what if Adam was really defying Dad? I mean, how do we know that it's correct?

THERAPIST: Good question, Rob. We gather information to support our alternative beliefs, and so one of the things that your dad could do is, as he said on the sheet, talk to Adam about what his intentions were in arriving home late. This could be applied to all of you at one time or the other as you recognize yourselves engaging in distorted thinking. We want to begin to examine your mode of thought and really question the validity of what you tell yourselves. This may make a monumental difference in how you interact.

From this point, the therapist begins to monitor the family members in challenging their belief statements in the fashion demonstrated above. During this process, feelings and emotions are also addressed, as well as communication skills and problem-solving strategies. Regular homework assignments are also employed in order to aid family members in learning to challenge their distorted thoughts more spontaneously. Eventually, the therapist walks each family member through this specific technique to ensure its correct use. In addition, the use of behavioral techniques, such as the reassignment of family members' roles and responsibilities, becomes an integral part of the treatment regime in this particular case. The general concept behind this is that with the change and modification of dysfunctional thinking and behaviors, there will be less family conflict.

A FAMILY SYSTEMS THERAPIST'S PERSPECTIVE ON RUTH, by Mary E. Moline, Ph.D.

Introduction

A systemic approach defines the client as being influenced by others within the individual's system, which includes the church, school, and workplace. Most often the system observed is the family. The transactions that occur between the individual and other family members shape the person's concept of self, relationships with others, and worldview.

For a family with members who demonstrate a poor sense of self, one might integrate a developmental approach and a systems model. In the case of Ruth, a systemic family approach requires an assessment of her family system, including her husband, her children, and her parents. An even more comprehensive systemic assessment could include examining her relationships (interactions) with other important units such as church, work, and friends. No rules dictate how much of her system of relationships the therapist must work with; rather, this will depend upon the therapist's clinical judgment. Conceptually (or symbolically), however, the therapist will make interventions with her that will enable her to deal with her husband, children, and parents, even though they may not be physically present in the therapy session.

Confidentiality as a Foundation for Therapy

A decision that family therapists often make prior to a client's first visit is whom they will see. Many insist that a client's entire family be seen during the first visit. Given the variety of systemic approaches available, one may decide to see only the concerned client in the beginning and later invite others in his or her system to attend therapeutic sessions. In that case, the matter of confidentiality must be addressed. The therapist needs to decide if what a client reveals in an individual session will be kept secret. It should be noted that many systems therapists avoid seeing the concerned client first, partially because of the problems involved with deciding how to deal in family therapy with this client's disclosures.

In my view, a safe rule in working with couples or families is not to keep secrets. This definitely applies in those situations where the law mandates that the therapist reveal information indicating that clients are likely to harm themselves or others and in child-abuse cases. Even in those situations where the law does not mandate the revealing of a secret, it is advisable to inform clients of any policies that apply to dealing with secrets. If secrets are kept, the therapist will certainly have a difficult time in doing effective therapy with various parts of a family system. Therapists can easily forget what they may not say when the entire family gets together. For this reason, many family therapists refuse to become entangled in keeping secrets, and they let this be known from the outset.

The matter of secrets is not a simple matter, as you can see in the following example. Assume that John has told you that he is having an affair, which started two years ago. At about this same time, Ruth began to have her panic attacks. You conclude that her reactions were a direct result of the changes that occurred between Ruth and John from the time he began the affair. However, John reveals his affair to you in private and tells you that he does not want to tell Ruth. You encourage him to do so, but he refuses. In fact, he lets you know that he is having an affair with another man and that they are not practicing safe sex. At the present time, there are no clear legal channels for sharing this information with Ruth. If you did not make it clear that you had a policy of not keeping secrets, John is clearly in control of the therapy sessions, and your therapeutic effectiveness is reduced.

If you decide to work within the framework of refusing to keep secrets, I suggest that you have this policy in writing and that you encourage your clients to discuss its ramifications. This contract informs your clients of the risks involved with the therapy process. Of course, clients in family therapy should be clearly informed about the legal limits of confidentiality from the beginning, just as would be the case for individual therapy.

Key Themes and Issues

If one views Ruth's problems from a developmental approach, the theme of family stages becomes central to the treatment process. One can also view the themes in her life from a structural perspective, in which case the boundaries of the system (rules for communicating) are also quite important. It may even hold true that the themes or issues to be examined determine the theoretical approach.

In Ruth's case, I would approach treatment from a structural-intergenerational model, which is my integration of models developed by Murray Bowen and Salvador Minuchin. My rationale for working from this integrated perspective is that Ruth's primary concern regarding change is how her going back to school and seeking a teaching job are likely to affect her husband and children. Thus, I view treatment in three phases. I approach the first two phases from an intergenerational (Bowen) model. The first phase involves having Ruth's husband, John, attend sessions, and the second phase includes assessing John's and Ruth's families of origin. The third phase entails bringing Ruth's entire family in for assessment and intervention. I approach these family sessions from a structural model. A more detailed explanation of these models is given in the section that deals with an assessment of Ruth.

Ruth appears to be unable to define herself separately from her husband and her children. Her struggle with her identity leads me to examine her process of *differentiation* (identity) as a central issue. Other key issues that I would assess and treat pertain to the ways in which anxiety is perpetuated through rigid (inflexible) patterns of three-person systems (known as triangulated interaction) across multiple family generations and to the ways in which her current family structures communication.

Differentiation.   Ruth appears, from a conversation we had over the telephone, to be struggling with developing a sense of self that is separate from her family and possibly from her family of origin. Her decision to develop an identity separate from her parents, husband, and children is known in Bowen's terminology as the process of differentiation. The less differentiated people are, the more they invest their energies in relationships; to the degree that they do not have a separate identity, they can be seen as lacking a sense of autonomy. For example, Ruth would like to pursue a career separate from being a mother and a wife. She appears to be most concerned, however, with how her husband and children will respond to her change. She is so concerned about what they think of her that she becomes immobilized. She wonders if she will lose her husband if she follows her goals. At present, she does not seem to have the sense of self to negotiate such a change with either her husband or her children.

The goal for Ruth from a systemic perspective is to increase her level of differentiation. This does not mean that she will selfishly follow her own directives but that she can determine the direction of her life.

What keeps Ruth from having a sense of self is that she usually interacts with others by triangulation. This is a process by which a person (A) does not directly communicate information with another person (B) but goes through another individual (C). Gossip is a form of triangulation. It is an indirect and often ineffective form of communication. For example, Ruth may wish to communicate that she is upset with her father, but she chooses to tell her mother instead. In turn, her mother relays the message to the father and adds, "How dare you make my daughter angry!" This results in a confused and poorly delivered message. Ruth needed another person to deliver her thoughts to her father because she was unable to do so herself. Her indirect communication is a manifestation of her lack of differentiation. Her style of communication keeps her emotionally fused to others, such as her parents, husband, and children. In her case, the more fused she has become with others, the less she has been able to understand what she values and believes. To some degree, her value system has become identical to those of the people with whom she is fused. Fortunately, it appears that she is at least examining a desire to become a separate individual from John and that she is considering what the consequences will be if she does acquire a new sense of identity.

Anxiety. Ruth's fused relationship with John gives her a sense of well-being. When she attempts to change her relationship to others in her system (parents, husband, and children), however, the level of stress (anxiety and emotional distress) increases in the system. Her inability to reduce anxiety and emotional distress is exhibited by physical symptoms such as panic attacks, difficulty in breathing, and inability to sleep. Her referring physician has determined that there is no organic or physical causation. Depending on the outcome of her medical evaluation, she may be given medication as a way to control her symptoms so that she will be more amenable to psychotherapy. Generally, I do not recommend medication for removing anxiety symptoms because of my belief in the value of working through the issues that are leading to panic attacks rather than merely numbing these symptoms.

Ruth is anxious that her movement away from homemaking to teaching may threaten her family. Such anxiety is typical of clients who exhibit little clear sense of self. A differentiated person makes decisions confidently about the direction of his or her life and is willing to face the consequences of those decisions as necessary. The anxiety that is manifested in Ruth's family system pertains to the intensity, duration, and types of tensions that are occurring between the members. Anxiety is occurring because John and the children fear the possible changes taking place with Ruth. They may assume that her changes imply that she no longer loves them. One way of examining this anxiety and how it is manifested is to work with her from a natural systems (Bowen) perspective. The goal is to explore the processes within the family system that bring about her symptoms, including the manner in which family members form triangles.

Transgenerational patterns of interaction. A triangle (three-person relationship), according to Bowen's theory, is the smallest stable unit of human relations. When a family system is calm, one cannot detect a triangle; when a system is under stress, this process can be observed. If a two-person system is threatened by conflict, a third person is introduced in an attempt to create an overt appearance of togetherness. Actually, the conflict and the focus on the third person serve the purpose of reducing the tension in the dyad.

This concept can be applied to Ruth's case. To assess her panic attacks and determine her level of differentiation, one can assess the patterns of interaction in her current family as well as the relational patterns that have occurred in previous generations and have been transmitted from generation to generation. As mentioned, this involves examining the triangular process.

Looking at the situation between Ruth and John provides examples of triangular relationships. Because this couple is not able to discuss emotionally charged issues, there has been a tendency to focus on a particular child within the family. Jennifer, who is seen as the rebel, gets considerable attention. John may not have learned how to share the feelings of loneliness that he experiences when he considers Ruth working outside the home. Likewise, she cannot share how angry she feels about his not accepting her need for a career apart from her role in the family. Instead of dealing directly with each other about their concerns as a couple, they argue about their daughter Jennifer.

Consider the following example as yet another illustration of the nature and functioning of triangles. Jennifer comes home and tells her mother that she is angry that there is no food on the table. She also begins to complain about all the time that her mother spends at school and accuses her of neglecting the children. If Ruth allows herself to become anxious about Jennifer's response, she may not be able to sit her down and tell her about her need to go to school. If her identity (self) is influenced strongly by Jennifer's values, she may go to John and say: "Jennifer is at it again. She doesn't appreciate me at all." Then she may begin to experience physical symptoms, including shortness of breath. In his attempt to reduce her anxiety, John may approach Jennifer and say: "You've made your mother very upset. You will stay home tonight."

This example provides a further illustration of the nature of interlocking triangles. These indirect relationships do not solve family problems; rather, they increase the chances that symptoms will be maintained. Ruth and Jennifer do not discuss their upset feelings toward each other, but instead John takes on their anxiety.

Every family system forms triangles, but when one triangle becomes the consistent or persistent pattern of communication, symptoms arise. Ruth's symptoms include panic attacks. Jennifer may not be allowed to have peer relationships, and any of her attempts to define herself separately from the triangle will lead to anxiety among key family members. Jennifer may be rebellious and act out or may turn her angry feelings inward and become depressed. It is likely that she will develop psychosomatic symptoms, since that is her mother's pattern of relieving stress.

I am particularly interested in observing Ruth's relationship with John. In order to help her attain her goal of determining her own direction without experiencing anxiety, I want to observe and understand the patterns that characterize their relationship. How and why do they avoid emotionally charged topics? With whom in the family do they form alliances? How are triangular relationships in Ruth's current family a manifestation of patterns that go back over one or two generations in Ruth's and John's families?

Whatever the marital relationship patterns are, it is most likely that they will become apparent by studying patterns that have been passed on over several generations. This method of interacting and relating is often referred to as the family emotional system. For example, in three generations it has been observed that eldest girls assumed masculine-oriented roles and became more aligned with the father than the mother. This will have significance only if it is important to the person exploring his or her family of origin. Perhaps such a pattern would explain to a woman the reasons why she has few female relationships. Patterns that prohibit an individual in a couple or family system from being who and what he or she wants to be are fertile material for exploration. Also, if there is reactivity (poor impulse control, or emotions easily aroused and displayed) toward certain people, it will be therapeutically explored. Perhaps the eldest daughter is reactive whenever a woman tries to form a relationship with her or when her mother shows signs of what she considers to be "weak" or "emotional" behavior.

An exploration of both John's and Ruth's families of origin may determine patterns of closeness, conflict, and distance that emerge from generations of interaction. I would work with those themes that emerge from an intergenerational perspective. The goal of therapy from this perspective, which is the reduction of anxiety expressed in the system so that all the members of the family can improve their sense of self, fits Ruth's case well.

Rigid boundaries.   Observed from a structural paradigm, a theme in Ruth's case is that the family structure appears to have rigid boundaries. Boundaries are the rules that define who participates and how members of a family interact with one another and with "outsiders." Ruth says on the phone that she is concerned about "losing" her children. They are appropriately trying to join peer groups outside the home, which worries her. They are at an age (16 to 19) when it is time for them to gain an identity outside of the family.

It appears that Ruth's family does not have mutually agreed-upon rules that would help it through this developmental stage. This is understandable, for her family of origin was characterized by rigid rules. Now her current family may be struggling with making the transition from a family with children to a family with adolescents and adults. Thus, the rules may be: "Adolescents will not challenge their parents." "The parents will decide what adolescents do with their time." These rules may be appropriate for children but not for adolescents. If a family keeps these rules and adolescents agree to abide by them, the family has rigid boundaries. Its rules for communication are closed. They do not change, even when the need to do so is appropriate to a developmental stage.

In working with Ruth's family, I want to ascertain who is interacting with whom and by what rules. I will be raising this question: Are coalitions of two people who join together against another occurring in this family? If Ruth is having a difficult time defining herself within this system, perhaps her children and her husband are having the same difficulty. I want to ascertain whether rules for communication are closed (no opportunity for change) or open (constantly changing) and whether relationships are distant or enmeshed. It is probable that it is not just John who is having difficulty with Ruth's need to change but that her children are having the same trouble. If she is having a hard time defining herself outside this system, it may be that her children and her husband are having the same struggle. I will examine her family system from a structural family therapy perspective.

Assessment of Ruth

The therapist brings to the therapeutic process his or her perceptions and interactive processes that have been influenced by an intergenerational system, as does the client. Together they form a new system. As within any system, a change in one part will influence the other. Ruth is embarking on a journey that will affect those closest to her: her husband, her family, her family of origin (parents and siblings), her peers, and her therapist. In addition, assessments made about her will evolve and change as the therapeutic process progresses.

As mentioned, Ruth's treatment process will have three phases. In phase 1 I will have John accompany her for the first visit. I will ask him to assist her in assessing her presenting problem by asking them about their marital history and about their children. My decision to include him is based on my limited phone conversation with her, in which she said she was aware not only that it frightened her to think of making changes in her life but also that he was resisting her changes and preferred that she remain her "old self."

It is my goal to assess Ruth and John's relationship and try to determine what influence each has on the other. What kind of relationship do they have that prevents her from changing and him from wanting change? Do they lack the ability to negotiate a different relationship, and if so, why? To address these questions and as a means of enhancing their relationship, I will encourage him to become interested in couples therapy and in therapy with the entire family. If he chooses to become involved in the process, I will continue to work with both Ruth and John and examine their families of origin (phase 2). In order to assess patterns that affect the presenting problem, it is necessary to assess one's family over a three-generation span.

Phase 3 will entail my bringing the entire family in for assessment. I may predict that if there are changes in Ruth and John, the other parts of the system will react. In our telephone conversation, Ruth indicated that she was concerned that her professional involvement would threaten her family. From my perspective, it is important to include John and, later, the entire family, because they appear to be part of the reason that her changes have been difficult. There are many ways to approach this case from a systemic perspective. One might start with the entire family and then go to the separate subsystems.

In addition to the descriptive assessment given above, I might be asked to provide a formal diagnosis for Ruth, depending on the setting in which I work. Just as the assessments made about Ruth are subject to change as the therapeutic process progresses, any diagnosis should be considered tentative at the initial phase of therapy. Using the DSM-IV framework, I would assign the following diagnoses to Ruth:

300.01: panic disorder without agoraphobia
V61.20: parent/child relational problem
V61.1: partner relational problem
301.6: dependent personality disorder

Ruth was referred to me because of her general anxiety symptoms, which interfered in many areas of her functioning. I justify her diagnosis of panic disorder without agoraphobia on the ground that her anxiety is not due to direct physiological effects of a substance or a general medical condition. She said that she had concerns about having additional anxiety attacks and that she sometimes felt that she was "going crazy."

Although Ruth's main reason for seeking therapy was her generalized anxiety, her relationship problems with her parents and with her spouse could certainly be underlying factors contributing to the symptoms of anxiety and panic. The diagnoses of Parent/Child relational problem and also partner relational problem seem appropriate due to a number of her behavioral patterns. Her relationships with her parents are characterized by impaired communication, rigid discipline, and overprotection, all of which are associated with clinically significant impairment of the way she functions as an individual and in her family. Likewise, her relationship with her husband is marked by ineffective communication and fear of losing his support, which also affect her functioning.

I gave the diagnosis of dependent personality disorder because Ruth has exhibited many of the traits associated with this condition since her childhood. The following criteria confirm this diagnosis:

- She has difficulty in making decisions without a great deal of advice from others.
- She expects others to assume responsibility for major areas of her life.
- She has difficulty in disagreeing with significant others because of her fear of losing their approval.
- Because of her lack of self-confidence in her judgment, she has trouble initiating projects and following through with them (such as completing her teaching credential and getting a teaching position).
- At those times when she is alone, she is anxious because of her insecurities in taking care of herself.

These traits, which were passed down from several generations, will, I hope, be reduced through family therapy. My initial assessment and tentative diagnosis of Ruth logically lead to several specific treatment goals.

The individual goal for this case is the reduction of Ruth's symptomatic behaviors (panic attacks). The family system goals include (1) reducing triangles that have prevented her and others from obtaining a confident position in the system; (2) restructuring her immediate system so autonomy by all family members will be encouraged; (3) changing patterns of interaction, not only among family members but also between her and John, so that the relationship can become more flexible and able to cope with changes as the family moves to the next developmental stage; (4) reducing the presenting symptoms; and (5) creating an environment in which all members of the system feel secure and, indeed, are reinforced as they make needed changes.

Phase 1: Session with Ruth and John

My goals for our first session are to (1) obtain a working and therapeutic relationship with Ruth and John (or "join the family," in Minuchin's terms); (2) assess his willingness to be involved in the treatment process; (3) encourage his participation as a critical actor in this family act; and (4) explore family-of-origin dynamics in order to shift the focus from symptoms (Ruth's panic attacks) to process (who says what to whom and under what circumstances). This shift will help put Ruth's problems in a larger context, minimize blame (rejecting that she, Jennifer, or Adam is a potential identified patient) and thereby reduce anxiety, especially hers. Another goal is to confirm or refute my stated hypotheses (described in the section on themes and issues).

After introductions, I begin with Ruth and John's concerns regarding this session. I address them individually and ask:

THERAPIST: How were you feeling before you got here, and how is it to be here?

RUTH: I'm a little nervous to have John here with me.

THERAPIST: Could you explain what you mean by a little nervous?

RUTH: I guess I'm afraid that he may be here to make sure I continue to do things his way.

THERAPIST: What do you mean by "doing things his way"?

RUTH: That he'll be upset if I talk about wanting to make changes such as going to work. And that he'll try to pressure me not to.

THERAPIST: John, to what degree do you think Ruth's concerns are realistic?

JOHN: Well, to some degree her concerns are realistic. At first when she asked me to come here, I was angry because I thought she was inviting me because I was the one with a problem. Then I decided that I'd like to know what this therapy stuff is all about and be a part of this with her instead of being left behind to wonder what she's saying or doing that will affect me or our family.

I am interested in their answer to the question "How were you feeling before you got here?" This question brings out in the open each person's reactions and gets dialogue going that makes it possible to discover what each needs in order to be more relaxed before treatment can begin. Their answers to this question tell me that John and Ruth are willing to be honest with each other. Neither hesitated, and yet both were nervous in sharing their concerns. His honesty and her willingness to share are signs that the prognosis for change in their relationship is good. Her anxiety may be reduced as they learn to negotiate a new relationship.

Other questions I pursue during the beginning of the first session are (1) "Who said what to whom in order to convince you both to come to this session?" and (2) "What do you both hope to have happen during this session, and what do you expect from me?" These questions help me ascertain how each sees the meaning of their being there. If it appears that John has a desire to be a part of the therapeutic relationship, I continue to gather background information on both of them. This is done in the form of a genogram.

A *genogram* is an organized map, or diagram, that demonstrates one's family over three generations. It is a method by which the therapist and the client(s) shift from examining a symptomatic individual (Ruth) to a family system conceptualization of the problem, and it often gives an indication of a solution. In obtaining this transgenerational history, I acquire a history of the nuclear family (Ruth and John's family), a history of her extended family, and a history of his extended family.

One goal in developing a genogram is to determine the following: (1) *relationship patterns* that have been repeated from one generation to the next, which explain the context in which the presenting problem or symptoms developed; (2) the occurrence, if any, of *emotional cutoffs,* which are a means by which people attempt to distance themselves from a fused, or overclose, relationship; (3) triadic relationships (triangles), which denote conflict, fusion, or emotional cutoffs; and (4) *toxic issues* such as religion, gender independence, money, politics, and divorce, which create in the client emotional reactivity with other parts of the system.

The therapist gathers from clients the following information about their current family, their family of origin, their mother's family, and their father's family: occupations; educational background; date of births of self and present children; dates of marriage, separation, or divorce; names of former spouses and children; miscarriages, stillbirths, and adopted and foster children; where all children now live; dates and types of severe illnesses; passages such as promotions and graduations; demographic data; cultural and ethnic data; socioeconomic data; military service; religion; addictions such as drugs, alcohol, and sex; abuse of old people, children, or adults; and retirement or unemployment dates. This information forms a data base that will be used to demonstrate family interaction patterns.

Symbols for mapping such a genogram include the following*:

1. On the left side go men and boys in a family, and the symbol is: □

2. On the right side go women and girls in a family, and the symbol is: ○

3. Marriage is symbolized by:
   Marriage line

4. Separation is symbolized by:

5. Divorce is symbolized by:

*From McGoldrick and Gerson (1985), *Genograms in Family Assessment.*

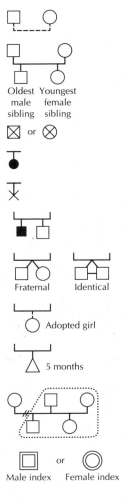

6. Living together is symbolized by:

7. Children are listed in birth order, beginning with the oldest on the left:

8. Death is symbolized by:

9. Spontaneous abortion is symbolized by:

10. Induced abortion is symbolized by:

11. Stillbirth is symbolized by:

12. Twins are symbolized by:

13. Adopted or foster children are symbolized by:

14. Pregnancy is symbolized by:

15. Persons living in the same household are circled:

16. The index person (the person on whom the genogram is focused) is symbolized by:

The following symbols are used to determine the emotional relationships found in a triangle. Each symbol demonstrates what kind of relationship two people have in a three-person relationship.

1. To demonstrate relationships in conflict:

2. To demonstrate relationships that are fused, or very close:

3. To demonstrate relationships that have cutoffs:

4. To demonstrate relationships that are fused and in conflict:

5. To demonstrate relationships that are distant:

Ruth and John's genogram

As we develop Ruth and John's genogram, the interview goes as follows:

THERAPIST: What is your age, Ruth?

RUTH: I'm 39.

THERAPIST: John, how old are you?

JOHN: I'm 45.

THERAPIST: When did you get married?

RUTH: June 17, 1974.

THERAPIST: Is this the first marriage for both of you?

JOHN: It is for Ruth, but I was married for a short period of time to a woman named Helen.

THERAPIST: When did you marry Helen?

JOHN: I married her in August 1971.

THERAPIST: Did you have any children?

JOHN: No, but Helen did have a miscarriage in December 1971.

THERAPIST: Is Helen still alive?

JOHN: Yes.

THERAPIST: How was this marriage for you?

JOHN: I was happy, but I never forgave her for what she did.

THERAPIST: What did she do that you couldn't forgive?

JOHN: She divorced me.

THERAPIST: When did she divorce you?

JOHN: July 1972.

THERAPIST: Did you know why she left you?

JOHN: No.

THERAPIST: Did you want to know?

JOHN: No.

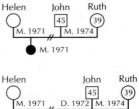

THERAPIST: How do you respond as you talk about this relationship?

JOHN: I'm irritated.

THERAPIST: Why do you get irritated?

JOHN: Because I think she's like many other women in my life who left me for no reason. [He becomes upset.]

THERAPIST: Who were some of these many women?

JOHN: My mother, for one. She left my dad when I was 8 years old. She returned two years later, but my father never forgave her. They never had a good relationship after that. They argued a lot. I've never forgiven her either.

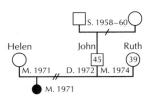

THERAPIST: Did she change her relationship with you as a mother?

JOHN: Not exactly. But I became very close to my father. He began to confide in me in a way that made me feel special.

THERAPIST: What do you mean by special?

JOHN: He would confide in me as if I were his friend about his relationship with my mother. He told me he had been glad when she left.

THERAPIST: How did your mother's absence affect you, and does this event affect you today?

JOHN [hesitant]: I guess I had a difficult time relating to women. I wanted to be close to them and at the same time I was turned off when they seemed eager to have a relationship. Helen just reinforced my belief that a good woman is hard to find.

THERAPIST: But you chose to marry again.

JOHN: Well, Ruth was different.

THERAPIST: What was different about Ruth?

JOHN: She was a devoted daughter to her parents, and she wanted the same things I wanted from life—a family and a stable life. We now have four children, two girls and two boys. Lately, though, Ruth has changed.

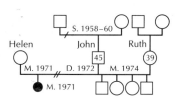

THERAPIST: How do you believe she has changed?

JOHN: She decided to go back to school and possibly work outside the home someday.

THERAPIST: How has her decision affected you?

JOHN: It brings up those old feelings I had when Helen decided to leave me and that I experience when I think about my mother.

THERAPIST: What are those old feelings?

JOHN: I don't know. I guess I get angry. I get upset that the women in my life, and this includes Ruth, will leave me.

THERAPIST: Whom do you talk to about your troubles with Ruth?

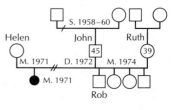

JOHN: Well, occasionally I talk to Rob.

THERAPIST [to Ruth]: Did you know that John confides in Rob?

RUTH: No, but I see Rob becoming closer to his father and more distant from me.

THERAPIST: What do you mean by distant?

RUTH: Rob doesn't talk to me. John and I argue a lot about Rob, and John always takes Rob's side.

JOHN: You know, as I hear Ruth talk, I realize that I'm partially responsible for Rob's being distant from Ruth. I've confided in him a lot about her, especially when I'm upset with her.

THERAPIST: Did you know that, Ruth?

RUTH: No, but it makes sense now why Rob would not want to be around me, especially if he hears a lot of negative things about me from his father.

THERAPIST: John, is it possible for you to tell Ruth when you're upset with her instead of telling Rob?

JOHN: It will be hard, but I'm going to try. I see for the first time that I'm doing to Rob what my father did to me.

THERAPIST: What did your father do to you?

JOHN: He made me his confidant. He was closer to me than to my mother. I knew that hurt her. Now, not knowingly, I'm telling Rob what I feel about his mother. I understand why it's important to talk to Ruth, but it will be hard.

THERAPIST: What makes it so difficult?

JOHN: I don't know.

THERAPIST: Pretend you know!

JOHN: Maybe she'll reject me if I tell her the truth. Maybe she'll leave me.

THERAPIST: Ruth, what do you think about John's notion that he needs to talk to you more, knowing that it will be difficult?

RUTH: I'm pleased and touched. We hardly talk about painful things. In fact, we've never talked about John's ex-wife or his mother. I certainly would prefer to have John talk to me instead of talking to Rob. I'd also like to stop arguing about Rob. For the first time, I feel there's hope for John and me. If he can be more honest with me, maybe I can be more honest with him.

Summary

This is an example of why using a genogram to examine a system is so valuable. Had I decided to bring only Ruth in, neither she nor I would have known about John's unresolved feelings. It is my new assumption that his triadic relationship (fused with his father and emotionally cut off from his mother) has kept him from forming a healthy individuated relationship with Ruth or with any other woman. His parents were unable to resolve their conflicts, and so one parent moved closer to him, just as the other was emotionally cut off in an effort to reduce the stress and anxiety in the marital dyad. John and Ruth discovered that they were continuing the same pattern that was evident in John's family of origin. Their identities were blended (fused) to the extent that they were unable to discuss the emotionally laden issue of gender independence, and therefore they chose not to relate to each other. In an attempt to dissipate their anxiety, they triangled Rob into their relationship (see Figure 10-2). John, like his father before him, chose to tell his son about his unresolved feelings toward his wife. Rob began to distance himself from his mother, most likely for reasons he cannot completely understand. His distancing is being influenced by his father and not by a personal experience with his mother. This triangle left Ruth feeling isolated and without support. She felt that

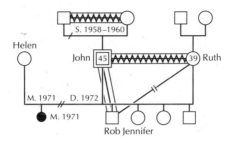

FIGURE 10-2   Multigenerational triangles, showing repeated structural patterns with emphasis on John's family

her family really did not appreciate her. But the emotional revelation during therapy helped give Ruth and John a new perspective on the family's problems.

In addition, a new option for interacting was opened up. John found he was able to break the *family rule* of not discussing emotionally charged issues, especially with a woman, a rule that prohibited Ruth from exploring with him how each of them felt as she was trying to become a more independent person within this system. When she decided to make some changes, she inadvertently influenced him to change. This is a perfect example of how change in one part of the system will result in other parts of the system being changed.

Phase 2: Ruth's Genogram

I assign Ruth to gather information from her parents and siblings and any other family member who is willing to discuss her family's story. I ask John to collect the same information from his family. I tell them that the purpose of gathering such data is not to help them change others in the system but to assist them in making individual changes that can also result in a healthy relationship. After phase 1, both John and Ruth say they feel a strengthened sense of commitment to their marriage.

Ruth finds in going to her parents' home and separately approaching each of them that her mother is freer to discuss the family and their issues than her father. However, he does give her some illuminating details about himself. The process of gathering information is an intervention within itself. Ruth is breaking the family taboo of asking questions of her superiors and also inquiring about their own feelings in regard to others. Gathering all of the needed information occurs over a four-month period.

Mother's family.   Ruth discovers that her mother is relieved to tell her about the family. Her mother, Edith, says she is the eldest of three siblings. She explains that she felt burdened by the role of caretaker for her brother and sister. She also says her father was abusive toward her and punished her severely if she did not obey him. He was not a religious man and was a heavy drinker. Edith decided at an early age not to try to relate much to her father. Her family members never discussed their feelings about one another. Conflict arose when religion was brought up or when she talked of going on to college. Her father and mother sat down with her and explained that they could not afford to send her (but they did send her brother) and that she would not be permitted to bring the subject up again.

Edith tells Ruth that she never heard a supportive word from any member of the family. Also, there was a rumor that Edith's mother had been sent to a hospital for what was known then as a nervous breakdown. This incident was never discussed among family members, and Ruth had never heard about it. She asks why her mother never spoke about this incident, and Edith weeps, saying that she was never allowed to discuss it. This is the first time Ruth has seen her mother cry, much less express emotions. In addition, her mother shares that she sees Ruth as the most stable person in the family. This is the first positive remark Ruth can remember receiving from her mother.

Father's family.   Ruth's father, Patrick, is less cooperative. He asks her a number of questions about her need to know family information. I advised her it was best not to tell the family that her questions were part of a therapeutic process. She chooses to say that they are part of an educational experience, which is true. Her father begins by saying that he is uncomfortable with giving her any information about his family. This is the first time he has admitted a feeling to her. When she asks about his reasons, he says families should keep their lives private. He believes that only God should know what really goes on inside a family. Ruth does not react to her father but simply accepts whatever he feels comfortable in revealing.

Patrick goes on to tell her that his older brother died at birth and that his youngest sister committed suicide. Her death left him as the only child of a fundamentalist minister and a mother that he knew little about. This is the first time her father has ever shared anything about himself. It allows Ruth to see her father in a different light. She also gains a sense about herself that she never had before. She discovers that she can handle discussing emotionally laden issues with her father. In the past, she would never have permitted herself to do so. She also feels more grown-up with her father. It is as if he is treating her as an equal for the first time. Her genogram evolves as shown in Figure 10-3.

Ruth's interpretation of her genogram.   Ruth develops her own insight regarding her place and process in the family. She discovers that:

- A toxic issue in this system over the years is a female notion of independence from the family.
- Over three generations the eldest daughters have emotionally cut off from their fathers and have remained distant with their mothers, while the mothers and fathers have stayed in conflicted marriages. One hypothesis regarding this pattern is that the binder of anxiety (what keeps the system homeostatic, or a couple appearing to be together) is for a husband and wife to deflect their attention to the eldest daughter. The toxic issue that

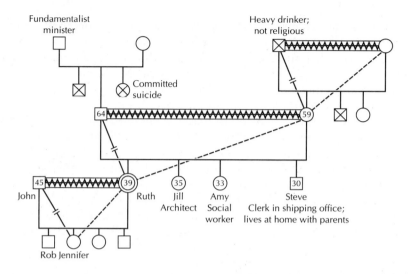

FIGURE 10-3   Multigenerational triangles and
repeated structural patterns in Ruth's genogram

evokes the process is the desire of the eldest daughter to move physically
and emotionally away from the fused triad (mother/father/daughter).

Ruth begins to understand that when she became the focus of attention
in her family, her parents' communication with each other increased.
When she tried to move out on her own (emotionally and physically), her
parents would focus on her. They were unable to work out their personal
conflicts and instead chose to argue about her. When Ruth complied and
the family appeared calm, her mother and father approved of her and had
little more to say to each other.

In a therapy session we discuss Ruth's understanding of patterns
carried on from one generation to the next:

THERAPIST: Ruth, what are you learning from the work you're doing with
your family?

RUTH: I'm beginning to realize that whenever I made an independent
move, I began to feel guilty. My movement created a great deal of
reactivity from my parents, and in my desire to reduce their anxiety I
decided not to have a career. In some ways, I believe, I was keeping
them together. Maybe the role of the eldest daughter was to keep the
parents together whatever the cost.

THERAPIST: Do you see any correlations between what you did in your
family of origin and what you're currently doing in your own family?

RUTH: I'm seeing that I've continued the pattern. If John even hints at
being uncomfortable with my making decisions independently from
the family, I feel guilty, and I believe I feel responsible for his feelings
and reducing his stress. Also, I'm continuing this pattern with my
children. I make them feel guilty if they try to become independent

from the family. Jennifer is a perfect example. If she chooses to wear clothes I disapprove of, I think she's being rebellious, and now that I think about it, she's distancing herself from me as I did with my mother. I argued with John over this. Perhaps John and I avoid working on our issues when we argue about Jennifer. Also, I'm beginning to realize that I could be helping Jennifer continue the same pattern. In other words, if she doesn't compromise for the family, she's made to feel guilty. Fortunately, Jennifer is not completely like me. She fought my intention to have her feel guilty when I told her that she didn't appreciate me. My mother would often tell me that I didn't appreciate her.

THERAPIST: Maybe that's what Jennifer's gift is to this family, not to comply, so that the pattern doesn't continue.

RUTH: I believe you're right.

THERAPIST: Do you still believe that John doesn't want you to become your own person?

RUTH: Not anymore. He has been working on his own problems in therapy, and we've seen how we've brought the patterns of our own families of origin into our marriage. We're getting along much better. In fact, John has actually encouraged me to take courses next semester. Also, I feel I can now support my children's activities outside our home without feeling abandoned by them.

THERAPIST: Have your panic attacks continued during this time?

RUTH: I still get anxious, but now that I'm beginning to see what this is all about, I haven't had a panic attack in four months. My relationship with John has improved a great deal. And with this recent insight about my interactions with my children, I'm hoping my relationship with them will also improve.

This work accomplished with John and Ruth is a condensed example. It could take months before someone would come to these conclusions. For a time I might meet weekly with the family, and then at a later time meet less frequently. The therapeutic process of working with the family might last between six and ten months.

Phase 3: Presenting Ruth with the Idea of Family Therapy

Ruth reports that since she and John began to come to therapy, Adam has been acting out more at home and at school. He and Ruth are having more arguments, usually centering on her request to have him clean up his room or do his homework. Before she entered treatment, they were very close, going to the movies and attending school events. John is frustrated with Adam, who has been having trouble at school. According to John, Adam does not clean his room when asked.

I recommend to Ruth that she consider bringing her entire family into the therapeutic process. She and John, having explored their intergenerational dynamics in depth, have made some significant changes. According to both of them, their relationship has improved, and she is feeling far less guilt and anxiety about her decision to return to school. However, she complains that their children are still resisting change, and especially her changes. Adam and Jennifer have told her that they prefer the "old Mom" and do not want their lives to become unsettled.

Based on our discussion, Ruth decides to ask her family to join her in therapy. The entire family is asked to attend the first session. All of the children agree to participate, which can be considered a good sign. But Rob, the elder son, is reluctant. He feels that he does not have any problems, and he does not understand why he should attend.

With the family's permission, I ask Jerry Corey to attend the meeting as my co-therapist. The luxury of having female and male co-therapists can be most therapeutic. Because I have been working with John and Ruth, we have a relationship that the children might perceive as a coalition, with their parents against them. Having a neutral person as part of a therapeutic team can counterbalance this situation. Choosing a co-therapist of the opposite gender allows for working with transference and also provides opportunities for the co-therapist to model behaviors during the session.

The first session

Jerry asks the family members to be seated wherever they want. I thank the family for coming and address each member by first name. I say that the purposes of this first meeting are to establish the goals for treatment and to assess with them whether further sessions might be helpful to the family. We also discuss the limits of confidentiality and the reporting laws for the state.

The presenting complaint.   It is apparent that there is some confusion over why everyone needs to be present. Therefore, we ask Ruth to explain her concerns to the family and her hopes for these sessions.

RUTH: Since John and I have been in therapy, I've seen this family change. Adam, you've been more moody. We've been arguing more, and you seem unwilling to take any suggestions of mine to get your homework done or to clean your room. I believe our marriage is improving, but my relationship with the children, especially Adam, is getting worse.

Jerry and I observe that Ruth and Adam sit next to each other. John sits next to me, and Jennifer sits between Adam and Susan, who is 18. Rob, who is 19, sits away from the rest of the family. Jerry and I ask each member for his or her observations regarding the family. We also ask them: "If you could get something from this session for yourself, what might that be? Would you like to have a different relationship with anyone in your family?"

The family interaction.   What follows are excerpts of a dialogue among the family members, Jerry, and myself during this first session with the family.

JOHN: We're here because you asked us to come together as a family. If we can help, we'd be glad to do that. I personally have been learning about having a better relationship with Ruth, but I have no goals for myself with this family gathering. But she and I are concerned about Adam. I think she is more concerned than I am. Since she and I began to improve our relationship through counseling, he has become less obedient and cooperative, especially with her. Yesterday, he yelled at Jennifer, and when I tried to punish him, Ruth told me to leave him alone and let them work it out by themselves. I disagree with her new idea of how to discipline these children. I think they should be punished if they do something wrong. I was brought up never to disobey my parents.

ROB [interrupting]: This is weird! We never talk about family stuff. The only time we ever get together is when we go to church. Sometimes I'm glad that Mom is more independent. She's not on my case as much as she was before.

JERRY COREY: Rob, would you tell your mother what you mean by "being on your case"?

ROB: She would always want to know where I was going and what I was doing. Mom would always tell me if she didn't like the girls I was going with.

JERRY: Rob, you're talking about your mother as though she weren't in the room. How about talking directly to her over here?

ROB: That's kind of hard for me to do. It's not something that I usually do.

MARY MOLINE: I can understand that, Rob. But in these sessions I'd like for each of you to talk directly to each other. That would help me understand you better.

ROB: I also want to say something about Dad. I feel he's too hard on Adam.

JERRY: So, Rob, there sits your dad. Can you tell him directly what you mean by your statement that he's too hard on Adam?

ROB [reluctantly]: Dad, you're always upset when Adam starts arguing with his sisters or me. And you're getting on my case lately. If I'm not home by 10, you get all bent out of shape, just like Mom used to do. You're right, Dad, Adam has become a real pain in the neck since you and Mother began seeing a counselor. But can't you show a little patience with him?

JERRY: John, how is it for you to hear what Rob is saying to you?

JOHN [looking to me]: I don't believe I have to take this. I never corrected my father.

MARY: How does this affect you to hear what Rob just said to you?

JOHN: Well, it does make me upset. Don't you know how much your mother and I care for you?

MARY: It seems that the two of you have more to talk about. I'm hoping we
can continue this dialogue at some future time, but I'd like to make
sure that we get to each person in the family. [She turns to Jennifer.]
What would you like to say about being here, and what you would like
for yourself in these sessions?

JENNIFER [looking to Ruth and Susan]: Susan and I like the idea of coming
here, because the family seems so different since Mom and Dad went
to counseling. But we feel that Mom has abandoned the family.

JERRY: Would you tell your mother what you mean by "abandoning the
family"?

JENNIFER: Well, Mother, you don't do our wash anymore. You tell us to do
our own wash. We have to make our own lunches. You seem to have
many more opinions. I agree with Rob that you and Dad seem to be
getting along better, but you're arguing more with Adam and me. I
want to stay out of the house when the bickering begins, especially
between you and Adam.

MARY: Ruth, how do you respond to what Jennifer just said to you?

RUTH: It's hard to hear Jennifer disapproving of my going to college or my
wanting her and the children to become more independent from me. I
think that's why it's so difficult for me to get a job outside the home.
I'm torn between making myself happy or my family happy. I'm
feeling less guilty about my decision, but I'm frustrated to see that the
children are becoming more upset. Originally, they wanted me to leave
them alone, and I was afraid I was losing them. Now they seem to be
afraid they're losing *me*.

MARY: How do you respond to what your mother just said, Jennifer?

JENNIFER: I'd rather not respond right now.

MARY: That's OK, you don't need to answer now. Hopefully, we can get
back to what's going on between you and your mother later in this
session. [She turns to Susan.] How, specifically, would you like things
to be different for yourself with each member of your family?

SUSAN: Jennifer and I would like more of Mom's time.

JERRY: Instead of talking for Jennifer, perhaps you could talk for yourself.
Later, Jennifer can say what she would like to be different.

MARY: Susan, is there anything that you want to add?

SUSAN: Well, I'd like to say that I agree with Rob that Dad is not as nice as
he used to be since Mom got into counseling. He's nicer to Mom but
seems more upset with all of us and . . .

JOHN [interrupting]: How can you say that I'm not nice to you? I do the
best I can, and nobody appreciates that!

JERRY: Is that what you were trying to tell your father, Susan? Did he hear
you right?

SUSAN [turning to Jerry]: No.

JERRY: Would you mind telling your father what you'd like from him?

SUSAN [with tears in her eyes]: Dad, it's not that we don't appreciate how
hard you work. It's just that I don't hear anything nice from you
anymore.

MARY: Susan, if you could have one thing different with your father, what would that be?

SUSAN: That we could do something together without getting into a fight.

MARY: How would that be for you, John?

JOHN: Well, if I could find the time, I'd like to do more with Susan. I'm spending more time with Ruth, and that has had an effect on my relationship with Susan and Jennifer. Sometimes, though, I don't know what a father does with a 17-year-old.

MARY: Why don't you ask her?

JOHN [looking at Susan, after a long pause]: Well, what do you think?

SUSAN: We could go to a movie.

MARY: Is that something you'd like to do with Susan?

JOHN: Yeah, if we could ever agree on a movie.

MARY: It sounds good, and I hope the two of you will make the time to talk with each other about what both of you want. [She turns to Adam.] Adam, what would you like to say about yourself?

ADAM: I think it's unfair that my family picks on me.

MARY: Who in this room picks on you, and would you tell them directly?

ADAM: Susan, you've been picking on me. And Jennifer just sits around and smiles. And, well . . . [fidgeting and looking to the floor] Dad and Mom have been upset with me a lot lately and . . .

JOHN [interrupting]: When have I been upset with you that you didn't deserve it?

RUTH [interrupting and turning to John]: I think you ought to let Adam finish.

MARY: Ruth, how about letting John speak for himself. [She looks to John.] What would you like to say to Adam?

JOHN: I feel that everyone is picking on me, and it's getting me mad! We're supposed to be here for Ruth, not me!

JERRY: John, I can understand that you might feel as if you're being picked on. But another way to look at this is to consider that what they're telling you is a sign that they trust you enough to be open and honest with you about their feelings. Maybe these are things that they haven't been able to express to you until now.

JOHN: Well . . . I don't know . . . But I do want my kids to be able to talk to me.

JERRY: If you could be more open with them, that would allow them to be more open with you. A short time ago, Adam said some things to you, and you seemed to be very emotionally moved. Is there anything you'd like to say to Adam?

JOHN: It's very difficult to hear what you had to say, Adam. [He turns to Jerry laughingly.] Did I do it right this time?

JERRY: I hope you'll continue to talk. [He addresses all the family members except for Ruth.] Several of you have mentioned that your mother's counseling has affected your lives. Some of you have even said that you felt abandoned by her. Would each of you be willing to talk to your mother?

SUSAN: Mom, it's hard to see you being different. I was so used to you taking an interest in us, even though at times I complained. You did so much for us, but I guess you have a life of your own, too.

ROB: I think you're right on, Susan!

JOHN: I think Susan has made a good point.

ADAM: Mother, I miss you not sticking up for me more. I think I don't like fighting with you, but at times I find myself starting a fight with you.

MARY: Do you think the fighting and missing your mom are related?

ADAM [thinking for a while]: Maybe!

JENNIFER: I like talking like this. We never do this at home, and we're not even fighting right now.

MARY [turning to Ruth]: How is it for you to hear that?

RUTH: It feels good to see my family talking about themselves and realizing that I don't have to take so much care of them anymore.

JERRY: Our time is almost up, but before we close, I'd like to ask each of you if there are reasons you might want to return.

All of the family members feel that it is important to return, because they like what has happened during the session. They are agreeable to attending another session the following week. Jerry then explains to them the value of doing some homework before the next session. Because the family members are open to this idea, he suggests the following assignments:

- *For Ruth.* Avoid interfering when one of the children is attempting to interact with John.
- *For Susan and John.* Decide on an activity that you're willing to do together before the next session.
- *For Rob.* Take some more time to let your father know what you'd like with him. It's important that you don't tell him how he should be different but instead talk about yourself with him.
- *For Jennifer.* Take the initiative to ask your mother to do something with you before next week, such as going shopping or spending 20 minutes together.
- *For Ruth and John.* Continue to discuss what you would like to do with each other and what you would like to do separately. When you do start to focus on the children, try to talk instead about yourselves.

The family members are asked if they have any objections to these assignments and if they would be willing to follow through with them by the following week, at which time they will meet again with both therapists. All feel that they can complete the assignments.

It is important that families work on issues outside of therapy as well as during therapy. In this way they can observe that they have the strength to make their own changes. By taking this responsibility, they empower themselves. The only family member not given an assignment is Adam. This is an attempt to keep the other family members focusing away from him and keep him from continuing to be identified as a *patient* in this family.

Process commentary

The co-therapists set out to observe the structure of the family by (1) allowing the members to sit where they wanted to and (2) attempting to get a clearer picture of the family's transactional patterns. We assume, in observing the structure, that Ruth's change has produced stress in the sibling subsystem. There was stress in the spousal subsystem, but including John in the beginning session reduced it. Ruth appears to have rigid boundaries with Adam. Her ability to make changes has strengthened her boundary with Adam, and he is reacting to those changes. No longer does she feel the need to give in to his demands. But conflicts have increased in their relationship. Her changes are resulting in new strains on this relationship. If Adam can have a closer relationship with his siblings or other peer groups, he may be able to better adjust to this change. Jennifer also appears to be having difficulty with the changes, not only with Ruth but also with the fact that the spousal subsystem is becoming stronger. We repeat, *If change occurs in any one part of the system, change will occur in the other parts.* In other words, changes in Ruth and the rudimentary changes in the spousal subsystem have affected the equilibrium of this family. Whenever possible, therefore, it is important to have the whole family enter treatment so that the changes that occur are productive for the system as well as each individual within it.

In this family there is an enmeshment among members. They lack a clear sense of their individuality and roles in the family. Families such as this one are prone to conflict and confusion, and the behavior of one member or unit, in this case both Ruth and John, immediately affects the other members of the family.

Through a Bowenian process, Ruth and John are learning new behaviors. She is learning not to maintain her role as peacemaker, and he is learning to be more supportive of her. As a result, the other family members are being forced to learn to deal with one another. Up to this session they have been increasing the conflict among themselves and with Ruth in order to bring her back into her previous role as mediator. In family-therapy terms this is known as an attempt to maintain homeostasis, which involves prompting a return of the family to the former status.

This system (family) is relatively functional. Its members were able to make some strides in communicating in the session, especially considering that they generally have not expressed their own feelings with one another. John and Ruth's exploration of transgenerational patterns has assisted them in learning how to express these feelings, and that change helped them facilitate the children's flexibility, difficult as it has been at times. Intergenerational patterns of not expressing feelings and allowing independent thought are not likely to continue. Because these patterns do not change overnight, the family still has considerable work to do. The committed effort aimed at modifying these patterns will not only free this family to be more honest and open but will benefit future generations.

The family has an excellent chance of making structural changes. These include:

- becoming more direct with one another
- taking the focus off of Adam as a problem
- reducing the coalition that Adam and Ruth have against John
- reducing the enmeshed (overclose) relationship Ruth has with Adam, so she can have a closer relationship with John and so Adam can have appropriate closer relationships with his siblings and other peers

The chances are that the entire family will not always be included in future therapy sessions. Instead, therapy may include parts of the system (John and Rob), the spousal subsystem (Ruth and John), or the sibling subsystem (Rob, Jennifer, Susan, and Adam). Ruth and John will need to continue strengthening their independence with each other and their togetherness.

Questions for Reflection

Regarding family therapy with Ruth, consider some of the similarities and the differences between Dattilio's cognitive-behavioral approach and Moline's systemic approach. Reflect on the following questions as you study these two approaches:

1. What differences do you see between working with Ruth in individual counseling and using family therapy? Do you think that including her family in a few sessions will promote or inhibit her progress in individual therapy? Do you see any disadvantages in not meeting with her individually in therapy?
2. If Ruth were your client, what advantages and disadvantages would there be in working exclusively with her in the context of family therapy? Would you be interested in having at least one session with her family of origin, as Dattilio did? What connections do you see between her family of origin and her current family structure?
3. What possible ethical issues are involved if you do not suggest family therapy for Ruth, given clear indications that some of her problems stem from conflicts within her family?
4. If you were conducting family therapy in this case, whom would you consider to be your primary client? Would your client be the family as a system? Ruth? John? Jennifer? Adam? Susan? Rob? Can you see any ethical binds if you develop an alliance with certain members of this family?
5. Dattilio focused on Ruth's family schemata, including beliefs from her family of origin and those in her current family. Moline focused on genograms, which involved working with Ruth's family of origin and seeing connections with her present family. What advantages

can you see in working with family schemata and in utilizing genograms?

6. How do you think that your own relationships in your family of origin
   might either help or hinder you in working with this family? Can you
   see any possible sources of problems or potential countertransfer-
   ences? If you become aware that you have unfinished business with
   either your family of origin or your present family, what course would
   you probably take?

7. If you were working with Ruth's family, with whom might you be
   most inclined to form an alliance? With which person do you think you
   would have the most difficulty in working, and why?

8. What do you think you would do if the tension within Ruth's family
   increased as she continued to make changes for herself? If she decided
   to file for a divorce or said that she intended to leave her family, what
   reactions would you have?

9. At this point in your professional development, how ready are you to
   work with the entire family? Do you feel competent to do marital or
   family therapy? What further training would you need to feel ready to
   treat Ruth from these perspectives?

10. Do you see any difference in goals between individual counseling and
    family therapy? Do you notice any differences between the in-
    terventions that were made in these conjoint and family sessions and
    those in Ruth's individual sessions?

11. If you and Ruth were from different cultures, what factors would you
    as a family therapist want to address with both her and the members of
    her family? What role might cultural factors play in understanding the
    structure of this family? How might the interventions you make vary
    depending on the cultural background of the family involved in the
    therapeutic process?

12. Do you have any bias toward Ruth because of her desire to change her
    role within the family? Does her thinking fit with yours regarding
    female roles in the family? regarding male roles in the family?

EMPOWERING THE FIELD FAMILY:
A CASE USING BRIEF FAMILY TECHNIQUES,
by Jon L. Winek, Ph.D., and Susan C. Carlin-Finch, M.A., M.M.F.T.

Introduction

The presenting problem in this case was asthma, present in two of Betty
Field's four children. The Fields are a three-generation family, headed by
Annie, the matriarchal grandmother, age 61. Betty, her daughter, age 38, is
a divorced mother of four children: Andy, 16, John, 13, Mitch, 11, and
Elise, 8. This is a working-class African-American family, living in Annie's

home in an inner-city district of a large southwestern city. The family members report being very involved in their church, especially in the choir. Everyone in the family sings and plays a musical instrument. The intake interview presented a dispute between Betty and Andy over practicing his drums. She did not think that he was practicing enough; when she told him to do so, he would either resist or refuse. This upset Annie, because the household was constantly in turmoil. She was the initial contact, calling the counseling center for therapy for her daughter and two of her grandsons. The center's policy is to ask if the client has a preference regarding the gender of the therapist, and she requested a female therapist.

The case was originally assigned to one of the authors based on the grandmother's preference for a woman. The therapist made the decision for co-therapy following a discussion of the assignment in a case conference. Along with simple management issues, she considered the possible gender issues: All of the "authorities" in the sessions would be female, and three of the identified clients were male. The therapist was concerned that this could prevent her from "joining" with the identified clients—that is, building and maintaining a therapeutic alliance. Hence, she contacted the other author and asked him to function as a co-therapist with the family.

We entered the therapy with some degree of understanding of "typical" black, single-parent, three-generation families. With this in mind, we began to formulate some hypotheses that we would test throughout the therapeutic process. Truthfully, our aim was to set aside our hypotheses as we went into the initial session and to focus our energies on simply being with the family and focusing on what the members would bring to therapy. Within this framework, we were in a position to begin learning about their "family culture."

Highlights of the Family Therapy Sessions

Session 1.   We meet the family in the center's waiting room and introduce ourselves to each member, shaking hands and welcoming them. Four family members are present at this session: Annie, Betty, Andy, and John. After escorting them to the therapy room, we proceed with the administrative tasks of setting fees and signing releases. Annie expresses some concern over videotaping, but we make an effort to reassure her and make her comfortable before starting the session. We are beginning our attempts to join with the family even before we get down to therapeutic "business."

The session begins with the question "What brings you to therapy?" addressed to the four family members. Annie speaks first, reporting that the boys are asthmatic and that they are trying therapy as a possible solution. We generally follow the principle of allowing all to speak for themselves, which leads us to discuss the nature of the boys' asthma with them. As therapists, both of us share that we also were asthmatic as children. These are further attempts to join, and such a stance allows us to remain joined with the boys, even if they are scapegoated by the family. At this point Annie interrupts both boys, qualifying their answers for them and giving us a hint that power may be an issue for this family, providing us with diagnostic information. To remain symmetrical, we address the same question to Betty, who replies that the asthma is an issue but that there are also disciplinary problems. Once again, Annie interrupts, saying, "I agree with her, but with one exception . . ." Following Annie's qualification, we observe that Betty is crying, but we do not address her tears directly.

At this point, Betty introduces her depression, and we ask her what her ideal outcome of therapy would be. We feel that addressing a symptom before knowing the context that supports it further supports the symptom and continues the vicious circle accompanying the symptom. This is, as such, our first intervention. We do not buy into her depression, but we ask her what she wants rather than what she is. Betty answers that she desires more peace within the household because there is so much friction, particularly between herself and Andy. We try to investigate this issue a bit further, but Annie interrupts and captures our attention once again. However, we then begin to ask about Annie and Betty's relationship as a possible issue, providing further diagnostic material. As we do not wish to further feed into Betty's depression, we switch our focus over to the boys and begin eliciting more information from them, which serves to join a bit more with them. We discover that the boys have different fathers, and we explore their relationships with their fathers.

Turning to Betty, we ask about her relationships with the boys' fathers. She presents herself as powerless and says that her mother plays the role of husband and father as well as that of grandmother. At this point there is a danger of imposing our values on the family, so we ask directly what that means to her. She begins to cry and look away, and we turn to Annie and ask how well she performs the husband and father roles. She expresses displeasure at having those jobs but says that she feels obligated to take on these roles when Betty goes into "one of her moods." Betty leaves the room in tears, and we make no effort to stop her. All members present try to explain Betty's depression, but we disallow that, indicating that she should be present when she is being talked about. We intervene by asking them to take responsibility for their part in her depression, which is brought out by the boys' circumvention of her authority and their grandmother's permission to do so.

Betty returns to the session, and we do not address her leaving, once again avoiding labeling her as the patient. We decide at this point to deal directly with the issue of going around the mother. Here we use our power to change the system when it cannot change itself. We direct the children to stop going to Annie, direct Betty to make all of the decisions herself, and forbid Annie to make any decisions. We rehearse this in the session, providing them with reinforcement whenever they perform as prescribed. We conclude the session by sending them out to do their homework.

At the conclusion of the session, we felt joined with all of the members except Betty. We did not make more of an effort to join with her because we were unable to create an environment in which we could join with her on anything except her depression. Our assessment seemed reasonable and was accepted by the family. Our interventions produced some movement and reinforcement within the session. We were saddened by not connecting with Betty, but we were confident that our alliance with the others would ensure her return to therapy. The movement we saw in the session made us hopeful that their situation would improve, thus providing us a way to join with Betty over something other than her depression. We redistributed the power that Annie held as the matriarch, so that Betty could stop utilizing the power of her depression. Our interventions were designed to support this move by having the boys go to their mother and having the grandmother "bounce" them right back to their mother should they fail in their homework. We shared in the session a fantasy of the grandmother wielding a tennis racquet to return the boys to their mother as a tennis player returns a serve.

Session 2.   Annie, Betty, Andy, and John, as well as the remaining family members, Mitch and Elise, are present at this session. We both join with the two new children by shaking hands and introducing ourselves. We observe that the family members arrange themselves by gender and birth order. Annie, Betty, and Elise are seated together, as are Andy, John, and Mitch.

The family reports improvement concerning the children's circumvention of their mother. We then ask, "What would you like to work on today?" to which Betty answers: "Same things. Things are getting better, but we still need to work on them some more." Annie agrees with Betty rather than qualifying her answer as she usually had. We suggest that Betty describe to Mitch and Elise what happened in the last session. This intervention is designed to further remove Annie as the family head and give Betty control over the children.

Following this, we move into history-taking, informing the family that we are looking for the underlying causes of its difficulties. During this portion of the session, Betty introduces the physical abuse she endured at the hands of her second husband. She cites it as the main cause of her depression and as an important factor in her children's behavior, because the older ones witnessed some of the abuse. We reframe her self-identified weakness (staying in an abusive relationship) as a strength that was necessary for her children's well-being, and we admire her strength to leave in spite of the difficulties she would face without her husband's financial support. It is on this issue that we are finally able to connect with Betty.

During the remainder of this session we examine the children's relationships with their fathers and Betty's relationships with her ex-husbands and her mother. The family does a substantial amount of self-diagnosis, expressing that Betty's depression is situational and is the result of past manipulation by her second husband. Once the family has fleshed out the diagnosis, Betty seems to be relieved. During this process we observe that the children seem to circumvent their mother in order to protect her, which is, in fact, perpetuating the circle of powerlessness that she originally felt while she remained with her second husband. We conclude the session by calling attention to the progress that they made during the previous week and instructing them to continue with the homework, with the added message for each to be responsible for his or her part in the assignment. So that Betty can feel more in control of her own life and to reinforce the boundary between her and her children, we give her permission to find more time for herself by locking her children out of her room for a brief period that is to be "her time."

Session 3. All six family members are present at this session, and we begin by asking for a report on the homework. Annie and Betty agree that things are better at home but that there is still a way to go. Betty reports that she is also feeling better, because she has been getting out of the house, but that she is still feeling critical of herself because she is not more like her mother. She reports that the only good things she got out of her marriages were her four children but that for her to care for them without a husband is "cockeyed." We proceed to join with her a bit more, and in the process we examine her external support networks, or lack of them. She further sees her dependence on her mother as a near-fatal character flaw. Annie intervenes again by explaining to her that she got involved with the children only because Betty wasn't able to do so herself. This leads us to consider that Annie is overinvolved with the children and that we should intervene to reduce this.

We present this idea to Betty by saying, "I think the therapy is really about you and your mom, not your children." Both of them respond that it is not, but we decide to push them a bit more. Betty self-diagnoses the situation by adding, "The way I feel about my marriages is affecting my relationship with my children." Annie agrees, pointing out that when Betty is angry with the children "over nothing," they begin to "take up" for one another. We ask Annie why the children go to her, and she answers that it is because "She isn't around." Betty keeps insisting that the problem is that she is not enough like her mother, and we point out that she and her mother seem to play complementary roles. Betty then turns to her desire to have some time for herself, which we reinforce by suggesting that it should be built into her homework assignment again. This seems effective, and it serves to get us back on track with the family's agenda rather than our own. We were meeting with so much resistance because we had mis-diagnosed the problem as being primarily between mother and daughter.

We are also faced with the issue of Betty's wanting a husband follow-ing her two divorces. This can be interpreted as both a racial and a gender issue, because she is a middle-aged African-American woman with four children. What we have not yet addressed with her completely is the reality of women in her situation who are looking for an eligible man to marry. There is a relative dearth of eligible men in her age group who would be willing to take on the responsibility that comes with this family. Since she feels it is a problem, we owe it to her to address the issue fully. On the other hand, we don't wish to feed into her depression by pointing out how unlikely it is that she will find a husband. Because of this, we decide to table that issue until such time as she has regained some control over her symptom and family.

The remainder of the time is spent reconnecting with everyone and reinforcing the interventions we have made. Betty is told to go out by herself once during the coming week, and the children are told that they may go only to their mother for decisions and that they have no choice in the matter. We further reinforce our interventions by explaining their purpose to the family. We reinforce Betty's new position of power by saying, after she makes a statement that reflects her will to control her children, how well she is doing.

Session 4.   This is the first session after the family canceled two consecutive appointments, the first due to a conflict with a church activity and the second because of car problems. Betty looks much better and seems rather "up" when we meet the entire family in the center's waiting room.

We open the session by asking the family members what they want to work on in the session. Betty spends the next several minutes reporting on the change that has occurred over the previous three weeks. This part of the session is light, and she reports improvement in her children's behavior. Andy and John report an improvement in their asthma. This portion of the session serves to reinforce their change. Betty introduces her need for more time to herself so she can work on finding some companionship for herself outside of the family.

When Betty expresses her desire to find a mate, Andy interjects that "two is enough." The other children agree with Andy on this issue. We observe that the children have taken on the job of being their mother's protectors. We make interventions designed to allow them to give up this job and to put Betty in charge of finding time for herself as well as becoming more socially active with the ultimate goal of locating a mate. It is suggested that she take steps to build a social life outside of the family and that the children concern themselves with being "selectors rather than protectors."

During the remainder of the session we address Betty's fear about becoming more social; we also explore her reactions to her children's resistance. As the session concludes, we give her the homework of going out on her own. We remind her that the children took over the role of protectors and that part of her depression stems from her overinvolvement with them. This overinvolvement was originally functional following her abuse and divorce, but it became dysfunctional when the family became locked into this pattern.

Session 5.   We start this session without John because he is busy studying for a test the following day. From the outset of the session, it is clear that Betty has become more depressed since our last session. Gone are the family's smiles and laughter, and she appears to be on the verge of tears. She reports that her children continue to circumvent her by going to Annie when decisions need to be made. She starts to cry and says: "It's like I'm not even here. We've come a long way from where we were before, but it's like I'm not even here." We follow her lead and begin to empathically explore the nature of her powerlessness, which serves the function of joining with her and also provides us with diagnostic material. Annie becomes frustrated with her daughter and defends her actions in terms of the importance of meeting the children's needs when Betty cannot do so. She says that Betty could control and demand respect from her children. At this point, however, Annie has failed to recognize the role she plays in making it impossible for her daughter to demand respect.

We observe that out of concern for Betty's safety in seeking a new mate, the system returned to the original behavior pattern to prevent such a move on her part. One of us moves next to her and points out that the discussion the previous week scared her children into acting out. Together, we explain that the early success resulted from our power in making the homework assignments. We say that such power lasts for only a short period and that now she will have to become more powerful to make the changes stick. We then model her taking a firm stance with the children, encouraging her to make demands on them.

After these interventions, we try to focus further on the issue of Betty becoming involved with a man. At this point, Annie interrupts to report that she cannot understand why Betty has not mentioned a relationship in which she is involved. We intervene by discussing the process, saying that Annie is acting like the children and treating us as the authority to run to. We refuse to take part in that process, which provides insight for Annie into her role in Betty's powerlessness. The balance of the session is spent encouraging Betty to take power for herself and reinforcing the generational boundaries.

Session 6.   The family arrives a half-hour late due to traffic difficulties. Everyone is present except Andy, who is home studying. Betty begins the session, reporting that she has been able to give the boys a new responsibility around the home. She further reports that things in general are improving, but she expresses the desire to get out on her own more often. During this portion of the session, she describes her difficulties in achieving this change, which we reinforce by praising her efforts and her success. We share that we see the children's acting-out behavior as a manifestation of their efforts to care for her. The children reject our position, but she accepts it and argues with her children about its validity.

We then focus our interventions on the children, teasing John about his skill at being a parent. The other children laugh quite hard about this, embarrassing John in the process, but we intervene by pointing out that his skill is also theirs. Betty sees her children's need to protect her as a result of the abuse they witnessed. She further describes her improved relationship with Andy. We then conclude the session by further empowering her and giving her the homework assignment of going out socially as well as excluding the children from accompanying her on her errands.

Behaviorally, we see improvement in the fact that Betty set the agenda for the session and dominated the interaction, instructing her children rather than reacting to them. We observe that Annie remained outside of the interaction between Betty and the children.

Session 7. Betty opens the session, reporting improvement in socializing and controlling her children's behavior. We reinforce her through praise and having her describe the benefits she received from making those changes. We then call Annie into the session by saying that "we haven't heard from you in a while." She responds by smiling and saying: "I know. It's great being just Grandma." She shares her perceptions on the family's improvement, which acts as a reinforcer. We then discuss the changes with the children. John reports that he initially missed going out with his mother but that he no longer pouts when left behind but spends time with his friends, which he greatly enjoys. The other children do not seem disturbed by the changed pattern but rather enjoy the freedom that the change allows.

We feel that we have been successful, and we ask Betty what we should do next. She agrees that we are through with this aspect of therapy, but she introduces new personal issues that she wants dealt with and says she wants the continued support of therapy. Thus, we make a new contract to continue therapy.

Follow-Up: You Continue as the Therapist with This Family

1. How would you continue working with the Field family?
2. If at the conclusion of this course of treatment Betty asked about individual counseling with the female therapist to work on "women's issues," what would be an appropriate response?
3. How would this treatment have been different if during the first session we had encouraged Betty to get in touch with her depressive feelings?
4. What would have been different if this family had been seen only by a male therapist? only by a female therapist?
5. What cultural issues might be operating in this case? If you were providing therapy for this family, what would you want to know about

the culture of the family? What problems, if any, might you have in joining with the members of the family because of cultural differences?

6. The family first asked for help with asthma in two of the children. The therapists, besides sharing that they, too, had struggled with asthma as children, did not talk further about this issue. What are the pragmatic and ethical ramifications for this course of treatment?

7. What would you have done differently with this family?

MARIA: TORN BETWEEN HERSELF AND HER FAMILY

Some Background Data

Maria is a 32-year-old Latina whose parents were born in Mexico.* She and her parents now live in Arizona, where she is pursuing graduate study in social work, but her ultimate goal is to make her home in Mexico and to work in the management of social-service agencies. She sees a great need for counseling and social work in Mexico, and she is committed to helping her people. Maria has completed all her course work in the doctoral program in social work. To get her degree, she needs to turn in her dissertation, which is almost finished. Of course, she will have an oral examination in which her doctoral committee questions her about the dissertation. She has been putting off the final phase of this project for well over a year despite promptings from her chairperson.

Maria is seeking therapy with me because she wants to work on her fears of succeeding and her struggles because her parents do not accept her professional strivings. During the intake interview, Maria tells me that a negative experience she had with another therapist made it extremely difficult for her to seek help again. She feels that her former therapist was not at all sensitive to her cultural background and did not understand the nature of her struggles. Moreover, she felt a great deal of pressure to accept his views on life, because, as she puts it: "He acted as though I should accept what he wanted for me, rather than helping me figure out what was best for myself. He'd tell me that it was about time that I grew up and thought about myself, and forgot what my parents and family wanted of me. He just wouldn't listen to me when I tried to explain that in my family you simply don't say aloud everything you think and feel."

Because I am not Mexican-American and Maria's experiences with her previous therapist were not satisfactory, she is concerned about my ability to relate to her situation. She lets me know that she places great value on her family, on respect for her parents, and on remaining true to the values espoused by her religion. Although she struggles with her parents, she has no intention of cutting them out of her life. She has decided to come to me

*I wish to thank my students Toni Muñoz and Nancy Zybala, who reviewed this case and provided insightful comments.

because she knows that I favor working with individuals from a family systems perspective. Maria has a particular interest in family therapy, both personally and professionally. She even chose to study one facet of systems theory as the basis for her dissertation. Assuming a systemic orientation, I will describe how I work with Maria and her significant others, even though they are not present at her therapy sessions.

Identifying Goals as a Starting Place

In Maria's case, a general goal from a systemic perspective is to increase her level of differentiation. This does not mean that she will selfishly follow her own directives; it means that she will be able to determine the direction of her life. Some family therapists maintain that in the process of determining her direction in life, she also needs to find a balance between what is beneficial for her individually and what is beneficial for her family. The notion of achieving her individuality at the expense of the good of her family is not likely to sit well with Maria, and certainly not with her family. Indeed, in her culture the notion that she can determine the course of her life is almost sacrilegious.

It becomes apparent that Maria has learned about systemic therapy on an intellectual level but has not integrated her insights on an emotional level. Although she has studied therapeutic approaches, she lacks a personal awareness of her internal conflicts. Moreover, in spite of her interest in family systems, she says that she cannot imagine her parents coming to a therapy session with her. She is frightened over the thought of approaching her parents with the request that they join her in therapy. But she is willing to explore the impact that growing up in her family is having on her today.

From the outset, I stress a therapeutic contract setting the focus for counseling. Maria will have to decide specifically what beliefs, feelings, and behaviors she wants to change. In her family she has been told what is best for her, which makes it difficult for her to identify what she wants for herself. Early in the sessions I will encourage her to explore her wants within the context of her culture. I hope that she will gradually begin to identify *what* she hopes to change about herself and *how* she can accomplish her stated goals.

However, Maria is vague in stating what she wants. She tells me that she is confused about her desires. She finally says that she wants to "be myself around my father" and also to "feel free to live my own life, rather than doing what my family expects of me." She appears to have a difficult time in asking for what she wants. In working toward the goal of "being myself around my father," it is important that she balance the processes of individuation and interdependence. Although her striving toward individuation can be a source of empowerment, it will also be important to consider her respect for her father, and it is essential to explore how her academically or professionally. Her parents actively encouraged and supported her older brothers' educational and professional endeavors, and both of them became highly successful, one as a physician and the other as an architect. The daughters in the family, however, were expected to get a well-paying job in business for a time, save their earnings, and then marry and have children.

MARIA: Both of my parents, and especially my mother, would tell me that it was a waste of my time to think of going on to college. They thought it was fine that I had graduated from high school, but they asked what I was trying to prove when I kept up my interest in college. To their way of thinking, I should learn all the domestic talents, and I should set my sights on some desirable and successful man. Marriage was seen as the ultimate in my parents' plan for me. From their perspective, a daughter who doesn't marry is a great concern. Since they will not be around forever to take care of their daughter, it's important that they leave her in capable hands. My parents believe that women need to be taken care of. Any hint on my part that I wanted to get not only a bachelor's degree but also a doctorate in social work was unthinkable. They didn't want to hear about any of my academic accomplishments. In so many ways I tried to get my parents to understand how important my profession was to me. When I tried to tell them about professional opportunities that I'd accepted as a social worker, they abruptly changed the subject, often talking about the successes of my brothers.

In exploring family rules and the messages that Maria received, it becomes clear that her relationship with her parents is making it difficult for her to create a life of her own, or at least the kind of life she indicates that she wants. For instance, she lives in fear of meeting the wrath of her father. At a later point in her therapy, I again suggest that she attempt to bring her parents in for one of her therapy sessions. She continues to be hesitant, and she again assures me that her parents will have nothing to do with her therapy. Although I suggest a number of ways in which she might approach members of her family to include them in a few of her sessions, she says that she is not ready to risk this step now, even though she would like to be.

In lieu of working with her and her family together, I suggest a number of therapeutic exercises in which she can bring significant others into her sessions in symbolic ways. She is willing to do a variety of role playing in which she addresses her mother, father, and some of her siblings in symbolic and psychological ways. Thus, even though the work with Maria is individual therapy, we are dealing with her reactions to members of her immediate and extended family, though they are not present in the sessions. Our work together consists of discovering ways in which her family influences her now and ways in which she might change, even if her parents do not.

individuation can present potential problems in relating to other members of her family.

One way in which I can assist Maria in becoming more personal is to ask her specific questions that call on her to use descriptive language:

JERRY: What do you hear your parents telling you now?
MARIA: They say: "Why do you want so much education? If you're too educated, you'll scare all the men off. As your parents, we want to know that you're protected and will be taken care of. That's what marriage is about. Someday your father will be gone. Who will protect you and love you then?"
JERRY: When you say you want to become your own person, what would this person be like? What aspects of your life do you like?
MARIA: I'm never alone when facing tragedy. My family is always there. I love the family at holidays and special occasions.
JERRY: What are some of the changes that you most want to make?
MARIA: What I'd like to change is the feeling that my life is not my own, and my unsatisfactory way of dealing with my father. I know I don't have much self-confidence, and that I hope to change.

Such questions show respect for Maria, yet at the same time she is learning how to think in more personal and concrete terms. Her answers to these questions provide material for further exploration. Our therapeutic work continues to focus on the issue of defining what Maria wants and what she is willing to do to get it. After we work together to narrow down her goals, she finally comes up with a clearer statement of her personal goals: "I want to take whatever steps are necessary to complete the writing of my dissertation and to apply for my oral and written doctoral examinations." She agrees to do this within a particular time frame, and together we outline specific steps she will take to accomplish her objectives. As important as it is, however, completing her doctoral dissertation is not the total answer to her problems. She recognizes her pattern of avoiding completion of projects. She enthusiastically initiates diverse projects, and then just as she is at the point of successfully finishing them, she typically finds some way to put off whatever is needed for completion. As a part of her therapeutic work, she wants to explore the meaning and the implications of this pattern in her life. She hopes to become her own person and still maintain a relationship with her family.

Exploration of Maria's Family History and Family Patterns

Early in our therapy sessions, Maria begins exploring the meaning of her failure to complete projects, which leads us to discuss her role in her family of origin. In exploring her family history, she will bring to the surface salient life events that have had an impact on her. She has accepted and learned definite roles, and she now rehearses and acts out these roles according to the expectations of her parents. I am especially interested in assisting her in taking a look at her family structure (a term that refers to the social and psychological organization of her family system, including factors such as birth order and her perception of herself in the family context). Some of the questions that I raise with Maria are:

- "In what type of family structure did you grow up?"
- "What is your current family structure? Have you carried certain patterns from your original family into your current family?"
- "When you compare yourself with each of your siblings, what stands out for you? Which sibling is the most like you? least like you?"
- "In reviewing your early years, what are a few events that seem most significant to you now, and why?"

In working with Maria in the context of her family and cultural background, I take into account certain cultural values that she expresses early in the course of our work together. By way of summary, the following are some of these key values:

- Her extended family is of great importance to her, as well as her immediate family.
- The value she places on family life emphasizes interdependence over independence, affiliation over confrontation, collective values over self-interest, and cooperation over competition.
- Her family structure is patriarchal, which in her case is characterized by an authoritarian father and a submissive mother.
- Her culture has contributed to her view of herself as a woman, for she learned clear expectations of appropriate role behavior that separates the sexes. In her culture, women are traditionally expected to be submissive, docile, intuitive, feeling, gentle, caring, sentimental, and dependent. Her culture taught her that men are supposed to be strong, determined, authoritarian, independent, courageous, rational, objective, and forceful.

Family rules and basic life decisions.   Although from the outset I encourage Maria to invite her parents to attend a family session with her, she decides that neither she nor they are ready yet for this kind of meeting. However, she is willing to explore the ways in which her "family rules" have affected her. She understands that family rules consist of what a family expects children to do or be in order to gain recognition and acceptance. She has probably heard many verbal and direct messages, as well as some subtle ones that she inferred from her parents' actions. Examples of these messages are:

- Men need to be taken care of.
- Men are more important than women.
- Women must silently endure the hardships of life and marriage.
- A woman's place is at home with the children, creating the perfect environment for her husband.

We will certainly take into account the power that cultural injunctions continue to wield in her life today. For instance, simply coming to therapy proved to be extremely difficult:

MARIA: In my culture, to talk about one's personal problems is to demonstrate weakness. It is extremely difficult for me to have to ask for help. I feel that revealing my problems to you is making myself vulnerable. It's very hard for me to express my feelings, especially to show tears or to show you what I consider my weakness. My father always told me that I shouldn't cry, and he liked me when I was happy. I saw my mother as strong, and she never cried in front of me.

It is considered highly inappropriate for her to seek help with her problems outside of the church or her family. Merely coming to therapy goes against her cultural grain. Although it is acceptable for her to study psychotherapy and practice it with others as a helper, she feels it is not acceptable for her to need this help or to reveal her deeper problems to others. Her negative experience with her previous therapist has compounded her reluctance to explore her own psychological world.

Maria realizes that she has internalized many traditional Mexican values. This is fine with her, for there is much that she appreciates in her family and her culture. Moreover, she often wonders if she really fits in the dominant Anglo culture. She is caught between two cultures. If she does accept some of the values of the dominant culture, she wants to do so without losing her Mexican-American cultural traits. She is having a difficult time in balancing the demands of her traditional family against the dominant culture in which she lives, and she is experiencing even more trouble in defining what she expects for herself. Whether Maria marries into her culture will be a key to which direction she will go. However, given her present leanings, it will be quite surprising if she can live in a strictly traditional environment without resentment and frustration.

Maria says that growing up in her family, she heard a lot of "Don't make it" or "Don't succeed" messages. One of the cultural messages she grew up with was the notion that education was for boys more than it was for girls, that her place was to create an identity by being a homemaker, that having a profession was not necessary, and that she should be loyal to the traditional ways of her family. In our work together, Maria and I identify and explore some of these family messages and rules in our early sessions by reviewing selected events that she remembers from her childhood and adolescent years. She was actually given more attention for *not* succeeding, and on those occasions when she did succeed, she was *negatively* recognized (which in essence says, "I don't like you").

In several of our sessions we review Maria's memories, and she reports that in many situations her parents ignored her when she was successful. Once, her folks gave no verbal response when she announced to them that she had been given a grant to pursue her graduate studies in Arizona. Her perception is that she was not supposed to go on to college and succeed

Fear of success.   A major theme for Maria in growing up in her family was "Don't make it!" Based on this strong parental message, we discovered, she decided very early something about herself and her role in life: "Although I'll go ahead and do what I want, I won't complete important ventures." That decision follows Maria to this day. Even though she is mostly finished with a doctoral program, which far exceeds the programming in her life by her parents, she finds some way *not* to ultimately succeed. She can always use as an excuse that she is not yet finished with something and that *if* she did finish, *then* she would be successful. Although she incorporated certain drives and ambitions from her family, she also made a decision early in her life not to fully experience the satisfaction that comes from completing projects. It is clear that she is afraid of how others would react if she were to be truly successful. From the vantage point of her traditional culture, it would be shameful if she achieved more than the men in the family.

In Maria's culture, success is considered as being in direct conflict with humility. Thus, we explore her fear of success in light of cultural messages that she has received. We devote some time to looking at her anxiety over going beyond what her parents actually accomplished in their own lives and beyond *their expectations* of her. Furthermore, we look at the power of the cultural messages that reinforced the messages of her parents and downplayed professional success. We talk about the many ways in which she sabotaged herself so that she would somehow fail in endeavors that had meaning for her. She begins to see how she limits her capacity to enjoy success.

We Move toward Action

Understanding the patterns that fit into her early family experiences is one matter. Yet if Maria hopes to change, she will have to take *action* and do something about changing, not merely talk about the prospects of change. Because family therapy is action-oriented, Maria and I think of ways in which she can practice some behavior that will challenge the early decisions she made. We begin to plan for how she can, for a change, actually complete a very meaningful project—in the situation at hand, her doctorate. The therapy involves going through each of the steps and practicing what she has typically done to procrastinate and what she can do differently now. Also, I encourage her to predict problems in finishing her dissertation, such as finding a good typist. She looks at ways to overcome barriers that will prevent her from completing this important task. We explore her fears of the board of examiners and predict the worst outcomes she can imagine. She is convinced of the importance of finishing her dissertation, and she makes a commitment to stick to her contract.

I also use a future-projection technique and ask her to imagine talking to each member of her family, letting them know that she has completed her doctorate. I ask her to talk to me as her father, mother, and each of her brothers. I also ask her to "become each family member" and say to me what she expects they might tell her; then she also says what she hopes each of them would say. This provides fertile ground for discussion, and it is a way of working with Maria in the context of her family system. I suggest several homework assignments at various sessions. One is to write a letter to each family member (but not to send the letter); another involves her initiating a discussion in real life with each member of her family. She is at least taking steps in opening doors that could lead to enhanced communication. Another assignment involves having her contact her grandparents and interview them to gain more familiarity with her roots and uncover patterns that have been passed down from the generations. She makes no attempt to change her grandparents; rather, the aim is for her to initiate a different kind of contact with some important members of her extended family. The material from these homework assignments proves to be useful in our therapy sessions.

A Closing Commentary

If we meet for enough sessions, I will work with Maria on the process of becoming separate from her parents, largely because this is what she continues to say she wants. We will also examine the potential consequences if she adopts values for herself that are contrary to the values of her parents. It seems crucial that she explore the price she is paying both for remaining as she is and the price she would pay for becoming a different person.

I think that an important aspect of our work would be to help Maria find some way that satisfactorily blends her Mexican-American cultural values and the dominant cultural values into a new synthesis. Ideally, she can find some way to remain true to the values she acquired from her family yet also modify some traditions that are not meaningful for her. If she wants to pursue a profession, she will probably have to come to grips with the reality that her culture does not put a great deal of emphasis on individuality, autonomy, assertion, accomplishing, and thinking about what is best for oneself. She will surely have conflicts as she attempts to integrate some of her new ways when she encounters her family. Thus, in our sessions we practice various ways to respond when others in her family do not accept the changes that she is making.

Follow-Up: You Continue as Maria's Therapist

Assume that Maria continues counseling with the goal of working toward making decisions that are best for her, even if they are different from those her family expects. On my referral she comes to see you. Show how you would work with her from a systemic perspective.

1. Maria really lives in two cultures. Do you have any thoughts on how you might help her work through what seem to her to be insurmountable conflicts? How might you help her respect and appreciate the values she acquired from her family?
2. Do you have any ideas of how to proceed if what Maria wanted was diametrically opposed to what would be acceptable in her culture? What might you suggest if you saw that her progress in attaining her personal goals would result in alienating her from her family and from her culture?
3. What ethical and clinical issues are involved in dealing with Maria's negative reactions to her previous therapist? If she told you that she was reluctant to get involved in therapy with you because she wondered if you could understand her struggles with her culture, how would you address her concern?
4. What specific knowledge would you want to have about Mexican-American traditions and the culture in which Maria grew up as a child and as a youth? What mistakes might you make if you attempted to counsel her without taking into account her family and cultural background?
5. Assume that you talked to a colleague about this case and this person said: "Maria is going to have to realize that if she's going to live and study in Arizona, she'll have to give up many of the ways she was brought up with in her traditional family. After all, she's going to have to face reality." What attitudes might your colleague be expressing? What would you want to say to this person?
6. Do you think there is a way to help Maria make the transition when she leaves Arizona and goes to Mexico to work?
7. Do any of Maria's early experiences and decisions touch off any associations with your life? To what degree have you faced, or do you now face, similar issues? How do you think this will either facilitate or interfere with your work with her?
8. Can you see different directions from those I began in which you would like to take Maria? What are some of the most pressing themes in her life that you think need attention? What family therapy techniques might you draw on in helping her in this exploration?
9. What advantages and disadvantages do you see to beginning therapy with a contract? If Maria failed to complete her dissertation by the time she had said she would, what might you say and do?
10. Family therapy encourages working with the entire family, if at all possible. As you recall, Maria expressed hesitation both times when I encouraged her to ask her parents to come with her for a family session. Do you think I was being too confrontive in asking her at different times to attempt to involve her parents in her therapy? How

might you approach her in working with her to include her family? What resistance might you expect from her and from her parents, and how do you think you would deal with such resistance?

RECOMMENDED SUPPLEMENTARY READINGS

Baucom, D. H., & Epstein, N. (1990). *Cognitive-behavioral marital therapy*. New York: Brunner/Mazel. This work is considered by many to be the bible of cognitive-behavioral marital therapy. It provides the reader with a wealth of assessment techniques, strategies, and case vignettes with couples.

Bedrosian, R. C., & Bozicas, G. D. (1994). *Treating family of origin problems: A cognitive approach*. New York: Guilford Press. This excellent book suggests cognitive-behavioral techniques as a supplementary component to family-of-origin problems. It does a nice job of dovetailing the two modalities into a unique and effective approach.

Dattilio, F. M. (1994). *Cognitive therapy with couples: Initial phase of treatment* [Videotape]. Sarasota, FL: Professional Resource Press (56 minutes). This professionally made videotape (VHS, 1/2 inch) is a clear example of the initial stage of treating couples. It demonstrates assessment techniques and several strategies used with dysfunctional couples. It also provides video graphics along with a summary of each session in an accompanying booklet. This is an excellent training tape for both the introductory- and the intermediate-level professional.

Dattilio, F. M., & Padesky, C. A. (1990). *Cognitive therapy with couples*. Sarasota, FL: Professional Resource Exchange. This little book packs a great deal of information into a concise description of applying cognitive therapeutic strategies to couples. It provides the reader with history and philosophy, assessment techniques, and specific strategies used in all aspects of the treatment phase. A full-length case vignette is provided at the end to demonstrate the nuts-and-bolts application of this modality.

Goldenberg, H., & Goldenberg, I. (1994). *Counseling today's families* (2nd ed.). Pacific Grove, CA: Brooks/Cole. This book deals with the family as a social system, the process of appraising family functioning, and counseling today's changing families. The book offers a useful perspective on counseling families with alternative lifestyles. The authors discuss implications for the following family structures: the single-parent family, the remarried family, the cohabiting heterosexual couple, gay and lesbian couples, and the dual-career family. In this new edition an excellent chapter has been added on counseling ethnically diverse families. Guidelines are provided for counseling African-American, Latino, and Asian-American families.

Kerr, M., & Bowen, M. (1988). *Family evaluation*. New York: Norton. This book presents a comprehensive examination and discussion of Bowen's family system theory. It also assists readers in understanding the integration of theory and practice. (In her contribution in this chapter, Mary Moline draws heavily from Bowenian concepts such as the differentiation of self, triangles, the multi-generational transmission process, and emotional cutoffs.)

McGoldrick, M., & Gerson, R. (1985). *Genograms in family assessment*. New York: Norton. This is a reference guide for those interested in constructing genograms. It provides a standard format for genogram symbols. Moreover, it describes various methods for developing underlying assumptions and for interpreting data.

Minuchin, S. (1974). *Families and family therapy*. Cambridge, MA: Harvard University Press. This is considered the most important book describing structural family therapy. The author discusses the therapeutic implications of a structural approach. He explores the dynamics of change, examining the variety of restructuring operations that can be employed to challenge a family and to change its basic patterns. (Moline's treatment of Ruth also borrows concepts from Minuchin's structural approach.)

Minuchin, S., & Fishman, H. C. (1981). *Family therapy techniques*. Cambridge, MA: Harvard University Press. This practical book is a companion to Minuchin's earlier book. In this volume the authors discuss the main concepts of the structural approach: understanding the family, joining the family, and treating the family.

Nichols, M. P., & Schwartz, R. C. (1995). *Family therapy: Concepts and methods* (3rd ed.). Boston: Allyn & Bacon. This highly readable introductory textbook presents the historical and conceptual context of family therapy. Theory chapters deal with systems of family therapy including the psychoanalytic, experiential, behavioral, Bowenian, strategic, and structural approaches. The final chapter, a comparative analysis, does a splendid job of bringing together common concepts of various family system theories.

Schwebel, A. I., & Fine, M. A. (1994). *Understanding and helping families: A cognitive-behavioral approach*. Hillsdale, NJ: Erlbaum. This is one of the few books that comprehensively addresses the cognitive-behavioral approach to family therapy. (In his contribution in this chapter, Frank Dattilio draws concepts from this source.) The book provides step-by-step instruction along with the philosophy and theory of the cognitive-behavioral approach. A number of case vignettes are interspersed throughout the text, which makes it enjoyable reading for the basic- to intermediate-level practitioner.

CHAPTER ELEVEN

Bringing the Approaches Together and Developing Your Own Therapeutic Style

This chapter focuses on how to work with the themes of Ruth's life from a variety of therapeutic perspectives. I want to reemphasize that one approach does not have a monopoly on the truth. There are many paths to the goal of providing Ruth with insight and mobilizing her resources so that she can take constructive action to give new direction to her life. These therapeutic perspectives can actually complement one another. Before demonstrating my own integrative style with Ruth, I will discuss counseling her from a multicultural perspective.

WORKING WITH RUTH FROM A MULTICULTURAL PERSPECTIVE

I discussed Ruth and other cases in this book with Jerome Wright, Ph.D., a colleague and a friend who teaches human services at California State University at Fullerton, specializing in courses in cultural diversity. Wright conceived of a way to encourage his students to appreciate the subtle aspects of working with cultural themes in the lives of clients. He gave Ruth's case to his students and asked them to form small study groups to research the cultural variables that would apply to her if she were from each of these ethnic groups: Asian American, Latino, African American, and Native American. The students were also asked to think of issues that would be involved if she were being counseled from a feminist perspective and special issues to consider if she were a lesbian. Each of the study groups had the freedom to present its findings in any way it saw fit, as long as the members did so as a group. I attended my colleague's class for two weeks and heard each of the group's presentations. Some did role-playing situations, others invited guest speakers who represented the group they were studying, and others found interesting ways to involve the class in their presentation. I was impressed with the value of this approach in teaching multicultural awareness to counseling students, and it gave me some new ideas for the revision of Ruth's case. Before exploring themes in her life and demonstrating my eclectic approach to working with her, I'd like to raise a few issues that should be considered if she and her therapist were from different cultural backgrounds. Issues such as race, ethnicity, gender, age, socioeconomic status, religion, lifestyle, and sexual orientation are crucial when establishing a therapeutic relationship with clients.

Becoming immersed in the study of cultural diversity is not without its dangers, however. There is a problem in accepting stereotypes and applying general characteristics of a particular group to every individual within that group. Indeed, the differences among individuals within a given ethnic group can be as great as the differences between populations. What is important to keep in mind is that knowledge about the client's culture provides counselors with a conceptual framework that they can use in making interventions. But knowledge of a client's cultural values is only the beginning. Counselors need to be aware of the ways in which their own culture has influenced their behavior. It is especially important that they be aware of their assumptions and biases and how these factors are likely to influence the manner in which they work with clients who differ culturally from them. Counseling across cultures is personally demanding, but it can also be exciting.

A guiding principle that I try to build into my practice is that I allow my client to teach me what is relevant to our relationship. It would be impossible for me to have comprehensive and in-depth knowledge of the cultural backgrounds of all of my clients. However, it is not unrealistic to expect my client to teach me about those aspects of his or her culture that are important for us to attend to in our work together. I have become convinced that universal human themes unite people in spite of whatever factors differentiate them. Regardless of our culture, we have a need to receive and give love, to make sense of our psychological pain, and to make significant connections with others. Besides these universal themes that transcend culture, we need to be aware of specific cultural values as we counsel people from various backgrounds. This discussion is not limited merely to cultural differences but to any kind of difference between the counselor and client that has the capacity to create a gap in understanding. Thus, differences in age, gender, lifestyle, socioeconomic status, religion, and sexual orientation are all essential to explore within the context of the client/therapist relationship.

The Many Faces of Ruth

Let's assume that Ruth is an Asian American. Depending on her degree of acculturation, I want to know something about the values of her country of origin. I may anticipate that she has one foot in her old culture and another foot in her new one. She may experience real conflicts, feeling neither fully Asian nor fully American, and at some points she may be uncertain about the way to integrate the two aspects of her life. She may be slow to disclose personal material, but this is not necessarily a reflection of her unwillingness to cooperate with the counseling venture. Rather, her reluctance is likely to reflect a cultural tradition that has encouraged her to be emotionally reserved. Knowing something about her case and about her background, I am aware that shame and guilt may play a significant role in her behavior. Talking about family matters is often considered to be something shameful and to be avoided. Furthermore, in her culture stigma and shame may arise over experiencing psychological distress and feeling the need for professional help.

As another example, consider the importance of accurately interpreting nonverbal behavior. Let's assume now that Ruth is a Latina and that she is cautious in attempting to maintain eye contact because her therapist is a man. I would probably err if I assumed that this behavior reflected resistance or evasiveness. Instead, she is behaving in ways that she thinks are polite, for direct eye contact could be seen as disrespectful. Also, I would need to be patient while developing a working alliance with her. As is true of many ethnic groups, Latinos have a tendency to reveal themselves more slowly than do many Anglo clients. Again, this does not mean that Ruth is being defensive, but it can reflect different cultural norms. She may not relate well to a high level of directness, because in her culture she has learned to express herself in more indirect ways.

If Ruth were a Native American and if I were unfamiliar with her culture, I could err by interpreting her quiet behavior as a sign that she was stoic and unemotional. Actually, she may have good reason to be emotionally contained, especially during the initial meeting with a non-Indian. Her mistrust does not have to be a sign of paranoia; rather, it can be a realistic reaction based on numerous experiences that have conditioned her to be cautious. If I did not know enough about her culture, it would be ethically imperative that I either learn some of its basic aspects or that I refer her to a counselor who was culturally skilled in this area. I don't burden myself with the unrealistic standard that I should know everything. It would be acceptable to admit to her that I lacked knowledge about her culture and then proceed to find a way to remedy this situation. Openness with a client can certainly be the foundation for a good relationship. Ruth can educate me about what would be important to know about her cultural background.

If Ruth is a member of a minority group, as distinct from being a member of the WASP majority, she is likely to have encountered her share of discrimination based on being different. This factor will need to be addressed if her counselor is of a different ethnic or racial group. As an African American, Latina, Native American, Asian American, or Pacific Islander, Ruth will share the experience of institutional oppression. She will know what it means to struggle for empowerment. Chances are that being both a woman and a member of one of these minority groups, she will experience a compounding of the problems that have previously been described in her case. This experience is bound to be reflected in the dynamics of our therapeutic relationship. I will need to somehow demonstrate my good faith and my ability to enter her world and understand the nature of her concerns. If I ignore these very real cultural realities, the chances are that she will not stay in therapy with me very long. However, I cannot emphasize enough the guiding principle of letting her provide me with the clues for the direction of therapy. In our initial encounter I will want to know what it was like for her to come to the office and why she is there. Rather than having prior conceptions of what we should be doing in this venture, I will ask her what she wants and why she is seeking help from me at this time in her life. If cultural issues are present, I expect that they will emerge very soon if I am listening sensitively to her and attempting to understand her world. As you read about the themes in Ruth's life in the following pages, be aware of how cultural variations could easily be woven into the fabric of the counseling process.

Questions for Reflection

1. If your cultural background and life experiences are very different from Ruth's, do you see it as presenting any particular problems in establishing a therapeutic relationship? If you do differ from her on any of these dimensions—race, culture, ethnicity, socioeconomic status, value system, religion, lifestyle, or sexual orientation—would you feel a need to discuss these differences with her? From your perspective might any of these differences incline you to refer her to another therapist? If you were to make a referral, what are the ethical and legal considerations?
2. In examining your own belief system and life experiences, do you think you would have any difficulty working therapeutically with any particular racial, ethnic, or cultural group? If you expect that you might have difficulty, what are your concerns, and what might you do about them?
3. What specific aspects about each culture do you feel a need to understand in order to develop a therapeutic alliance and work effectively with a client? If you do not have this knowledge, how could you go about acquiring it?
4. From your perspective how important is it that you be like your client in each of the following areas: age? gender? race? ethnicity? culture? socioeconomic status? religion? values? sexual orientation? education? marital status? family status?
5. Are you aware of referral sources for clients from various ethnic and cultural backgrounds? If so, what are they? If not, how could you find out about such referrals?

MY INTEGRATIVE APPROACH TO WORKING WITH RUTH

In this section I work toward an integration of concepts and techniques from the various schools of therapy by demonstrating the progression of Ruth's counseling. I will then ask you to work with her by drawing particular aspects from each of the models and applying them to her.

Each therapy approach has something unique to offer in understanding Ruth. My attempt will be to use a combination of approaches by working with her on a *thinking, feeling,* and *behaving* basis. Table 11-1 shows

Table 11-1.   Major areas of focus in Ruth's therapy

Orientation	*Areas of Focus*
Psychoanalytic therapy	My focus is on ways in which Ruth is repeating her early past in her present relationships. I have a particular interest in how she brings her experiences with her father into the session with me. I concentrate on her feelings for me, because working with transference is a major way to produce insight. I am also interested in her dreams, any resistance that shows up in the sessions, and other clues to her unconscious processes. One of my main goals is to assist her in bringing to awareness buried memories and experiences, which I assume have a current influence on her.
Adlerian therapy	My focus is on determining what Ruth's lifestyle is. To do this, I examine her early childhood experiences through her early recollections and family constellation. My main interest is in determining what her goals and priorities in life are. I assume that what she is striving toward is equally as valid as her past dynamics. Therapy consists of doing a comprehensive assessment, helping her understand her dynamics, and then helping her define new goals.
Existential therapy	My focus is on challenging the meaning in Ruth's life. What does she want in her life? I am interested in the anxiety she feels, her emptiness, and the ways in which she has allowed others to choose for her. How can she begin to exercise her freedom? I assume that our relationship will be a key factor in helping her take actual risks in changing.
Person-centered therapy	I avoid planning and structuring the sessions, because I trust Ruth to initiate a direction for therapy. If I listen, reflect, empathize, and respond to her, she will be able to clarify her struggles. Although she may be only dimly aware of her feelings at the beginning of therapy, she will move toward increased clarity as I accept her fully, without judgment. My main focus is on creating a climate of openness, trust, caring, understanding, and acceptance. Then she can use this relationship to move forward and grow.

Table 11-1.   Major areas of focus in Ruth's therapy *(continued)*

Orientation	Areas of Focus
Gestalt therapy	My focus is on noticing signs of unfinished business for Ruth, as evidenced by ways in which she reaches impasses in her therapy. Because she has never worked through her feelings of not being accepted, these issues appear in her therapy. I ask her to bring them into the present by reliving them, rather than by merely talking about past events. I am mainly interested in helping her experience her feelings fully, instead of developing insight or speculating about why she behaves as she does. The key focus is on *how* she is behaving and *what* she is experiencing.
Reality therapy	Our focus is guided by the principles of control therapy. First we work on our relationship. Key questions are "What are you doing now?" and "Is this behavior helping you?" Once Ruth has made an evaluation about her own current behavior, we make plans. I get a commitment from her to follow through with these plans and never accept excuses.
Behavior therapy	My initial focus is on doing a thorough assessment of Ruth's current behavior. I ask her to monitor what she is doing so that we can have baseline data. We then develop concrete goals to guide our work, and I draw on a wide range of cognitive and behavioral techniques to help her achieve her goals—for example, stress-reduction techniques, assertion training, role rehearsals, modeling, coaching, systematic desensitization, and relaxation methods. I stress learning new coping behaviors that she can use in everyday situations. She practices these in our sessions and elsewhere.
Cognitive-behavior therapy	My interest is focused on Ruth's internal dialogue and her thinking processes. I uncover the ways in which she is creating her own misery through self-indoctrination and retention of beliefs that are not rational or functional. By use of Socratic dialogue, I try to get her to spot her faulty thinking, to learn ways of correcting her distortions, and to substitute more effective self-statements and beliefs. I am willing to use a wide range of cognitive, behavioral, and emotive techniques to accomplish our goals.
Family systems therapy	My focus is on the degree to which Ruth has become differentiated from her significant others. We also examine ways in which anxiety is perpetuated by rigid interactional patterns and by her family's structure, and ways in which she can balance her role as a mother with taking care of herself.

what I am likely to borrow from each of the therapies as I conceptualize Ruth's case. As I describe how I would proceed with her, based on the information presented in her autobiography and the additional data from the nine theory chapters, I make parenthetical comments that indicate from what theoretical orientations I am borrowing concepts and techniques in any given piece of work. Thus, in addition to seeing a sample of my style of working with Ruth, you will have a running commentary on what I am doing, why I am using particular techniques, and what directions I am going in. As you read, think about what you might do that is similar to or different from my approach.

Initial Stages of Work with Ruth

After reading Ruth's autobiography before our initial session, I feel excited about working with her. I like her ability to pinpoint many of her concerns, and the data she provides are rich with possibilities. From these data alone I do not have a clear idea of where our journey together will take us, for a lot will depend on *how far* she wants to go and *what* she is willing to explore. From the data alone, though, I do have many ideas of how I want to proceed.

Our beginning.   I assume that Ruth, too, has some anxiety about initiating therapy. I want to provide her with the opportunity to talk about what it is like for her to come to the office today. That in itself provides the direction for part of our session. I surely want to get an idea of what has brought her to therapy. What is going on in her life that motivates her to seek therapy? What does she most hope for as a result of this venture? I structure the initial session so that she can talk about her expectations and about her fears, hopes, ambivalent feelings, and so forth. Because I will be an important part of the therapy process, I give her the chance to ask me personally and professionally how I will work with her. I do not believe in making therapy into a mysterious adventure. I think that clients have a right to know about the process that they are about to become involved with. Further, I think that Ruth will get more from her therapy if she knows how it works, if she knows the nature of her responsibilities and mine, and if she is clear on what she wants from this process. (This way of thinking is typical of models such as Adlerian therapy, behavior therapy, cognitive-behavior therapy, and reality therapy.)

The contract.   Again drawing on the above-mentioned models, I begin formulating a working contract, one that will give some direction to our sessions. As a part of this contract, I discuss what I see as my main responsibilities and functions, as well as Ruth's responsibilities in the process. I want her to know at the outset that I expect her to be an *active* party in this relationship, and I tell her that I function in an active and directive way (which is characteristic of most of the cognition/behavior/action-oriented therapies).

I see therapy as a significant project—an investment in the self, if you will—and I think that Ruth has a right to know what she can expect to gain as well as some of the potential risks. I begin by getting some sense of her goals, and though they are vague at first, I work with her to get them as specific and concrete as possible. (This process is especially important in Adlerian therapy, behavior therapy, cognitive-behavior therapy, and reality therapy.) I will come back to goals in a bit.

Letting Ruth tell her story.   I do not begin with a gathering of life-history data, though I do think this is important. I see value in first letting Ruth tell her story in the way she chooses. The way in which she walks into the office, her nonverbal language, her mannerisms, her style of speech, the details that she chooses to go into, and what she decides to relate and not to relate provide me with a valuable perspective from which to understand her. I am interested in how she perceives the events in her life and how she feels in her subjective world. (This is especially important in the existential and person-centered models.) If I do too much structuring initially, I interfere with her typical style of presenting herself. So I give everything to listening and letting her know what I am hearing (something that person-centered therapists put a premium on, and something I especially value in the initial stages of therapy). I want to avoid the tendency to talk too much during this initial session. It is not easy giving my full attention to Ruth, yet doing so will pay rich dividends in terms of the potential for therapy. If I listen well, I will get a good sense of what she is coming to therapy for. If I fail to listen accurately and sensitively, there is a risk of going with the first problem she states instead of waiting and listening to discover the depth of her experience.

Gathering data.   I mentioned earlier that I would not begin the session by asking Ruth a series of questions pertaining to her life history. After letting her tell her story in her way, I ask questions to fill in the gaps. This method gives a more comprehensive picture of how she views her life now, as well as events that she considers significant in her past. Rather than making it a question-and-answer session, I like the idea of using an *autobiographical approach,* in which she writes about the critical turning points in her life, events from her childhood and adolescent years, relationships with parents and siblings, school experiences, current struggles, and future goals and aspirations, to mention a few. I ask her what she thinks would be useful for her to recall and focus on and what she imagines would be useful to me in gaining a better picture of her subjective world. In this way she does some reflecting and sorting out of life experiences outside of the session, she takes an active role in deciding what her personal goals will be for therapy, and I have access to rich material that will give me ideas of where and how to proceed with her. (This unstructured, or open-ended, autobiography could fit into existential and the person-centered models, in which the emphasis is on the subjective world of the client. Also, psychoanalytic practitioners would want to know a lot about her developmental history.)

Therapy Proceeds

I favor integrating cognitive work into therapy sessions, and because I see therapy as a *learning* experience, I recommend some books to Ruth to supplement her therapy. These may include novels, books that deal with central areas of concern to her personally, and something on the nature of therapy. For example, I suggest that she read some books about women (and men) facing midlife crises, about parent/child relationships, about enhancing one's marriage, about sex, and about special topics related to her concerns. (This is consistent with approaches such as behavior therapy, reality therapy, and, especially, rational emotive behavior therapy.) I find that this type of reading provides a good catalyst for self-examination, especially if these books are read in a personal way—meaning that Ruth would apply their themes to her life.

Clarifying therapy goals.   During the beginning stages I assist Ruth in getting a clearer grasp of what she most wants from therapy, as well as seeing some steps she can begin to take in attaining her objectives. Like most clients she is rather global in stating her goals in her autobiography, so I work with her on becoming more concrete. When she looks in the mirror, Ruth says, she does not like what she sees. She would like to have a better self-image and be more confident. I am interested in knowing specifically *what* she does not like, the ways in which she now lacks confidence, and what it feels like for her to confront herself by looking at herself and talking to me about what she sees.

Ruth reports that she would like to be more assertive. She can be helped to pinpoint specific instances in which she is not assertive and to describe what she actually does or does not do in such circumstances and how she feels at these times. We consistently move from general to specific, for the more concrete she is, the greater are her chances of attaining what she wants. (It is from behavior therapy that I have learned the value of specifying goals.)

Importance of the client/therapist relationship.   I am convinced that one of the most significant factors determining the degree to which Ruth will attain her goals is the therapeutic relationship that she and I will create. (This element is given primary emphasis in the person-centered, existential, Adlerian, and Gestalt approaches. Therapy is not seen as something that the therapist *does to* a passive client, using skills and techniques. It is a deeply *personal* relationship that Ruth can use for her learning.) Thus,

I think that the person who I am is just as important as my knowledge of counseling theory and the level of my skills. Although I see it as essential that I am able to use techniques effectively—and that I have a theoretical base from which to draw a range of techniques—this ability becomes meaningless in the absence of a relationship between Ruth and myself that is characterized by a mutual respect and trust. (I am influenced by the person-centered approach, which emphasizes the personal characteristics and attitudes of the therapist. Some questions I see as vital are the following: To what degree can I be real with Ruth? To what degree can I hear what she says and accept her in a nonjudgmental way? To what degree can I respect and care for her? To what degree can I allow myself to enter her subjective world? To what degree am I aware of my own experiencing as I am with her, and how willing am I to share my feelings and thoughts with her?) I can help her to the degree that I am authentic myself with her. This relationship is vital at the initial stages of therapy, but it must be maintained during all stages if therapy is to be effective.

Working with Ruth in Cognitive, Emotive, and Behavioral Ways

As I mentioned earlier, my eclectic style is a blend of concepts and techniques from many therapeutic approaches. As a basis for selecting techniques to employ with Ruth, I look at her as a *thinking, feeling,* and *behaving* person. Although for purposes of teaching in this illustration I may have to describe the various aspects of what I am doing separately, do keep in mind that I tend to work in an integrated fashion. Thus, I would not work with Ruth's cognitions, then move ahead to her feelings, and finally proceed to behaviors and specific action programs. All of these dimensions would be interrelated. When I am working with her on a cognitive level (such as dealing with decisions she has made or one of her values), I am also concerned about the feelings generated in her at the moment and about exploring them with her. And in the background I am thinking of what she might actually *do* about the thoughts and feelings she is expressing. This *doing* would involve new behaviors that she can try in the session to deal with a problem and new skills that she can take outside and apply to problems that she encounters in real-life situations. (As a basis for this integrative style I am drawing on the cognitive and emotional insight-oriented approach of psychoanalysis; on the experiential therapies, which stress the expression and experiencing of feelings; on the cognitive therapies, which pay attention to the client's thinking processes, affecting behavior and beliefs; and to the action-oriented therapies, which stress the importance of creating a plan for behavioral change.)

Exploring Ruth's fears related to therapy.   Ruth begins a session by talking about her fears of coming to know herself and by expressing her ambivalent feelings toward therapy:

RUTH: Before I made the decision to enter therapy, I had worked pretty hard at keeping problems tucked away neatly. I lived by compartmentalizing my life, and that way nothing became so fearsome that I felt overwhelmed. But this reading that I'm doing, writing in my journal, thinking about my life, talking about my feelings and experiences in here—all this is making me uncomfortable. I'm getting more and more anxious. I suppose I'm afraid of what I might find inside of me if I keep searching.

I see this anxiety as something realistic, and I surely do not want to merely reassure Ruth that everything will turn out for the best if she will only trust me and stay in therapy. I want to explore in depth with her the *decision* that she must now make. Looking at her life in an honest way is potentially frightening. There *are* risks attached to this process. Although she has security now, she is paying the price in terms of boredom and low self-respect. Yet her restricted existence is a safe one. The attractions of getting to know herself better and the possibilities for exercising choice and control in her life can be very exciting, yet also frightening. At this point I hope that she will look at this issue and take a stand on how much she wants for herself and the risks that she is willing to take in reaching for more.

Ruth decides to continue.   Being in therapy is a series of choices. Not only does therapy open Ruth up to new possibilities by expanding her awareness and thus widening the brackets of her freedom to choose, but she makes choices all during the therapy process itself. I respect her choices, and I support her when she is struggling with difficult ones; I also push her gently and invite her to ask for more and take more risks. Ultimately, she is the one who decides many times during our sessions the depth to which she is willing to go. (This is very much an existential concept.)

Ruth works to become free.   In one session Ruth expresses her desire to be liberated:

RUTH: All my life I've felt unfree. I've had to be the person that my parents wanted me to be, I've had to be the wife that John expected me to be, and I've had to be what my kids expected as a mother. I'd like to be free and feel that I can live for me, but so far I don't seem to be able to.
JERRY: Between now and our next session I'd like to suggest that you do several things. In your journal let yourself imagine all the ways you've felt unfree in your life. Just write down phrases or short sentences. It might help if you could write down messages that you've heard from your parents. What have they said they wanted of you? It might help if you actually imagine that you *are* for a time your father and just write as fast as you can all the things he might say about all he expects. Then let yourself write to Ruth as your mother. Again, without thinking

much, just let her words and thoughts come to the paper. If you do that several times this week, we can pursue it more next week.

(Here is the idea of "homework assignments," borrowed from the cognitive and behavioral therapies, only I am stressing the feelings that go with such an exercise. In this way Ruth can review some earlier experiences, and I hope she will stir up some old feelings associated with these memories.)

At the following session Ruth brings her journal and says she would like to talk about what it was like to write herself letters (as her father and as her mother), saying all that was expected of her. I ask her to share what this was like, and I pay attention to her body as well as her words. (Like the Gestalt therapist, I think that the truth of one's messages is conveyed in voice inflections, postures, facial features, and the like. If I listen only to her words, I am likely to miss a deeper level of meaning. Like the person-centered therapist I value listening to what she is feeling and expressing.) Although I think it is important that I reflect and clarify (a person-centered technique), I deem it crucial that I bring myself into a dialogue with Ruth. If I am having reactions to what she is saying or if she is touching something within me, sharing my present experience with her can facilitate her work. (This is valued in both the existential and the person-centered approaches.) My own disclosure, at timely and appropriate moments, can lead to a deeper self-exploration on Ruth's part. I must take care not to disclose merely for its own sake; nor is it well to take the focus off of her. But even a few words can let her know that I understand her.

Ruth is talking about her mother's messages to her. As I listen to her, I notice that there is a critical tone and a sharpness to her voice, and she makes a pointing gesture with her finger. I get an idea that I want to pursue, and I say:

JERRY: Would you sit in this red rocking chair? Actually rock back and forth, and with a very critical voice—pointing your finger and shaking it—deliver a lecture to Ruth, who is sitting in this other chair.

RUTH: I want you to work hard and never complain. Look at how I've slaved, and look at how moral I've been. Life is hard and don't forget that. You're put on earth here to see if you can pass the test. This life is merely a testing place. Bear all your burdens well, and you'll be rewarded in the next life—where it counts! Work hard! Keep pure—in mind, spirit, and body. Look what I've done in life—you can too.

There are many possibilities of places to go from here. (So far I have been using a Gestalt technique of asking her to "become" her mother in the hope that she can actually *feel* what this brings up in her as she relives the scene.) I ask her to sit in the other chair and be Ruth and respond to her mother's lecture. The dialogue continues with exchanges between Mother and Ruth, and finally I ask her to stop and process what has gone on. This technique can also be done with her father.

We work on Ruth's cognitions.   I see Gestalt techniques as very useful for assisting Ruth to get an experiential sense of what might be called "toxic introjects." These are the messages and values that she has swallowed whole without digesting them and making them her own. My goal is to help her externalize these introjections so that she can take a critical look at them. I have an investment in getting her to look at this process and make her values truly her own. (This is very much an existential notion. Authenticity consists of living by one's own values, not living blindly by values given by others.)

So I ask Ruth to identify as many family rules as she can that she recalls having grown up with as a child. She recollects parental messages such as these: "Don't think for yourself." "Follow the church obediently, and conform your will to God's will." "Never question the Bible." "Live a moral life." "Don't get close to people, especially in sexual ways." "Always be proper and appropriate."

In addition to working with Ruth's feelings, I find it essential to work with her *cognitive structures*, which include her belief systems, her thoughts, her attitudes, and her values. (In family systems therapy attention would be given to family rules; in behavior therapy attention would be given to beliefs and assumptions that have an influence on her behavior; in rational emotive behavior therapy attention would be paid to irrational beliefs and self-indoctrination; in Adlerian therapy we would look at her basic mistakes; and in reality therapy the focus would be on values.) Whatever terms are used, I tend to focus on the underlying messages that Ruth pays attention to now in her life. I assume that her self-talk is relevant to her behavior.

Ruth brings up her father.   As we explore the messages that Ruth was reared with, one theme seems to emerge. She has lived much of her life in ways that were designed to get her father's approval. She feels that unless she gets her father's acceptance and approval, she will never have "arrived." She reasons that if the father who conceived her could not love her, then nobody ever could. If *this* man does not show her love, she is doomed to live a loveless life! I proceed by getting her to look at the Adlerian family systems and cognitive-behavioral concepts and techniques to get her to critically evaluate some invalid assumptions she continues to make.

As much as possible without pushing Ruth away, I challenge and confront her thinking and her value system, which appear to be at the root of much of her conflict. It is not so much a matter of my imposing my values on her; rather, it is a matter of getting her to look at beliefs and values that she has accepted to determine if she still wants to base her life on them. Does she want to spend the rest of her life in a futile attempt to "win over" her father? Does she want to continue making all men into her father? What will it take for her to finally gain her father's acceptance and love—if this is possible? What might she think of the person she had to become to gain his acceptance? I take this line of questioning in an attempt to get her to *think*, to *challenge* herself, and to *decide* for herself her standards for living.

Dealing with Ruth's past in understanding her decisions.   I have been talking about some of the early decisions that Ruth made in response to messages that she received from her parents. I very much value the exploration of a client's early childhood experiences as a basis for understanding present pressing issues. (The psychoanalytic approach emphasizes a reconstruction of the past, a working through of early conflicts that have been repressed, and a resolution of these unconscious conflicts. Family approaches encourage her to work through conflicts with her parents.) I accept that Ruth's childhood experiences were influential factors in contributing to her present development, although I do not think that these factors have *determined* her or that she is fixed with certain personality characteristics for life unless she goes through a long-term analytic reconstructive process. (I favor the Gestalt approach to working with her past.) I ask her to bring any unresolved conflicts from her past into the here and now through fantasy exercises and role-playing techniques. In this way her past is being dealt with in a powerful way as it is being manifested in her current problems.

In Ruth's attempt to face her past I expect some *resistance*—hesitation, defenses, and barriers at certain anxiety-provoking points. (Psychoanalysis has resistance as a central concept; Gestalt therapy mentions the "impasse.") In working with resistance, I attempt to respect it. In other words, I see that Ruth's resistance is an inevitable part of how therapy proceeds. To some extent it is healthy to resist. Resistance shows that she is aware of the risks of changing and the anxiety that coming to terms with unknown parts of herself brings up. Thus (in a psychoanalytic view), I do not see resistance necessarily as conscious defiance or unwillingness to cooperate. (Behavior therapists often assume that "resistance" is an excuse on the therapist's part for poor management of techniques. They see it as a function of failure by the therapist to make a correct assessment and apply an appropriate treatment plan. I agree with the psychoanalytic concept of resistance as a fundamental part of therapy and as something that needs to be recognized and dealt with.)

Overall, Ruth is a willing and motivated client. She is insightful, courageous, able to make connections between current behavior and past influences, willing to try risky behaviors both in the session and out of the session, and willing to face difficult issues in her life. Even under such favorable (and almost ideal) circumstances I still think that she will experience some resistance. She debated about whether to continue therapy; at times she blames her parents for her present problems, and at other times she chooses to stay comfortable because of her fear of plunging into unknown territory. In short, I work with whatever resistance she shows by pointing out its most obvious manifestations first and encouraging her to talk about her fears and explore them. I think an effective way to deal with resistance is to recognize it and deal with it directly. This can be done in a gentle yet confrontational way, along with providing support to face issues that she might otherwise avoid.

Working toward redecisions.   As much as possible I structure situations in the therapy session that will facilitate new decisions on Ruth's part. I think that her redecisions have to be made on both the emotional and cognitive levels. (In encouraging Ruth to make new decisions, I draw on cognitive, emotive, and behavioral techniques. I use role-playing procedures, fantasy and imagery, assertion-training procedures, Gestalt techniques, and family systems therapy methods, to mention a few. She can spend years in getting insights into the cause of her problems, but I think it is more important that she commit herself to some course of action. Here I like the Adlerian and reality-therapy emphasis on getting the client to decide on a plan of action and then make a commitment to carrying it out.)

Encouraging Ruth to act.   In many ways I look at therapy as a place of safety where clients can experiment with new ways of being to see what behavioral changes they really want to make. The critical point consists of actually taking what is learned in the sessions and applying it to real-life situations. I consistently encourage Ruth to carry out homework assignments geared to having her challenge her fears and inhibitions in a variety of practical situations. Thus, if she says that she is yearning for a weekend alone with her husband yet fears asking for it because she might be turned down and the rejection would hurt, I challenge her: "If you don't bother to ask, chances are you won't have this weekend you say you want with John. You've constantly brought up in here that you don't ask for what you want, suffer in silence, and then end up depressed and unloved. Here's your chance to actually *do* something different instead of what you typically do. What stops you from asking for what you want?"

Ruth has a long list of excuses to justify her lack of willingness to initiate a weekend alone with John. A few of them are that they do not have the money, their children would miss them, he is too busy, and they might find that they were bored with each other's company. In reality-therapy fashion I tell her that I don't want to settle for excuses. I argue with her on each point, attempting to convince her that if she does want to change her situation, she has to actually take risks and try new behavior. (This fits into most of the action-oriented behavioral approaches.) I ask Ruth to decide if she *really* wants to make changes in her life or merely *talk about* making changes. Because she sincerely wants to be different, we use session time in much role playing and behavioral rehearsal, and then I ask her to try out her new learning in different life situations, especially with her family. For me, translating what is learned in the sessions into daily life is the essence of what therapy is about.

Evaluating Ruth's Therapy Experience

My style of counseling places emphasis on continuing assessment by both the counselor and the client from the initial to the final session. In my work with Ruth I bring up from time to time the topic of her progress in therapy. We openly discuss the degree to which she is getting what she wants from the process (and from me). If she is not successfully meeting her objectives, we can explore some factors that might be getting in the way of her progress. I could be a restricting factor. This is especially true if I am reacting to her strictly from a technical approach and am withholding my own reactions from her. If I am being inauthentic in any way in the sessions, I am certain that this will show up in a failure on her part to progress to the degree to which she might have.

I also explore with Ruth some of the circumstances in her life that may be contributing to what appears to be slow or nonexistent progress. She has done a lot of changing, which may itself be creating new problems in her home relationships, and she may feel a need to pull back and consolidate her gains. There may be a plateau for a time before she is ready to forge ahead with making other major life changes. Still another factor determining her progress or lack of it lies within herself—namely, her own decision and commitment of how far she wants to go in therapy. Is she willing to make some basic changes in her personality and create a new identity for herself? Is she willing to pay the price that changing entails? Does she merely want to solve some pressing problems on the surface, while remaining personally unchanged? These are but a few of the factors that we have to consider in understanding any failure in the therapy process.

How do Ruth and I determine the degree to which she is progressing? What criteria do we use to make this determination? (Behavior therapy is built on the assumption that assessment and evaluation are basic to the therapy process. Techniques must be continually verified to determine if they are working. Behavior changes in the client are a major basis for making this evaluation.) From my vantage point I look at Ruth's work in the sessions and what she is doing outside of them as a measure of the degree to which therapy is working. Another important index is our relationship. If it is one of trust and if she is dealing with difficult personal issues in her therapy and also working on these issues outside of the sessions, then therapy is working. Also, her own evaluation of how much progress she sees and how satisfied she is by the outcomes is a major factor in assessing therapeutic results.

When is it time for Ruth to terminate therapy? This, too, is a matter that I openly evaluate at appropriate times. Ultimately, I see it as her choice. My hope is that once she attains a degree of increased self-awareness *and* specific behavioral skills in meeting present and future problems, she might well be encouraged to end formal therapy and begin to become her own therapist. (This is a cognitive-behavioral approach.) To keep her beyond this point could result in needlessly fostering her dependence on me, which is not too unlike the problem that brought her to therapy in the first place.

How Would You Work with Ruth Using Your Own Approach?

At this time you are challenged to try your hand at achieving some synthesis among the nine approaches by drawing on each of them in a way that seems meaningful to you—one that fits your own personality and your view of people and the nature of therapy. I am providing some questions to help you organize the elements of your approach.

1. What would you be thinking and feeling as you approached your initial session with Ruth? Use whatever you know about her from the material presented about her and her autobiography in the first chapter, from the nine chapters on her work with various therapists, and from my eclectic approach in working with her in this chapter.
2. Briefly state how you see Ruth, in terms of her current dynamics and most pressing conflicts. How would you feel in working with her as a client? How do you view her capacity to understand herself and to make basic changes?
3. How much direction do you see Ruth needing? To what degree would you take the responsibility for structuring her sessions? Where would you be on a continuum of highly directive to very nondirective?
4. Would you be inclined toward short-term therapy or long-term therapy? Why?
5. What major themes do you imagine that you would focus on in Ruth's life?
6. In what ways might you go about gathering life-history data in order to make an initial assessment of her problems and to determine which therapy procedures to use?
7. How might you help Ruth clarify her goals for therapy? How would you help her make her goals concrete? How would you assess the degree to which she was meeting her goals?
8. How much interest would you have in working with Ruth's past life experiences? her current issues? her future aspirations and strivings? Which of these areas do you favor? Why?
9. What value do you place on the quality of your relationship with Ruth? How important is the client/therapist relationship for you as a determinant of therapeutic outcomes?
10. Would you be more inclined to focus on Ruth's feelings? her thought processes and other cognitive factors? her ability to take action as measured by her behaviors?
11. How supportive might you be of Ruth? How confrontational might

you be with her? In what areas do you think you would be most supportive? most confrontational?

12. How much might you be inclined to work toward major personality reconstruction? toward specific skill-development and problem-solving strategies?

13. How might you explore Ruth's major fears, both about therapy and about her life?

14. What life experiences have you had that would most help you in working with Ruth? What personal characteristics might hinder your work with her?

15. How might you proceed in dealing with Ruth's parents and the role she feels that they have played in her life? How important would it be to focus on working through her attitudes and feelings toward her parents? Do you think that this can be done symbolically (through role playing), or for her to resolve her problems is it necessary that she deal directly with her parents? In what ways might you want to work with Ruth's family of origin?

16. To what degree would you strive to involve Ruth's current family in her therapy?

17. How much might you structure outside-of-therapy activities for Ruth (homework, reading, journal writing, and so forth)?

18. What values do you hold that are similar to Ruth's? How do you expect that this similarity would either get in the way of or facilitate therapy?

19. What specific techniques and concepts might you derive from the psychoanalytic approach? from the experiential approaches? from the cognition/behavior/action-oriented approaches? from systemic approaches?

20. Would you orient Ruth's therapy more toward insight or toward action? What balance might you seek between the cognitive aspects and the feeling aspects? How might you make the determination of when Ruth was ready to end therapy?

AN EXERCISE: THEMES IN RUTH'S LIFE

A few of the major themes that have therapeutic potential for further exploration are revealed in the following statements that Ruth made at one time or another:

1. "You seem so distant and removed from me. You're hard to reach."
2. "In spite of my best attempts, I still feel a lot of guilt that I haven't done enough."
3. "I just don't trust myself to find my own answers to life."
4. "I'm afraid to change for fear of breaking up my marriage."
5. "It's hard for me to ask others for what I want."
6. "I feel extremely tense, and I can't sleep at night."

7. "All my life I've tried to get my father's approval."
8. "It's hard for me to have fun. I'm so responsible."
9. "I've always had a weight problem, and I can't seem to do much about it."
10. "I'm afraid to make mistakes and look like a fool."
11. "My daughter and I just don't get along with each other."
12. "I give and give, and they just take and take."
13. "I've lived by the expectations of others for so long that I don't know what I want anymore."
14. "I don't think my marriage is the way it should be, but my husband thinks it's just fine."
15. "I'm afraid to tell my husband what I really want with him, because I'm afraid he'll leave me."
16. "I fear punishment because I've given up my old religious values."
17. "I wear so many hats that sometimes I feel worn out."
18. "There's not enough time for me to be doing all the things I know I should be doing."
19. "I'm afraid of my feelings toward other men."
20. "When my children leave, I'll have nothing to live for."

Look over the list of Ruth's statements above. Select the ones that you find most interesting. Here are three suggestions for working with them: (1) For each of the themes you select, show how you would begin working with Ruth from *each* of the nine perspectives. (2) If you prefer, take only two contrasting approaches and focus on these. (3) You might want to attempt to combine several therapeutic models and work with Ruth using this synthesis.

Attempt to work with a few of Ruth's statements after reading about my integrated way of working with her in this chapter. This would make interesting and lively material for role playing and discussion in small groups. One person can "become" Ruth while others in the group counsel her from the vantage point of several different therapeutic perspectives. Practicing a variety of approaches will assist you in discovering for yourself ways to pull together techniques that you consider to be the best.

CONCLUDING COMMENTS

The process of beginning to develop a counseling style that fits you is truly a challenge. It entails far more than picking bits and pieces from theories in a random and fragmented manner. As you take steps to develop an integrated perspective, you might ask: Which theories provide a basis for understanding the *cognitive* dimension? Which theories help you understand the *feeling* dimension? And what about the *behavioral* dimension? As you are aware, most of the nine therapies you have studied focus primarily on one of these dimensions of human experience. The task is to wisely and creatively select therapeutic procedures that you can employ in working with a diverse population. Knowing the unique needs of your clients, your own values and personality, and the theories themselves is a good basis for beginning to develop a theory that is an expression of yourself.

By now, I am sure, it is evident that it requires knowledge, skill, art, and experience to be able to determine what techniques work best with particular clients and with certain problems. It is also an art to know *when* and *how* to use a particular therapeutic intervention. Because building your personalized theory of counseling is a long-term venture, I do hope that you will be patient with yourself as you continue to grow through your reading, thinking, and experience in working with clients and through your own personal struggles and life experiences.

RECOMMENDED SUPPLEMENTARY READINGS

These sources will help you develop a basis for integrating diverse therapeutic approaches and dealing with counseling in a multicultural context.

Atkinson, D. R., Morten, G., & Sue, D. W. (Eds.). (1993). *Counseling American minorities: A cross-cultural perspective* (4th ed.). Dubuque, IA: Brown & Benchmark. This work has excellent sections dealing with counseling Native Americans, Asian Americans, African Americans, and Latinos, and it deals with implications for minority group and cross-cultural counseling.

Lazarus, A. A. (1989). *The practice of multimodal therapy.* Baltimore: Johns Hopkins University Press. This book presents a practical approach that is highly readable. The author develops his own systematic and comprehensive therapy and describes a wide variety of techniques. He endorses and expands on the stance he calls "technical eclecticism."

Norcross, J. C. (Ed.). (1987). *Casebook of eclectic psychotherapy.* New York: Brunner/Mazel. This casebook is a compendium that was designed as an extension of the *Handbook of Eclectic Psychotherapy.* Thirteen case histories concretely illustrate the practice of a systematic eclectic therapy in its varied manifestations.

Norcross, J. C., & Goldried, M. R. (Eds.). (1992). *Handbook of psychotherapy integration.* New York: Basic Books. This is an excellent handbook that deals with the conceptual aspects of psychotherapeutic integration, describes some of the main integrative approaches, and discusses future directions.

Pedersen, P. (1994). *A handbook for developing multicultural awareness* (2nd ed.). Alexandria, VA: American Counseling Association. This work is based on the assumption that all counseling is to some extent multicultural. The author contends that we can either choose to attend to the influence of culture or we can ignore it. In this useful handbook, he heals with topics such as developing multicultural awareness, becoming aware of our culturally biased assumptions, acquiring knowledge for effective multicultural counseling, and learning skills to deal with cultural diversity.

TO THE OWNER OF THIS BOOK:

I hope that you have found *Case Approach to Counseling and Psychotherapy,* Fourth Edition, useful. So that this book can be improved in a future edition, would you take the time to complete this sheet and return it? Thanks.

School and address: _____

Department: _____ Instructor's name: _____

1. What I like *most* about this casebook is: _____

_____

_____

2. What I like *least* about this casebook is: _____

_____

_____

3. My general reactions to Ruth's case are: _____

_____

4. My general reactions to the experts who worked with Ruth are: _____

_____

5. Other specific cases in the book I found most helpful are: _____

_____

6. Specific cases I found least useful or would suggest deleting in future editions are:

_____

7. The kinds of cases I would like to see added are: _____

_____

8. My general reaction to this book is: _____

_____

9. The name of the course in which I used this book is: _____

10. On a separate sheet of paper, please write specific suggestions for improving this book and anything else you'd care to share about your experience in using the book.

Optional:

Your name: _____   Date: _____

May Brooks/Cole quote you, either in promotion for *Case Approach to Counseling and Psychotherapy,* Fourth Edition, or in future publishing ventures?

Yes: _____   No: _____

Sincerely,

Gerald Corey

FOLD HERE

NO POSTAGE
NECESSARY
IF MAILED
IN THE
UNITED STATES

BUSINESS REPLY MAIL

FIRST CLASS   PERMIT NO. 358   PACIFIC GROVE, CA

POSTAGE WILL BE PAID BY ADDRESSEE

ATT: *Dr. Gerald Corey*

Brooks/Cole Publishing Company
511 Forest Lodge Road
Pacific Grove, California 93950-9968

FOLD HERE

Brooks/Cole Publishing is dedicated to publishing quality books for the helping professions. If you would like to learn more about our publications, please use this mailer to request our catalogue.

Name: _____

Street Address: _____

City, State, and Zip: _____

FOLD HERE

BUSINESS REPLY MAIL

FIRST CLASS   PERMIT NO. 358   PACIFIC GROVE, CA

POSTAGE WILL BE PAID BY ADDRESSEE

ATT: *Human Services Catalogue*

Brooks/Cole Publishing Company
511 Forest Lodge Road
Pacific Grove, California 93950-9968

FOLD HERE